TRAVELS IN TARTARY, THIBET AND CHINA

THE BROADWAY TRAVELLERS

THE BROADWAY TRAVELLERS
In 26 Volumes

I	An Account of Tibet	*Desideri*
II	Akbar and the Jesuits	*du Jarric*
III	Commentaries of Ruy Freyre de Andrada	*de Andrada*
IV	The Diary of Henry Teonge	*Teonge*
V	The Discovery and Conquest of Mexico	*del Castillo*
VI	Don Juan of Persia	*Juan*
VII	Embassy to Tamerlane	*Clavijo*
VIII	The English-American	*Gage*
IX	The First Englishmen in India	*Locke*
X	Five Letters	*Cortés*
XI	Jahangir and the Jesuits	*Guerreiro*
XII	Jewish Travellers	*Adler*
XIII	Memoirs of an Eighteenth Century Footman	*Macdonald*
XIV	Memorable Description of the East Indian Voyage	*Bontekoe*
XV	Nova Francia	*Lescarbot*
XVI	Sir Anthony Sherley and His Persian Adventure	*Sherley*
XVII	Travels and Adventures	*Tafur*
XVIII	Travels in Asia and Africa	*Battúta*
XIX	Travels in India, Ceylon and Borneo	*Hall*
XX	Travels in Persia	*Herbert*
XXI	Travels in Tartary, Thibet and China Vol. I	*Huc and Gabet*
XXII	Travels in Tartary, Thibet and China Vol. II	*Huc and Gabet*
XXIII	Travels into Spain	*D'Aulnoy*
XXIV	The Travels of an Alchemist	*Li*
XXV	The Travels of Marco Polo	*Benedetto*
XXVI	The True History of His Captivity	*Staden*

TRAVELS IN TARTARY, THIBET AND CHINA

1844-1846

Volume Two

HUC AND GABET

LONDON AND NEW YORK

First published 1928 by RoutledgeCurzon

Published 2014 by Routledge
2 Park Square, Milton Park, Abingdon, Oxfordshire OX14 4RN
711 Third Avenue, New York, NY 10017
First issued in paperback 2014

*Routledge is an imprint of the Taylor & Francis Group,
an informa business*

All rights reserved. No part of this book may be reprinted or reproduced or utilized in any form or by any electronic, mechanical, or other means, now known or hereafter invented, including photocopying and recording, or in any information storage or retrieval system, without permission in writing from the publishers.

The publishers have made every effort to contact authors/copyright holders of the works reprinted in *The Broadway Travellers*. This has not been possible in every case, however, and we would welcome correspondence from those individuals/companies we have been unable to trace.

These reprints are taken from original copies of each book. In many cases the condition of these originals is not perfect. The publisher has gone to great lengths to ensure the quality of these reprints, but wishes to point out that certain characteristics of the original copies will, of necessity, be apparent in reprints thereof.

British Library Cataloguing in Publication Data
A CIP catalogue record for this book
is available from the British Library

Travels in Tartary, Thibet and China VII

The Broadway Travellers
ISBN 978-0-415-34484-5 (hbk)
ISBN 978-1-138-86772-7 (pbk)

THE BROADWAY TRAVELLERS

EDITED BY SIR E. DENISON ROSS
AND EILEEN POWER

HUC AND GABET

TRAVELS IN TARTARY THIBET AND CHINA
1844–1846

*Translated by William Hazlitt
Now edited with an Introduction
by Professor Paul Pelliot*

VOLUME TWO

Published by
GEORGE ROUTLEDGE & SONS, LTD.
BROADWAY HOUSE, CARTER LANE, LONDON

First published in this Series in 1928

PRINTED IN GREAT BRITAIN BY HEADLEY BROTHERS,
18, DEVONSHIRE STREET, E.C.2; AND ASHFORD, KENT.

CONTENTS OF VOLUME II

CHAPTER ONE

Caravan of Khalkha Tartars—Son of the King of Koukou-Noor—Sandara the Bearded—Two thousand Oxen are stolen from the Houng-Mao-Eul, or Long Hairs—Fearful Tumult at Tang-Keou-Eul—Description and character of the Long Hairs—Feasts of the First Day of the Year—Departure for the Lamasery of Kounboum—Arrival at Night—Old Akayé—The Kitat-Lama—The Stammerer—Pilgrims at Kounboum—Description of the Feast of Flowers 1

CHAPTER TWO

Marvellous birth of Tsong-Kaba—His preparation for the Apostleship—He departs for the West—His interview with the Grand Lama of Thibet—He reforms the Lamanesque worship—Numerous analogies between the Catholic religion and reformed Buddhism—Origin of these analogies—Tree of the Ten Thousand Images—Lamanesque Teaching—Faculty of Prayer—Government of the Lamasery of Kounboum—Offerings of the Pilgrims—Industry of the Lamas—The Adventures of Sandara the Bearded—Favourable disposition of the Lamas towards Christianity—Singular practice for the relief of Travellers—Nocturnal Prayers—Departure for the Lamasery of Tchogortan 45

CHAPTER THREE

Aspect of the Lamasery of Tchogortan—Contemplative Lamas—Lama Herdsmen—The " Book of the Forty-two Points of Instruction, delivered by Buddha "—Extract from the Chinese Annals, with relation to the Preaching of Buddhism in China—The Black Tents—Manners of the Si-Fan—Long-haired Oxen—Adventures of a stuffed Karba—Lamanesque Chronicle of the Origin of Nations—Alimentary Diet—Valuable discoveries in the Animal Kingdom—Manufacture

CONTENTS

of Camel-hair Cord—Frequent visits to Tchogortan—Classification of Argols—Brigand Anecdote—Elevation of the Pyramid of Peace—The Faculty of Medicine at Tchogortan—Thibetian Physicians—Departure for the Blue Sea . . 80

CHAPTER FOUR

Aspect of the Koukou-Noor—Tribes of Kolos—Chronicle of the Origin of the Blue Sea—Description and March of the Great Caravan—Passage of the Pouhain-Gol—Adventures of the Altère-Lama—Character of our pro-cameleer—Mongols of Tsaidam—Pestilential Vapours of the Bourhan-Bota—Ascent of the Chuga and Bayen-Kharat Mountains—Wild Cattle—Wild Mules—Men and Animals killed with the Cold—Encounter with Brigands—Plateau of Tant-La—Hot Springs—Conflagration in the Desert—Village of Na-Ptchu—Sale of Camels, and Hiring of Long-tailed Oxen—Young Chaberon of the Kingdom of Khartchin—Cultivated Plains of Pampou—Mountain of the Remission of Sins—Arrival at Lha-Ssa 115

CHAPTER FIVE

Lodgings in a Thibetian House—Appearance of Lha-Ssa—Palace of the Talé-Lama—Picture of the Thibetians—Monstrous Toilet of the Women—Industrial and Agricultural Productions of Thibet—Gold and Silver Mines—Foreigners resident at Lha-Ssa—The Pebouns—The Katchis—The Chinese—Position of the relations between China and Thibet—Various speculations of the Public respecting us—We present ourselves to the Authorities—Form of the Thibetian Government—Grand Lama of Djachi-Loumbo—Society of the Kalons—Thibetian Prophecy—Tragical Death of three Talé-Lamas—Account of Ki-Chan—Condemnation of the Nomekhan—Revolt of the Lamasery of Sera 168

CHAPTER SIX

Visit of Five Spies—Appearance before the Regent—Ki-Chan makes us undergo an Examination—Supper at the expense of the Government—A night of imprisonment with the Regent

CONTENTS

PAGE

—*Confidential communications of the Governor of the Katchi—Domiciliary Visit—Seals affixed to all our effects—Sinico-Thibetian Tribunal—Inquiry about the Geographical Maps—Homage paid to Christianity, and to the French name—The Regent assigns to us one of his Houses—Erection of a Chapel—Preaching of the Gospel—Conversion of a Chinese Doctor—Religious Conferences with the Regent—Recreation with a Magnifying Glass—Conversations with Ki-Chan—Religious character of the Thibetians—Celebrated formula of the Buddhists—Buddhist Pantheism—Election of the Talé-Lama—The Small-pox at Lha-Ssa—Sculptures in use among the Thibetians* 207

CHAPTER SEVEN

Notice of Moorcroft the English Traveller—Routes between Lha-Ssa and Europe—Discussion with the Chinese Ambassador—Contest between the Regent and Ki-Chan about us—Our expulsion from Lha-Ssa determined on—Protest against this arbitrary measure—Report of Ki-Chan to the Emperor of China—System of Chronology in use in Thibet—New Thibetian year—Festivals and rejoicings—Buddhist Monasteries of the Province of Oui—Khaldan—Preboung—Sera—Farewell of the Regent—Separation from Samdadchiemba—Ly, the Pacificator of Kingdoms—Triple Address of the Chinese Ambassador—Picturesque adieu between the Ly-Kouo-Ngan and his Wife—Departure from Lha-Ssa for Canton—Crossing a river in a leathern boat . . . 253

CHAPTER EIGHT

Chinese account of Thibet—Mountain of Loumma-Ri—Arrival at Ghiamda—Visit of two Military Mandarins—Accident on a wooden bridge—The Unicorn—Passage of a Glacier—Appearance of Lha-Ri—Ascent of Chor-Kou-La—Frightful Road to Alan-To—Village of Lang Ki-Tsoung—Famous Mountain of Tanda—Catastrophe of Kia-Yu-Kiao—Passage of the celebrated Plateau of Wa-Ho—Arrival at Tsiamdo . . 294

CONTENTS

CHAPTER NINE

Glance at Tsiamdo—War between two Living Buddhas—We meet a small Caravan—Calcareous Mountains—Death of the Mandarin Pey—The great chief Proul-Tamba—Visit to the Castle of Proul-Tamba—Buddhist Hermit—War among the tribes—Halt at Angti—Thibetian Museum—Passage of the Mountain Angti—Town of Djaya—Death of the son of the Mandarin Pey—Musk Deer—River with Gold Sands—Plain and Town of Bathang—Great Forest of Ta-So—Death of Ly-Kouo-Ngan—Interview with the Mandarins of Lithang—Various bridges of Thibet—Arrival on the Frontiers of Chian—Residence at Ta-Tsien-Lou—Departure for the capital of the Province of Sse-Tchouan 342

INDEX 393

Travels in Tartary, Thibet, and China

VOLUME II

CHAPTER I

THE Houses of Repose are very numerous in the small town of Tang-Keou-Eul, by reason of the great number of strangers, who are drawn thither from all quarters by commerce. It was in one of these establishments, kept by a family of Mussulmen, that we went to lodge. As we had nothing to do with trade, we felt called upon candidly to communicate the fact to the host, and to arrange the terms of our living in his house; it was agreed that we should be there as in a common hotel. All this was very well; but the question was, what were we to do afterwards; what was to become of us? This question incessantly engrossed our minds, and tormented us not a little.

As far as Tang-Keou-Eul we had followed, with sufficient continuity, the route we had traced out for ourselves; we might even say that this portion of our journey had been successful beyond all expectations. Now the business was to carry out our plan, and to penetrate to Lha-Ssa, the capital of Thibet; an undertaking which appeared bristling with almost insuperable difficulties. Tang-Keou- Eul was our columns of Hercules, with their depressing *ne plus ultra* "No farther shalt thou go." However, we had already

TRAVELS IN TARTARY,

vanquished too many obstacles, to be easily overcome by discouragement. We heard that almost every year caravans proceeded from Tang-Keou-Eul, and penetrated into the very heart of Thibet. We wanted nothing more to confirm our determination. Whatever other people had undertaken and executed, we assumed also to undertake and to execute, as not being, probably, beyond our power. It was therefore settled that the journey should be carried out to the end, and that no one should say that Catholic missionaries had less courage for the interest of the faith than merchants for a little profit. The possibility of departure being thus determined we had nothing to seek but the opportunity.

Our great business, therefore, was to collect all possible information respecting this famous route into Thibet. We heard terrible things about it; we should have to travel for four months through a country absolutely without inhabitants, and should have, accordingly, to lay in before our departure, all the necessary provisions. In the season of winter, the cold was so horrible that it often happened that travellers were frozen to death or buried beneath the avalanches of snow; while, in summer, a great number were drowned, for they had to cross large streams, without bridge or boat, without other aid than that of animals, which themselves often could not swim. Moreover, there were hordes of brigands, who at certain periods of the year prowled about the desert and stripped travellers and abandoned them, without clothes or food, amidst these frightful plains; in short, there was no end of stories, enough to make our hair stand on end; and these stories, fabulous as they seemed, or, at least much exaggerated, were the same on every tongue—were all of a frightful uniformity. Besides, there were to be seen and questioned in the streets of Tang-Keou-Eul some

THIBET, AND CHINA

Tartar-Mongols, who were standing evidence of the truth of these long narratives, being the remnants of a large caravan, which had been attacked in the preceding year by a troop of brigands. These had contrived to escape, but their companions had been left to the mercy of the Kolo [Kolo (mGo-log, Ngo-log)] "brigands." This information, while ineffectual to shake our resolution, induced us to remain where we were until a favourable opportunity for departure should present itself.

We had been six days at Tang-Keou-Eul, when a small caravan of Tartar-Khalkhas arrived at our House of Repose. It came from the frontiers of Russia, and was on its way to Lha-Ssa to offer up its adorations to a young child, which, the people were informed, was the famous Guison-Tamba newly transmigrated. When the Tartars learned that we were awaiting a favourable opportunity for proceeding towards Thibet, they were delighted, fully appreciating the fact that their troop, in this unexpected accession of three pilgrims, received an accession, also, of three combatants in the event of a fight with the Kolo. Our beards and mustachios inspired them with an exalted idea of our valour, and we were forthwith decorated by them with the title of *Batourou* "braves." This was all exceedingly honourable and seductive; but still, before we finally decided upon joining the cavalcade, we thought it expedient to consider the various aspects of the matter gravely and maturely.

The caravan, which occupied the great court-yard of the House of Repose, counted only eight men; the rest was camels, horses, tents, baggage, and kitchen utensils; but then the eight men, according to their own account, were perfect war dragons. At all events, they were armed up to the teeth, and made a grand display before us of their matchlocks, lances, bows and arrows, and above all, a piece of artillery, in

TRAVELS IN TARTARY,

the shape of a small cannon, of the size of one's arm ; it had no carriage but mounted between the two humps of a camel it produced a very formidable effect. All this warlike apparatus failed to inspire us with confidence, and, on the other hand, we placed but slight reliance upon the moral effect of our long beards. It was necessary, however, to adopt a decided course ; the Tartar-Khalkhas urged us pressingly, assuring us of complete success. Of the lookers-on, disinterested in the matter one way or the other, some told us that the opportunity was altogether eligible, and that we ought by all means to avail ourselves of it ; while others assured us that it would be the extreme of imprudence to proceed, for that so small a party would be inevitably eaten up by the Kolo ; and that it would be far better, as we were in no immediate hurry, to wait for the great Thibetian embassy.

Now this embassy having only just quitted Peking, would not reach Tang-Keou-Eul for fully eight months, a delay which it seemed absolutely ruinous for us to undergo. How, with our modest means, were we to maintain ourselves and our five animals for so long a time in an inn ? After maturely calculating and weighing everything : let us confide in the protection of God, said we, and go forth. We announced our resolution to the Tartars, who were highly delighted. We immediately requested the host of the House of Repose to purchase for us four months' provision of meal. "What do you want with four months' meal ? " asked the Tartars. "They say the journey is of at least three months' duration, and it is expedient, therefore, to provide for four months to meet the chance of accidents." "Ay, the Thibetian embassy occupies a long time on the journey, but we Tartars travel in quite a different manner ; we do the distance in a moon and a-half at the very outside ; we gallop the whole way, so that we get over nearly

THIBET, AND CHINA

200 lis (twenty leagues) a day." This intimation at once caused us to change our resolution. It was manifestly quite impossible for us to keep up with this caravan. In the first place, as to ourselves, never having been accustomed, like the Tartars, to forced marches, we should have been dead in three days; and as to our animals, weary and worn with four months' incessant toil, they could not have for any length of time borne up against the pace of our proposed companions. The Tartars having forty camels could afford to knock up one half of them. Indeed, they themselves admitted that with our three camels, it was impossible for us to undertake the journey with them, and they accordingly advised us to buy a dozen others. The advice, excellent in itself, was, with reference to the state of our exchequer, absolutely absurd. Twelve good camels would have cost us three hundred ounces of silver; now the total amount of our funds was under two hundred ounces.

The eight Tartar-Khalkhas were all of princely blood, and, accordingly, on the evening preceding their departure, they received a visit from the son of the King of Koukou-Noor, who was then at Tang-Keou-Eul. As the room we occupied was the handsomest in the establishment, it was arranged that the interview should take place there. The young Prince of Koukou-Noor surprised us by his noble mien and the elegance of his manners; it was obvious that he spent considerably more of his time at Tang-Keou-Eul than in the Mongol tent. He was attired in a handsome robe of light blue cloth, over which was a sort of jacket of violet cloth, with a broad border of black velvet. His left ear was decorated, in Thibetian fashion, with a gold earring from which hung several trinkets; his complexion was almost as fair as our own, and his countenance admirably gentle in its expression: in utter contradistinction from ordinary

Tartars, his garments were exquisitely clean. As the visit of a Prince of Koukou-Noor was quite an event, we determined to be wholly regardless of expense in celebrating it; and Samdadchiemba received, accordingly, orders to prepare a banquet for his royal highness, that is to say, a great pitcher of good, hot tea, with milk. His royal highness deigned to accept a cup of this beverage, and the remainder was distributed among his staff, who were in waiting outside. The conversation turned upon the journey into Thibet. The prince promised the Tartar Khalkhas an escort throughout his estates. " Beyond that point," said he, " I can answer for nothing; you must take your chance, good or bad, as shall happen." Then addressing us, he advised us by all means to wait for the Thibetian embassy, in whose company we should be able to travel with greater ease and security. On taking leave, the royal visitor drew from a purse elegantly embroidered, a small agate snuff-box, and graciously offered to each of us a pinch.

Next morning the Tartar-Khalkhas proceeded on their journey. When we saw them depart, a feeling of sorrow came over us, for we would gladly have accompanied them had it been at all practicable; but the sentiment soon subsided, and we applied our thoughts to the best use we should make of our time while we remained at Tang-Keou-Eul. It was at last determined that we should procure a master, and devote ourselves entirely to the study of the Thibetian language and of the Buddhist books.

At eleven leagues from Tang-Keou-Eul there is, in the land of the Si-Fan, or Eastern Thibetians, a Lamasery, whose fame extends not merely throughout Tartary, but even to the remotest parts of Thibet. Thither pilgrims flock from all quarters, venerating; for there was born Tsong-Kaba-Remboutchi [Tsong-kha-pa Rim-po-ch'ê], the famous reformer of Buddhism.

THIBET, AND CHINA

The Lamasery bears the name of Kounboum [Kumbum], and its Lama population numbers no fewer than 4,000 persons, Si-Fan, Tartars, Thibetians, and Dchiahours. It was determined that one of us should visit this place, and endeavour to engage a Lama to come and teach us for a few months the Thibetian language. M. Gabet, accordingly, departed on this mission, accompanied by Samdadchiemba, while M. Huc remained at Tang-Keou-Eul, to take care of the animals and of the baggage.

After an absence of five days, M. Gabet returned to the House of Repose, eminently successful, having secured at the Lamasery of Kounboum a perfect treasure in the person of a Lama who had passed ten of the thirty-two years of his life in a grand Lamasery at Lha-Ssa itself. He spoke pure Thibetian perfectly, wrote it with facility, and was very learned in the Buddhist books; moreover, he was quite familiar with several other idioms, Si-Fan, Mongol, Chinese, and Dchiahour; in a word, he was a philologist of the first water. This young Lama was a Dchiahour by birth, and a cousin-german of Samdadchiemba; his name was Sandara, and in the Lamasery he was called Sandara the Bearded, by reason of the remarkable length of that appendage in which he luxuriated.

The devotion which Samdadchiemba's cousin forthwith manifested in our favour made us rejoice that we had not adventured with the Tartar-Khalkhas caravan, for here we were placed in the precise position for procuring every requisite information about Thibet, and of making ourselves acquainted at the same time with the language and religion of that celebrated region.

We applied ourselves to study with perfect enthusiasm. First, we composed in Mongol two dialogues, comprehending the most familiar conversational phrases. These Sandara translated into Thibetian with scrupulous attention. Every morning he wrote out a page in our presence, giving us a grammatical commentary upon each expression as he proceeded; this was our lesson for the day, which we first transscribed several times, in order to break our hand into the Thibetian writing, and then chanted, in the manner of the Lamaseries, until the whole page was thoroughly impressed upon the memory. In the evening our master heard us recite the portion of dialogue he had written for us in the morning, and rectified our defects of pronunciation. Sandara acquitted himself of his task with talent and amiability. From time to time in the course of the day, he would, by way of recreation, give us details full of interest respecting Thibet and the Lamaseries he had visited. It was impossible to listen to the descriptions given by this young Lama without admiration; nowhere had we heard a person express himself with greater facility or a more winning manner; the simplest, commonest things became in his mouth picturesque and full of charm; he was especially remarkable when he sought to induce upon others any particular view of his own upon some subject in which he really felt an interest. His eloquence was then really powerful.

After having surmounted the first difficulties of the Thibetian language, and familiarized ourselves with the expressions in ordinary use, we proceeded to give our studies an altogether religious direction. We got Sandara to translate for us into the sacred style of his language some of the leading Catholic forms, such as the Lord's Prayer, the Salutation, the Apostles' Creed, the Commandments; and thereupon we took occasion to explain to him the general truths of the Christian religion. He seemed all at once struck with this new doctrine, so different from the vague, incoherent propositions of Buddhism. Before long he attached so much importance to the study of the Christian religion that he entirely laid aside the Lama books he had brought with him, and applied himself to the acquisition of our prayers with an ardour that made us truly joyful. From time to time in the course of the day he would interrupt what he was about in order to make the sign of the cross, and he practised this religious act in a manner so grave and respectful that we thoroughly believed him to have become a Christian at heart. The excellent tendencies he manifested filled us with the most lively hopes, and we gratefully viewed in Sandara an incipient apostle, destined one day to labour with success in converting the sectaries of Buddha.

While we three, master and pupils, were thus absorbed in studies so important, Samdadchiemba, who had no sort of vocation for things intellectual, passed his time lounging about the streets of Tang-Keou-Eul and drinking tea. Not at all pleased with this occupation of his time, we devised to withdraw him from his idleness, and to utilize him in his special character of cameleer. It was according arranged that he should take the three camels and pasture them in a valley of Koukou-Noor, noted for the excellence and the abundance of its pasturage. A Tarter of the locality promised to receive him into his tent, and we rejoiced in the arrangement, as effecting the double advantage of supplying Samdadchiemba with an occupation in conformity with his tastes, and of giving our camels better and less costly fodder.

By degrees, all the fine things we had imagined in Sandara vanished like a dream. This young man, apparently of devotion so pure and disinterested, was in reality a dissipated knave, whose only aim was to ease us of our sapeks. When he thought he had rendered himself essential to us, he threw aside the mask, and placed himself undisguisedly before us in all the detestability of his character; he became insolent, haughty, overbearing. In his Thibetian lessons, he substituted for the mild, gentle, insinuating tone of his former instruction, manners the most insufferably harsh and brutal, such as the worst tempered pedagogue would not betray towards the poorest of his pupils. If we asked him for an explanation which perhaps he had previously given, he would assail us with such amenities as these: "What! you learned fellows want to have the same thing told you three times over! Why, if I were to tell a donkey the same thing three times over, he'd remember it." We might easily, no doubt, have cut short these impertinences by sending the man back to his Lamasery; and, more than once, we were strongly inclined to adopt this course, but, upon the whole, we thought it better to undergo a little humiliation than to deprive ourselves of the services of a Lama whose talents were indisputable, and who, therefore, might be of the greatest utility to us. His very rudeness, we considered, would aid our progress in acquiring the Thibetian language, for we were sure that he would not pass over the most trivial fault in grammar or pronunciation, but, on the contrary, would rate us for any such defects, in a style eminently calculated to produce an abiding impression. This system, though somewhat tedious, and decidedly displeasing to one's self-love, was incomparably superior to the method practised by the Chinese Christians towards the European missionaries in giving them Chinese lessons. Partly from politeness, partly from religious respect, they affect to be in ecstacies with whatever their spiritual father-pupil says; and, instead of frankly correcting the faults which naturally occur in his expressions, they are rather disposed to imitate his defective language, so that he may, with the less trouble to himself, understand them, the result of which excessive complaisance is that the missionaries are put to grave inconvenience when they seek to converse with pagans who, not having the same devotion towards them, do not admit in them a fine pronunciation, or a masterly knowledge of words. Upon such occasions, how one regrets that one had not for a teacher some Sandara the Bearded! Upon such considerations, we resolved to keep our master with all his defects, to endure his abuse, and to make the best and most we could of him. As we found that our sapeks were his object, it was agreed that we should pay him handsomely for his lessons; and moreover, we made up our minds to wink at his little knaveries, and to affect to have no idea that he had an understanding with the people who sold us our daily provisions.

Samdadchiemba had not been gone many days before he suddenly re-appeared amongst us. He had been robbed by brigands who had taken from him his entire provision of meal, butter and tea. For the last day and a half he had eaten nothing whatever, and of consequence, his voice was hollow, and his face pale and haggard. Only seeing one camel in the court-yard, we imagined that the two others had become the prey of the brigands, but Samdadchiemba relieved us by the assurance that he had confided them to the Tartar family who had granted him their hospitality. Upon hearing this statement, Sandara knitted his brows. "Samdadchiemba," said he, "you are my younger brother, as it were; I have therefore a right to ask you a few questions." And thereupon he submitted the cameleer to an interrogatory characterized by all the depth and subtlety of an able advocate cross-examining some cunning offender. He demanded the minutest details, and applied himself with infinite ingenuity to work up the contradictions into which he involved the questioned party, and to put forward in prominent relief the apparent improbability of the story. How was it, he asked, that the robbers had stolen the butter, yet left the bag in which the butter was carried? How was it they had respected the little snuff-bottle, yet carried off the embroidered purse which served it as a cover? When he had finished his inquiries, he added, with a malicious smile, "I have put these few questions to my brother out of pure curiosity; I attach no importance to them. It is not I who have to disburse the wherewithal to buy him fresh provisions."

Samdadchiemba, meantime, was dying with hunger, so we gave him some sapeks, and he went to dinner in a neighbouring eating-house. As soon as he had quitted the room, Sandara proceeded: "Nobody shall ever persuade me that my brother has been robbed. The brigands in this part of the country don't do their work in the way he wants to make out. The fact is, that Samdadchiemba, when he got among the Tartars, wanted to show off, and distributed his provisions right and left in order to make friends. He had no reason to fear being lavish; what he gave away cost him nothing." The probity of Samdadchiemba was a fact so thoroughly impressed upon our convictions that we altogether repudiated this wicked insinuation, which we clearly saw proceeded at once from Sandara's jealous annoyance at the confidence we reposed in his cousin, and from a cunning desire, in giving us the idea that he was warmly attached to our interest, to divert our attention from his own petty peculations. We gave Samdadchiemba, who did not at all perceive his relative's treachery, some more provisions, and he returned to the pastures of Koukou-Noor.

Next day, the town of Tang-Keou-Eul was the scene of terrible disorder. The brigands had made their appearance in the vicinity, and had driven off 2,000 head of cattle belonging to the tribe called Houng-Mao-Eul "Long Hairs." These Eastern Thibetians quit once a year the slopes of the Bayen-Kharat [Bayen-khara] mountains, in large caravans, and come to Tang-Keou-Eul to sell furs, butter, and a kind of wild fruit that grows in their diſtriƈt. While they are engaged in these commercial operations, they leave their large herds in the vast prairies that abut upon the town, and which are under the jurisdiƈtion of the Chinese authorities. There was no example, we heard, of the brigands having ventured to approach so close as this to the frontiers of the empire. This present audacity of theirs, and more especially the known violence of charaƈter of the Long Hairs, contributed to throw the whole town into utter dismay and confusion. Upon hearing of their loss, the Long Hairs had tumultuously rushed to the Chinese tribunal, and, their long sabres in their hands, lightning in their eyes, and thunder in their mouths, had demanded juſtice and vengeance. The terrified Mandarin inſtantly dispatched 200 soldiers in pursuit of the robbers. But the Long Hairs, seeing that these foot soldiers could never overtake the brigands, who were well mounted, threw themselves into their saddles, and dashed off in search of the thieves. They returned next day with no other result attained than that their fury was redoubled. Altogether deſtitute of foresight, these half-savages had gone off without any provisions whatever, never thinking that, in the desert, they would find nothing to eat. Accordingly, after a day's forced march, hunger had compelled them to return. Not so the Chinese soldiers. These worthies, knowing much better what they were about, had provided themselves for their warlike expedition with infinite asses and oxen laden with apparatus for the kitchen, and with ammunition for the mouth. As they felt no sort of desire to go and fight for 2,000 cattle that did not belong to them, after a very brief military progress they halted on the banks of a river, where they spent several days, eating, drinking and amusing themselves, and giving no more heed to the brigands than though there had never been such personages in the world. When they had consumed all their provisions they returned quietly to Tang-Keou-Eul, and declared to the Mandarin that they had scoured the desert without being able to come up with the robbers : that once, indeed, these had seemed within their grasp, but that, availing themselves of their magic powers, they had vanished. At Tang-Keou-Eul everybody is persuaded that the brigands are all more or less sorcerers, and that in order to render themselves invisible all they have to do is to exhale in a particular manner, or to throw some sheep's treddles behind them. It is probably the Chinese soldiers who have brought these fables into vogue ; at all events they certainly make excellent use of them in all their expeditions. The Mandarins, doubtless, are not their dupes ; but provided the victims of the robbers are content with these tales, that is all the Chinese authorities care about.

For several days the Houng-Mao-Eul were perfectly furious. They ran about the streets like madmen, flourishing their sabres and vociferating a thousand imprecations against the brigands. All the townspeople got carefully out of their way, respecting their anger with entire veneration. The appearance of these fellows, even at their very best, when they are perfectly calm and good humoured, is sufficiently alarming. They are clothed at all seasons of the year in a great sheepskin robe, rudely drawn up round the waist by a thick camel-hair rope. Left to itself this robe would drag along the ground, so that when raised by the cord above the knees it communicates to the chest a most rotund, stuffed and awkward appearance. They have great leather boots, which come up to just below the knees, so that, as they wear no trousers, their legs are

THIBET, AND CHINA

always half bare. Their hair, black and greasy, hangs in long matted locks down their shoulders, and, in fact, falling over the brow, half conceals the face. The right arm is always bare, the sleeve being thrown quite back. A long broad sabre is passed through their girdle just below the chest, and the right hand scarcely ever quits its hilt. The manners and movements of these inhabitants of the desert are abrupt and jerking, their speech brief and energetic. The tones of their voice have something about them metallic and deafening. Many of them are wealthy, and with these display consists in decorating the sheath of the sword with precious stones, and their own robes with borders of tiger-skin. The horses which they bring to Tang-Keou-Eul are remarkably beautiful, vigorous and well-made, and of great grandeur in the step: in all respects far superior to those of Tartary, and fully justifying the Chinese phrase, *Sima* [*hsi-ma*], *toung-nieou* [*tung-niu*], "Western horses—eastern oxen."

The Houng-Mao-Eul, being famous for their bravery and for an independence which amounts to the ferocious, it is they who give the *ton* to the people of Tang-Keou-Eul, who all essay to catch their air and gait, and to acquire a reputation for valour and devil-may-carishness. The result is, that Tang-Keou-Eul bears a strong family resemblance to a great den of thieves. Everybody there makes it his business to have his hair and clothes in utter disorder, everybody bawls at everybody, everybody pushes against everybody, everybody fights everybody, so that everybody from time to time draws everybody's blood. In the depth of winter, though the winter here is desperately cold, people go about with their arms and half their legs bare. To wear clothing adapted to the icy season would be considered a mark of pusillanimity. A good, brave fellow, they say, should fear nothing, neither men nor elements. At Tang-Keou-Eul the Chinese themselves have loſt much of their urbanity and of the polished forms of their language, having involuntarily undergone the influence of the Houng-Mao-Eul, who converse together in much the same ſtyle that we can imagine tigers in the woods to converse. On the day of our arrival at Tang-Keou-Eul, a few minutes before we entered the town, we met a Long Hair who had been giving his horse drink in the river Keou-Ho. Samdadchiemba, who was always attraƈted by anything having an eccentric air, cautiously approached the man, and saluted him in the Tartar fashion, saying, " Brother, art thou at peace ? " The Houng-Mao-Eul turned fiercely towards him : " What business of thine is it, tortoise-egg," cried he, with the voice of a Stentor, " whether I am at peace or at war ? And what right haſt thou to address as thy brother a man who knows nothing about thee ? " Poor Samdadchiemba was taken all aback at this reception, yet he could not help admiring, as something very fine, this haughty insolence of the Long Hair.

Tang-Keou-Eul, in consequence of its dirt and its excessive population, is a very unwholesome place to live in. There is an universal odour of grease and butter about, that is enough to make you sick. In certain quarters, more particularly where the especial poor and the especial vagabonds congregate, the ſtench is insupportable. Those who have no house wherein to shelter themselves colleƈt in the nooks of ſtreets and squares, and there they lie, higgledy-piggledy, and half naked, upon filthy ſtraw, or rather, dung-heaps. There are ſtretched together the sick young, and the infirm old, the dying man, sometimes the dead, whom no one takes the trouble to bury, until, at length, putrefaƈtion manifeſting itself, the bodies are dragged into the middle of the ſtreet, where the authorities remove them, and have them thrown into some general pit. From amid this hideous misery there pullulates into the bosom of the population a crowd of petty thieves and swindlers, who, in their address and audacity, leave far behind the Robert Macaires of the weſtern world. The number of these wretched creatures is so great, that authority, weary of contending with them, has left them to take their own course, and the public to guard their own sapeks and goods. These worthies work, as a matter of preference, in the houses of repose and the inns. Their *modus operandi* is this :—Two of them, associated together for the purpose, hawk about various articles of merchandise, boots, skin-coats, bricks of tea, and what not. They offer these for sale to travellers. While one of them engages the attention of the deſtined viƈtim, by displaying his goods and bargaining, the other ferrets about and pockets whatever he can lay his hands on. These rascals have inconceivable skill in counting your sapeks for you, in such a way as to finger fifty or a hundred or more of them without your having the slighteſt notion as to what is going on. One day, two of these little thieves came to offer for our purchase a pair of leathern boots. Excellent boots ! said they; boots such as we could not find in any shop in the whole town ; boots that would keep out the rain for days ; and as to cheapness, perfeƈtly unexampled. If we missed this opportunity, we should never have such another. Only juſt before they have been offered 1,200 sapeks for them ! As we did not want boots, we replied that we would not have them at any price. Thereupon the aƈting merchant assumed a lofty tone of generosity. We were foreigners ; we should have them for 1,000 sapeks, 900, 800, 700. " Well," said we, " we certainly don't want any boots juſt now, yet, doubtless, as you say, these are very cheap, and it will be worth while to buy them as a reserve." The bargain was accordingly concluded; we took our purse, and counted out 700 sapeks to the merchant, who counted them over himself, under our very eyes, pronounced the amount correct, and once more laid the coin before us. He then called out to his companion who was poking about in the court-yard: "Here, I've sold those capital boots for 700 sapeks." "Nonsense," cried the other, "700 sapeks! I won't hear of such a thing." "Very well," said we; "come, take your boots and be off with you." He was off, and so quickly, that we thought it expedient to count our sapeks once more; there were a hundred and fifty of them gone, and that was not all; while one of the rascals had been pocketing our money under our very nose, the other had bagged two great iron pins that we had driven into the court-yard for the purpose of our camels. Therefore we took a resolution—better late than never—to admit, in future, no merchant whatever into our room.

The House of Repose, as we have already indicated, was kept by Mussulmen. One day, their Mufti who had recently arrived from Lan-Tcheou [Lan-chou], the capital of Kan-Sou, attended at the house, in order to preside over some religious ceremony, the nature and object of which they would not explain to us. Sandara the Bearded, however, had an explanation of his own, which was, that the Grand Lama of the Hoei-Hoei attended on these occasions to teach his sectaries the latest improvements in the art of cheating in trade. For two days, the principal Mussulmen of the town assembled in a large apartment, contiguous to our own. There they remained for a long time, squatting on the ground, with their heads resting on their knees. When the Mufti appeared, all sent forth groans and sobs. After they had sufficiently lamented in this fashion, the Mufti recited, with a perfectly alarming volubility of tongue, several Arabic prayers; then everybody had another turn at lamenting, after which the cheerful assembly separated. This doleful ceremony was performed thrice in each of the two firſt days. On the morning of the third day, all the Mussulmen ranged themselves in the court-yard round the Mufti, who was seated on a ſtool, covered with a fine red carpet. Then the hoſt of the House of Repose brought in a fine sheep, adorned with flowers and ribbons. The sheep was laid on its side, the hoſt held it by its head, and two other Mussulmen by the legs, while a fourth presented to the Mufti a knife on a silver dish. He took the knife with great gravity, and approaching the victim, thruſt the weapon up to the hilt into its neck. Thereupon cries and groans once more resounded on all sides. These ceasing, the sheep was skinned, cut up, and taken into the kitchen to be cooked, and, by-and-by, a grand entertainment of boiled mutton, presided over by the Mufti, closed the ceremony.

The Mussulmen, or Hoei-Hoei, are very numerous in China. It is said that they penetrated thither under the dynaſty of the Thang [T'ang], which began in 618, and terminated in 907. They were received by the Emperor, who at that period resided at Si-Ngan-Fou [Hsi-an-fu], the present capital of Chan-Si. They were kindly entertained, and the Emperor, ſtruck with their fine features and forms, loaded them with favours, and entreated them to settle in his dominions. At firſt, it is ſtated, they were only 200 in number, but they have since so multiplied that they now conſtitute a large population, eminently formidable to the Chinese. Kan-Sou, Yun-Nan, Sse-Tchouan, Chan-Si, Chen-Si, Chan-Toung, Pe-Tche-Li, and Liao-Toung [Liao-tung] are the provinces in which they are moſt numerous. In some particular localities, indeed, they form the majority of the population, as compared with the

TRAVELS IN TARTARY,

Chinese. They have, however, become so mingled, so fused with the native people, that it would be difficult now-a-days to recognize them, were it not for the small blue cap which they all conſtantly wear, to diſtinguish themselves from the Chinese. Their physiognomy has retained no veſtige of its original type. Their nose has become flat, their eyes have sunk in, their cheek-bones ſtarted out. They do not know a single word of Arabic—a language which their prieſts alone are bound to learn, and this only so as to read it. Chinese has become their ſtep-mother tongue; yet they have preserved a certain energy of charaƈter which you seldom find among the Chinese. Though few in number, as compared with the enormous general population of the empire, they have ensured for themselves the fear and respeƈt of all about them. Closely united among themselves, the entire community always takes up any matter affeƈting one of its members. It is to this spirit of association that they owe the religious liberty which they enjoy through all the provinces of the empire. No person would venture, in their presence, to cavil at their religious creed, or their religious praƈtices. They abſtain from smoking, from drinking wine, from eating pork, from sitting at table with pagans; and no one presumes to find fault with these peculiarities. They do not even hesitate to contravene the laws of the empire, if these contravene their freedom of worship. In 1840, while we were on our mission to Tartary, the Hoei-Hoei of the town of Hada, built a mosque, or *Li-Pai-Sse* [*li-pai-ssŭ*], as the Chinese called it. When it was completed, the Mandarins of the place wanted to demolish it, because, contrary to the law, it rose higher than the Tribunal of Juſtice. Upon this intention becoming known, all the Mussulmen of the locality rose in arms, assembled, swore to prosecute in common a suit againſt the Mandarins, to impeach them

THIBET, AND CHINA

at Peking, and never to lay down their arms until they had effected the removal of the offending dignitaries. As in China, money has the preponderant influence in all matters of this kind, the Mussulmen of Hada raised a subscription among all their co-religionists in the empire, and by its means defeated the Mandarins, who had desired to demolish their mosques, and effected their deposition and banishment. We have often asked each other how it was that the Christians in China live in a state of oppression, wholly at the arbitrary disposition of the tribunals, while the Mussulmens march about with heads erect, and constrain the Chinese to respect their religion. It certainly is not because the religion of Mahomet is, more than Christianity, in harmony with Chinese manners; quite the contrary, for the Chinese [Christians] may, without any compromise of their religious duties, live in intimacy with the pagans, eat and drink with them, interchange presents with them, and celebrate in common with them the Festival of the New Year, all which things are forbidden to the Hoei-Hoei by the despotic and exclusive spirit of their religion. No: that the Christians are everywhere oppressed in China is to be attributed to the great isolation in which they live. If one of them is taken before a tribunal, all his brethren in the locality get out of the way, instead of coming in a body to his aid and awing by their numbers the aggressive Mandarins. Now, more especially, that imperial decrees have been issued favourably to Christianity, if the Christians were to rise simultaneously in all parts of the empire, were energetically to assume possession of their rights, giving publicity to their worship, and exercising fearlessly, and in the face of day, their religious practices, we are satisfied that no one would venture to interfere with them. In China, as everywhere else, men are free who manifest the will to be so; and that will can only be effectively developed by the spirit of association.

We were now approaching the first day of the Chinese year, and in every direction people were preparing for its celebration. The sentences, written on red paper, which decorate the fronts of houses, were renewed; the shops were filled with purchasers; there was redoubled activity of operations in every quarter, while the children, ever eager to anticipate holidays and entertainments, were discharging, each evening, preliminary fireworks in the streets. Sandara informed us that he could not pass the Festival of the New Year at Tang-Keou-Eul, being obliged to return to the Lamasery, where he had duties to fulfil towards his masters and superiors. He added, that on the third day of the new moon, when he had satisfied all his obligations, he would come back and resume his services. He spoke in a tone of intense kindliness, in order to make us forget the daily impertinences he had been guilty of towards us. We did not at all urge him to return. Though delighted at the prospect of renewing our studies with him, we were determined not to seem anxious about the matter, lest we should raise still higher the already preposterous estimate he had of his own importance. We told him that since propriety recalled him to the Lamasery for the first day of the year, he ought by all means to obey the call. We then offered him three rolls of sapeks, saying, according to the custom in such cases, that it was to enable him to drink with his friends a cup of high-coloured tea. For some minutes he feigned that he would not accept the coin, but at last we overcame his exquisite delicacy, and he consented to put the sapeks in his pocket. We then lent him Samdadchiemba's mule, and he left us.

The last days of the year are ordinarily, with the Chinese, days of anger and of mutual annoyance; for having at this period made up their accounts, they are vehemently engaged in getting them in; and every Chinese being at once creditor and debtor, every Chinese is juſt now hunting his debtors and hunted by his creditors. He who returns from his neighbour's house, which he has been throwing into utter confusion by his clamorous demands for what that neighbour owes him, finds his own house turned inside out by an uproarious creditor, and so the thing goes round. The whole town is a scene of vociferation, disputation, and fighting. On the laſt day of the year disorder attains its height; people rush in all directions with anything they can scratch together, to raise money upon, at the broker's or pawnbroker's, the shops of which tradespeople are absolutely besieged throughout the day with profferers of clothes, bedding, furniture, cooking utensils, and moveables of every description. Those who have already cleared their houses in this way, and yet have not satisfied the demands upon them, poſt off to their relations and friends to borrow something or other which they vow shall be returned immediately, but which immediately takes its way to the *Tang-Pou,* or pawnbroker's. This species of anarchy continues till midnight; then, calm resumes its sway. No one, after the twelfth hour has ſtruck, can claim a debt, or even make the slighteſt allusion to it. You now only hear the words of peace and good-will; everybody fraternizes with everybody. Those who were juſt before on the point of twiſting their neighbour's neck, now twine their friendly arms about it.

The new year is celebrated in much the same way as in Europe. Everybody dresses as fine as he possibly can; formal and informal visits are exchanged; presents circulate; dinners and parties are given; people go to see the play, the jugglers and so on. Fireworks ſtartle you at every turn; there is nothing going on but merry-making. After a few days the shops are once more opened, and business imperceptibly resumes its course; at least with those who can carry it on; those who can't, declare themselves bankrupt, or, as the Chinese phrase it, leave the door open.

The Hoei-Hoei do not keep the new year at the same time with the Chinese, for in their special calendar they observe the Hegira of Mahomet. Owing to this circumstance, we passed these days of disorder and tumult in the greatest tranquillity. The epoch assigned for the recovery of debts was, in the place where we lodged, indicated merely by a few disputes, followed immediately by profound quiet. The House of Repose was not even disturbed by fire-works. We availed ourselves of this tranquillity, and of the absence of Sandara, to go thoroughly over our Thibetian lessons. The two dialogues we possessed were analysed, decomposed [parsed], subjected to the intellectual alembic, in every way and in every detail. Housekeeping cares occupied, indeed, a portion of our daytime: but we made up for this by borrowing a few hours from the night, an arrangement which did not at all suit our host, who, finding that it involved him in an extra outlay for light, not only cut off our supplies, by removing the oil bottle, but, like the regular Turk he was, put on a charge per diem for light. As we did not choose to be condemned to darkness in this way, we bought a packet of candles, and constructed, with a long nail and the half of a carrot, a candlestick, not remarkable, indeed, for elegance or costliness, but which perfectly fulfilled its office. When the Turk's dole of oil was consumed, we lighted our candle, and we were thus able to give free course to the ardour of our Thibetian studies. Sometimes we would interrupt our labours to indulge in the relaxation of talking about France; and, after this rambling for awhile, in spirit, over our dear native land, it was with a certain amount of difficulty only, that we could assume the realities of our position. It seemed strange, impossible almost, that we two should be seated there, amid the silent night, poring over Thibetian characters, in a country well nigh at the extremity of the world, and practically unknown to Europeans.

On the third day of the first moon, Sandara the Bearded reappeared. During his absence we had enjoyed such delightful calm, that his aspect occasioned within us a very painful sensation; we felt like schoolboys alarmed at the approach of a severe preceptor. Sandara, however, was charmingly amiable. After gracefully wishing us a happy new year, in the most paternal, the most sentimental of phraseology, he proceeded to discourse upon the little mule we had lent him. First, on their way out, the little mule had thrown him a dozen times, so that at last he had resolved to walk; but then the creature was so droll, so fantastic in its ways, had so amused him, that he had not had time to grow tired. After this and similar small talk, we proceeded to business. Sandara said, that since we were determined to wait for the Thibetian embassy, he invited us to go and reside meanwhile in the Lamasery, at Kounboum; and thereupon, with his accustomed eloquence, he descanted upon the advantages presented by a Lamasery to men of study and prayer. The proposition met the very wish of our hearts; but we took care not to manifest any enthusiasm in the matter, contenting ourselves with replying, coldly: "Well, we'll see how we like it."

The next day was devoted to the preparations for departure. Not having our camels with us, we hired a car, on which to transport our baggage. In announcing our departure to the host of the House of Repose, we claimed our tent, which we had lent him twelve days before, for a pic-nic party that he said he had formed with some friends into the Land of Grass; he replied, that he would send for it immediately to the friend's house, where it was carefully ſtowed away. We waited, but in vain; night came, the tent did not. At laſt, the hoſt told us that his friend had left home for a day or two, and that the tent was locked up; but that it should be sent after us as soon as his friend returned. Sandara had hitherto said nothing; but when night came, and he found that we were not ready, he could no longer reſtrain his impatience. "It's quite obvious," said he to us, "that you are people altogether of another world; why don't you underſtand that your tent is at the pawnbroker's?" "At the pawnbroker's? Impossible!" "It is not at all impossible; it is considerably more than probable; the Hoei-Hoei wanted money wherewith to pay his debts at the end of the twelfth moon; he was delighted to find you with him in the emergency; he borrowed your tent, and he took it ſtraight—not to the land of Grass, but to the House of Pledges; and now he hasn't got the money to redeem it with. Juſt have him up: I'll put the matter to him, and you'll see." We requeſted the hoſt to come to us. As soon as he entered the chamber, Sandara the Bearded commenced his interrogatory with imposing solemnity. "Liſten to me," said he; "this evening I have a few words to say to you. You are a Turk—I a Lama, yet the laws of reason are the same for both of us. You have taken our tent, and you have carried it to the pawnbroker's; if you were in an embarrassed position, you did quite right; we do not reproach you; but we depart to-morrow, and our tent is not yet here. Which of us has reason on his side? we in claiming our property, or you in not reſtoring it? Do not tell us that the tent is at a friend's: I tell you that it is at the pawnbroker's. If, by the time we have drunk this jug of tea, our tent is not brought back, I will myself go to the magiſtrate to demand that it be given up to us, and we shall see whether a Lama-Dchiahour is to be oppressed by a Turk." By way of peroration to this harangue, Sandara gave such a thump with his fiſt upon the table that our three cups performed a caper in the air. The Turk had nothing to say, and it was manifeſt that our tent was really at the pawnbroker's. After a moment's pause, the hoſt assured us that we should have our property immediately, and he entreated us earneſtly not to mention the matter abroad, leſt it should compromise his eſtablishment. We had scarcely quitted our room, before there arose a grand confusion in the court-yard; the attendants were collecting everything they could lay their hands upon, saddles, bed-clothes, candleſticks, kitchen utensils, wherewith to redeem the tent, which, before we slept, we saw securely packed on the car which was to convey it to the Lamasery.

Next morning, at daybreak, we proceeded on our journey. The country through which we passed is occupied here by the Si-Fan, who lead a nomad life, and merely use the land as paſturage for their cattle,—whereas the Chinese, as in Eaſtern Tartary, are gradually encroaching upon the desert, building houses, and bringing into cultivation portions of the Land of Grass. Our brief voyage presented nothing remarkable, except, indeed, that in crossing a small river, upon the ice the car turned over and went to pieces. In France, in order to continue our journey, we should have needed a wheelwright and a smith to repair the damage; but fortunately our Phaeton was a Chinese, that is to say, a man who is never at a loss; and, accordingly, with a large ſtone, some bits of ſtick, and some ends of rope, he soon put everything to rights, and we merely loſt a little time.

TRAVELS IN TARTARY,

At the distance of a li from the Lamasery we found four Lamas, friends of Sandara, who had come to meet us. Their religious costume, the red scarf that enveloped them, their mitre-shaped yellow caps, their modest mien, the low, grave tones of their voices, all this produced a marked impression upon us, and we felt as though a perfume of religious and cenobitic life was diffused around us. It was past nine in the evening when we reached the first dwellings of the Lamasery. To avoid disturbing the profound silence which reigned everywhere about, the Lamas made the carman stop, and filled with straw the interior of the bells which hung from the horses' necks. We then advanced slowly, and without saying a word, along the calm deserted streets of this great Lamanesque city. The moon was not present; but the sky was so clear, so pure, and the stars were so brilliant, that we could perfectly distinguish the cottages of the Lamas spread over the sides of the mountain, and the grand, though fantastic outlines of the Buddhist temples, standing out in the air like gigantic phantoms. That which most struck us at the moment, was the majestic and solemn silence which prevailed throughout the Lamasery, and which was interrupted only by the short sleepy bark of some half-wakened dog, like the scream of the sea-eagle, or the melancholy sound of a marine shell marking, at intervals, the watches of the night. We at length reached Sandara's cottage. As it was too late for us to seek a suitable lodging, our teacher gave us up his own habitation, and himself sought the hospitality of a neighbour. The Lamas who had accompanied us did not withdraw until they had made for us some tea with milk, and set before us some mutton, some fresh butter, and some exquisite rolls. We supped with excellent appetite, for we were thoroughly hungry, and, moreover, we experienced in our inmost heart a feeling of

THIBET, AND CHINA

peculiar contentment, for which it seemed difficult to account.

We attempted to sleep, but it was in vain; slumber would not come near us; our minds, indeed, were too full of the strange position in which we now found ourselves. The whole thing appeared quite inconceivable. There were we, in this land of Amdo, unknown to Europe; in this great Lamasery of Kounboum, so famous, so venerated among Buddhists, in the cell of one of its ablest Lamas, amidst conventual manners although new to us; all these and analogous considerations whirled through and about the brain, like the vague intangible forms of a dream. We passed the night framing all sorts of plans.

As soon as day began to dawn we were on foot. Around us all was still silent. We offered up our morning prayer, our hearts agitated with sentiments altogether new to us in their peculiar character; with mingled joy and pride that it had been thus vouchsafed to us to invoke the true God in this famous Lamasery, consecrated to a lying and impious worship. It seemed to us as though we were about to grasp universal Buddhism within the paternal arms of the Christian faith.

Sandara soon made his appearance, and prepared for our breakfast some tea with milk, raisins, and cakes fried in butter. While we were occupied with our meal, he opened a small cupboard, and took out a wooden plate, highly polished, and decorated with gilding and flowers upon a red ground. After wiping it carefully with his scarf, he placed upon it a broad sheet of pink paper, then, upon the paper, he symmetrically arranged four fine pears, which he had directed us to buy at Tang-Keou-Eul, and then he covered the whole with a silk handkerchief, of oblong form, called in these countries *Khata* [*kha-btags*].

TRAVELS IN TARTARY,

"With this," said he, "we will go and borrow a lodging for you."

The *Khata*, or Scarf of Blessings, is so prominent a feature in Thibetian manners that we may as well give an account of it. The *Khata*, then, is a piece of silk, nearly as fine as gauze, and of so very pale a blue as to be almoſt white. Its length about triples its breadth, and the two extremities are generally fringed. There are *Khatas* of all sizes and all prices, for a *Khata* is an objeċt with which neither poor nor rich can dispense. No one ever moves unless provided with a supply. When you go to pay a visit, when you go to ask a favour, or to acknowledge one, you begin with displaying the *Khata* ; you take it in both hands, and offer it to the person whom you desire to honour. When two friends who have not seen each other for a long time, meet, their firſt proceeding is to interchange a *Khata* ; it is as much a matter of course as shaking hands in Europe. When you write, it is usual to enclose a *Khata* in the letter. We cannot exaggerate the importance which the Thibetians, the Si-Fan, the Houng-Mao-Eul, and all the people who dwell towards the weſtern shores of the Blue Sea, attach to the ceremony of the *Khata*. With them, it is the pureſt and sincereſt expression of all the nobleſt sentiments. The moſt gracious words, the moſt magnificent presents go for nothing, if unaccompanied with the *Khata* ; whereas, with the *Khata*, the commoneſt objeċts become of infinite value. If any one comes, *Khata* in hand, to ask you a favour, to refuse the favour would be a great breach of propriety. This Thibetian cuſtom is very general among the Tartars, and especially in their Lamaseries ; and *Khatas* accordingly form a very leading feature of commerce with the Chinese at Tang-Keou-Eul. The Thibetian embassy never passes through the town without purchasing a prodigious number of these articles.

THIBET, AND CHINA

When we had finished our modest breakfast, we issued forth in search of a lodging. Sandara the Bearded preceded us, bearing gravely on both hands the famous dish of four pears. This proceeding seemed to us so strange, that we were altogether confused, imagining that the entire population would have their eyes fixed upon us. Nothing of the sort: the Lamas, whom we met, passed silently on, without even turning their heads, or paying the slightest attention to us in any way. The little *chabis*, harum-scarum rogues in common with schoolboys all over the world, alone seemed to notice our presence. At last we entered a house. The master was in the court-yard, drying horse-droppings in the sun. Upon perceiving us, he immediately enveloped himself in his scarf, and entered his cell. We followed him thither, and Sandara presented to him the *Khata* and the plate of pears, accompanying the present with an harangue in the East Thibetian tongue, of which we did not understand one single word. Meanwhile we stood humbly apart, like poor wretches incapable even of soliciting a favour for themselves. When the harangue was completed, the host invited us to seat ourselves on the carpet, presented to each a cup of tea with milk, and told us, in Mongol, that he was rejoiced that strangers, come from such a distance, that Lamas of the Western Heaven, should deign to cast their eyes upon his poor dwelling. Had he understood our European idioms, our answer would have been: Pray don't mention it; but as we had to speak in Mongol, we told him that we had, indeed, come from a great distance, but that, in great measure, we seemed once more at home when we had the good fortune to meet with hospitality such as his. After having sipped the tea, and conversed for a while about France, Rome, the Pope, and the cardinals, we got up, in order to visit the place destined for us, which, for poor wanderers like us, seemed perfectly magnificent. Our host assigned to us a large room, with an ample *kang*, a separate kitchen, with stove, kettle, and other utensils, and, lastly, a stable for the horse and the mule. We almost wept with joy, and infinitely regretted that we had not another *Khata* at hand, wherewith at once to express our warm gratitude to the excellent Lama.

How potent is the empire of religion over the heart of man, even though that religion be false, and ignorant of its true object! How great was the difference, for example, between these Lamas, so generous, so hospitable, so fraternal towards strangers, and the Chinese, that thorough nation of shopkeepers, with hearts dry as a ship-biscuit, and grasping as a monkey, who will not give a traveller even a cup of water except for money or money's worth. The reception given to us in the Lamasery of Kounboum at once recalled to our thoughts those monasteries, raised by the hospitality of our religious ancestors, in which travellers and the poor ever found refreshment for the body and consolation for the soul.

We moved into our new dwelling the same day, the Lamas, more immediately neighbours of Sandara, cordially giving us their assistance. It was obviously with genuine pleasure that they carried for us, on their shoulders, the various articles composing our baggage; that they swept the room, lighted the fire, and arranged the stable for the reception of the animals. When all these matters were completed, the master of the house had, according to the rules of hospitality, to prepare an entertainment for us, since people, who are moving, are supposed to have no time for anything else.

Our readers will probably not be displeased at our giving them here a sketch of our new house and of

THIBET, AND CHINA

its inhabitants. Immediately within the entrance gate was an oblong court, surrounded with stables commodiously arranged. On the left of the gate, a narrow passage led to a second square court, the four sides of which were occupied with the cells of Lamas. The side opposite the corridor constituted the abode of the master of the house, named Akayé [aka-yeh] "old brother." Akayé was a man of sixty odd years, tall, and so very thin and dry that he seemed a living skeleton. His long face was a mere framework of bones, covered with a baked, wrinkled skin. When he threw aside his scarf, and showed his arms, blackened with the sun, you might very well have taken them for two old bare vine sticks. Though he still managed to keep himself tolerably straight upon his legs, his step itself was tottering. Altogether he looked like some antique piece of mechanism convulsively put in motion from time to time by the operation of a piston. For thirty-eight years Akayé had been employed in the temporal administration of the Lamasery. He had in this occupation amassed a tolerable fortune, but it had all gone in charitable gifts and in charity loans never returned, so that he was now reduced to great poverty, nothing remaining to him but this house, which he had built in the time of his prosperity, and which no one would purchase from him. To let it was against the rules of the Lamasery, which admit no medium between absolute sale or absolute gift, except gratuitous loan. To complete his misfortunes, Akayé was unable to profit by the extraordinary offerings which from time to time are distributed among the Lamas who have attained certain grades in the hierarchy. Having been completely occupied throughout life with temporal matters, he had had no time for study, so that he was altogether illiterate, and could neither read nor write. This did not, however, prevent him from praying, morning, noon, and night; he had his chaplet conſtantly in his hand, and pass him when you might, you would hear him mumbling various forms of prayer. This man was a creature of excellent heart, but nobody seemed to take any heed to him—he was old and penniless.

To the right of Akayé, in another side of the court, lodged a Lama of Chinese origin, who was accordingly called the Kitat-Lama (Chinese Lama). Though seventy years old, he was in far better condition than poor Akayé; for though his frame was somewhat bent, it was ſtill comfortably filled out; his face, replete with animation, was adorned with a fine white beard, somewhat yellowish towards the extremity. The Kitat-Lama was a man eminent among the Lama *savants ;* he wrote and spoke perfeƈtly Chinese, Mongol, and Thibetian. During a long residence in Thibet and in several kingdoms of Tartary, he had amassed a large fortune; it was said that in his cell were several cheſts full of silver ingots; yet his avarice continued of the moſt sordid character; he lived wretchedly, and clothed himself in rags; he was always turning his head about on one side or the other, like a man in perpetual fear of being robbed. In Tartary he had been considered a Grand Lama, but in Kounboum, where Lamanesque notables abound, he was merely one of the crowd. The Kitat-Lama had with him a *Chabi* (pupil) eleven years old, a sharp, mischievous little vagabond, though with a good heart at bottom. Every evening we heard him at high words with his maſter, who regularly reproached him at night for the monſtrous extravagances of the day, in respeƈt of too much butter, too much tea, too much oil, too much everything.

Opposite the dwelling of the Kitat-Lama was the lodging of the two French missionaries; and beside their apartment was a small cell, wherein modeſtly dwelt a young student of medicine, in his second year. This young Lama was a tall, broad-shouldered fellow of twenty-four, whose, dull, lead-coloured, fat face convicted him of effecting in his small abode a very considerable consumption of butter. We never saw him poking his nose from his hole without thinking of [La] Fontaine's rat, which, out of devotion, had retired into a great Dutch cheese. This young man was afflicted with a convulsive stammering, which sometimes almost choked him when he talked, and this infirmity, in rendering him timid and reserved, had also, perhaps, contributed to develop in him a certain amiability of manner and readiness to oblige. His great horror was the little *Chabi*, who took a malicious pleasure in imitating his manner of speaking.

The portion of the court which faced the residence of old Akayé was composed of a range of small kitchens, quite separate the one from the other. The master of the house, the Kitat-Lama, the stutterer, the missionaries, each had a kitchen of his own. In the phrase of the Lamasery, we were four distinct families in the house. Notwithstanding the collection of several families within one enclosure, there prevails throughout the most perfect order and silence ; the inmates seldom interchange visits, and each attends to his own affairs without in the smallest degree interfering with those of his neighbour. In the house where we were located, we never saw our co-dwellers except on very fine days. It being now the depth of winter, whenever the sun favoured our court-yard with its rays, the four families forthwith issued from their respective apartments, and sat themselves down before their doors on their felt mats. The Kitat-Lama, whose eyes were still very good, would occupy himself in mending his wretched garments with bits of old rags, Akayé would murmur his prayers, scratching all the while his arms, the skin of which was so rough that it almoſt resounded to the touch. The ſtudent in medicine would chant, in order to avoid ſtammering, his lesson of therapeutics. As to ourselves, it was no easy matter to divert our attention from the singular speƈtacle around us ; we had, indeed, on our knees our book of Thibetian dialogues, but our eyes were more frequently direƈted to the three families basking in the sun.

The Lamasery of Kounboum contains nearly 4,000 Lamas ; its site is one of enchanting beauty. Imagine in a mountain's side a deep, broad ravine, adorned with fine trees, and harmonious with the cawing of rooks and yellow-beaked crows, and the amusing chattering of magpies. On the two sides of the ravine, and on the slopes of the mountain, rise, in an amphitheatrical form, the white dwellings of the Lamas of various sizes, but all alike surrounded with a wall, and surmounted by a terrace. Amidſt these modeſt habitations, rich only in their intense cleanliness and their dazzling whiteness, you see rising, here and there, numerous Buddhiſt temples with gilt roofs, sparkling with a thousand brilliant colours, and surrounded with elegant colonnades. The houses of the superiors are diſtinguished by ſtreamers floating from small hexagonal turrets ; everywhere the eye is attraƈted by myſtic sentences, written in large Thibetian charaƈters, red or black, upon the doors, upon the walls, upon the poſts, upon pieces of linen floating like flags from maſts upon the tops of the houses. Almoſt at every ſtep you see niches in form resembling a sugar-loaf, within which are burning incense, odoriferous wood, and cypress leaves. The moſt ſtriking feature of all, however, is to see an exclusive population of Lamas walking about the numerous ſtreets of the Lamasery, clothed in their uniform of red dresses and yellow mitres. Their face is ordinarily grave ; and though silence is not prescribed, they speak little, and that always in

THIBET, AND CHINA

an undertone. You see very few of them at all about the ſtreets, except at the hours appointed for entering or quitting the schools, and for public prayer. During the reſt of the day, the Lamas for the moſt part keep within doors, except when they descend by narrow, tortuous paths to the bottom of the ravines, and return thence, laboriously carrying on their shoulders a long barrel containing the water required for domeſtic purposes. At intervals you meet ſtrangers who come to satisfy a devotional feeling, or to visit some Lama of their acquaintance.

The Lamasery of Kounboum, indeed, enjoys so high a reputation that the worshippers of Buddha resort thither in pilgrimage from all parts of Tartary and Thibet, so that not a day passes in which there are not pilgrims arriving and departing. Upon the great feſtivals, the congregation of ſtrangers is immense, and there are four of these in the year, the moſt famous of all being the Feaſt of Flowers, which takes place on the fifteenth day of the firſt moon. Nowhere is the feſtival celebrated with so much pomp and solemnity as at Kounboum. Those which take place in Tartary, in Thibet, and even at Lha-Ssa itself, are not at all comparable with it. We were inſtalled at Kounboum on the sixth of the firſt moon, and already numerous caravans of pilgrims were arriving by every road that led to the Lamasery. The feſtival was in everyone's mouth. The flowers, it was said, were this year of surpassing beauty: the Council of the Fine Arts, who had examined them, had declared them to be altogether superior to those of preceding years. As soon as we heard of these marvellous flowers, we haſtened, as may be supposed, to seek information respeƈting a feſtival hitherto quite unknown to us. The following are the details with which we were furnished, and which we heard with no little curiosity.

TRAVELS IN TARTARY,

The flowers of the fifteenth of the first moon consist of representations, profane and religious, in which all the Asiatic nations are introduced with their peculiar physiognomies and their distinguishing costumes. Persons, places, apparel, decorations—all are formed of fresh butter. Three months are occupied in the preparations for this singular spectacle. Twenty Lamas, selected from among the most celebrated artists of the Lamasery, are daily engaged in these butter-works, keeping their hands all the while in water, lest the heat of the fingers should disfigure their productions. As these labours take place chiefly in the depth of the winter, the operators have much suffering to endure from the cold. The first process is thoroughly to knead the butter, so as to render it firm. When the material is thus prepared, the various portions of the butter work are confided to various artists, who, however, all alike work under the direction of a principal who has furnished the plan of the flowers for the year, and has the general superintendence of their production. The figures, etc., being prepared and put together, are then confided to another set of artists, who colour them, under the direction of the same leader. A museum of works in butter seemed to us so curious an idea that we awaited the fifteenth of the moon with somewhat of impatience.

On the eve of the festival, the arrival of strangers became perfectly amazing. Kounboum was no longer the calm, silent Lamasery, where everything bespoke the grave earnestness of spiritual life, but a mundane city, full of bustle and excitement. In every direction you heard the cries of the camels and the bellowing of the long-haired oxen on which the pilgrims had journeyed thither; on the slopes of the mountain overlooking the Lamasery arose numerous tents wherein were encamped such of the visitors as had not

THIBET, AND CHINA

found accommodation in the dwellings of the Lamas. Throughout the 14th, the number of persons who performed the pilgrimage round the Lamasery was immense. It was for us a strange and painful spectacle to view that great crowd of human creatures prostrating themselves at every step, and reciting in undertones their form of prayer. There were among these Buddhist zealots a great number of Tartar-Mongols all coming from a great distance. They were remarkable, alike, for their heavy, awkward gait, and for the intense devotion and scrupulous application with which they fulfilled the exact rules of the rite. The Houng-Mao-Eul, or Long Hairs, were there too, and, their manners being in no degree better here than at Tang-Keou-Eul, the haughty uncouthness of their devotion presented a singular contrast with the fervent, humble mysticism of the Mongols. They walked proudly, with heads erect, the right arm out of the sleeve and resting on their sabre hilts, and with fusils at their backs. The Si-Fan of the Amdo country formed the majority of the pilgrims. Their physiognomy expressed neither the rough recklessness of the Long Hairs, nor the honest good faith and good nature of the Tartars. They accomplished their pilgrimage with an air of ease and nonchalance which seemed to say, " We are people of the place ; we know all about the matter, and need not put ourselves at all out of the way."

The head-dress of the Amdo women occasioned us an agreeable surprise ; it was a little bonnet of black or grey felt, the form of which was identical with that of the bonnets which were once all the fashion in France, and which were called, if we remember aright, *Chapeaux à la trois pour cent.* The only difference was that the riband by which the bonnet was tied under the chin, instead of being black, was red or yellow. The hair was allowed to fall from under the bonnet over the shoulders, in a number of minute braids, decorated with mother-of-pearl and coral beads. The rest of the costume was like that of the Tartar women, the weighty effect of the great sheepskin robe being, however, mightily modified by the little *Chapeaux à la trois pour cent*, which communicates a most coquettish air. We were greatly surprised to find among the crowd of pilgrims several Chinese who, chaplet in hand, were executing all the prostrations just like the rest. Sandara the Bearded told us they were *Khata* merchants, who, though they did not believe in Buddha at all, pretended intense devotion to him, in order to conciliate custom among his followers. We cannot say whether this was calumny on Sandara's part; but certainly his representation concurred altogether with our knowledge of the Chinese character.

On the 15th, the pilgrims again made the circuit of the Lamasery, but by no means in such numbers as on the preceding days. Curiosity impelled the great majority rather towards the points where preparations were making for the Feast of Flowers. When night fell, Sandara came and invited us to go and see the marvellous butter works of which we had heard so much. We accordingly proceeded with him, accompanied by the Stutterer, the Kitat-Lama, and the *Chabi*, leaving old Akayé to take care of the house. The flowers were arranged in the open air, before the various Buddhist temples of the Lamasery, and displayed by illuminations of the most dazzling brilliancy. Innumerable vases of brass and copper, in the form of chalices, were placed upon slight framework, itself representing various designs; and all these vases were filled with thick butter, supporting a solid wick. The illuminations were arranged with a taste that would have reflected no discredit on a Parisian decorator.

THIBET, AND CHINA

The appearance of the flowers themselves quite amazed us. We could never have conceived that in these deserts, amidst a half savage people, artists of such eminent merit could have been found. From the paintings and sculptures we had seen in various Lamaseries, we had not in the slightest degree been led to anticipate the exquisite finish which we had occasion to admire in the butter works. The flowers were bas-reliefs, of colossal proportions, representing various subjects taken from the history of Buddhism. All the personages were invested with a truth of expression that quite surprised us. The features were full of life and animation, the attitudes natural, and the drapery easy and graceful. You could distinguish at a glance the nature and quality of the materials represented. The furs were especially good. The various skins of the sheep, the tiger, the fox, the wolf, etc., were so admirably rendered that you felt inclined to go and feel them with the hand, and ascertain whether, after all, they were not real. In each bas-relief you at once recognized Buddha; his face, full of nobleness and majesty, appertained to the Caucasian type, the artists conforming therein to the Buddhist traditions, which relate that Buddha, a native of the Western Heaven, had a complexion fair, and slightly tinged with red, broad, full eyes, a large nose, and long, curling, soft hair. The other personages had all the Mongol type, with the Thibetian, Chinese, Si-Fan, and Tartar shadings, so nicely discriminated that, without any reference whatever to the costume, you recognized at once to what particular tribe each individual belonged. There were a few heads of Hindoos and negroes, excellently represented. The latter excited a good deal of curiosity among the spectators. These large bas-reliefs were surrounded with frames, representing animals and flowers, all in butter, and all admirable, like the works they enclosed, for their delicacy of outline and the beauty of their colouring. On the road which led from one temple to another, were placed, at intervals, small bas-reliefs representing, in miniature, battles, hunting incidents, nomadic episodes, and views of the most celebrated Lamaseries of Thibet and Tartary. Finally, in front of the principal temple, there was a theatre, which, with its personages and its decorations, was all of butter. The *dramatis personæ* were a foot high, and represented a community of Lamas on their way to solemnize prayer. At first, the stage is empty, then, a marine conch is sounded, and you see issuing from two doors two files of minor Lamas, followed by the superiors in their state dresses. After remaining, for a moment, motionless on the stage, the procession disappears at the sides, and the representation is over. This spectacle excited great enthusiasm; but, for ourselves, who had seen rather better mechanism, we regarded these mannikins, that moved on the stage and then off it without stirring a limb, as decidedly flat. One representation of the play, therefore, amply sufficed for us, and we went about admiring the bas-reliefs.

Whilst we were examining a group of devils, as grotesque, at all events, as those of Callot, we heard behind us a tremendous flourish of trumpets and marine conches, and, upon enquiry, were informed that the Grand Lama was issuing forth from his sanctuary to visit the flowers. We desired nothing better, for the Grand Lama of Kounboum was a great object of curiosity with us. He soon reached the place where we stood. He walked in the centre of the principal dignitaries of the Lamasery, preceded by minor Lamas, who cleared the way with great black whips. This Living Buddha appeared to us to be, at the outside, forty years old; he was of ordinary size, with a very flat and very common face, and of a very dark complexion. As he passed on he gave a vague glance at the bas-reliefs; when he saw that fine face of Buddha so repeatedly presented to his observation, he muſt, we thought, have said to himself that by dint of transmigrations he had dolefully degenerated from his original type. If the person of the Grand Lama, however, did not particularly ſtrike us, his coſtume did, for it was ſtrictly that of our own bishops: he bore on his head a yellow mitre, a long ſtaff in the form of a cross was in his right hand, and his shoulders were covered with a mantle of purple-coloured silk, faſtened on the cheſt with a clasp, and in every respect resembling a cope. Hereinafter we shall have occasion to point out numerous analogies between the Roman Catholic worship and the Lamanesque ceremonies.

The spectators generally appeared to give very slight heed to their Living Buddha, their attention being much more closely applied to the Buddhas in butter, which, in truth, were much better worth looking at. The Tartars alone manifeſted any tokens of devotion; they clasped their hands, bowed their heads in token of respect, and seemed quite afflicted that the pressure of the crowd prevented them from proſtrating themselves at full length.

When the Grand Lama had made his circuit, he returned to his sanctuary, a proceeding which was adopted by all the spectators as a signal for abandoning themselves without reserve to transports of the moſt frantic joy. They sang themselves out of breath, danced themselves out of breath, they pushed one another about, they shouted and bawled loud enough to frighten the desert itself, they seemed all at once to have become a collection of lunatics. As, with all this disorder, there was risk of the illuminations and the butter works being overturned, Lamas armed with great lighted torches were ſtationed at intervals to ſtay the waves of the immense mass that rolled to and fro like a sea beaten by the tempeſt. We could not long endure the pressure, and the Kitat-Lama, perceiving the oppression under which we laboured, invited us to return home. We adopted the proposition all the more readily that the night was far advanced, and we felt the need of repose.

Next morning, when the sun rose, not a trace remained of the Feaſt of Flowers. All had disappeared; the bas-reliefs had been demolished, and the immense colleɛtion of butter had been thrown down a ravine to feed the crows withal. These grand works, on which so much pains, so much time, we may also say so much genius had been expended, had served merely as a speɛtacle for a single evening. Every year they make new flowers, and every year upon a new plan.

With the flowers disappeared also the pilgrims. Already, at daybreak, you saw them slowly ascending the tortuous paths of the mountain, returning to their homes in the desert sorrowfully and silently; for the heart of man can endure so little of joy in this world that the day succeeding a feſtival is generally full of bitterness and melancholy.

CHAPTER II

THE country of Amdo, situate south of Koukou-Noor, is inhabited by Eastern Thibetians, who, like the Mongol Tartars, lead a pastoral and nomadic life. The aspect of the country is wild and dismal. In all directions the eye discerns nothing but mountains of red and yellow ochre, almost destitute of vegetation, and intersected by deep ravines. It is only here and there, in this sterile and desolate region, that you find valleys tolerably supplied with pasturage, and hither the nomad tribes lead their flocks.

According to the Lamanesque chronicles, towards the middle of the fourteenth century of our era a shepherd of the land of Amdo, named Lombo-Moke [Lubumge (kLu-bum-dge)], had set up his black tent at the foot of a mountain, near the entrance to a deep ravine, through which, over a rocky bed, meandered an abundant stream. Lombo-Moke shared with his wife, Chingtsa-Tsio [Shing-bza-'ach'os] the cares of pastoral life. They possessed no numerous flocks; some twenty goats and a few *sarligues* [*sarlik*] or long-haired cattle, constituted all their wealth. For many years they had lived alone and childless in these wild solitudes. Each day Lombo-Moke led his animals to the neighbouring pastures, while Chingtsa-Tsio, remaining alone in her tent, occupied herself with the various preparations of milk, or with weaving, after the manner of the women of Amdo, a coarse linen with the long hair of the *sarligues*.

One day, Chingtsa-Tsio having descended to the bottom of the ravine to draw water, experienced a faintness, and fell senseless on a large stone which bore inscribed on it various characters in honour of the Buddha Chakdja-Mouni [Sâkya-muni]. When Chingtsa-Tsio came to herself, she felt a pain in her side, and at once comprehended that the fall had rendered her fruitful. In the year of the Fire Hen (1357), nine months after this mysterious event, she brought into the world a son, whom Lombo-Moke named Tsong-Kaba, from the appellation of the mountain, at whose feet his tent had stood for several years past. The marvellous child had, at his birth, a white beard, and his face wore an air of extraordinary majesty. There was nothing childlike about his manners. So soon as he saw the light, he was capable of expressing himself with clearness and precision in the language of Amdo. He spoke little, indeed, but his words always developed a profound appreciation of the nature and destiny of man.

At the age of three, Tsong-Kaba resolved to renounce the world, and to embrace the religious life. Chingtsa-Tsio, full of respect for the holy project of her son, herself shaved his head, and threw his fine long flowing hair outside the tent. From this hair there forthwith sprang a tree, the wood of which dispensed an exquisite perfume around, and each leaf of which bore, engraved on its surface, a character in the sacred language of Thibet. Tsong-Kaba himself withdrew into the most absolute retirement, avoiding even the presence of his parents. He took up his position on the summits of the wildest mountains, or in the depths of the profoundest ravines, and there passed whole days and nights in prayer and in the contemplation of eternal things. His fastings were long and frequent. He respected the life even of the humblest insect, and rigorously interdicted himself the consumption of any sort of flesh whatever.

THIBET, AND CHINA

While Tsong-Kaba was thus engaged in purifying his heart by assiduity and prayer, and the practices of an auſtere life, a Lama, from one of the moſt remote regions of the Weſt, casually visited the land of Amdo, and received the hospitality of Lombo-Moke's tent. Tsong-Kaba, amazed at the science and the sanctity of the ſtranger, proſtrated himself at his feet, and conjured him to become his inſtructor. The Lamanesque traditions relate that this Lama of the weſtern regions was remarkable not only for his learning, the profundity of which was unfathomable, but for the singularity of his appearance. People especially remarked his great nose, and his eyes that gleamed as with a supernatural fire. The ſtranger being, on his part, not less ſtruck with the marvellous qualities of Tsong-Kaba, did not hesitate to adopt him as his disciple, and for this purpose took up his abode in the land of Amdo, where, however, he only lived a few years. After having initiated his pupil in all the doctrines recognized by the most renowned saints of the Weſt, he fell asleep one day, on a ſtone, on the summit of a mountain, and his eyes opened not again.

Tsong-Kaba, deprived of the holy ſtranger's lessons, became all the more eager for religious inſtruction, and ere long he formed the resolution of abandoning his tribe, and of going to the further weſt, to drink at their very source the pure precepts of sacred science. He departed, ſtaff in hand, alone, and without a guide, but his heart filled with superhuman courage. He firſt proceeded due south, and reached, after long and laborious journeyings, the frontiers of the province of Yun-Nan, quite at the extremity of the Chinese empire. Then, inſtead of pursuing the previous directions, he turned towards the north-weſt, along the banks of the great river Yarou-Dsangbo [Yarudzang-po]. He reached at length the sacred town of the kingdom of Oui [Wei (Dbus; Üi)].[1] As he was about to continue on his way, a *Lha* "spirit" all radiant with light, stayed him, and prohibited his further progress. "Oh, Tsong-Kaba," said he, " all these vast regions belong to the great empire which has been granted to thee. It is here thou art ordained to promulgate the rites of religion and its prayers. It is here will be accomplished the last evolution of thy immortal life." Tsong-Kaba, docile to the supernatural life, entered the Land of Spirits (Lha-Ssa), and selected an humble dwelling, in the most solitary quarter of the town.

The monk of the tribe of Amdo soon attracted disciples; and before long his new doctrine and the innovations which he introduced into the Lamanesque ceremonies created considerable excitement. At length, Tsong-Kaba resolutely put himself forward as a reformer, and began to make war upon the ancient worship. His partisans increased from day to day, and became known as the Yellow Cap Lamas, in contradistinction to the Red Cap Lamas, who supported the old system. The king of the country of Oui, and the Chakdja, the Living Buddha, and chief of the local Lamanesque hierarchy, became alarmed at this new sect that was introducing confusion into religious ceremonies. The Chakdja sent for Tsong-Kaba, in order to ascertain whether his knowledge was so profound, so marvellous, as his partisans pretended; but the reformer refused to accept the invitation. Representing a religious system which was to supersede the old system, it was not his business, he considered, to perform an act of submission.

Meantime the Yellow Caps became by degrees the predominant sect, and the homage of the multitude was

[1] Oui, in Thibetian, means centre, middle; and hence the name was given to the province which occupies the centre of Thibet, and the capital of which is Lha-Ssa.

turned towards Tsong-Kaba. The Buddha Chakdja, finding his authority repudiated, made up his mind to go and visit the little Lama of the province of Amdo, as he contumeliously designated the reformer. At this interview, he proposed to have a discussion with his adversary, which he flattered himself would result in the triumph of the old doctrine. He repaired to the meeting with great pomp, surrounded with all the attributes of his religious supremacy. As he entered the modest cell of Tsong-Kaba, his high red cap struck against the beam of the door, and fell to the ground, an accident which everybody regarded as a presage of triumph for the Yellow Cap. The reformer was seated on a cushion, his legs crossed, and apparently took no heed to the entrance of Chakdja. He did not rise to receive him, but continued gravely to tell his beads. The Chakdja, without permitting himself to be disconcerted either by the fall of his cap, or by the cold reception that was given him, entered abruptly upon the discussion, by a pompous eulogium of the old rites, and an enumeration of the privileges which he claimed under them. Tsong-Kaba, without raising his eyes, interrupted him in these terms : " Let go, cruel man that thou art, let go the louse thou art crushing between thy fingers. I hear its cries from where I sit, and my heart is torn with commiserating grief." The Chakdja, in point of fact, while vaunting his own virtues, had seized a louse under his vest, and in contempt of the doctrine of transmigration, which forbids men to kill anything that has life in it, he was endeavouring to crack it between his nails. Unprovided with a reply to the severe words of Tsong-Kaba, he prostrated himself at his feet, and acknowledged his supremacy.

Thenceforward, the reforms proposed by Tsong-Kaba encountered no obstacle ; they were adopted throughout Thibet, and afterwards became, by imperceptible degrees, established in all the kingdoms of Tartary. In 1409, Tsong-Kaba, then fifty-two years old, founded the celebrated monastery of Kaldan, three leagues from Lha-Ssa; it still flourishes, containing upwards of 8,000 Lamas. In 1419, the soul of Tsong-Kaba, who had become Buddha, quitted the earth and returned to the Celestial Realm, where it was admitted into the Heaven of Rapture. His body, which remained in the Lamasery of Kaldan, preserves to this day, it is alleged, all its original freshness, and, moreover, by a perennial miracle, lies a little above the earth, without being supported or raised upon anything. It is added that the mouth still, from time to time, addresses words of encouragement to those Lamas who have made marked progress towards perfection—words altogether inaudible for the less eminent of the community.

Besides the reformation which Tsong-Kaba introduced into the liturgy, he rendered himself further famous by a new edition of the *Body of Doctrine*, left by Chakdja-Mouni. The most important of his works is entitled *Lam-Rim-Tsien-Bo* [*Lam-rim-ch'en-po*] " the Progressive Path to Perfection."

Upon the most superficial examination of the reforms and innovations introduced by Tsong-Kaba into the Lamanesque worship, one must be struck with their affinity to Catholicism. The cross, the mitre, the dalmatica, the cope which the Grand Lamas wear on their journeys, or when they are performing some ceremony out of the temple; the service with double choirs, the psalmody, the exorcisms, the censer, suspended from five chains, and which you can open or close at pleasure, the benedictions given by the Lamas by extending the right hand over the heads of the faithful; the chaplet, ecclesiastical celibacy, spiritual retirement, the worship of the saints, the feasts, the processions, the litanies, the holy water,

THIBET, AND CHINA

all these are analogies between the Buddhists and ourselves. Now, can it be said that these analogies are of Christian origin? We think so. We have indeed found neither in the traditions nor in the monuments of the country any positive proof of their adoption, still it is perfectly legitimate to put forward conjectures which possess all the characteristics of the most emphatic probability.

It is known that, in the fourteenth century, at the time of the domination of the Mongol emperors, there existed frequent relations between the Europeans and the peoples of Upper Asia. We have already, in the former part of our narrative, referred to those celebrated embassies which the Tartar conquerors sent to Rome, to France, and to England. There is no doubt that the barbarians who thus visited Europe must have been struck with the pomp and splendour of the ceremonies of Catholic worship, and must have carried back with them into the desert enduring memories of what they had seen. On the other hand, it is also known that, at the same period, brethren of various religious orders undertook remote pilgrimages for the purpose of introducing Christianity into Tartary; and these must have penetrated at the same time into Thibet, among the Si-Fan, and among the Mongols on the Blue Sea. Jean de Montcorvin, Archbishop of Peking, had already organized a choir of Mongol monks, who daily practised the recitation of the Psalms, and the ceremonies of the Catholic faith. Now, if one reflects that Tsong-Kaba lived precisely at the period when the Christian religion was being introduced into Central Asia, it will be no longer matter of astonishment that we find, in reformed Buddhism, such striking analogies with Christianity.

And may we not proceed to lay down a proposition of a more positive character? This very legend of Tsong-Kaba, which we heard in the very place of his birth, and from the mouth of several Lamas, does it not materially ſtrengthen our theory? Setting aside all the marvellous features which have been added to the ſtory by the imagination of the Lamas, it may be fairly admitted that Tsong-Kaba was a man raised above the ordinary level by his genius, and also, perhaps by his virtue; that he was inſtructed by a ſtranger from the Weſt; that after the death of the maſter the disciple, proceeding to the Weſt, took up his abode in Thibet, where he diffused the inſtruction which he himself had received. May it not be reasonably inferred that this ſtranger with the great nose was an European, one of those Catholic missionaries who at the precise period penetrated in such numbers into Upper Asia. It is by no means surprising that the Lamanesque traditions should have preserved the memory of that European face, whose type is so different from that of the Asiatics. During our abode at Kounboum, we, more than once, heard the Lamas make remark upon the singularity of our features, and say, roundly, that we were of the same land with the maſter of Tsong-Kaba. It may be further supposed that a premature death did not permit the Catholic missionary to complete the religious education of his disciple, who himself, when afterwards he became an apoſtle, merely applied himself, whether from having acquired only an incomplete knowledge of Chriſtian doctrine, or from having apoſtatized from it, to the introduction of a new Buddhiſt liturgy. The feeble opposition which he encountered in his reformation would seem to indicate that already the progress of Chriſtian ideas in these countries had materially shaken the faith of Buddha. We shall by-and-by inquire whether the numerous analogies between the Buddhiſts and the Catholics are an obſtacle or an aid to the propagation of the faith in Tartary and Thibet.

THIBET, AND CHINA

The reformation of Tsong-Kaba triumphed in all the regions comprised between the Himalaya mountains, the frontiers of Russia, and the Great Wall of China. It even made its way into some provinces of the Celestial Empire, into Kan-Sou, for example, Chan-Si, Pe-Tche-Li, and all Mantchouria. The Bonzes have retained the ancient rites, with the exception only of a few innovations which have been adopted in particular localities. There is now a regular distinction understood between the two classes of Lamas, the yellow and the grey; that is to say, those who follow the reformation and those who persist in the elder worship. These two sects, which no doubt at one time treated each other as rivals, and made war upon each other, now live in perfect harmony. The Bonzes and the Lamas regard themselves as all of the same family.

The tribe of Amdo, previously altogether obscure and of no importance whatever, has, since the reformation of Buddhism, acquired a prodigious celebrity. The mountain at the foot of which Tsong-Kaba was born became a famous place of pilgrimage. Lamas assembled there from all parts to build their cells, and thus by degrees was formed that flourishing Lamasery, the fame of which extends to the remotest confines of Tartary. It is called Kounboum, from two Thibetian words signifying Ten Thousand Images, and having allusion to the tree which, according to the legend, sprang from Tsong-Kaba's hair, and bears a Thibetian character on each of its leaves.

It will here be naturally expected that we say something about this tree itself. Does it exist? Have we seen it? Has it any peculiar attributes? What about its marvellous leaves? All these questions our readers are entitled to put to us. We will endeavour to answer as categorically as possible.

Yes, this tree does exist, and we had heard of it too

often during our journey not to feel somewhat eager to visit it. At the foot of the mountain on which the Lamasery stands, and not far from the principal Buddhist temple, is a great square enclosure, formed by brick walls. Upon entering this we were able to examine at leisure the marvellous tree, some of the branches of which had already manifested themselves above the wall. Our eyes were first directed with earnest curiosity to the leaves, and we were filled with an absolute consternation of astonishment at finding that, in point of fact, there were upon each of the leaves well-formed Thibetian characters, all of a green colour, some darker, some lighter than the leaf itself. Our first impression was a suspicion of fraud on the part of the Lamas; but, after a minute examination of every detail, we could not discover the least deception. The characters all appeared to us portions of the leaf itself, equally with its veins and nerves. The position was not the same in all; in one leaf they would be at the top of the leaf; in another, in the middle; in a third, at the base, or at the side; the younger leaves represented the characters only in a partial state of formation. The bark of the tree and its branches, which resemble that of the plane tree, are also covered with these characters. When you remove a piece of old bark, the young bark under it exhibits the indistinct outlines of characters in a germinating state, and, what is very singular, these new characters are not unfrequently different from those which they replace. We examined everything with the closest attention, in order to detect some trace of trickery, but we could discern nothing of the sort, and the perspiration absolutely trickled down our faces under the influence of the sensations which this most amazing spectacle created. More profound intellects than ours may, perhaps, be able to supply a satisfactory explanation of the mysteries of this singular tree; but as to us, we altogether give it up. Our readers possibly may smile at our ignorance; but we care not, so that the sincerity and truth of our statement be not suspected.

The Tree of the Ten Thousand Images seemed to us of great age. Its trunk, which three men could scarcely embrace with outstretched arms, is not more than eight feet high; the branches, instead of shooting up, spread out in the shape of a plume of feathers, and are extremely bushy: few of them are dead. The leaves are always green, and the wood, which is of reddish tint, has an exquisite odour, something like that of cinnamon. The Lamas informed us that in summer, towards the eighth moon, the tree produces large red flowers of an extremely beautiful character. They informed us also that there nowhere else exists another such tree; that many attempts have been made in various Lamaseries of Tartary and Thibet to propagate it by seeds and cuttings, but that all these attempts have been fruitless.

The Emperor Khang-Hi, when upon a pilgrimage to Kounboum, constructed, at his own private expense, a dome of silver over the Tree of the Ten Thousand Images; moreover, he made a present to the Grand Lama of a fine black horse, capable of travelling a thousand lis a day, and of a saddle adorned with precious stones. The horse is dead, but the saddle is still shown in one of the Buddhist temples, where it is an object of special veneration. Before quitting the Lamasery, Khang-Hi endowed it with a yearly revenue, for the support of 350 Lamas.

The fame of Kounboum, due in the first instance to the celebrity of Tsong-Kaba, is now maintained by the excellent discipline of the Lamasery, and the superiority of its teaching. Its Lamas are deemed students throughout their lives, for religious knowledge is reputed inexhaustible. The students are distributed into four sections, or faculties, according to the nature of the special studies to which they desire to apply themselves. 1. The Faculty of Mysticism, which comprehends the rules of contemplative life, and the examples exhibited in the career of the Buddhist saints. 2. The Faculty of Liturgy, comprising the study of religious ceremonies, with the expounding of all that appertains to Lamanesque worship. 3. The Faculty of Medicine, which applies itself to the four hundred and forty maladies of the human frame, to medical botany, and to the pharmacopœia. 4. The Faculty of Prayers, the most esteemed of all, the best paid, and, as a matter of course, the most numerous.

The voluminous works which serve as the basis of instruction in prayers, are divided into thirteen series, which represent, as it were, so many degrees in the hierarchy. The place which each student occupies in the schoolroom and the temple service depends upon the series of theological works through which he has passed. Among the Lamas, you see old men proclaiming, by their low position in the hierarchy, their idleness or incapacity; and, on the other hand, mere youths elevated, by their application and their ability, to the highest ranks.

In order to obtain a degree in the Faculty of Prayers, all that is required from the student is to recite, without stopping, the books he has been directed to study. When he believes himself quite up, he gives intimation of this belief to the Grand Lama of prayers, in the form of a rich *khata*, a dish of raisins, and some ounces of silver, in ingots, the amount depending upon the degree at which he aims; he also makes presents to the Lama-examiners. Although it is, of course, perfectly understood that the judges are incorruptible, yet at Kounboum, as elsewhere, people do say that a few offerings to the academy are not without their effect at an examination. Men are men everywhere!

Before the principal temple of the Lamasery there is a large square court, paved with broad stones, and surrounded with twisted columns, covered with coloured sculptures. It is in this enclosure that the Lamas of the Faculty of Prayers assemble at the lecture hour, which is announced to them by the sound of a marine conch; here they sit, according to their rank, upon the bare stones, undergoing, in winter, the cold, the frost and the snow; and in summer, the rain, and the sun's heat. The professors alone are under shelter; they sit upon a sort of platform, covered with a tent. It is a singular spectacle to see all these Lamas with their red scarves and great yellow mitres, so huddled together that you cannot see the flag-stones on which they sit. After some of the students have given out the lesson of the day, the professors, in turn, give commentaries, vague and incomprehensible as the text itself, but nobody makes any objection; the explanation is quite near enough. Besides, the universal conviction is that the sublimity of a doctrine is in exact proportion to its obscurity and its unintelligibility.

The lesson generally concludes with a thesis, supported by a student previously named for that purpose, and whom the other students are entitled to question upon whatever subject comes into their heads at the time. There is nothing more preposterous than these theses, which nearly remind one of those famous discussions of the schools in the middle ages, where there were such furious argumentations *de omni re scibili*. At Kounboum the rule is for the conqueror to mount on the shoulders of the conquered, and to be carried by him in triumph right round the walls of the school. One day Sandara the Bearded came home from lecture, his face radiant with unwonted

TRAVELS IN TARTARY,

smiles. We soon learned that he had been the hero of the theses; he had defeated his competitor upon the important question why poultry and other winged creatures are destitute of one of the vital functions common to all other animals. We mention this particular instance because it will give an idea of the elevation and grandeur of Lamanesque education.

At certain periods of the year, the Living Buddha, the Grand Superior of the Lamasery, himself appears in person, and gives, in state, official expoundings of the Sacred Books. These commentaries, though not a bit more learned or more lucid than those of the professors, are received as authority. The Thibetian language is alone used in the schools.

The discipline of the Lamasery is vigilant and severe. In the faculties, during the lectures, and in the temples, during the recitation of prayers, you see Lama censors leaning upon long iron rods, and maintaining order and silence among the students. The least infraction of the rules is at once visited with a reprimand, and, if necessary, with blows of the iron rod, the old Lamas being equally liable to both the one and the other with the young *Chabis*.

A certain number of Lamas form the police of the Lamasery; they are attired in the same manner as the other Lamas, only their dress is grey and their mitre black. Day and night they perambulate the streets of the city, armed with a great whip, and re-establish order wherever their interposition has become necessary. Three tribunals, presided over by Lama judges, have jurisdiction in all matters that are above the immediate authority of the police. Those who are guilty of theft, to however trifling an amount, are first branded on the forehead and on each cheek with a hot iron, and then expelled from the Lamasery.

The Buddhist monasteries, though similar in many

respects to our own, exhibit essential differences. The Lamas are subject, it is true, to one same rule, and to one same discipline, but it cannot be said that they live in community. You will find among them all the graduated shades of poverty and wealth that you see in mundane cities. At Kounboum we often observed Lamas clothed in rags, begging, at the doors of their rich brethren, a few handfuls of barley meal. Every third month the authorities make a distribution of meal to all the Lamas of the Lamaseries, without distinction, but the quantity is altogether inadequate. The voluntary offerings of the pilgrims come in aid, but, besides that these offerings are uncertain, they are divided among the Lamas according to the position which each occupies in the hierarchy, so that there are always a great many who never receive anything at all from this source.

Offerings are of two sorts, tea offerings and money offerings. The first is operated in this fashion: the pilgrim who proposes to entertain the brotherhood waits upon the superiors of the Lamasery, and, presenting to them a *khata*, announces that he shall have the devotion to offer to the Lamas a general or special tea. The tea-general is for the whole Lamasery without distinction; the tea-special is given only to one of the four faculties, the selection being with the pilgrim. On the day fixed for a tea-general, after the repetition of morning prayer, the presiding Lama gives a signal for the company to retain their seats. Then forty young *Chabis*, appointed by lot, proceed to the great kitchen, and soon return laden with jars of tea with milk; they pass along the ranks, and as they come to each Lama, the latter draws from his bosom his wooden tea-cup, and it is filled to the brim. Each drinks in silence, carefully placing a corner of his scarf before his cup, in order to modify the apparent anomaly of introducing so material a proceeding as tea-drinking into so spiritual a spot. Generally there is tea enough presented to go round twice, the tea being ſtronger or weaker according to the generosity of the donor. There are some pilgrims who add a slice of fresh butter for each Lama, and magnificent Amphytrions go the length, further, of oatmeal cakes. When the banquet is over, the presiding Lama solemnly proclaims the name of the pious pilgrim who has done himself the immense credit of regaling the holy family of Lamas; the pilgrim donor proſtrates himself on the earth; the Lamas sing a hymn in his favour, and then march out in procession paſt their proſtrate benefaƈtor, who does not rise until the laſt of the Lamas has disappeared.

Offerings of this sort are very little for each individual Lama; but when you refleƈt that on such occasions there are assembled together more than 4,000 tea-drinkers, you may easily eſtimate that the aggregate expense becomes a very serious affair. In the Lamasery at Kounboum, one single tea-general, without either butter or cakes, coſts fifty ounces of silver, or about twenty pounds.

Money offerings are ſtill more expensive, for they are always accompanied with a tea-general. The money is not diſtributed at service time. After prayers, the presiding Lama announces that such a pilgrim, of such a place, has offered so many ounces of silver to the holy family of Lamas, and that the whole sum equally divided produces such a quotient. In the course of the day, the Lamas proceed to the Offering-office, where their respeƈtive proportion is scrupulously delivered to them.

There is no particular period or day fixed for the reception of offerings; they are always welcome; however, at the four great feſtivals of the year they are more numerous and more important than at other times, on account of the greater number of pilgrims.

THIBET, AND CHINA

After the Feaſt of Flowers, the King of Souniot, who was at Kounboum, made an offering, before he returned to Tartary, of six hundred ounces of silver, and a tea-general for eight days! with butter and cakes; the total expense amounting to six hundred pounds! When the offering is made by a diſtinguished personage, it is cuſtomary for the Living Buddha to be present at the ceremony, and he receives for his especial share an ingot of silver weighing fifty ounces, a piece of red or yellow silk, a pair of boots, and a mitre, arranged in a basket decorated with flowers and ribands, and covered with a rich *khata*. The pilgrim proſtrates himself on the ſteps of the altar, where the Living Buddha is seated, and places the basket at his feet. A *Chabi* takes it up, and in return presents to the pilgrim a *khata* in the name of the Living Buddha, whose business throughout is to preserve the impassibility and dignity befitting his assumed divinity.

Besides the diſtributions and the offerings, the Lamas of Kounboum employ various means of improving their temporal condition. Some of them keep cows, and sell to the colleagues their milk and butter which helps to season their tea and oatmeal. Others form themselves into a joint ſtock company, and undertake the preparation of the teas-general which the pilgrims present to the community: others are tailors, dyers, bootmakers, hatters, and so on, and make up, for a fixed remuneration, the clothes of the Lamas. Laſtly, a few of the number have shops, wherein they sell, at enormous profits, various goods which they procure from Tang-Keou-Eul or Si-Ning-Fou.

In the class of induſtrial Lamas there is, however, a certain number who derive their livelihood from occupations which seem more conformable with the spirit of a religious life, namely, the printing and transcribing the Lamanesque books. Our readers are, perhaps, aware that the Thibetian writing proceeds horizontally, and from left to right. Though the idiom of the Lamas is alphabetical, much in the manner of our European languages, yet they make no use of moveable type; stereotype printing on wood is alone practised. The Thibetian books resemble a large pack of cards; the leaves are moveable, and printed on both sides. As they are neither sewn nor bound together, in order to preserve them they are placed between two thin boards, which are fastened together with yellow bands. The editions of the Thibetian books printed at Kounboum are very rude, the letters are sprawling and coarse, and in all respects very inferior to those which emanate from the imperial printing press at Peking. The manuscript editions, on the contrary, are magnificent; they are enriched with illustrative designs, and the characters are elegantly traced. The Lamas do not write with a brush like the Chinese, but use little sticks of bamboo cut in the form of a pen; their inkstand is a little copper box resembling a jointed snuff-box, and which is filled with cotton saturated with ink. The Lamas size their paper, in order to prevent its blotting; for this purpose, instead of the solution of alum used by the Chinese, they sprinkle the paper with water mixed with one-tenth part of milk, a simple, ready, and perfectly effective process.

Sandara the Bearded did not belong to any of the classes of industrials that we have enumerated; he had a business of his own, namely, that of *taking in* the strangers whom devotion or other motives brought to the Lamasery. The Mongol-Tartars in particular afforded him profitable employment in this way. On their arrival he would introduce himself in the character of *cicerone*, and, thanks, to the easy, seductive elegance of his manners and conversation, he always managed to get engaged as their man of business during their

THIBET, AND CHINA

ſtay. At Kounboum itself Sandara's reputation was by no means unequivocal. The better Lamas shunned him, and some of them went so far as to give us a charitable hint not to confide too much in his fine words and always to keep an eye upon our purse when in his company. We learned that, compelled to quit Lha-Ssa for some knavery, he had vagabondized for three years through the provinces of Sse-Tchouan and Kan-Sou, as a ſtrolling player and fortune-teller. We were not at all surprised at this information. We had ourselves remarked that whenever Sandara became frankly himself, his manner was always that of an aƈtor.

One evening, when he seemed in a more amiable humour than ordinary, we thought we could extraƈt from him some of his old adventures. "Sandara," said we, "the chattering Lamas here pretend that on your way from Thibet you remained three years in China." "The words are truth." "They say, too, that you are a capital hand at ſtage recitations." Sandara rose, clacked a sort of prelude with his fingers, threw himself into a theatrical attitude, and recited, with emphasis, some Chinese verses. "A Lama comedian!" said we, laughingly; "this is a marvel indeed!" "No, no!" cried he; "I was firſt a Lama, then a comedian, and now I am a Lama again. Come," continued he, resuming his accuſtomed seat, "since the chatterers have spoken to you of my adventures, I will give you the real hiſtory of them.

"After remaining for ten years at Lha-Ssa, in the Lamasery of Sera, a longing for my country took possession of my thoughts: the Three Valleys occupied my soul. The malady at length became so powerful, that I could not resiſt it. I accordingly departed, having as my travelling companions four Lamas of Amdo, who were also returning home. Inſtead of pursuing the eaſtern route we proceeded southwards, for in that direction the desert is not wholly uninhabited. We journeyed, pack on back, and staff in hand. If on our way we came to a black tent, we sought its hospitality, otherwise we had to pass the night in the depths of some ravine, or beneath some rock. You know that Thibet is a country covered with great mountains; we had accordingly a continuous series of ascendings and descendings. Although it was summer, we frequently encountered heavy falls of snow. The nights were very cold, but during the day, especially in the valleys, we were almost killed with the heat.

" We walked on merrily, however. We were all in good health and in good humour, more particularly when the shepherds had made us a present of a kid, or a good lump of butter. In the country through which we passed we saw some very singular animals; they were not so big as an ordinary cat, and they were covered with a sort of hair as hard as iron needles. Whenever one of these creatures perceived us, it immediately rolled itself up, so that you could no longer distinguish head, tail, or feet, and became, as it were, a great ball, all bristling with long hard thorns. At first these beasts frightened us; we could not comprehend at all what they were, for the books of prayer say not a word about them. However, by degrees we got courage enough to examine them closely. As these balls were too prickly to be touched with the hand, we placed a stick horizontally across one of them, and then pressed down both ends, until we made the ball open itself a little, and then there came out a little face, like a man's, that looked at us fixedly. We cried out in great terror, and ran away as hard as we could. At last, however, we grew accustomed to the little animals, and they even served us for an amusement, for it was good fun to turn them over and over down the hills, with the iron ends of our staves.

THIBET, AND CHINA

"We also met with worms of a very surprising kind. One day when it was very hot, we were journeying along a little stream that meandered through a valley in which the grass grew very high. Towards noon, after drinking tea, we lay down and slept on the edge of the ſtream. You know that, according to the rule of Tsong Kaba, the yellow-mitred Lamas do not wear trousers. When we woke up we found a number of worms ſticking to our legs; they were of a grey colour, and as big as one's finger. We tried to get them off, but could not; and as we did not experience any pain from them, we waited to see what would be the end of the affair. By-and-by the beaſts swelled, and when they had become quite round and large, they dropped oft themselves. Oh! Thibet is a singular country. You see animals there that are found nowhere else. Lamas who have not travelled in the country won't believe what we tell them about it." "They are wrong, then," said we, "for what you have juſt said is in perfect conformity with the truth. These curious animals that you describe are not inhabitants of Thibet only; they are very common in our country. Those which are enveloped with sharp thorns we call hedgehogs; and the great worms we call leeches." "What, have you seen animals of the kind?" "Often." "I'm glad to hear it, for you'll be able to confirm what we say to any Lamas that don't believe us.

"Well, we went on quite comfortably, till we came to the Eul [Ol (? or Erh)] Mountain. This mountain is very lofty, and covered with a great foreſt of pine and holly; we reſted at the foot of it during a whole day, in a black tent. When night came, two of our number said: 'The evening is fine, the moon bright; we can't do better than cross the mountain in the cool of the night. In the morning it will grow hot, and we shall find it much more laborious to climb the mountain then.' 'No,' objected the others, 'night is for wild beasts; men should only travel by day.' Thus, you see, we disagreed about the matter. The two first persisted; they took up their iron-pointed staves, fastened their packs on their shoulders, and went their way. This, you will admit, was an ill step to take. When pilgrims have said: 'Let us journey together,' they should not part company.

"Well, when day broke, we also went on our way —we three who remained of the five. Just as we were reaching the summit of the Eul Mountain, 'Tsong-Kaba!' cried I, 'here is an iron-pointed staff on the ground.' 'Why,' said one of my companions, looking at the staff, 'this is Lobzan's [Lobzang (Blobzang)] staff.' We examined it closely, and clearly recognized it. 'This,' said we, 'is what people get by travelling at night. They drop something or other, and there is not light enough for them to find it again.' We went on. After a short further and very rugged ascent, we stepped on the plateau of the mountain. We had no sooner done so than all three sent forth a cry of terror; for we saw before us another iron-pointed staff, Lama's clothes torn in pieces, pieces of human flesh, and bones broken and gnawed. The earth torn up, and the grass trodden down, indicated that a severe struggle had taken place on the spot. It was obvious at once that some wild beasts, tigers or wolves, had killed and devoured our companions. I stood for a moment panic-struck at the horrible spectacle. Then I wept like a child. We rushed down the other side of the mountain with fear-impelled speed. From that moment our journey was a sad and silent one. Only, when we came to a black tent, we would recount to the shepherds the awful catastrophe of our poor comrades, and the relation afforded some slight alleviation of our grief.

"Three moons after our departure from Lha-Ssa

THIBET, AND CHINA

we arrived at the frontiers of China. There we separated; the two Lamas of Amdo turned to the north, towards their own country; while I, crossing the wall of Ten Thousand Lis, entered the province of Sse-Tchouan. After a few days' march, I found in an inn a company of comedians. All night these people did nothing but sing, joke and drink rice-wine. ' In this country of Sse-Tchouan,' said the manager of the company to me, ' there are no Lamas. What do you propose to do with that red robe and that yellow hat of yours?' ' You are quite right,' said I; ' in a country of Lamas, to be a Lama is well; but in a land of comedians, one must be a comedian. Will you take me into your company?' ' Bravo! bravo!' cried everybody; ' you shall be one of us.' And so saying, each made me a low bow, which I returned by putting my tongue in my cheek, and scratching my ear, according to the Thibetian manner of saluting. At first, I took the matter as a joke; but by-and-by upon reflecting that I had no means left, I thought I might as well take the manager at his word, and accordingly I became a member of the corps.

"Next day I packed up my religious costume, and assumed a mundane suit. As my memory had been long disciplined by the study of prayers, I found little trouble in learning a part in a play, and in a few days I became quite a first-rate comedian. We gave representations, during upwards of a year, in all the towns and villages of Sse-Tchouan. The company then resolving to visit the province of Yun-Nan, I quitted them, because that expedition would have carried me too far from my native Three Valleys. After the feast of separation, accordingly, I proceeded on my way to the paternal roof. The journey occupied nearly two years. At every place I came to, I stopped a few days and gave representations, practising as a merry-andrew, and making a comfortable thing enough of it, for one always gets more by performing on one's own account. I entered my native village in grand ſtyle, mounted on a magnificent ass I had bought at Lan-Tcheou and with twelve ounces of silver in my pocket. I gave a few representations to my countrymen who were amazed at my skill; but I had soon to give up my new profession.

"One evening when the family were assembled to hear some of my Thibetian ſtories, my mother maintained profound silence and her face manifeſted utter grief; soon I observed the tears trickling down her cheeks. 'Mother,' asked I, 'why do you weep? In my ſtory was there anything to excite your tears?' 'Thy ſtory,' she replied, 'produces upon me no impression whatever, agreeable or disagreeable; it ſtrikes upon my ears, but makes no way to my heart. That which moves, that which afflicts me, is the thought that when you left us, fourteen years ago, to visit the Land of Saints, thou were clad in the sacred habit of the Lamas, and that now thou art a layman and a buffoon.' These words confounded me. After a moment's silence I rose and cried emphatically: 'It is written in the Holy Doctrine that it is better to honour one's father and mother than to serve the spirits of heaven and earth. Therefore, mother, say what you would have me do, and your son will reverentially obey you.' 'Throw aside those mundane clothes,' said my mother, 'cut off that tress of hair, and re-enter the family of the saints.' I had nothing to say in reply, but proſtrated myself thrice on the ground, in token of submission. When a mother speaks, one muſt obey; filial piety is the basis of all good doctrine. In translating for you the ten great commandments of Jehovah, I remembered that the fourth said: 'Thou shalt honour thy father and thy mother.'

"Next morning I resumed my Lama dress, and a

few days after proceeded to Kounboum, where I am labouring to sanctify myself."

These last words of Sandara the Bearded clearly merited to be received with a horse laugh, but we restrained ourselves by dint of biting our lips, for we had experienced that, notwithstanding his immense zeal for sanctification, our worthy tutor had not as yet attained any very great results in the matter of patience and mildness.

This summary of the adventures of Sandara at once explained to us how it was that upon all occasions he manifested such marked predilection for the men and things of China. The rules bequeathed by Tsong-Kaba interdicted to the Lamas the use of garlic, brandy and tobacco; garlic being prohibited because it is unbecoming to present one's self before the image of Buddha with bad breath, offensive in itself, and capable of infecting the perfume of the incense; brandy, because this fatal liquor disturbs the reason and excites the passions; and tobacco, because it engenders idleness, and absorbs precious hours that ought to be devoted to the study of prayers and of doctrine. Despite these prohibitions, so soundly based, the Lamas—such of them, at least, as sanctify themselves after the manner of Sandara—do not hesitate to smoke, to drink, and to season their oatmeal with garlic. All this, however, is done secretly, and without the knowledge of the police. In the Lamasery of Kounboum, Sandara was the patron and introducer of the Chinese hawkers who deal in these contraband articles, and aided them in the sale of their goods for a small commission.

A few days after the Feast of Flowers, we vigorously resumed our Thibetian studies under the direction of Sandara, who came every morning to work with us. We occupied ourselves in the translation of an abridgement of Sacred History from the creation to the preaching of the Apostles. We gave to this work the dialogue form; the two interlocutors being a Lama of Jehovah and a Lama of Buddha. Sandara fulfilled his functions altogether as a matter of business. The favourable tendencies which he at first manifested, when we were at Tang-Keou-Eul, his crossings, his admiration of the Christian doctrine, had been all a mere farce. Religious feelings had no hold upon his grasping, hardened heart. He had acquired, by his long abode among the Chinese, a sneering, cold-blooded, carping incredulity, which he seemed to delight in parading upon all occasions. In his estimation, all religions were so many devices invented by the wise for the more facile and effective despoilment of the witless. Virtue, with him, was a vain word, and the man of merit he who had made the most of his fellow men.

Despite, however, these sceptical and impious opinions, Sandara could not prevent himself from feeling high admiration of the Christian doctrine. He was especially struck with the concatenation of the historical facts which he translated for us. He found in them a character of authenticity, of which the fables accumulated in the Buddhist books are wholly destitute; he admitted this, not unfrequently, but always in an unguarded moment, for his aim was to support in our presence his melancholy part of a free-thinker. When he was with the Lamas, he was more at his ease; and there he did not hesitate to declare that as to religious doctrine, we knew more about it than all the living Buddhas put together.

After some time, we began to make a certain sensation in the Lamasery; the Lamas talked a good deal to one another about the two Lamas of Jehovah, and the new doctrine they taught. It was remarked that we were never seen to prostrate ourselves before Buddha; that, thrice a day, we said prayers which were not Thibetian prayers; that we had a language of our own, which nobody else understood, but that with other people we talked Tartarian, Chinese and a little Thibetian. Here was more than enough to excite the curiosity of the Lamanesque public. Every day we had visitors, and the conversation with them always and altogether turned upon religious questions. Among all the Lamas who visited us, we did not find one of the same incredulous stamp with Sandara the Bearded; they all, on the contrary, seemed sincerely religious and full of faith; many of them attached the utmost importance to the study and knowledge of truth; and we found the same men coming again and again to seek instruction from us in our holy religion.

The instruction we communicated was altogether historical in its plan, everything being carefully excluded which could suggest dispute, or arouse the spirit of contention; we gave our friends a simple and concise outline of our religion, leaving them to derive thence, for themselves, conclusions against Buddhism. Proper names and dates, precisely set forth, produced more effect upon them than the most logical reasoning. When they had thoroughly mastered the names of Jesus, of Jerusalem, of Pontius Pilate, the date of four thousand years since the creation of the world, and the names of the twelve Apostles, they had no longer any doubts as to the redemption, or as to the preaching of the Gospel. The connection which they observed between the history of the Old Testament and that of the New, amounted, in their eyes, to demonstration. The mysteries and the miracles created no difficulty in their minds.

After all we have seen in our long peregrination and especially during our abode in the Lamasery of Kounboum, we are persuaded that it is by instruction, and not by controversy, that the conversion of the heathen is to be efficaciously operated. Polemics may reduce an adversary to silence, may often humiliate him, may sometimes irritate him, but they will never convince him. When Jesus Chriſt sent forth his disciples, he said to them: Go forth and teach all nations, which does not mean: go forth and hold controversies with all nations. In our days, two schools of philosophy, the one recognizing Descartes for its head, the other Lamennais, have much disputed the queſtion whether paganism is a crime or an error; it appears to us to be neither the one nor the other, but simply the effeċt of ignorance. The spirit of a pagan is enveloped in darkness. Carry light within that darkness, and the darkness will disappear: the pagan needs neither the thesis of the Cartesians, nor the requisitory of the Lamennaisians: all he wants is inſtruċtion.

The eagerness of the Lamas to visit us, and especially their favourable tendencies towards Chriſtianity, gave, after a while, umbrage to the zealous tenacity of Sandara; he turned desperately sulky, and after going through the lesson of the day, in the drieſt and briefeſt manner possible, he would say not another word to us for the reſt of the twenty-four hours, but observe towards us the moſt contumelious silence. If we asked him in the humbleſt manner the Thibetian name of some object, or the meaning of some particular phrase in the Dialogues, he would not condescend to a word of reply. In this extremity, we usually had recourse to our neighbour, the young ſtudent in medicine, who always gave us the information we needed with the most frank cordiality; and although he was not very learned in Thibetian, we found him of very great utility. His open, good-natured character, moreover, encouraged us to ask him many questions respeċting some of the Lama praċtices which we desired to underſtand. In return for these services, we aided, with all our hearts, his desire to become acquainted with the Chriſtian religion. Far different

THIBET, AND CHINA

from Sandara, he was full of respect for the truths we announced to him; but his timid, irresolute temperament kept him from openly abjuring Buddhism. His idea was, that he could be, at one and the same time, a good Christian and a fervent Buddhist; in his prayers, he invoked alternately Tsong-Kaba and Jehovah, and he carried his simplicity so far as to ask us sometimes to take part in his religious practices.

One day he proposed to us a service of devotion in favour of all the travellers throughout the whole world. "We are not acquainted with this devotion," said we; "will you explain it to us?" "This is it: you know that a good many travellers find themselves, from time to time, on rugged, toilsome roads. Some of these travellers are holy Lamas on a pilgrimage; and it often happens that they cannot proceed by reason of their being altogether exhausted; in this case we aid them by sending horses to them." "That," said we, "is a most admirable custom, entirely conformable with the principles of Christian charity; but you must consider that poor travellers such as we are not in a position to participate in the good work; you know that we possess only a horse and a little mule, which require rest, in order that they may carry us into Thibet." "Tsong-Kaba!" ejaculated the Lisper, and then he clapped his hands together, and burst into a loud laugh. "What are you laughing at? What we have said is the simple truth: we have only a horse and a little mule." When his laughter at last subsided: "It was not that I was laughing at," said he; "I laughed at your misconceiving the sort of devotion I mean; what we send to the travellers are paper horses." And therewith he ran off to his cell, leaving us with an excellent occasion for laughing in our turn at the charity of the Buddhists, which we thus learned consisted in giving paper horses to travellers. We maintained our gravity, however, for we had made it a rule never to ridicule the practices of the Lamas. Presently the Lisper returned, his hands filled with bits of paper, on each of which was printed the figure of a horse, saddled and bridled and going at full gallop. "Here!" cried the Lisper, "these are the horses we send to the travellers. To-morrow we shall ascend a high mountain, thirty lis from the Lamasery, and there we shall pass the day, saying prayers and sending off horses." "How do you send them to the travellers?" "Oh! the means are very easy. After a certain form of prayer, we take a packet of horses which we throw up into the air, the wind carries them away, and by the power of Buddha they are then changed into real horses, which offer themselves to travellers." We candidly told our dear neighbour what we thought of this practice, and explained to him the grounds upon which we declined to take any part in it. He seemed to approve of our sentiments on the subject; but this approval did not prevent him from occupying a large portion of the night in fabricating, by means of the press, a prodigious number of horses.

Next morning, before daybreak, he went off, accompanied by several colleagues, full, like himself, of devotion for poor travellers. They carried with them a tent, a boiler and some provisions. All the morning the wind blew a hurricane; when, towards noon, this subsided, the sky became dark and heavy, and the snow fell in thick flakes. We awaited, with anxious impatience, the return of the Stutterer. The poor wretch returned in the evening, quite worn out with cold and fatigue. We invited him to rest for awhile in our tent, and we gave him some tea with milk, and some rolls fried in butter. "It has been a dreadful day," said he. "Yes, the wind blew here with great violence." "I'll venture to affirm it was nothing here to what we found it on the top of the mountain: the tent, the boiler—everything we had with us was carried away by a regular whirlwind, and we were obliged to throw ourselves flat on the ground in order to save ourselves from being carried away too." "It's a sad pity you've loſt your tent and boiler." "It is, indeed, a misfortune. However, it muſt be admitted that the weather was very favourable for conveying horses to the travellers. When we saw that it was going to snow, we threw them all up into the air at once, and the wind whisked them off to the four quarters of the world. If we had waited any longer, the snow would have wetted them, and they would have ſtuck on the sides of the mountain." Altogether this excellent young man was not dissatisfied with his day's work.

The twenty-fifth of each moon is the day devoted to the transmission of horses to poor travellers. The practice is not a general rule; but it is left to the devotion of individuals. The twenty-eighth of the moon is set apart for another species of religious exercise, in which all the Lamas are required to participate. On the twenty-seventh the Stammerer gave us notice of the ceremony in these words: "To-morrow night we shall, perhaps, prevent your sleeping, for we shall have to celebrate our nocturnal prayers." We paid no special attention to this intimation, conceiving that it simply meant that in the course of the night the Lamas would recite prayers in their cells, as they not unfrequently did. We accordingly retired to reſt at our usual hour, and fell asleep.

Conformably with the warning of the Stammerer, our slumbers did not remain long uninterrupted. Firſt we seemed to dream that we heard a sort of concert by a great multitude of voices up in the air. Imperceptibly these vague, confused sounds became loud and distinct. We awoke and heard clearly enough the chanting of Lamanesque prayers. In the twinkling of an eye, we were up and dressed and out in the courtyard, which was illumined with a pale light that appeared to descend from above. In his wonted corner sat old Akayé, telling his beads. "Akayé," asked we, "what is this strange noise?" "The nocturnal prayers. If you want to see more of them you had better go on to the terrace." There was a ladder resting in the most accommodating manner against the wall. We hastily ascended it, and became spectators of a most singular sight. The terraces were illuminated by red lanterns suspended from long poles, and all the Lamas, attired in their state mantles and yellow mitres, were seated on the roofs of their houses chanting their prayers with a slow and monotonous voice. On the roof of our own house we found the Stammerer, the Kitat-Lama, and his *Chabi*, wholly absorbed with the ceremony. We took care not to disturb them, and contented ourselves with merely looking on and listening. These innumerable lanterns, with their red, fantastic glare, the buildings of the Lamasery vaguely illumined by the reflection of their trembling light, the four thousand voices combining in one immense concert, accompanied from time to time by the sound of trumpets and marine conches—all this produced an effect that agitated the soul with a sort of vague terror.

After having gazed for a while at this strange spectacle, we descended into the courtyard, where we found old Akayé still in the same place and in the same position. "Well," said he, "you have seen the ceremony of nocturnal prayers?" "Yes, but we don't understand what they precisely mean. Would it be troubling you too much to ask from you some explanation of the matter?" "Not at all. These prayers were instituted for the purpose of driving

THIBET, AND CHINA

away demons. You muſt know that this country was once fearfully infeſted with demons, who caused maladies in the herds and spoiled the milk of the cows; they often invaded the cells of the Lamas, and at times carried their audacity to the excess of penetrating into the temple in the hour of general prayer, their presence being indicated by the confusion and discordance which immediately prevailed in the psalmody. During the night they assembled in large numbers in the ravine, where they frightened everybody with cries and howlings so ſtrange in their charaćter that no man could imitate them. A Lama, full of learning and piety, invented the noćturnal prayers, and the demons have since almoſt entirely disappeared from the diſtrićt. A few come here occasionally, but they don't do any mischief as they used to do." "Akayé," asked we, "have you ever chanced to see any of these demons?" "No, never; and I'm sure you have not seen any of them." "What makes you suppose so?" "Because the demons only appear to wicked Lamas, and the good Lamas never see them." At this moment the prayer of the Lamas on the house-tops ceased, the trumpets, the bells, the drums, and the marine conches sounded all at once three different times; the Lamas, then, all sent forth together hideous cries and yells, like those of wild beaſts, and the ceremony terminated. The lanterns were extinguished, and silence resumed its sway. We bade old Akayé good-night, and once more went to sleep.

We had been residing at Kounboum more than three months, enjoying the friendly sympathy of the Buddhiſt monks and the protećtion of the authorities. But for some time paſt we had been in flagrant opposition to a leading rule of the Lamasery. Strangers who pass through Kounboum, or who merely reside there for a short time, may dress as they please. Those persons on the contrary, who are connected in any way with the Lamasery, or who are making any stay in the place, are required to wear the sacred dress of the Lamas, that is to say, a red gown, a small dalmatica without sleeves and showing the arm, a red scarf, and a yellow mitre. This rule of uniformity is very strictly enforced; and accordingly, one fine morning, the Grand Discipline Lama sent an official formally to request that we should observe the statutes of the Lamasery. We replied that, not being of the religion of Buddha, we could not adopt the sacred dress of the Lama, without insulting our own holy religion; but that as we did not wish to create the slightest confusion in the establishment, we were ready to quit it, if we could not obtain a dispensation in the matter of costume.

Several days passed without anything further being said on this unpleasant subject. Meantime Samdadchiemba arrived with the three camels, which he had been pasturing in a valley of Koukou-Noor. If we had to remove, it was clear that his return was most opportune. By-and-by, the Lamanesque government once more sent us their envoy, to say that the rule of the Lamasery was inflexible; that they grieved that our sublime and sacred religion did not permit us to comply with it; but that although we could not remain in the Lamasery of Kounboum, they would gladly retain us in the neighbourhood, and that to this end they invited us to go and take up our abode at Tchogortan [ch'u-'khor-tang], where we might wear what dress we pleased.

We had heard a great deal about the little Lamasery of Tchogortan, which serves as a sort of country house and botanical garden for the Faculty of Medicine. It stands within half-an-hour's walk of Kounboum. The Grand Lamas and students of the medical section proceed thither every year, towards the close of the summer, and remained generally for about a fortnight, collecting medicinal plants on the surrounding hills. During the remainder of the year most of the houses are empty, and you scarcely see a single soul, except a few contemplative Lamas who have hollowed out cells for themselves in the most rugged declivities of the mountain.

The proposition of the Lamanesque government appeared to us altogether eligible, for the fine weather was just setting in; winter in town, spring in the country—this was admirable! Our three months' abode at Kounboum had made us tolerably conversant with Lama manners; we accordingly purchased a *khata* and a small dish of raisins, with which we repaired to the Lama administrator of Tchogortan, who received us in the most affable manner, and promised at once to give orders for the preparation of a suitable abode for us. After giving a splendid Feast of Farewell to old Akayé, the Kitat-Lama, and the Stammerer, we loaded our camels with our baggage and gaily proceeded on our way to the little Lamasery.

CHAPTER III

A HALF HOUR sufficed for us to effect our removal from Kounboum to Tchogortan. After skirting for some time the arid sides of a lofty mountain, we descended into a broad valley, through which flowed a rivulet, the banks of which were still covered with ice. The place seemed full of good pasturage, but in consequence of the coldness of the climate, vegetation is very slow and very late in the locality. Although it was near the month of May, the nascent germs scarcely as yet coloured the surface of the soil.

A Lama, with red, round face, came to meet us, and conducted us to the habitation which the administrator of the Lamasery had prepared for our reception. We were installed in a large apartment which, only the evening before, had served as the abode of sundry juvenile calves, too young and too weak to follow the parent cows to the mountains. Every pains had been taken to clean the apartment, but the success had not been so perfect as to preclude our distinguishing on the floor many traces of the late occupants; however, the authorities had assigned to us the best accommodation that the Lamasery afforded.

Tchogortan is, as we have before stated, the country house of the Faculty of Medicine of Kounboum: its aspect is tolerably picturesque, especially in summer. The habitations of the Lamas, constructed at the foot of a mountain that terminates in a peak, are shaded by ancient trees, the great branches of which afford a retreat to infinite kites and crows. Some feet below these cottages runs an abundant stream, interrupted by various dams which the Lamas had constructed for the purpose of turning their *tchukor*, or praying mills. In the depths of the valley, and on the adjacent hills, you see the black tents of the Si-Fan, and a few herds of goats and long-haired cattle. The rocky and rugged mountain which backs the Lamasery serves as an abode for five contemplative monks, who, like the eagles, have selected as the site of their aeries the most elevated and most inaccessible points. Some have hollowed out their retreat in the living rock; others dwell in wooden cells, stuck against the mountain like enormous swallows' nests; a few pieces of wood, driven into the rock, form the staircase by which they ascend or descend. One of these Buddhist hermits, indeed, who has entirely renounced the world, has voluntarily deprived himself of these means of communication with his fellows; a bag, tied to a long string, served as the medium for conveying to him the alms of the Lamas and shepherds.

We had frequent conversations with these contemplative Lamas, but we could never exactly ascertain what it was they contemplated up there in their nests. They themselves could give nothing like a clear idea of the matter; they had embraced this manner of life, they told us, because they had read in their books that Lamas of very great sanctity had lived in that way. However, they were worthy folk, of peaceful, simple, easy temperaments, who passed their waking hours in prayer, and when they were tired of praying relaxed with sleep.

Besides these five hermits, who always dwelt in the rocks above, there were, below, several Lamas who had charge of the unoccupied houses of the Lamasery. These by no means, like the former, looked at life in its fine and mystical aspect; they were, on the contrary, absorbed in the realities of this world; they were, in fact, herdsmen. In the great house where we were installed there were two big Lamas who poetically passed their time in herding some twenty cattle, in milking the cows, making butter and cheese, and looking after the juvenile calves. These bucolics seemed little to heed contemplation or prayer: they sent forth, indeed, frequent invocations to Tsong-Kaba but this was always on account of their beaſts, because their cows mutinied and would not be milked, or because the calves capered out of bounds over the valley. Our arrival afforded them a little diversion from the monotony of paſtoral life. They often paid us a visit in our chamber, and always passed in review the volumes of our small travelling library with that timid and respectful curiosity which simple and illiterate persons ever manifeſt towards the productions of the intellect. When they found us writing they forgot cows, and calves, and milk, and cheese, and butter, and would ſtand for hours together motionless, their eyes fixed upon our crow-quill as it ran over the paper, and left impressed there characters, the delicacy and novelty of which were matters of ecſtatic amazement to these simple creatures.

The little Lamasery of Tchogortan pleased us beyond our hopes. We never once regretted Kounboum any more than the prisoner regrets his dungeon after he has attained liberty. The reason was that we, too, felt ourselves emancipated. We were no longer under the ferule of Sandara the Bearded, of that hard and pitiless taskmaſter, who, while giving us lessons of Thibetian, seemed to have undertaken also to discipline us in patience and humility. The desire to attain knowledge had made us submit to his ill-treatment, but our departure from Kounboum afforded a joyful opportunity of throwing off this leech which had, for five whole months, obſtinately remained ſtuck to our exiſtence. Besides, the success we had already achieved in the ſtudy of the Thibetian tongue exempted us from the future necessity of having a master at our shoulder; we were quite strong enough now to walk alone and unaided.

Our hours of labour were employed in revising and analysing our dialogues, and in translating a small Thibetian work entitled *The Forty-two Points of Instruction, delivered by Buddha*. We possessed a magnificent edition of this work, in four languages, Thibetian, Mongol, Mantchou, and Chinese; so that, thus aided, we had no occasion to recur to the learning of the Lamas. When the Thibetian version presented any difficulty, all we had to do, in order to remove it, was to consult the three other versions with which we were familiarly acquainted.

The book in question, which is attributed to Chakdja-Mouni, is a collection of precepts and sentences, urging men, and especially religious persons, to the practice of piety. In order to give our readers an idea of the morality of the Buddhists, we will extract a few passages from this work, which is of high authority in Lamanism.

I

" Buddha, the Supreme of Beings, manifesting his doctrine, pronounced these words: There are, in living creatures ten species of acts which are called good, and there are also ten species of acts which are called evil. If you ask, what are the ten evil acts; there are three which appertain to the body: murder, theft and impurity. The four appertaining to speech are: words sowing discord, insulting maledictions, impudent lies, and hypocritical expressions. The three appertaining to the will are: envy, anger, and malignant thoughts.

II

" Buddha, manifesting his doctrine, pronounced these words: The wicked man who persecutes the good man, is like a madman, who, throwing back his head, spits against heaven ; his spittle, incapable of sullying heaven, merely falls back upon himself. And, again, he is like one who, the wind opposing him, throws dust at men ; the dust does not touch the men at whom it was aimed, but flies back into the eyes of him who threw it. Beware of persecuting good men lest calamities exterminate you.

III

"Buddha, etc. Beneath heaven there are twenty difficult things. 1, Being poor and indigent, to grant benefits is difficult. 2, Being rich and exalted, to study doctrine is difficult. 3, Having offered up the sacrifice of one's life, to die veritably, is difficult. 4, To obtain a sight of the prayers of Buddha is difficult. 5, To have the happiness to be born in the world of Buddha, is difficult. 6, To compound with voluptuousness and to be delivered from one's passions, is difficult. 7, To behold an agreeable object, and not to desire it, is difficult. 8, To resist a tendency for the lucrative and exalting, is difficult. 9, To be insulted, and abstain from anger, is difficult. 10, In the whirlwind of business to be calm, is difficult. 11, To study much and profoundly, is difficult. 12, Not to scorn a man who has not studied, is difficult. 13, To extirpate pride from the heart, is difficult. 14, To find a virtuous and able master, is difficult. 15, To penetrate the secrets of nature and the profundities of science, is difficult. 16, Not to be excited by prosperity, is difficult. 17, To leave wealth for wisdom, is difficult. 18, To induce men to follow the dictates of conscience, is difficult. 19, To keep one's heart always in equal motion, is difficult. 20, Not to speak ill of others, is difficult.

IV

"The man who seeks riches is like a child that, with the sharp point of a knife, attempts to eat honey ;

ere he has time to relish the sweetness that has but touched his lips, nothing remains to him but the poignant pain of a cut in the tongue.

V

"There is no passion more violent than voluptuousness! Nothing exceeds voluptuousness! Happily there is but one passion of this kind; were there two, not a man in the whole universe could follow the truth.

VI

"Buddha pronounced these words in the presence of all the *Charmanas* [*sramana*]:[1] 'Beware of fixing your eyes upon women! If you find yourself in their company, let it be as though you were not present. Take care how you speak with women. If you talk with them, guard well your hearts; let your conduct be irreproachable, and keep ever saying to yourselves: we who are *Charmanas*, residing in this world of corruption, must be like the flower of the water-lily, which, amid muddy water, contracts no stain.'

VII

"The man who walks in the path of piety must look upon the passions as dry grass near a great fire. The man who is jealous of his virtue, should flee on the approach of the passions.

VIII

"A *Charmana* who passed whole nights chanting prayers, manifested one morning, by his sad suppressed voice, great depression and the desire to withdraw from his calling. Buddha sent for this *Charmana*, and said to him, 'When you were with your family, what used you to do?' 'I was always playing on the guitar.' Buddha said to him, 'If the strings

[1] *Charmanas* (in Sanscrit, *S'raman'as*) are monks in the Lamanesque hierarchy.

of the guitar became loose, what happened?' 'I obtained no sound from them.' 'If the strings were too tight, what happened then?' 'The sounds were broken.' 'When the strings obtained the exact equilibrium between tension and flexibility, what happened then?' 'All the sounds accorded in perfect harmony.' Hereupon Buddha pronounced these words: 'It is the same with the study of doctrine; after you shall have achieved dominion over your heart, and regulated its movements to harmony, it will attain the acquisition of the truth.'

IX

"Buddha put this question to a *Charmana:* 'How long a time is fixed for the life of man?' He replied: 'It is limited to a few days.' Buddha pronounced these words: 'You have not yet acquired the knowledge of the doctrine.' Then addressing himself to another *Charmana*, he put this question: 'How long a time is fixed for the life of man?' He replied: 'It is limited to the time that suffices for a meal.' Buddha pronounced these words: 'So neither hast thou, as yet, the knowledge of the doctrine.' Then addressing himself to a third *Charmana*, he put to him this question: 'How long a time is fixed for the life of man?' He replied: 'It is limited to the time that suffices to emit a breath.' After he had thus spoken, Buddha pronounced these words: ' 'Tis well: thou mayest be said to have acquired the knowledge of the doctrine.'

X

"The man who, practising piety, applies himself to extirpate the roots of his passions, is like a man passing between his fingers the beads of a chaplet. If he proceeds by taking them, one after the other, he easily attains the end; so, by extirpating, one after the other, one's evil tendencies one attains perfection.

THIBET, AND CHINA
XI

" The *Charmana* who practises piety may compare himself with the long-haired ox, which, laden with baggage, is making its way through a marsh; it dares look neither to the right nor to the left, but goes straight on, hoping to get clear of the mud and to reach a place of rest. The *Charmana*, regarding his passions as more terrible than this mud, if he never diverts his eyes from virtue will assuredly attain the height of felicity."

We will not prolong these extracts. The few we have given will suffice to convey an idea of the matter and manner of this book, which is accepted as an authority alike by the Bonzes and the Lamas. It was conveyed from India to China in the 65th year of the Christian era at the epoch when Buddhism was beginning to make its way in the Celestial Empire. The Chinese annals relate this event in the following terms:—

"In the 24th year of the reign of Tchao-Wang [Chao-wang], of the dynasty of the Tcheou (which corresponds to the year 1029 B.C.), on the eighth day of the fourth moon, a light, coming from the south-west, illumined the palace of the king. The monarch, beholding this splendour, interrogated concerning it the sages who were skilled in predicting the future. These presented to him the books wherein it was written that this prodigy would announce that a great saint had appeared in the west, and that in a thousand years after his birth his religion would spread into those parts.

"In the 53rd year of the reign of Mou-Wang which is that of the Black Ape (951 B.C.), on the fifteenth day of the second moon, Buddha manifested himself (*i.e.* died.) A thousand and thirteen years afterwards, under the dynasty of Ming-Ti, of the

TRAVELS IN TARTARY,

dynasty of the Han in the seventh year of the reign of Young-Ping [Yung p'ing] (A.D. 64), on the fifteenth day of the first moon, the king saw in a dream, a man of the colour of gold, glittering like the sun, and whose stature was more than ten feet. Having entered the palace of the king, this man said, ' My religion will spread over these parts.' Next day, the king questioned the sages. One of these, named Fou-Y [Fu-I], opening the annals of the time of the Emperor Tchao-Wang, of the dynasty of the Tcheou, pointed out the connection between the dream of the king and the narrative in the annals. The king consulted the ancient books, and having found the passage corresponding with the reign of Tchao-Wang, of the dynasty of the Tcheou, was filled with gladness. Thereupon he dispatched the officers Tsa-In [Ts'ai-Yin] and Thsin-King [Ch'in-Ching], the man-of-letters Wang-Tsun, and fifteen other persons into the west, to obtain information respecting the doctrines of Buddha.

" In the tenth year (A.D. 67), Tsa-In and the rest, having arrived in Central India, among the great Youei-Tchi, met with Kas'yamatanga [Kâśyapamatanga] and Tcho-Fa-Lan [Chu-Fa-lan] and procured a statute of Buddha, and books in the language of Fan (Fan-Lan-Mo, or Brahma, that is to say, in Sanscrit), and conveyed them on a white horse to the city Lo-Yang. Kas'yamatanga and Tcho-Fa-Lan paid a visit to the Emperor, attired as religious persons, and were lodged in the Hong-Lon-Ssé [Hung-lu-ssŭ], called also Sse-Pin-Ssé [Ssŭ-pin-ssŭ] ('Hotel of the Strangers').

" In the 11th year (A.D. 68), the emperor ordered the construction of the monastery of the White Horse, outside the gate Yong-Mon [Yung-men], west of the city of Lo-Yang. Matanga [Kâśyapamatanga] there translated the *Sacred Book of Forty-two Articles*.

Six years after, Tsa-In and Tcho-Fa-Lan converted certain Tao-Ssé [*Tao-shih*] to Buddhism. Rising afterwards into celeſtial space, they caused the king to hear the following verses :—

" ' The fox is not of the race of the lions. The lamp has not the brightness of the sun or moon. The lake cannot be compared with the sea ; the hills cannot be compared with the lofty mountains.

" ' The cloud of prayer spreading over the surface of the earth, its beneficial dew fecundating the germs of happiness, and the divine rites operating everywhere marvellous changes, all the nations will advance according to the laws of reintegration.' "

Our firſt days at Tchogortan were entirely devoted to the translation of the *Book of Buddha;* but we soon found ourselves compelled to devote a portion of our time to the occupations of paſtoral life. We had remarked that every evening our animals had returned half-ſtarved, that inſtead of growing fatter and fatter they were daily becoming leaner and leaner: the simple reason was that Samdadchiemba took no sort of pains to find paſturage for them. After driving them out somewhere or other, he cared not whither, he would leave them to themselves on some arid hillside, and himself go to sleep in the sun, or ſtroll about chattering and tea-drinking in the black tents. It was to no purpose we lectured him ; he went on juſt the same as before, his reckless, independent character having undergone no modification whatever. Our only mode of remedying the evil was to turn herdsmen ourselves.

Moreover, it was impossible to remain pertinaciously and exclusively men of letters when all around seemed inviting us to make some concessions to the habits of this paſtoral people. The Si-Fan, or Eaſtern Thibetians, are nomads, like the Tartar-Mongols, and pass their lives solely occupied in the care of their flocks and herds. They do not live, however, like the Mongol tribes, in huts covered with felt. The great tents they construct with black linen are ordinarily hexagonal in form; within you see neither column nor woodwork supporting the edifice; the six angles below are fastened to the ground with nails, and those above are supported by cords which, at a certain distance from the tent, rest horizontally on strong poles, and then slope to the ground, where they are attached to large iron rings. With all this strange complication of sticks and strings, the black tent of the Thibetian nomads bears no slight resemblance to a great spider standing motionless on its long lanky legs, but so that its great stomach is resting on the ground. The black tents are by no means comparable with the tents of the Mongols; they are not a whit warmer or more solid than ordinary travelling tents. They are very cold, on the contrary, and a strong wind knocks them down without the least difficulty.

It may be said, however, that in one respect the Si-Fan seem more advanced than the Mongols, and to have a tendency for approximating to the manners of sedentary nations. When they have selected an encampment, they are accustomed to erect around it, a wall of from four to five feet high, and within their tents they construct furnaces, which are destitute neither of taste nor of solidity. These arrangements, however, do not create in them any attachment to the soil which they have thus occupied. Upon the slightest caprice they decamp, pulling down their walls and other masonry work, and carrying the principal stones with them to their next settlement, as part of their furniture. The herds of the Eastern Thibetians consist of sheep, goats and long-haired cattle; they do not breed as many horses as the Tartars, but those which they do breed are stronger and better formed; the camels we find in their country belong, for the moſt part, to the Tartar-Mongols.

The long-haired cattle, in Chinese *Tchang-Mao-Nieou* [*ch'ang-mao-niu*], is called *yak* by the Thibetians, *sarligue* by the Tartars, and *bœuf grognant* by the French naturaliſts. The cry of this animal does, in faɛt, resemble the grunting of a hog; but louder in tone and longer in duration. The yak is short and thick, and not so big as an ordinary ox; its hair is long, fine and shining, that under the belly aɛtually trailing on the ground. Its hoofs are meagre, and crooked, like those of goats; and, like the goats, it delights in clambering up rocks, and impending over the moſt rugged precipices. When at play, it twiſts and turns about its tail, which terminates in a broad tuft, like a plume of feathers. The flesh is excellent; the milk delicious, and the butter made of that milk beyond all praise. Malte-Brun, indeed, says, that the milk of this animal smacks of tallow. Matters of taſte are generally open queſtions, but in this particular inſtance we may anticipate that the presumption will be somewhat in favour of our opinion, since, as we believe, the learned geographer has not had the same opportunities with ourselves of drinking the milk in the black tents, and appreciating its savour at leisure.

Among the herds of the Si-Fan you find some yellow cattle, which are of the same family with the ordinary cattle of France, but in general poor and ugly. The calf of a long-haired cow and a yellow bull is called *Karba;* these seldom live. The long-tailed cows are so reſtive and so difficult to milk, that to keep them at all quiet the herdsman has to give them a calf to lick meanwhile. But for this device, not a single drop of milk could be obtained from them.

One day, a Lama herdsman, who lived in the same house with ourselves, came with a long, dismal face to announce that one of his cows had calved during the night and that unfortunately the calf was a *karba*. The calf died in the course of the day. The Lama forthwith skinned the poor beast, and stuffed it with hay. This proceeding surprised us at first, for the Lama had by no means the air of a man likely to give himself the luxury of a cabinet of natural history. When the operation was completed, we remarked that the hay-calf had neither feet nor head; hereupon it occurred to us that, after all, it was merely a pillow that the Lama contemplated. We were in error, but the error was not dissipated until the next morning, when our herdsman went to milk his cow. Seeing him issue forth, his pail in one hand, the hay-calf under the other arm, the fancy occurred to us to follow him. His first proceeding was to put the hay-*karba* down before the cow; he then turned to milk the cow herself. The mamma at first opened enormous eyes at her beloved infant; by degrees, she stooped her head towards it, then smelt at it, sneezed three or four times, and at last proceeded to lick it with the most delightful tenderness. This spectacle grated against our sensibilities; it seemed to us that he who first invented this parody upon one of the most touching incidents in nature must have been a man without a heart. A somewhat burlesque circumstance occurred one day to modify the indignation with which this trickery inspired us. By dint of caressing and licking her little calf, the tender parent one fine morning unripped it; the hay issued from within, and the cow, manifesting not the smallest surprise or agitation, proceeded tranquilly to devour the unexpected provender.

The Si-Fan nomads are really distinguishable from the Mongols by a more expressive physiognomy and by a greater energy of character; their features are not so flat, and their manners are characterized by an

THIBET, AND CHINA

ease and vivacity that form a strong contrast with the heavy uncouthness of the Tartars. Merry-makings, noisy songs, and joyous laughter animate their encampments, and banish melancholy; but with this turn for gaiety and pleasure, the Si-Fan are at the same time indomitably brave, and exceedingly addicted to warfare. They accordingly manifest the most profound contempt for the Chinese authority and authorities, and though inscribed in the imperial list of tributary nations, they absolutely refuse to render either obedience or tribute. There are among them, indeed, several tribes that constantly exercise their brigandage up to the very frontiers of the empire, the Chinese mandarins never venturing to encounter them. The Si-Fan are good horsemen, though not equal to the Tartars. The care of their herds does not prevent them from carrying on a little trade in the hair of their cattle and the wool of their sheep. They weave a sort of coarse linen, of which they make tents and clothing. When they are assembled round their great pot of milk tea, they give themselves up, like the Tartars, to their gossiping humour, and their passion for narratives of the adventures of Lamas and brigands. Their memory is full of local anecdotes and traditions; once put them on the track, and they will go on with an interminable series of tales and legends.

One day, while our camels were tranquilly browsing some thorny shrubs in the depth of the valley, we sought an asylum from the north wind in a small tent, whence issued a thick smoke. We found in it an old man who, knees and hands on the ground, was puffing with all his might at a heap of *argols* which he had just placed on the fire. We seated ourselves on a yak skin. The old man crossed his legs, and held out his hand to us. We gave him our tea-cups, which he filled with milk-tea, saying, "*Temouchi*" [*temushi*(? *bde* . . . *bshes*)] "drink in peace." He then gazed at us, alternately, with an air of some anxiety. "*Aka* (brother)," said we, "this is the firſt time we have come to seat ourselves in your tent." " I am old," he replied ; " my legs will scarce suſtain me; otherwise, I should have come to Tchogortan to offer you my *khata*. According to what the shepherds of the black tents have told me, you are from the farther Weſtern Heaven." " Yes, our country is far hence." " Are you from the kingdom of the Samba [San-pa (Zam-pa)] or from that of the Poba ? " " From neither ; we come from the kingdom of the French." " Ah, you are Franba [Framba] ? I never before heard of them. 'Tis such a great place, that Weſt ! The kingdoms there are so numerous. But-after all, it matters not : we are all of the same family, are we not ? " " Yes, assuredly all men are brothers, in whatever kingdom each is born." " That is true : what you say is founded on reason ; all men are brothers. Yet we know that, under heaven, there exiſt three great families : we men of the weſt are all of the great Thibetian family, as I have heard." "*Aka*, do you know whence come the three great families that are beneath the heaven ? " " This is what I have heard about it from Lamas learned in the things of antiquity. In the beginning, there was on the earth but one single man ; he had neither house nor tent ; for in those days winter was not cold nor summer hot ; the wind did not blow with violence, and there fell neither rain nor snow ; tea grew of itself on the mountains, and the cattle had nothing to fear from maleficent animals. This man had three children, who lived a long time with him, feeding upon milk and fruits, After attaining a very great age, this man died. The three children consulted what they should do with the body of their father ; they could not agree on the point, for each had a different opinion. One of them wanted to put him in a coffin and bury him; the second proposed to burn him; the third said it would be better to expose him on the top of a mountain. In the end, they resolved to cut the body into three pieces, to take each of them one piece, and then to separate. The eldeſt had the head and arms for his share : he was the anceſtor of the great Chinese family; and this is why his descendants have become celebrated in arts and induſtry, and remarkable for their intelligence, and for the devices and ſtratagems they can invent. The youngeſt, who was the father of the great Thibetian family, had the cheſt and ſtomach for his share, and this is why the Thibetians are full of heart and courage, fearing not to encounter death, and ever having among them indomitable tribes. The middle son, from whom descend the Tartar peoples, received as his inheritance the lower part of the body. You, who have travelled much in the deserts of the Eaſt, muſt know that the Mongols are simple and timid, without head and without heart; their only merit consiſting in keeping themselves firm on their ſtirrups, and solid on their saddles. This is how the Lamas explain the origin of the three great families that are beneath heaven, and the difference of their charaƈter. This is why the Tartars are good horsemen, the Thibetians good soldiers, and the Chinese good traders." As a return to the old man for his intereſting chronicle, we related to him the hiſtory of the firſt man, Adam, of the Deluge, and of Noah and his three children. He was at firſt extremely pleased to find in our ſtory also his three great families; but his surprise was immense when he heard us ſtate that the Chinese, the Tartars, and the Thibetians were all children of Shem, and that besides these, there were innumerable nations who composed the two other families of Cham [Ham] and Japhet. He looked at us fixedly, his mouth half open, and his head, from time to time, thrown up in amazement, as much as to say: I never thought the world was so big.

The time had passed rapidly during this archaiological sitting; so, after saluting the old man, we went to our camels, which we drove home to Tchogortan, where, fastening them to a stake at the door of our residence, we proceeded into our humble kitchen to prepare our evening meal.

Culinarily speaking, we were far better off at Tchogortan than at Kounboum. In the first place, we had milk, curds, butter, and cheese, *à discretion*. Then we had discovered a perfect mine, in a hunter of the vicinity. A few days after our arrival, this Nimrod entered our room and, taking a magnificent hare from a bag he carried at his back, asked us whether the *Goucho* [*gushri*][1] of the Western Heaven ate the flesh of wild animals. "Certainly," said we; "and we consider hares very nice. Don't you eat them?" "We laymen do, sometimes, but the Lamas, never. They are expressly forbidden by the Book of Prayers to eat black flesh." "The sacred law of Jehovah has prescribed no such prohibition to us." "In that case keep the animal; and, as you like hares, I will bring you as many of them every day as you please; the hills about Tchogortan are completely covered with them."

Just at this point a Lama chanced to enter our apartment. When he saw, stretched at our feet, the still warm and bleeding form of the hare, "Tsong-Kaba! Tsong-Kaba!" exclaimed he, starting back, with a gesture of horror, and veiling his eyes with both hands. Then, after launching a malediction against the poor hunter, he asked us whether we should dare to eat that black flesh? "Why not," rejoined we, "since it can injure neither our bodies nor our souls?"

---

[1] Goucho is a title of honour, given to the Lamas by the Thibetians.

And thereupon we laid down certain principles of morality, to the purport that the eating of venison is, in itself, no obstacle to the acquisition of sanctity. The hunter was highly delighted with our dissertation: the Lama was altogether confounded. He contented himself with saying, by way of reply, that in us, who were foreigners and of the religion of Jehovah, it might be no harm to eat hares; but that the Lamas must abstain from it, because, if they failed to observe the prohibition and their dereliction became known to the Grand Lama, they would be pitilessly expelled from the Lamasery.

Our thesis having been thus victoriously sustained we next proceeded to entertain the proposition of the hunter to provide us every day with as many hares as we pleased. First, we asked him whether he was in earnest. Upon his replying in the affirmative, we told him that every morning he might bring us a hare, but on the understanding that we were to pay him for it. "We don't sell hares here," replied he; "but since you will not accept them gratuitously, you shall give me for each the value of a gun-charge." We insisted upon a more liberal scale of remuneration, and, at last, it was arranged that for every piece of game he brought us, we should give him forty sapeks, equivalent to about four French sous.

We decided upon eating hares for two reasons. First, as a matter of conscience, in order to prevent the Lamas from imagining that we permitted ourselves to be influenced by the prejudices of the sectaries of Buddha; and, secondly, upon a principle of economy; for a hare cost us infinitely less than our insipid barley-meal.

One day, our indefatigable hunter brought us, instead of a hare, an immense roebuck, which is also black flesh and prohibited. In order not to compound in the least degree with Buddhist superstitions, we purchased the roebuck, for the sum of three hundred sapeks (thirty French sous.) Our chimney smoked with venison preparations for eight consecutive days, and all that time Samdadchiemba was in a moſt amiable frame of mind.

Leſt we should contraƈt habits too exclusively carnivorous, we resolved to introduce the vegetable kingdom into our quotidian alimentation. In the desert, this was no easy matter. However, by dint of induſtry, combined with experience, we ultimately discovered some wild plants, which, dressed in a particular manner, were by no means to be despised. We may be permitted to enter into some details on this subjeƈt. The matter in itself is of slight intereſt ; but it may have its use in relation to travellers who at any future time may have to traverse the deserts of Thibet.

When the firſt signs of germination begin to manifeſt themselves, if you scratch up the ground to the depth of about an inch, you will find quantities of creeping roots, long and thin like dog-grass. This root is entirely covered with little tubercles, filled with a very sweet liquid. In order to make an extremely nice dish of this vegetable, you have only to wash it carefully and then fry it in butter. Another dish, not less diſtinguished in our eſteem than the preceding, was furnished by a plant very common in France, and the merit of which has never yet been adequately appreciated : we refer to the young ſtems of fern. When these are gathered quite tender, before they are covered with down, and while the firſt leaves are bent and rolled up in themselves, you have only to boil them in pure water to realize a dish of delicious asparagus. If our words were of any effeƈt, we would earneſtly recommend to the attention of the Miniſter of Agriculture this precious vegetable, which abounds, as yet to no purpose, on our mountains and in our foreſts. We would also

THIBET, AND CHINA

recommend to him the nettle (*urtica urens*), which, in our opinion, might be made an advantageous substitute for spinage; indeed, more than once, we proved this by our own experience. The nettle should be gathered quite young when the leaves are perfectly tender. The plant should be pulled up whole with a portion of the root. In order to preserve your hands from the sharp biting liquid which issues from the points, you should wrap them in linen of close texture. When once the nettle is boiled, it is perfectly innocuous, and this vegetable, so rough in its exterior, then becomes a very delicate dish.

We were able to enjoy this delightful variety of esculents for more than a month. Then, the little tubercles of the fern became hollow and horny, and the stems themselves grew as hard as wood; while the nettles, armed with a long white beard, presented only a menacing and awful aspect. Later in the year, when the season was more advanced, the perfumed strawberry of the mountain and the white mushroom of the valley became valuable substitutes for fern and nettle. But we had to wait a long time for these luxuries, the cold in these countries being of protracted duration, and the vegetation, of consequence, exceedingly late. Throughout June there is snow still falling, and the wind is so cold that you cannot, without imprudence, throw aside your fur coats. With the first days of July, the warmth of the sun begins to be felt, and the rain falls in heavy showers; no sooner has the sky cleared up than a warm vapour rises from the earth, in surprising abundance. You see it first skimming the surface of the valleys and the low hills; then it condenses, and oscillates about somewhere above the surface, becoming, by degrees, so thick that it obscures the light of day. When this vapour has ascended high enough in the air to form great clouds, the south wind rises, and the rain again pours down upon the earth. Then the sky becomes clear once more, and once more the vapour rises and rises, and so it goes on. These atmospheric revolutions continue for a fortnight. Meanwhile, the earth is in a sort of fermentation; all the animals keep crouching on the ground, and men, women, and children feel, in every limb, vague, indescribable discomfort and disability. The Si-Fan call this period the season of land vapours.

Immediately that the crisis is past, the grass in the valley grows visibly, and the mountains and hills around are covered, as by enchantment, with flowers and verdure. The period was also one of palingenesis for our camels. They became wholly divested of their hair, which fell from them in large flakes, like rags, and for a few days they were as bare as though they had been closely shaved from the muzzle of the nose to the tip of the tail. In this condition they were perfectly hideous. In the shade they shook with cold in every limb, and at night we were obliged to cover them with a great piece of felt to keep them from dying with cold. After four days had elapsed, their hair began to re-appear. First, it was merely a red down, extremely fine and curling, like lamb's wool. The intense ugliness of the animals during their state of nudity made them appear perfectly beautiful in their new attire, which was completed in a fortnight. Thus, new dressed, they rushed with ardour to the pasturages, in order to get up respectable dimensions and adequate strength for their autumnal journey. To sharpen their appetites, we had purchased some sea salt, of which we gave them a large dose every morning, before they went into the valley: and every evening, on their return, we gave them another dose, to aid them to ruminate, during the night, the immense mass of forage which they had amassed in their stomachs during the day.

The new coating of our camels had enriched us with an immense quantity of hair; we exchanged one half of it for barley-meal, and the question then arose, what was the best use we could make of the remainder? A Lama, who was a skilful ropemaker, suggested an excellent idea: he pointed out that during the long journey through Thibet we should need a large supply of cord wherewith to fasten our luggage, and that ropes made of camel's hair were, on account of their flexibility, the best for cold countries. The suggestion, so full of wisdom, was at once adopted. The Lama gave us, gratuitously, a few lessons in his art, and we set to work. In a very short time we were able to twist our material tolerably well, so as to give it a form approximately, at least, resembling rope. Every day when we went out to tend our cattle, each of us took under his arm a bundle of camel's hair, which on his way he twisted into the smaller strings, that, on our return, we combined into larger cords.

Samdadchiemba contented himself with looking on as we worked, and with an occasional smile at our slips. Partly through idleness, partly through vanity, he abstained from lending us a hand. "My spiritual fathers," said he, one day, "how can people of your quality demean yourselves by rope-making? Would it not be much more proper to buy what ropes you require, or to give the materials out to be made by persons in the trade?" This question afforded us an opportunity of giving our cameleer a sound rating. After having emphatically impressed upon him that we were in no position to play the fine gentleman, and that we must closely study economy, we cited to him the example of St. Paul, who had thought it no derogation from his dignity to labour with his hands, in order to avoid being of charge to the faithful. So soon as Samdadchiemba learned that St. Paul had been at the same time a currier and an apostle, he forthwith abdicated his idleness and his self-sufficiency, and applied himself with ardour to rope-making. What was our astonishment on seeing the fellow at work, to find that he was a first-rate braider, for not an inkling had he ever given us to that effect! He selected the finest wool, and with it wove bridles and halters, that were really quite masterpieces of art. It is almost unnecessary to add that he was forthwith placed at the head of our rope-making establishment, and that we submitted ourselves altogether to his directorship.

The fine weather brought to Tchogortan a great number of visitors from Kounboum, who sought at once change of air and temporary relaxation from their studies. Our apartment now became a point of pilgrimage, for no one thought of spending a day at Tchogortan without paying a visit to the Lamas of the Western Heaven. Those Lamas with whom we had formed a more intimate acquaintance at Kounboum, and who had begun there to inform themselves as to the truths of the Christian religion, were attracted by a far higher motive than curiosity; they desired to discourse further of the holy doctrines of Jehovah, and to seek from us explanations of difficulties which had occurred to them. Oh! how our hearts were penetrated with ineffable joy when we heard these Buddhist monks pronounce with respect the sacred names of Jesus and of Mary, and recite, with manifest devotion, the prayers we had taught them. The great God, we doubt not, will place to their favourable account these first steps in the path of salvation, and will not fail to send shepherds to bring quite home to the fold these poor wandering sheep.

Among the Lamas who came to recreate for awhile at Tchogortan, we remarked especially a number of Tartar-Mongols, who, bringing with them small tents, set them up in the valley along the stream, or upon the sides of the moſt picturesque hills. There they passed whole days revelling in the delight of the independent life of the nomads, forgetting for awhile, the constraint and confinement of the Lamanesque life, in the enjoyment of the free life of the tent. You saw them running and frolicking about the prairie like children, or wreſtling and exercising the other sports which recalled the days and the land of their boyhood. The reaction with many of these men became so ſtrong that even fixity of tent became insupportable, and they would take it down and set it up again in some other place, three or four times a day; or they would even abandon it altogether, and taking their kitchen utensils and their pails of water and their provisions on their shoulders, would go, singing and dancing as they went, to boil their tea on the summit of some mountain, from which they would not descend till nightfall.

We observed, also, flocking to Tchogortan, another class of Lamas not less interesting than the Mongols; they always arrived at daybreak; their garments were tucked up to the knees, and on their backs were large osier baskets; all day long they would traverse the valley and the adjacent hills, collecting, not strawberries and mushrooms, but the dung which the herds of the Si-Fan deposit in all directions. On account of this particular occupation, we named these Lamas Lama-Argoleers, from the Tartar word *argol*, which designates animal excrement, when dried and prepared for fuel. The Lamas who carry on this class of business are in general idle, irregular persons, who prefer vagabondizing about on the hills to study and retirement; they are divided into several companies, each working under the direction of a superintendent, who arranges and is responsible for their operations. Towards the close of the day, each man brings the portion he has collected to the general depot, which is always situate at the foot of some well, or in the hollow of some valley. There the raw material is carefully elaborated; it is pounded and moulded into cakes, which are placed to dry in the sun, and when completely dessicated, are symmetrically piled, one on the other, the ſtack, when formed, being covered with a thick layer of dung to protect it from the dissolving aċtion of the rain. In the winter, this fuel is conveyed to Kounboum, and there sold.

The luxurious variety of combuſtibles which the civilized nations of Europe enjoy have exempted us from the necessity of making any very profound researches into the divers qualities of *argols*. Such has not been the case with the shepherd and nomadic peoples. Long experience has enabled them to classify *argols*, with a perspicuity of appreciation which leaves nothing to be desired in that particular respeċt. They have eſtablished four grand divisions, to which future generations will scarcely be able to apply any modification.

In the firſt rank are placed the *argols* of goats and sheep; a glutinous subſtance that enters largely into its composition communicates to this combuſtible an elevation of temperature that is truly aſtonishing. The Thibetians and Tartars use it in the preparation of metals; a bar of iron placed in a fire of these *argols* is soon brought to white heat. The residuum deposited by the *argols* of goats and sheep after combuſtion is a sort of green vitreous matter, transparent, and brittle as glass, which forms a mass full of cavities and very light; in many respeċts closely resembling pumice ſtone. You don't find in this residuum any ash whatever, unless the combuſtion has been mixed with foreign matter. The *argols* of camels conſtitute the second class; they burn easily, and throw out a fine flame, but the heat they communicate is less vivid and less intense than that given by the preceding. The reason of this difference is, that they contain in combination a smaller proportion of glutinous substance. The third class comprehends the *argols* appertaining to the bovine species; these, when thoroughly dry, burn readily, and produce no smoke whatever. This is almost the only fuel you find in Tartary and Thibet. Last come the *argols* of horses and other animals of that family. These *argols*, not having, like the others, undergone the process of rumination, present nothing but a mass of straw more or less triturated; they throw out a great smoke when burning, and are almost immediately consumed. They are useful, however, for lighting a fire, filling the office of tinder and paper to the other combustibles.

We perfectly understand that this rapid and incomplete essay on *argols* is not of a character to interest many readers; but we did not feel justified in either omitting or abridging it, because it has been an object with us to neglect no document that might be of assistance to those who, after us, may venture upon nomadic life for awhile.

The inhabitants of the valley of Tchogortan, though in the apparent enjoyment of profound peace are, nevertheless, an incessant prey to the fear of the brigands, who, they informed us, make periodical incursions from the mountains, and carry off all the cattle they can find. It was stated that in 1842, these had come in a large body, and devastated the whole of the surrounding country. At a moment when they were least expected, they issued from all the outlets of the mountain, and spread over the valley, sending forth fearful cries, and discharging their matchlocks. The shepherds, terror-struck by this unforeseen attack, had not even thought of the slightest resistance, but had fled in disorder, carrying with them only that which they happened to lay their hands upon at the moment. The brigands, profiting by this panic fear, burned the tents, and collected in one large enclosure, formed with ropes, all the cattle and sheep they found in and about the place. They then proceeded to the Little Lamasery of Tchogortan. But the Lamas had already disappeared, with the exception of the hermits, who remained perched on their nests on the rocks. The brigands carried off or demolished everything they came to : they burned the idols of Buddha, and broke down the dams that had been constructed for the purpose of turning the praying-mills. Three years after the event, we still saw the marked traces of their ferocious devastations. The Buddhist temple, which had stood at the foot of the mountain, had not been rebuilt. Its ruins, blackened with their conflagrations, and some calcined portions of the idols lay strewed upon the grass. The Lama hermits were spared, indeed ; but this, no doubt, was simply because the brigands saw it would be too protracted and too arduous a labour to achieve the tormenting them in their lofty and almost inaccessible abodes. The excesses which they perpetrated against the black tents and against the temple of Buddha itself showed that, if they left the poor recluses unscathed, it was by no means from respect or compassion.

So soon as the news of the arrival of the brigands reached Kounboum, the whole Lamasery was afoot, and in commotion. The Lamas rushed to arms with loud vociferations. They caught up whatever in the shape of a weapon first came to hand, and dashed off, confusedly, towards the Lamasery of Tchogortan. But they arrived there too late ; the brigands had disappeared, carrying off all the flocks and herds of the Si-Fan, and leaving behind them in the valley nothing but smoking ruins.

The shepherds who, since this event, had returned and set up their tents amidst the pasturages of

THIBET, AND CHINA

Tchogortan, were always on the watch, fearful of a new aggression. From time to time, some of them armed with lances and guns would patrol the neighbourhood ; a precaution which, though it would certainly have by no means intimidated the brigands, had at leaſt the advantage of communicating a certain degree of fancied security to the population.

Towards the end of August, while we were quietly occupied in the manufacture of our ropes, siniſter rumours began to circulate ; by degrees they assumed all the charaéter of certain intelligence, and no doubt was entertained that we were threatened with a new and terrible invasion of brigands. Every day we were alarmed with some fresh faét of a formidable nature. The shepherds of such a place had been surprised, their tents burned, and their flocks driven off. Elsewhere there had been a tremendous battle, in which a number of persons had been killed. These rumours became so subſtantially alarming that the adminiſtrators of the Lamasery felt bound to adopt some measures on the subjeét. They dispatched to Tchogortan a Grand Lama and twenty ſtudents of the Faculty of Prayers, charged with the task of preserving the locality from any unpleasant occurrence. On their arrival, these Lamas convoked the chiefs of the Si-Fan families, and announced that now they were come the people had nothing to fear. Next morning, they all ascended the higheſt mountain in the neighbourhood, set up some travelling tents there, and proceeded to recite prayers to the accompaniment of music. They remained in this encampment two whole days, which they occupied in prayer, in exorcising, and in conſtruéting a small pyramid of earth, whitened with lime, and above which floated, at the end of a maſt, a flag on which were printed various Thibetian prayers. This modeſt edifice was entitled the Pyramid of Peace. These ceremonies completed, the Lamas, great and small, folded their tents, descended from the mountain, and quietly returned to Kounboum, fully persuaded that they had opposed to the brigands an impassable barrier.

The Pyramid of Peace did not appear, however, to have infused equal confidence into the hearts of the herdsmen; for, one fine morning, they all decamped together, bag and baggage, and went with their herds and flocks to seek a less dangerous position elsewhere. They invited us to follow their example, but we preferred to remain where we were, for in the desert there is scarcely one place more secure than another. The flight of the shepherds, besides, seemed to us a guarantee that our tranquillity would not be disturbed, for we considered that the brigands, when they learned that no flocks remained in the valley of Tchogortan, would feel no interest in paying us a visit. We, therefore, in our turn, raised up in our hearts a Pyramid of Peace, in the form of a firm reliance on the divine protection; and, thus fortified, we abode calm and fearlessly in our adopted home.

For some days we enjoyed the most profound solitude. Since the disappearance of the herd and flocks, the argoleers, having nothing to do, had kept away. We were alone with a Lama, left in charge of the Lamasery. Our animals profited by the change, for now all the pasturages of the valley were theirs; they could browse wherever they liked over the valley, fearless of meeting a single competitor.

The desert, however, became after a time, once more alive, and towards the commencement of September the Lamas of the Faculty of Medicine repaired to Tchogortan, for the purpose of botanizing. The disposable houses received all they could contain, and the rest dwelt in tents, sheltered by the great trees of the Lamasery. Every morning, after they had recited their prayers in common, drunk their buttered tea, and eaten their barley-meal, all the students in medicine tuck up their garments, and go forth on the mountains, under the guidance of one of their professors. They are each provided with a long iron-pointed stick, and a small pick-axe; a leathern bag, filled with meal, is suspended from the girdle, and some carry at their backs great tea-kettles, for the Faculty spend the entire day on the mountain. Before sunset, the Lama physicians return laden with perfect faggots of branches, and piles of plants and grasses. As you see them wearily descending the mountains, supported by their long staves and bearing these burdens, they look more like poaching wood-cutters than like future doctors in medicine. We were often obliged to escort in person those of the number who had special charge of the aromatic plants; for our camels, which, attracted by the odour, always put themselves in pursuit of these personages, would otherwise inevitably, and without the smallest scruple, have devoured those precious simples, destined for the relief of suffering humanity. The remainder of the day is occupied in cleaning and spreading out on mats these various products of the vegetable kingdom. The medical harvest lasted eight whole days. Five other days are devoted to the selection and classification of the various articles. On the fourteenth day a small portion is given to each student, the great bulk remaining the property of the Faculty of Medicine. The fifteenth day is kept as a festival, in the form of a grand banquet of tea with milk, barley-meal, little cakes fried in butter, and boiled mutton. This terminates this botanico-medical expedition, and the illustrious Faculty gaily returns to the Grand Lamasery.

The drugs collected at Tchogortan are deposited in the general drug-room of Kounboum. When they have been thoroughly dried in the heat of a moderate fire, they are reduced to powder, and then divided into small doses, which are neatly enveloped in red paper, and labelled with Thibetian characters. The pilgrims who visit Kounboum buy these remedies at exorbitant prices. The Tartar-Mongols never return home without an ample supply of them, having an unlimited confidence in whatever emanates from Kounboum. On their own mountains and prairies they would find exactly the same plants, the same shrubs, the same roots, the same grasses; but then how different must be the plants, shrubs, roots, and grasses that grow and ripen in the birth-place of Tsong-Kaba!

The Thibetian physicians are as empirical as those of other countries—possibly somewhat more so. They assign to the human frame four hundred and forty maladies, neither more nor less. The books which the Lamas of the Faculty of Medicine are obliged to study, and to learn by heart, treat of these four hundred and forty maladies, indicating their characteristics, the means of identifying them, and the manner of combating them. These books are a hotch-potch of aphorisms, more or less obscure, and of a host of special recipes. The Lama physicians have not so great a horror of blood as the Chinese physicians have—they bleed sometimes and cup often. In the latter operation, they first subject the skin of the part to slight excoriations; and afterwards place over it a bullock's horn, open at the point. They exhaust the air within, and when a sufficient vacuum is obtained, stop up the hole with a pellet of chewed paper. When they wish to remove the cup they have only to remove this mastic.

The Lama physicians attach extreme importance to the inspection of the patient's water. They always require various specimens of it, collected at different hours of the day and night. They examine it with the most minute attention, and take the greatest heed to all the changes undergone by its colour. They whip it, from time to time, with a wooden spatula, and then put it up to the ear to ascertain what degree, if any, of noise it makes; for, in their view, a patient's water is mute or silent, according to his state of health. A Lama physician, to attain the character of thorough ability in his profession, must be able to treat and cure a patient without having ever seen him, the inspection of the water sufficing as a guide in the preparation of his prescriptions.

As we have said elsewhere, in speaking of the Tartar-Mongols, the Lamas introduce many superstitious practices into medicine. Yet, notwithstanding all this quackery, there is no doubt that they possess an infinite number of very valuable recipes, the result of long experience. It were, perhaps, rash to imagine that medical science has nothing to learn from the Tartar, Thibetian and Chinese physicians, on the pretext that they are not acquainted with the structure and mechanism of the human body. They may, nevertheless, be in possession of very important secrets, which science alone, no doubt, is capable of explaining, but which, very possibly, science itself may never discover. Without being scientific, a man may very well light upon extremely scientific results. In China, Tartary and Thibet, everybody can make gunpowder; yet it may be safely propounded that not one of these powder-makers can explain scientifically this chemical operation; each man has a good recipe for making the powder, and he makes it.

Towards September we received the joyful intelligence that the Thibetian embassy had arrived at Tang-Keou-Eul, where it was to remain for several days, in order to lay in a stock of provisions, and arrange its order of march. Thus, then, after long and annoying delay, we were about to proceed to the capital of Thibet. We made, without loss of time, all our necessary preparations. First we had to pay a visit to Kounboum, on order to purchase provisions for four months, since, on the whole route, there was not the least hope of finding anything to buy that we might want. Upon a careful calculation, we found that we should require five bricks of tea, two sheeps' paunches of butter, two sacks of flour, and eight sacks of tsamba [*tsam-pa*]. *Tsamba* is the name given here to barley-meal, the insipid article which constitutes the ordinary food of the Thibetians. They take a tea-cup half-filled with boiling tea; to this they add some pinches of *tsamba*, and then mix these materials together, with the finger, into a sort of wretched paste, neither cooked nor uncooked, hot nor cold, which is then swallowed, and is considered breakfast, dinner, or supper, as the case may be. If you desire to cross the desert to Lha-Ssa, you must perforce resign yourself to *tsamba*; 'tis to no avail the French traveller sighs for his accustomed knife and fork, and his accustomed knife and fork dishes : he must do without them.

Persons full of experience and philanthropy counselled us to lay in a good store of garlic, and every day to chew several cloves of it, unless we wished to be killed on our way by the deleterious vapours that emanated from certain elevated mountains. We did not discuss the merits of this hygeianic advice, but adopted it with absolute confidingness.

Our residence in the valley of Tchogortan had been in a high degree advantageous to our animals, which had become fatter than we had ever before known them; the camels, in particular, were magnificently stout; their humps, made firm with solid flesh, rose proudly on their backs, and seemed to defy the fatigues and privations of the desert. Still, even in their improved condition, three camels were not enough to carry our provisions and our baggage. We accordingly added to our caravan a supplementary camel and horse, which lightened our exchequer to the extent of twenty-five ounces of silver; moreover, we hired a young Lama of the Ratchico [Rachico] mountains, with whom we had become acquainted at Kounboum, and who was admitted into our party in the capacity of pro-cameleer. This appointment, while it raised the social condition of Samdadchiemba, diminished also the fatigues of his functions. According to this new arrangement, the little caravan was disposed in the following order: the pro-cameleer, Charadchambeul, went on foot, and led after him the four camels, who marched in Indian file, the one fastened to the tail of the other; Samdadchiemba, cameleer-in-chief, rode his little black mule beside the camels, and the two missionaries closed the procession, each mounted on a white horse. After having exchanged infinite *khatas* with our acquaintances and friends at Kounboum and Tchogortan, we proceeded on our route, directing our march towards the Blue Sea, where we were to await the Thibetian embassy.

From Tchogortan to the Koukou-Noor was four days' march. We passed on our way a small Lamasery, called Tansan, containing at most two hundred Lamas; its site is perfectly enchanting; rocky mountains, covered with shrubs and tall firs, form for it a circular enclosure, in the centre of which rise the habitations of the Lamas. A stream, bordered with willows and fine longwort, after tranquilly encircling the Lamasery, dashes over a rocky fall, and continues its course in the desert. The Buddhist monastery of Tansan is, they say, very rich, being largely endowed by the Mongol princes of Koukou-Noor with annual contributions.

On leaving the Lamasery of Tansan, we entered an extensive plain, where numerous Mongol tents and flocks of every kind picturesquely variegated the verdure of the pastures. We met two Lamas on horseback, who were seeking contributions of butter from the wealthy shepherds of the locality. Their course is this: they present themselves at the entrance of each tent, and thrice sound a marine conch. Thereupon some member of the family brings out a small roll of butter, which, without saying a word, he deposits in a bag, suspended from the saddle of each Lama's horse. The Lamas never once alight, but content themselves with riding up to each tent, and announcing their presence to the inmates by the sound of the shell.

As we advanced, the country became more fertile and less mountainous, until at length, we reached the vaſt and magnificent paſturage of Koukou-Noor. There vegetation is so vigorous that the grass rose up to the ſtomachs of our camels. Soon we discovered, far before us, quite on the horizon, what seemed a broad silver riband, above which floated light vapours that, rising, became loſt in the azure of the heavens. Our pro-cameleer informed us that this was the Blue Sea. His words filled us with a tremulous joy; we urged on our animals, and the sun had not set when we planted our tent within a hundred paces of the waters of the great lake.

CHAPTER IV

THE Blue Lake, in Mongol Koukou-Noor, in Thibetian Tsot-Ngon-Po [mTs'o-sngo-po], was anciently called by the Chinese Si-Haï [Hsi-hai] "Weſtern Sea"; they now call it Tsing-Haï "Blue Sea." This immense reservoir of water, which is more than a hundred leagues in circumference, seems, in faƈt, to merit the title of sea, rather than merely that of lake. To say nothing of its vaſt extent, it is to be remarked that its waters are bitter and salt, like those of the ocean, and undergo, in a similar manner, flux and reflux. The marine odour which they exhale is smelt at a great distance, far into the desert.

Towards the weſtern portion of the Blue Sea there is a small island, rocky and bare, inhabited by twenty contemplative Lamas, who have built thereon a Buddhist temple, and some modeſt habitations wherein they pass their lives, in tranquil retirement, far from the diſtraƈting disquietudes of the world. No one can go out and visit them, for, throughout the entire extent of the lake, there is not a single boat of any kind to be seen; at all events we saw none, and the Mongols told us that among their tribes no one ever thought of occupying himself in any way or degree with navigation. In the winter, indeed, at the time of the more intense cold, the water is frozen solidly enough to enable the shepherds around to repair in pilgrimage to the Lamasery. They bear to the contemplative Lamas their modeſt offerings of butter, tea and *tsamba*, and receive in exchange benediƈtions and prayers for good paſturage and prosperous flocks.

TRAVELS IN TARTARY,

The tribes of the Koukou-Noor are divided into twenty-nine banners, commanded by three *Kiun-Wang*, two *Beïlé*, two *Beïssé*, four Koung, and eighteen *Taï-Tsi*. All these princes are tributaries of the Chinese emperor, and, every second year, repair to Peking, whither they carry, as tribute, furs and gold-dust, which their subjects collect from the sands of the rivers. The vast plains which adjoin the Blue Sea are of very great fertility and of a most agreeable aspect, though entirely destitute of trees; the grass is of prodigious height, and the numerous streams which fertilize the soil, afford ample means to the numerous herds of the desert for satiating their thirst. The Mongols, accordingly, are very fond of setting up their tents in these magnificent pastures. The hordes of brigands harass them in vain: they will not quit the country. They content themselves with a frequent change of encampment, in order to baffle their enemies, but when they can no longer avoid the danger they encounter it with great bravery, and fight gallantly. The necessity under which they permanently exist of defending their property and their lives from the attacks of the Si-Fan, has, at length, rendered them intrepidly courageous. At any hour of the day or night they are ready for battle: they tend their cattle on horseback, lance in hand, fusil in sling, and sabre in belt. What a difference between these vigorous shepherds, with their long moustaches, and the languishing fiddle-faddles of Virgil, eternally occupied in piping on a flute, or in decorating with ribands and flowers their pretty straw hats.

The brigands, who keep the Mongol tribes of the Koukou-Noor always on the alert, are hordes of Si-Fan, or Eastern Thibetians, dwelling in the Bayen-Kharat mountains, towards the source of the Yellow River. In this part of the country they are known

THIBET, AND CHINA

under the generic appellation of Kolo. Their peculiar haunt, it is said, are the deep gorges of the mountain, whither it is impossible to penetrate without a guide, for all the approaches are guarded by impossible torrents and frightful precipices. The Kolos never quit these abodes except to scour the desert on a mission of pillage and devastation. Their religion is Buddhism; but they have a special idol of their own, whom they designate the Divinity of Brigandism, and who, assuredly, enjoys their most intense devotion, their most genuine worship. The chief business of their Lamas is to pray and offer up sacrifices for the success of their predatory expeditions. It is said that these brigands are in the revolting habit of eating the hearts of their prisoners, in order to fortify their own courage; but, for that matter, there is no monstrous practice which the Mongols of the Koukou-Noor do not unhesitatingly attribute to these people.

The Kolos are divided into several tribes, each bearing a particular name of its own; and it was only in the nomenclature of these tribes that we ever, in this part of the world, heard of the Khalmouks [Kalmuks], or Calmucks. That which we, in Europe, ordinarily conceive to be Khalmoukia, is a purely imaginary distinction; the Khalmouks are very far indeed from enjoying, in Asia, the importance which our books of geography assign to them. In the Khalmoukia of our imagining, no one ever heard of the Khalmouks. It was a long time before we could even discover the existence of the name at all; but, at last, we were lucky enough to meet with a Lama who had travelled extensively in Eastern Thibet, and he told us that among the Kolo, there is a small tribe called Kolo-Khalmouki [Kolo-Kalmuks]. It is just possible that at some former period the Khalmouks may have enjoyed great importance, and have occupied a large extent of country; but the great probability, at leaſt, is, that it was the travellers of the thirteenth century, who, relying upon some vague notions they had picked up, represented this petty tribe to be a great nation.

Neither does the Koukou-Noor country itself merit the importance given to it in our geographies: it occupies, in the maps, a far greater space than it really possesses. Though comprising twenty-nine banners, its limits are reſtricted: on the north it is bordered by Khilian-Chan [Ch'i-lien-shan], on the south by the Yellow River, on the eaſt by the province of Kan-Sou, on the weſt by the river Tsaidam, where begins another Tartar country, inhabited by tribes who bear the designation of Mongols of the Tsaidam.

According to the popular tradition of the Koukou-Noor, the Blue Sea did not always occupy its present site : that great mass of water originally covered, in Thibet, the place where the city of Lha-Ssa now ſtands. One fine day it abandoned its immense reservoir there, and, by a subterranean march, travelled to the place which now serves as its bed. The following is the narrative of this marvellous event that was related to us.

In ancient times the Thibetians of the kingdom of Oui resolved to build a temple in the centre of the great valley which they inhabited; they collected, at vaſt expense, the richeſt materials, and the edifice rose rapidly; but, juſt on the point of completion, it suddenly crumbled to pieces, without anyone having the least idea as to the cause of this disaſter. Next year, they made new preparations, and laboured upon the conſtruction of the temple with equal ardour; the second temple, when juſt completed, fell to pieces as the firſt had done; a third attempt was made, the only result of which was a third cataſtrophe, exactly the same with the two preceding. Everybody was plunged in utter despair, and there was talk of abandoning the enterprise. The king consulted a famous diviner of the country, who replied that it had not been given to him to know the cause which opposed the construction of the temple, but this he knew : that there was a great saint in the East who possessed a certain secret, which secret, being once extracted from him, the obstacle would forthwith disappear. He could, however, give no exact information as to who the great saint was, or where he lived. After protracted deliberation, a Lama, of excellent address and great courage, was sent on a mission of inquiry. He traversed all the districts east of the kingdom of Oui ; he visited all the Tartar tribes, stopping for awhile wherever he heard speak of any man especially noted for his sanctity and knowledge. All his inquiries were fruitless : it was to no purpose he discoursed of the valley of the kingdom of Oui, and of the temple which it had been attempted to raise there : nobody comprehended at all what he was talking about. He was returning home, depressed and disappointed, when, in crossing the great plains which separate Thibet from China, the girth of his saddle broke, and he fell from his horse. Perceiving, near at hand, beside a small pond, a poor, dilapidated tent, he proceeded thither to get his saddle repaired. Having fastened his horse to a stake at the door of the tent, he entered, and found within a venerable old man, absorbed in prayer. " Brother," said the traveller, " may peace be ever in thy dwelling." " Brother," replied the old man, without moving, " seat thyself beside my hearth." The Thibetian Lama fancied he saw that the old man was blind. " I perceive, with grief," said he, " that thou hast lost the use of thy eyes." " Yes ; 'tis now many years since I was deprived of the happiness of contemplating the brightness of the sun, and the verdure of our beautiful plains ; but prayer is a great consolation in my affliction. Brother, it seems to me that thy tongue has a peculiar accent: art thou not a man of our tribes?" "I am a poor Lama of the East. I made a vow to visit the temples that have been raised in the Mongol countries, and to prostrate myself before the sainted personages I should meet on my way. An accident has happened to me near this spot; I have broken the girth of my saddle, and I have come to thy tent to mend it." "I am blind," said the old man; "I cannot myself help thee; but look round the tent, there are several straps, and thou canst take that which will best answer thy purpose." While the stranger was selecting a good strap, wherewith to make a new girth, the old man spoke: "O Lama of eastern lands; happy art thou to be able to pass thy days visiting our sacred monuments! The most magnificent temples are in the Mongol countries; the Poba (Thibetians) will never attain anything like them: 'tis in vain they apply their utmost efforts to build such in their beautiful valley; the foundations they put will always be sapped by the waves of a subterranean sea, of which they do not suspect the existence." After a moment's silence the old man added: "I have uttered these words because thou art a Mongol Lama; but thou must lock them up in thy heart, and never communicate them to a single person. If, in thy pilgrimages, thou meetest a Lama of the kingdom of Oui, guard well thy tongue, for the revealing my secret will cause the ruin of our country. When a Lama of the kingdom of Oui shall know that in his valley there exists a subterranean sea, the waters of that sea will forthwith depart thence, and inundate our prairies."

He had scarcely uttered the last word when the stranger rose and said to him, "Unfortunate old man, save thyself, save thyself in haste: the waters will speedily be here, for I am a Lama of the kingdom of Oui." So saying, he jumped on his horse, and disappeared over the desert.

These words struck like a thunderbolt upon the poor old man. After a moment of dull stupor he gave way to cries and groans. While yielding to this excess of grief his son arrived, bringing home from pasture a small herd of cattle. "My son," cried the old man, "saddle thy horse on the instant, take thy sabre, and gallop off towards the West: thou wilt overtake a foreign Lama, whom thou must kill, for he has stolen from me my strap." "How!" exclaimed the young man, terror-struck, "wouldst thou have me commit a murder? Wouldst thou, my father, whom all our tribes venerate for thy great sanctity, order me to kill a poor traveller, because he took from thy tent a strap of which he had, doubtless, need?" "Go, go, my son, hasten, I conjure thee," cried the old man, throwing his arms about in despair; "go and immolate that stranger, unless thou wouldst have us all buried beneath the waves." The young man, believing that his father laboured under a temporary fit of insanity, would not contradict him, lest he should exasperate him still more; he therefore mounted his horse and galloped after the Lama of the kingdom of Oui. He came up with him before the evening: "Holy personage," said he, "pardon me, that I interrupt your progress; this morning you rested in our tent, and you took thence a strap, which my father is making great outcry for; the fury of the old man is so excessive, that he has ordered me to put you to death; but it is no more permissible to execute the orders of a raving old man than it is to fulfil those of a child. Give me back the strap and I will return to appease my father." The Lama of the kingdom of Oui dismounted, took off the girth of his saddle, and gave it to the young man, saying, "Your father gave me this strap, but, since he regrets the gift, carry it back to him; old men are fanciful, but we muſt, nevertheless, respeƈt them, and carefully avoid occasioning them any annoyance." The Lama took off his own girdle, made a saddle-girth of it, and departed, the young man returning in all haſte to his tent.

He arrived in the night time, and found his dwelling surrounded by a multitude of shepherds, who, unable to comprehend the lamentations of the great saint of their diſtriƈt, were awaiting, in much anxiety, the return of his son. "My father, my father," cried the young man, dismounting, "be calm, here is what thou wantedſt." "And the ſtranger?" asked the old man, "haſt thou put him to death?" "I let him depart in peace for his own country. Should I not have committed a great crime, had I murdered a Lama who had done you no evil? Here is the ſtrap he took from you." And so saying, he put the ſtrap into his father's hands. The old man shuddered in every limb, for he saw that his son had been over-reached: the same word in Mongol signifies both ſtrap and secret. The old man had meant that his son should kill the man who had ſtolen his secret from him: but when he saw that his son brought back to him a ſtrap, he cried: "The Weſt triumphs; 'tis the will of heaven!" He then told the shepherds to flee with their cattle and sheep in all haſte, unless they desired to be swallowed up by the waters. As to himself, he proſtrated himself in the centre of his tent and there resignedly awaited death.

Day had scarce dawned when there was heard underground a rumbling but majeſtic sound, similar to the tumult of torrents rolling their waves over the mountain sides. The sound advanced with fearful rapidity, and the water of the pond, beside which the old man lived, was seen to be in great commotion:

THIBET, AND CHINA

then the earth opened with terrible shocks, and the subterranean waters rose impetuously, and spread, like a vast sea, over the plain, destroying infinite numbers of men and beasts who had not time to escape. The old man was the first who perished beneath the waves.

The Lama, who bore the secret of this great catastrophe, upon arriving in the kingdom of Oui, found his countrymen in utter consternation at fearful sounds they had heard beneath them in the valley, and the nature and cause of which no one could explain. He related the story of the blind old man, and all immediately comprehended that the uproar which had so alarmed them had been occasioned by the subterranean sea, on its removal to the East. They resumed, with enthusiasm, the labours of construction they had abandoned, and raised a magnificent temple, which is still standing. An immense number of families settled around the temple, and, by degrees, there was created a great city, which took the name of Lha-Ssa " Land of Spirits."

This singular chronicle of the origin of the Blue Sea was first related to us in Koukou-Noor; it was afterwards repeated to us at Lha-Ssa, in almost precisely the same terms; but we could nowhere discover traces of any historical fact with which the singular fable might be supposed to correspond.

We abode in Koukou-Noor for nearly a month. Continual rumours of the brigands compelled us to move our encampment five or six times, in order to follow the Tartar tribes, who, at the least suggestion of approaching assailants, change their quarters, taking care, however, never to remove altogether from the rich pastures which border the Blue Sea.

Towards the end of October, the Thibetian embassy arrived, and we joined the immense body, already swollen on its previous way by a great number of

TRAVELS IN TARTARY,

Mongol caravans, which, like ourselves, availed themselves of this favourable escort to Lha-Ssa. Formerly the Thibetian government sent an embassy every year to Peking. That of 1840 was attacked on its journey by a large body of Kolos. The engagement lasted a whole day, but, in the end, the Thibetians were victorious over their assailants, and continued their journey. Next morning, however, it was discovered that they had no longer amongst them the Tchanak-Kampo [rGya-nag-mkhan-po],[1] a Grand Lama, who accompanies these embassies to Peking, in the character of representative of the Talé-Lama. For several days he was sought all round, but to no effect, and the only conclusion was that during the fight he had been taken prisoner by the Kolos, and carried off. The embassy, however, proceeded on its way, and arrived at Peking without its official head. The emperor, of course, was tremendously afflicted.

In 1841, there was another battle with the brigands, and another catastrophe. This time, the Tchanak-Kampo was not carried off by the brigands, but he received from them a gash in the chest, of which he died in a few days afterwards. The emperor, on hearing these melancholy tidings, was, it is affirmed, altogether inconsolable, and forthwith sent dispatches to the Talé-Lama, setting forth that, considering the difficulties and dangers of the journey, he would thenceforth require the compliment of an embassy only once in three years. Accordingly, the present embassy was the first which had been dispatched from Lha-Ssa since 1841. On its journey out it had been fortunate enough to encounter no brigands, and, consequently, its Tchanak-Kampo had been neither stolen nor stabbed.

Next day, after our departure from Koukou-Noor,

Tchanak is the Mongol name of Peking ; Kampo means Pontiff.

THIBET, AND CHINA

we placed ourselves at the van of the caravan, and then halted on one side, in order to see the immense procession defile before us, and so make acquaintance with our travelling companions. The men and animals composing the caravan might be thus estimated: 1,500 long-haired oxen, 1,200 horses, 1,200 camels and 2,000 men, Thibetians and Tartars, some on foot, some on ox-back, but most of them on horses and camels. All the cavalry were armed with lances, sabres, bows and arrows, and matchlocks. The footmen, designated *lakto* (? *lag-'don*, a mistake for *rkang-'gro*), were charged with the conduct of the files of camels and of the capricious and disorderly march of the cattle. The Tchanak-Kampo travelled in a large litter, carried by two mules. Besides this multitude, whose journey extended to Lha-Ssa, there was an escort of 300 Chinese soldiers, furnished by the province of Kan-Sou, and 200 brave Tartars, charged by the prince of Koukou-Noor with the protection of the holy embassy of the Talé-Lama, to the frontiers of Thibet.

The soldiers of the province of Kan-Sou fulfilled their functions like thorough Chinese. In order to avoid any disagreeable encounter, they carefully kept at the rear of the caravan, where they sang, smoked, and joked at their ease, giving no sort of heed to any possible brigands. Every day they exhibited the remarkable peculiarity of waiting until the rest of the caravan had filed off, when they carefully searched all over the night's encampment in order to pick up anything that might have been left behind, and, of course travelling somewhat in the rear of the rest, they were further able to realize any matters that those preceeding them might drop during the progress of the day. The Tartar soldiers pursued a course precisely the reverse: they were ever in the van, and at the sides of the caravan, dashing about to the tops of the hills and the depths of the valleys to see that no ambush of brigands lay in wait there.

The general march and particular movements of the caravan were executed with tolerable order and precision, especially at the outset. Generally we ſtarted every morning two or three hours before sunrise, in order that we might encamp about noon, and give the animals full time to feed during the remainder of the day; the reveillé was announced by a cannon-shot; forthwith, everybody rose, the fires were lighted, and while some of each particular party loaded the beaſts of burden, the others boiled the kettle and prepared breakfaſt; a few cups of tea were drunk, a few handfuls of *tsamba* eaten, and then the tent was taken down, folded, and packed A second cannon-shot gave the signal for departure. A few of the more experienced horsemen took the lead as guides; these were followed by long files of camels, and then came the long-haired cattle, in herds of two or three hundred beaſts each, under the care of several *lakto*. The horsemen had no fixed place in the procession; they dashed here and there, up and down, juſt as their caprice suggeſted. The plaintive cries of the camels, the roaring of the bulls, the lowing of the cows, the neighing of the horses, the talking bawling, laughing, singing of the travellers, the whiſtling of the *lakto* to the beaſts of burden, and, above all, the innumerable bells tinkling from the necks of the yaks and the camels, produced together an immense, undefinable concert, which, far from wearying, seemed, on the contrary, to inspire everybody with fresh courage and energy.

The caravan went on thus across the desert, ſtopping each day, in plains, in valleys, and on the mountain sides, improvising, with its tents, so numerous and so varied in form and colour, a large town, which vanished each morning, to reappear further on each evening. What an astonishing thing it must have been for these vast and silent deserts, to find themselves, all of a sudden, traversed by so numerous and so noisy a multitude! When we viewed those infinite travelling tents, those large herds, and those men, in turns shepherds and warriors, we could not help frequently reflecting upon the march of the Israelites, when they went in search of the Promised Land, through the solitudes of Madian.

On quitting the shore of the Blue Sea, we directed our steps towards the west, with a slight inclination, perhaps, southward. The first days of our march were perfect poetry; everything was just as we could have wished; the weather was magnificent, the road excellent, the water pure, the pastures rich and ample. As to brigands, we lost all thought of them. In the night, it was, indeed, rather cold; but this inconvenience was easily obviated by the aid of our sheepskin coats. We asked one another what people could mean by representing this Thibet journey as something so formidable; it seemed to us impossible for any one to travel more comfortably, or more agreeably. Alas! this enchantment was not of long duration.

Six days after our departure we had to cross the Pouhain-Gol [Bukhaïn-gol], a river which derives its source from the slopes of the Nan-Chan [Nan-shan] mountains, and throws itself into the Blue Sea. Its waters are not very deep, but being distributed in some dozen channels, very close to one another, they occupy altogether a breadth of more than a league. We had the misfortune to reach the first branch of the Pouhain-Gol long before daybreak; the water was frozen but not thickly enough to serve as a bridge. The horses which arrived first grew alarmed and would not advance; they stopped on the bank and gave the cattle time to come up with them. The whole caravan thus became assembled at one point, and it would be impossible to describe the disorder and confusion which prevailed in that enormous mass, amid the darkness of night. At laſt, several horsemen, pushing on their ſteeds and breaking the ice, actually and figuratively, the whole caravan followed in their train: the ice cracked in all directions, the animals ſtumbled about and splashed up the water, and the men shouted and vociferated; the tumult was absolutely fearful. After having traversed the firſt branch of the river, we had to manœuvre, in the same way, over the second, and then over the third, and so on. When day broke, the Holy Embassy was ſtill dabbling in the water; at length, after infinite fatigue and infinite quaking, physical and moral, we had the delight to leave behind us the twelve arms of the Pouhain-Gol, and to find ourselves on dry land; but all our poetical visions had vanished, and we began to think this manner of travelling perfectly deteſtable.

And yet everybody about us was in a ſtate of jubilation, exclaiming that the passage of the Pouhain-Gol had been admirably executed. Only one man had broken his legs and only two animals had been drowned. As to the articles loſt or ſtolen during the protracted disorder, no one took any heed to them.

When the caravan resumed its accuſtomed march, it presented a truly ludicrous appearance. Men and animals were all, more or less, covered with icicles. The horses walked on, very dolefully, evidently much incommoded by their tails, which hung down, all in a mass, ſtiff and motionless, as though they had been made of lead inſtead of hair. The long hair on the legs of the camels had become magnificent icicles, which knocked one againſt the other, as the animals advanced, with harmonious discord. It was very manifeſt, however, that these fine ornaments were not at all to the wearers' taſte, for they endeavoured, from time to time, to shake them off by ſtamping violently on the ground. As to the long-haired oxen, they were regular caricatures; nothing can be conceived more ludicrous than their appearance, as they slowly advanced, with legs separated to the utmoſt possible width, in order to admit of an enormous syſtem of stalactites which hung from their bellies to the ground. The poor brutes had been rendered so perfectly shapeless by the agglomeration of icicles with which they were covered, that they looked as though they were preserved in sugar-candy.

During the firſt few days of our march we were somewhat isolated and lonely amid the multitude; without friends or even acquaintance. However, we soon acquired companions, for there is nothing like travelling to bring men together. The companions whom we entered into association with, and beside whose tent we each day set up our own, were neither merchants, nor pilgrims, nor members of the embassy itself, nor simple travellers, like ourselves; they were four Lamas, who conſtituted a category altogether apart. Two of them were from Lha-Ssa, one from Further Thibet, and the fourth from the kingdom of Torgot. On our way they related to us their long and picturesque hiſtory, of which the following is an outline.

The three Thibetian Lamas had become the disciples of a Grand Lama, named Altère [Altere], who proposed to erect, in the vicinity of Lha-Ssa, a Buddhiſt temple, which, in extent and magnificence was to surpass all those previously exiſting. One day he announced to his three disciples that all his plans were formed, and that they muſt all now proceed upon a grand queſt for subscriptions wherewith to defray the enormous expenses of the sacred conſtruction. They accordingly all four set forth, with hearts full of zeal and devotion. They firſt directed their

TRAVELS IN TARTARY,

steps towards the north, and traversing all Central Asia, reached the kingdom of Torgot, close to the Russian frontier. On their way, they called at the the Lamaseries, and at the abode of all the Thibetians and Tartar princes that lay near their route. Everywhere they received considerable offerings, for, besides that their object was of itself calculated to excite the warmest interest in well-disposed minds, Altère-Lama had letters of recommendation from the Talé-Lama, from the Bandchan-Remboutchi [Panch'en-Rimboch'ê], and from the heads of all the most famous Lamaseries of Thibet. In Torgot, a rich Mongol Lama, touched with the devotion of these intrepid collectors, offered them all his herds, and entreated Altère-Lama to admit him among his disciples, so that he might aid them in their mission through the countries of Tartary. Altère-Lama, on his part, moved with a zeal so pure, a disinterestedness so entire, consented to accept both his offerings and himself. The Lama collectors thus became five in number.

From Torgot they directed their march towards the east, going from one tribe to another, and everywhere augmenting their herds of cattle, sheep, and horses. On their way, they passed through the country of the Khalkhas, where they stayed for some time in the Lamasery of the Great Kouren, the offerings of the Tartar pilgrims flowing in abundantly. Hence, they turned south, to Peking, where they converted into gold and silver the innumerable animals which they had collected together from all parts. After an extended residence in the capital of the Chinese empire, they resumed their operations in the deserts of Tartary, and still seeking subscriptions, and still receiving them, arrived at Kounboum. In this famous and sainted Lamasery, capable of appreciating the merit of good Lamas, the zeal and devotion of the celebrated questors attained a colossal reputation;

they became the objects of the public veneration, and the professors, who aimed at perfection in their pupils, proposed to them these five men as models.

Altère-Lama, after three years of so meritorious a request, now only sighed for the hour when he should return to Lha-Ssa and consecrate to the construction of his temple all the rich offerings he had succeeded in collecting. Great, therefore was his joy, when he heard the intelligence that the Thibetian embassy was at hand. He resolved to avail himself of its escort, on its return from Peking, so as securely to convey his gold and his silver through the dangerous district of the Kolo. Meanwhile, he announced, he would apply all his attention to the preparations required for this important journey.

But, alas! the projects of men are often frustrated at the very moment when they seem on the point of succeeding in the most triumphant manner. One fine day there arrived at Si-Ning-Fou an imperial courier extraordinary, bearing dispatches by which the Grand Mandarin of that town was ordered to arrange with the superior of the Lamasery of Kounboum for the immediate arrest of Altère-Lama, charged with having, during the past three years, committed the most comprehensive swindling, by means of certain letters of recommendation, falsely attributed to the Talé-Lama. The orders of his imperial majesty were executed. One may easily imagine the stupefaction, on the occasion, of the poor Altère-Lama, and especially of his four disciples, who throughout the affair, had acted with the most entire good faith. The very embassy, on the protection of which Altère-Lama had so relied, was directed by the Thibetian government to take charge of the Grand Questor, whose marvellous successes had been published at Lha-Ssa, by the indiscreet laudations of the pilgrims.

Altère-Lama, having been arrested on the spot, was immediately forwarded, under safe escort, to Lha-Ssa, the route taken by his guard being that of the imperial couriers, through the province of Sse-Tchouan. Upon his arrival in the capital of Thibet, his case was to be inveſtigated by his natural judges. Meanwhile, his prodigious receipts were confiscated to the benefit of the Talé-Lama; for, obviously nothing could be more juſt than that he should be placed in possession of the gold and the silver which had been raised under the all-potent influence of his name. As to the Grand Queſtor's four disciples, it was arranged that they should await the return of the Thibetian embassy, and proceed with it to Lha-Ssa, taking with them fifty-eight magnificent camels which the Altère-Lama had procured, and which were to be at the disposal of the Thibetian government.

These four unfortunate disciples were the travelling companions whom good fortune had thrown in our way. The recollection of their fallen maſter was ever in their minds, but the sentiments which that recollection excited in them were not always the same. Sometimes they regarded their maſter as a saint, sometimes as a swindler; one day they would pronounce his name with veneration, raising their clasped hands to their forehead; another day they would curse him, and spit in the air, to show their contempt for him. The Lama of Torgot, however, always made the beſt of the matter. He reproached himself, sometimes, for having made an offering of all his herds to a man who now developed, pretty manifeſtly, every appearance of a rogue; but ſtill he consoled himself that after all the man's knavery had been the occasion of his seeing a good deal of the world, and visiting the moſt celebrated Lamaseries. These four young men were excellent fellows, and capital travelling companions. Every day they gave us some fresh details of their varied adventures, and their narratives frequently contributed to make us forget, for awhile, the fatigues and miseries of the journey.

A permanent cause of this suffering we had to endure was our pro-cameleer Charadchambeul. At first, this young Lama appeared to us a budding saint, but before long, we found that we had got amongst us a complete little demon with a human face. The following adventure opened our eyes to his character, and showed us what we should have to endure on his account.

The day after the passage of the Pouhain-Gol, when we had been marching for a part of the night, we remarked, on one of our camels, two great packages, carefully enveloped in wrappers, which we had not before seen. We thought, however, that some traveller, who had not been able to find room for them on his own sumpter animal, had asked Charadchambeul to take charge of them during the journey; and we, accordingly, quietly pursued our way, without, at the time, recurring to the circumstances. When we reached our encampment for the night, so soon as the baggage was taken down, we saw, to our great surprise, our Lama of the Ratchico mountains take the two packets, envelope them mysteriously in a piece of felt, and hide them in a corner of the tent. There was evidently something here which required explanation; and we accordingly desired Charadchambeul to inform us what was this new luggage that we saw in the tent. He approached us, and in a whisper as though fearing to be heard, told us that during the night Buddha had bestowed on him a special grace, in enabling him to find on the road a good thing, and then he added, with a knavish smile, that at Lha-Ssa, this good thing would sell for at least ten ounces of silver. We frowned and required to see this same good thing. Charadchambeul, having first carefully closed the door of the tent, uncovered, with infinite emotion, his pretended godsend. It consisted of two great leathern jars, full of a sort of brandy that is distilled in the province of Kan-Sou, and which is sold at a high price. On these two jars were Thibetian characters indicating the well-known name of the proprietor. We had the charity to reject the thought that Charadchambeul had stolen these jars during the night; and preferred to suppose that he had picked them up on the road. But our pro-cameleer was a casuist of very loose morality. He pretended that the jars belonged to him, that Buddha had made him a present of them, and that all which now required to be done was carefully to conceal them, lest the previous proprietor should discover them. Any attempt to reason such a worthy as this into morality and justice would have been simply lost labour and time. We therefore emphatically declared to him that the jars were neither ours nor his, that we would neither receive them into our tent nor place them on our camels during the journey, and that we had no desire whatever to arrive at Lha-Ssa with the character of being thieves. And in order that he might labour under no sort of misconception as to our feelings, we added, that unless he forthwith removed the jars from our tent, we should instantly proceed and give information of the circumstance to the proprietor. He seemed somewhat shaken by this intimation, and in order effectually to induce him to restitution, we advised him to carry what he had "found" to the ambassador, and request him to return it to the owner. The Tchanak-Kampo, we said, would not fail to be affected by his probity, and even if he did not give him a reward in hand, would bear him in mind, and when we reached Lha-Ssa would doubtless benefit him in some way. After an animated opposition, this advice was adopted. Charadchambeul presented himself before

THIBET, AND CHINA

the Tchanak-Kampo, who said to him, on receiving the jars : " Thou art a good Lama. A Lama who has justice in his heart is acceptable to the spirits." Charadchambeul returned perfectly furious, vehemently declaring that we had induced him to commit an imbecility in giving up the jars to the ambassador, who had presented him with nothing in return but empty words. From that moment he vowed an implacable hatred towards us. He did his work how and when he pleased ; he took a delight in wasting our provisions ; every day he loaded us with abuse, and in his rage often turning upon the poor animals, he would beat them about the head till he had half killed them. To discharge the wretch there, amid the desert, was impossible. We were fain therefore to arm ourselves with patience and resignation, and to avoid irritating still more the man's untamed ferocity.

Five days after the passage of the Pouhain-Gol, we reached Toulain-Gol [Taolai-yin-gol], a narrow, shallow river, which we crossed without any difficulty. The caravan halted shortly afterwards near a Lamasery, which had the appearance of former prosperity, but which was, at present, wholly deserted. The temples and the Lamas' cells, all tumbling in pieces, had become the abode of bats and of enormous rats. We heard that this Buddhist monastery, after having been besieged for three days by the brigands, had been taken by them, the greater portion of the inmates massacred, and the place itself plundered and demolished. From that time forth, no Lama had ventured to settle in the spot. The vicinity, however, was not so entirely uninhabited as we at first supposed. In walking over some rocky hills close by, we found a herd of goats and three miserable tents, concealed in a ravine. The poor inmates came out and begged for a few leaves of tea and a little *tsamba*. Their eyes were hollow, and their features pale and haggard. They knew not, they said, where to take refuge, so as to live in peace. The fear of the brigands was so powerful over them that it divested them even of the courage to flee away.

Next day, the caravan continued its route, but the Chinese escort remained encamped on the bank of the river; its task was completed, and after a few days rest it would return home. The Thibetian merchants, so far from being distressed at the circumstances, said that now the Chinese soldiers were no longer with them they should be able to sleep at night, freed from the fear of thieves.

On the 15th November, we quitted the magnificent plains of the Koukou-Noor, and entered upon the territory of the Mongols of Tsaidam. Immediately after crossing the river of that name, we found the aspect of the country totally changed. Nature becomes all of a sudden savage and sad; the soil, arid and stony, produces with difficulty a few dry, salt-petrous bushes. The morose and melancholy tinge of these dismal regions seems to have had its full influence upon the character of its inhabitants, who are all evidently a prey to the spleen. They say very little, and their language is so rude and guttural that other Mongols can scarcely understand them. Mineral salt and borax abound on this arid and almost wholly pastureless soil. You dig holes two or three feet deep, and the salt collects therein, and crystallizes and purifies of itself, without your having to take any trouble in the matter. The borax is collected from small reservoirs, which become completely full of it. The Thibetians carry quantities of it into their own country, where they sell it to the goldsmiths, who apply it to facilitate the fusion of metals. We stayed two days at the land of Tsaidam, feasting upon *tsamba* and some goats which the shepherds gave in exchange for some bricks of tea. The long-tailed oxen and the camels regaled themselves with the nitre and salt which they had everywhere about for the picking up. The grand object with the whole caravan was to get up its strength as much as possible, with a view to the passage of the Bourhan-Bota [Burkhan-Buddha], a mountain noted for the pestilential vapours in which, as we were informed, it is constantly enveloped.

We started at three in the morning, and after infinite sinuosities and meanderings over this hilly country, we arrived, by nine o'clock, at the foot of the Bourhan-Bota. There the caravan halted for a moment, as if to poise its strength ; everybody measured, with his eyes, the steep and rugged paths of the lofty ascent, gazed with anxiety at a light, thin vapour, which we were told was the pestilential vapour in question, and for awhile the entire party was completely depressed, and discouraged. After having taken the hygeianic measures prescribed by tradition, and which consisted in masticating two or three cloves of garlic, we began to clamber up the side of the mountain. Before long, the horses refused to carry their riders, and all, men as well as animals, advanced on foot, and step by step ; by degrees, our faces grew pale, our hearts sick, and our legs incapable of supporting us ; we threw ourselves on the ground, then rose again to make another effort ; then once more prostrated ourselves, and again rose to stumble on some paces farther ; in this deplorable fashion was it that we ascended the famous Bourhan-Bota. Heavens ! what wretchedness it was we went through ; one's strength seemed exhausted, one's head turning round, one's limbs dislocated ; it was just like a thoroughly bad seasickness ; and yet, all the while, one has to retain enough energy, not only to drag one's self on, but, moreover, to keep thrashing the animals which lie down at every step, and can hardly be got to move. One portion of the caravan, as a measure of precaution, stopped half way up the mountain, in a gully where the pestilential vapours, they said, were not so dense; the other portion of the caravan, equally as a measure of precaution, exerted their most intense efforts in order to make their way right up to the top, so as to avoid being asphyxiated by that dreadful air, so completely charged with carbonic acid. We were of the number of those who ascended the Bourhan-Bota at one stretch. On reaching its summit, our lungs dilated at their ease. The descent of the mountain was mere child's play and we were soon able to set up our tent far from the murderous air we had encountered on the ascent.

The Bourhan-Bota mountain has this remarkable particularity, that the deleterious vapour for which it is noted is only found on the sides faceing the east and the north; elsewhere the air of the mountain is perfectly pure and respirable. The pestilential vapours themselves would appear to be nothing more than carbonic acid gas. The people attached to the embassy told us that when there is any wind, the vapours are scarcely perceptible, but that they are very dangerous when the wind is calm and serene. Carbonic acid gas being, as the reader is aware, heavier than the atmospheric air, necessarily condenses on the surface of the ground, and remains fixed there until some great agitation of the air sets it in movement, disperses it in the atmosphere, and neutralizes its effects. When we crossed the Bourhan-Bota, the weather was rather calm than otherwise. We remarked that when we were lying on the ground, respiration was much more difficult; when, on the contrary, we raised ourselves on horseback, the influence of the gas was scarcely felt. The presence of the carbonic acid rendered it very difficult to light a fire; the *argols* burned without flame, and threw out great quantities of smoke. As to the manner in which the gas is formed, or as to whence it comes, we can give no sort of idea. We will merely add, for the benefit of those who are fond of seeking explanations of things in their names, that Bourhan-Bota means Kitchen of Bourhan; Bourhan being a synonyme of Buddha.

During the night we passed on to the other side of the mountain there fell a frightful quantity of snow. Our companions, who had not ventured to ascend the entire mountain at once, rejoined us in the morning; they informed us that they had effected the ascent of the upper portion of the mountain easily enough, the snow having dispersed the vapour.

The passage of the Bourhan-Bota was but a sort of apprenticeship. A few days after, Mount Chuga [Shugan] put our strength and courage to a still more formidable test. The day's march being long and laborious, the cannon-shot, our signal for departure, was heard at one o'clock in the morning. We made our tea with melted snow, ate a good meal of *tsamba*, seasoned with a clove of garlic, cut up into small bits, and started. When the huge caravan first set itself in motion, the sky was clear, and a brilliant moon lit up the great carpet of snow with which the whole country was covered. Mount Chuga being not very steep in the direction where we approached it, we were able to attain the summit by sunrise. Almost immediately afterwards, however, the sky became thickly overcast with clouds, and the wind began to blow with a violence which grew constantly more and more intense. The opposite sides of the mountain we found so encumbered with snow that the animals were up to their girths in it; they could only advance by a series of convulsive efforts, which threw several of them into gulfs from which it was impossible to extricate them, and where they accordingly perished. We marched in the very teeth of a wind so strong and so icy, that it absolutely at times choked our respiration, and despite our thick furs, made us tremble lest we should be killed with the cold. In order to avoid the whirlwinds of snow which the wind perpetually dashed in our faces, we adopted the example of some of our fellow travellers, who bestrode their horses' backs with their faces to the tail, leaving the animals to follow the guidance of their instincts. When we reached the foot of the mountain, and could use our eyes, we found that more than one face had been frozen in the descent. Poor M. Gabet, among the rest, had to deplore the temporary decease of his nose and ears. Everybody's chin was more or less chapped and cut.

The caravan halted at the foot of Mount Chuga, and each member of it sought refuge for awhile in the labyrinths of a number of adjacent defiles. Exhausted with hunger, and our limbs thoroughly benumbed, what we wanted to bring us to was a good fire, a good supper, and a good well-warmed bed; but the Chuga is far from possessing the comfortable features of the Alps; no Buddhist monks have as yet bethought themselves of taking up their abode there for the solace and salvation of poor travellers. We were, consequently, fain to set up our tent amid the snow, and then to go in search of what *argols* we could burn. It was a spectacle worthy of all pity to see that multitude, wandering about in all directions, and rummaging up the snow, in the hope of lighting upon some charming thick bed of *argols*. For ourselves, after long and laborious research, we managed to collect just enough of the article to melt three great lumps of ice, which we extracted by aid of an hatchet, from an adjacent pond. Our fire not being strong enough to boil the kettle, we had to content ourselves with infusing our *tsamba* in some tepid water, and gulping it down in order to prevent its freezing

THIBET, AND CHINA

in our hands. Such was all the supper we had after our frightful day's journey. We then rolled ourselves up in our goat-skins and blankets, and crouching in a corner of the tent, awaited the cannon-shot that was to summon us to our delightful *Impressions de Voyage*.

We left in this picturesque and enchanting encampment, the Tartar soldiers who had escorted us since our departure from Koukou-Noor; they were no longer able to extend to us their generous protection, for, that very day, we were about to quit Tartary, and to enter the territory of Hither Thibet. The Chinese and Tartar soldiers having thus left us, the embassy had now only to rely upon its own internal resources. As we have already stated, this great body of 2,000 men was completely armed, and everyone, with the merest exception, had announced himself prepared to show himself, upon occasion, a good soldier. But somehow or other the whilome so martial and valorous air of the caravan had become singularly modified since the passage of the Bourhan-Bota. Nobody sang now, nobody joked, nobody laughed, nobody pranced about on his horse; everybody was dull and silent; the mouftaches which heretofore had been so fiercely turned up, were now humbly veiled beneath the lamb-skins with which all our faces were covered up to the eyes. All our gallant soldiers had made up their lances, fusils, sabres, bows and arrows, into bundles, which were packed upon their sumpter animals. For that matter, the fear of being killed by the brigands scarcely occurred now to anyone: the point was to avoid being killed by the cold.

It was on Mount Chuga that the long train of our real miseries really began. The snow, the wind, and the cold there set to work upon us, with a fury which daily increased. The deserts of Thibet are certainly the most frightful country that it is possible to conceive. The ground continuing to rise, vegetation diminished as we advanced, and the cold grew more and more intense. Death now hovered over the unfortunate caravan. The want of water and of pasturage soon destroyed the strength of our animals. Each day we had to abandon beasts of burden that could drag themselves on no further. The turn of the men came somewhat later. The aspect of the road was of dismal auspice. For several days we travelled through what seemed the excavations of a great cemetery. Human bones and the carcases of animals presenting themselves at every step, seemed to warn us that, in this fatal region, amidst this savage nature, the caravans which had preceded us had preceded us in death.

To complete our misery, M. Gabet fell ill, his health abandoning him just at the moment when the frightful difficulties of the route called for redoubled energy and courage. The excessive cold he had undergone on the passage of Mount Chuga had entirely broken up his strength. To regain his previous vigour, he needed repose, tonic drinks, and a substantial nourishment, whereas all we had to give him was barley-meal, and tea made with snow water; and, moreover, notwithstanding his extreme weakness, he had every day to ride on horseback, and to struggle against an iron climate. And we had two months more of this travelling before us, in the depth of winter. Our prospect was, indeed, sombre!

Towards the commencement of September, we arrived in sight of the Bayen-Kharat, the famous chain of mountains, extending from south-east to north-west, between the Hoang-Ho and the Kin-Cha-Kiang [Ching-sha-chiang]. These two great rivers, after running a parallel course on either side of the Bayen-Kharat, then separate, and take opposite directions, the one towards the north, the other towards the south. After a thousand capricious meanderings in Tartary and Thibet, they both enter the Chinese empire; and after having watered it from west to east, they approach each other towards their mouths, and fall into the Yellow Sea very nearly together. The point at which we crossed the Bayen-Kharat is not far from the sources of the Yellow River; they lay on our left, and a couple of days' journey would have enabled us to visit them; but this was by no means the season for pleasure trips. We had no fancy for a tourist's excursion to the sources of the Yellow River: how to cross the Bayen-Kharat was ample occupation for our thoughts.

From its foot to its summit the mountain was completely enveloped in a thick coat of snow. Before undertaking the ascent, the principal members of the embassy held a council. The question was not whether they should pass the mountain: if they desired to reach Lha-Ssa, the passage of the mountain was an essential preliminary; nor was it the question whether they should await the melting of the snow; the point was simply whether it would be more advantageous to ascend the mountain at once or to wait till next day. The fear of avalanches filled everyone's mind, and we should all have gladly subscribed to effect an assurance against the wind. After the example of all the councils in the world, the council of the Thibetian embassy was soon divided into two parties, the one contending that it would be better to start forthwith, the other insisting that we ought, by all means, to wait till the morrow.

To extricate themselves from this embarrassment, they had recourse to the Lamas, who had the reputation of being diviners. But this expedient did not combine all minds in unity. Among the diviners there were some who declared that this day would be calm, but that the next day there would be a terrible wind, and there were others who announced an exactly contrary opinion. The caravan thus became divided into two camps, that of movement and that of non-movement. It will at once be understood that in our character of French citizens we instinctively placed ourselves in the ranks of the progressists; that is to say, of those who desired to advance, and to have done with this villainous mountain as soon as possible. It appeared to us, moreover, that reason was altogether on our side. The weather just then was perfectly calm; but we knew not what it might be on the morrow. Our party, therefore, proceeded to scale these mountains of snow, sometimes on horseback, but more frequently on foot. In the latter case, we made our animals precede us, and we hung on to their tails, a mode of ascending mountains which is certainly the least fatiguing of all. M. Gabet suffered dreadfully, but God, of his infinite goodness, gave us strength and energy enough to reach the other side. The weather was calm throughout, and we were assailed by no avalanche whatever.

Next morning, at daybreak, the party who had remained behind advanced and crossed the mountain with entire success. As we had had the politeness to wait for them, they joined us, and we entered together a valley where the temperature was comparatively mild. The excellence of the pasturage induced the caravan to take a day's rest here. A deep lake, in the ice of which we dug wells, supplied us with abundance of water. We had plenty of fuel, too, for the embassies and pilgrimages being in the habit of halting in the valley, after the passage of the Bayen-Kharat, one is always sure to find plenty of *argols* there. We all kept up great fires throughout our stay, burning all the burnable things we could find, without the smallest consideration for our successors, leaving it to our 15,000 long-haired oxen to supply the deficit.

We quitted the great valley of Bayen-Kharat, and set up our tents on the banks of the Mouroui-Oussou, or, as the Thibetians call it, Polei-Tchou [Polei-ch'u] "river of the Lord." Towards its source, this magnificent river bears the name of Mouroui-Oussou [Murui-usu] "tortuous river"; further on it is called Kin-Cha-Kiang "river of golden sand," and arrived in the province of Sse-Tchouan, it becomes the famous Yang-Dze-Kiang [Yang-tzŭ-chiang] "blue river." As we were passing the Mouroui-Oussou, on the ice, a singular spectacle presented itself. We had previously, from our encampment, observed dark, shapeless masses, ranged across this great river; and it was not until we came quite close to these fantastic islets that we could at all make head or tail of them. Then we found out that they were neither more nor less than upwards of fifty wild cattle, absolutely encrusted in the ice. They had no doubt attempted to swim across the river, at the precise moment of the concretion of the waters, and had been so hemmed in by the flakes as to be unable to extricate themselves Their fine heads, surmounted with great horns, were still above the surface; the rest of the bodies was enclosed by the ice, which was so transparent as to give a full view of the form and position of the unlucky animals, which looked as though they were still swimming. The eagles and crows had pecked out their eyes.

Wild cattle are of frequent occurrence in the deserts of Hither Thibet. They always live in great herds, and prefer the summits of the mountains. During the summer, indeed, they descend into the valleys in order to quench their thirst in the streams and ponds; but throughout the long winter season they remain on the heights, feeding on snow, and on a very hard rough grass they find there. These animals, which are of enormous size, with long black hair, are especially remarkable for the immense dimensions and splendid form of their horns. It is not at all prudent to hunt them, for they are said to be extremely ferocious. When, indeed, you find two or three of them separated from the main herd, you may venture to attack them; but the assailants muſt be numerous, in order to make sure of their game, for if they do not kill the animal at once there is decided danger of his killing them. One day we perceived one of these creatures licking up the nitre in a small place encircled with rocks. Eight men, armed with matchlocks, left the caravan, and poſted themselves in ambush, without being detected by the bull. Eight gun-shots were fired at once; the bull raised his head, looked round with fiery eyes in search of the places whence he had been assailed, and then dashed over the rocks into the plain, where he tore about furiously, roaring awfully. The hunters affirmed that he had been wounded, but that, intimidated by the appearance of the caravan, he had not ventured to turn upon his assailants.

Wild mules are also very numerous in Hither Tartary. After we had passed the Mouroui-Oussou we saw some almoſt every day. This animal, which our naturaliſts call *cheval hémione*, a horse half-ass, is of the size of an ordinary mule; but its form is finer and its movements more graceful and active; its hair, red on the back, grows lighter and lighter down to the belly, where it is almoſt white. The head, large and ugly, is wholly at variance with the elegance of its body; when in slow motion, it carries its head erect, and its long ears extended; when it gallops, it turns its head to the wind, and raises its tail, which exactly resembles that of the ordinary mule; its neigh is ringing, clear, and sonorous, and its speed so great that no Thibetian or Tartar horseman can overtake it. The mode of taking it is to poſt oneself in ambush near the places that lead to the springs where they drink, and to shoot it with arrows or bullets: the flesh is excellent, and the skins are converted into boots. The *hêmiones* are productive, and their young, from generation to generation, are always of the same species. They have never been tamed to domeſtic purposes. We heard of individuals having been taken quite young, and brought up with other foals; but it has always been found impracticable to mount them or to get them to carry any burden. With the firſt opportunity, they run away, and resume their wild ſtate. It did not, however, appear to us that they were so extremely fierce as they were represented: we have seen them frolicking about with the horses of our caravan, when paſturing; and it was only on the approach of man, whom they see and scent at a great diſtance, that they took to flight. The lynx, the chamois, the reindeer, and the wild goat abound in Hither Tartary.

Some days after the passage of the Mouroui-Oussou, the caravan began to break up; those who had camels went on a-head, refusing to be any longer delayed by the slow progress of the long-haired oxen. Besides, the nature of the country no longer permitted so large a body to encamp on one spot. The paſturages became so scarce and meagre that the animals of the caravan could not travel all together, without the danger of ſtarving all together. We joined the camel party, and soon left behind us the long-haired oxen. The camel party itself was before long fain to subdivide; and the grand unity once broken up, there were formed a number of petty caravans, which did not always concur, either as to the place of encampment or the hour of departure.

We were imperceptibly attaining the higheſt point of Upper Asia, when a terrible north wind, which lasted fifteen days, combined with the fearful severity of the temperature, menaced us with destruction. The weather was still clear; but the cold was so intense that even at mid-day we scarcely felt the influence of the sun's rays, and then we had the utmost difficulty in standing against the wind. During the rest of the day, and more especially during the night, we were under constant apprehension of dying with cold. Everybody's face and hands were regularly ploughed up. To give something like an idea of this cold, the reality of which, however, can never be appreciated, except by those who have felt it, it may suffice to mention a circumstance which seems to us rather striking. Every morning, before proceeding on our journey, we ate a meal, and then we did not eat again until the evening, after we had encamped. As *tsamba* is not a very toothsome affair, we could not get down, at a time, as much as was required for our nourishment during the day; so we used to make three or four balls of it, with our tea, and keep these in reserve, to be eaten, from time to time, on our road. The hot paste was wrapped in a piece of hot linen, and then deposited in our breast. Over it were all our clothes; to wit, a thick robe of sheep-skin, then a lamb-skin jacket, then a short fox-skin cloak, and then a great wool overall; now, upon every one of the fifteen days in question, our *tsamba* cakes were always frozen. When we took them out, they were merely so many balls of ice, which, notwithstanding, we were fain to devour, at the risk of breaking our teeth, in order to avoid the greater risk of starvation.

The animals, overcome with fatigue and privation, had infinite difficulty in at all resisting the intensity of the cold. The mules and horses, being less vigorous than the camels and long-haired oxen, required special attention. We were obliged to pack them in great pieces of carpet, carefully fastened round the body, the head being enveloped in rolls of camel's hair. Under any other circumstances this singular costume would have excited our hilarity, but just then we were in no laughing mood. Despite all these precautions, the animals of the caravan were decimated by death.

The numerous rivers that we had to pass upon the ice were another source of inconceivable misery and fatigue. Camels are so awkward and their walk is so uncouth and heavy, that in order to facilitate their passage, we were compelled to make a path for them across each river, either by strewing sand and dust or by breaking the first coat of ice with our hatchets. After this, we had to take the brutes, one by one, and guide them carefully over the path thus traced out; if they had the ill-luck to stumble or slip, it was all over with them; down they threw themselves on the ice, and it was only with the utmost labour they could be got up again. We had first to take off their baggage, then to drag them with ropes to the bank, and then to stretch a carpet on which they might be induced to rise; sometimes all this labour was lost: you might beat the obstinate animals, pull them, kick them; not an effort would they make to get on their legs; in such cases, the only course was to leave them where they lay, for it was clearly impossible to wait, in those hideous localities, until the pig-headed brutes chose to rise.

All these combined miseries ended in casting the poor travellers into a depression bordering on despair. To the mortality of the animals was now added that of the men, who, hopelessly seized upon by the cold, were abandoned, yet living, on the road. One day, when the exhaustion of our animals had compelled us to relax our march, so that we were somewhat behind the main body, we perceived a traveller sitting on a great stone, his head bent forward on his chest, his arms pressed against his sides, and his whole frame motionless as a statue. We called to him several times, but he made no reply, and did not even indicate, by the slightest movement, that he heard us. "How absurd," said we to each other, " for a man to loiter in this way in such dreadful weather. The wretched fellow will assuredly die of cold." We called to him once more, but he remained silent and motionless as before. We dismounted, went up to him, and recognized in him a young Mongol Lama who had often paid us a visit in our tent. His face was exactly like wax, and his eyes, half-opened, had a glassy appearance; icicles hung from his nostrils and from the corners of his mouth. We spoke to him, but obtained no answer; and for a moment we thought him dead. Presently, however, he opened his eyes, and fixed them upon us with a horrible expression of stupefaction: the poor creature was frozen, and we comprehended at once that he had been abandoned by his companions. It seemed to us so frightful to leave a man to die, without making an effort to save him, that we did not hesitate to take him with us. We took him from the stone on which he had been placed, enveloped him in a wrapper, seated him upon Samdad-chiemba's little mule, and thus brought him to the encampment. When we had set up our tent, we went to visit the companions of this poor young man. Upon our informing them what we had done, they prostrated themselves in token of thanks, and said that we were people of excellent hearts, but that we had given ourselves much labour in vain, for that the case was beyond cure. "He is frozen," said they, "and nothing can prevent the cold from getting to his heart." We ourselves did not participate in this despairing view of the case, and we returned to our tent, accompanied by one of our patient's companions, to see what further could be done. When we reached our temporary home, the young Lama was dead.

More than forty men of the caravan were abandoned still living, in the desert, without the slightest possibility of our aiding them. They were carried on horseback and on camelback so long as any hope remained, but when they could no longer eat, or speak, or hold themselves up, they were left on the way-side. The general body of the caravan could not stay to nurse them, in a barren desert, where there was hourly danger of wild beasts, of robbers, and, worse than all, of a deficiency of food. Yet, it was a fearful spectacle to see these dying men abandoned on the road! As a last token of sympathy, we placed beside each, a wooden cup and a small bag of barleymeal, and then the caravan mournfully proceeded on its way. As soon as the last straggler had passed on, the crows and vultures that incessantly hovered above the caravan would pounce down upon the unhappy creatures who retained just enough of life to feel themselves torn and mangled by these birds of prey.

The north wind greatly aggravated M. Gabet's malady. From day to day his condition grew more alarming. His extreme weakness would not permit him to walk, and being thus precluded from warming himself by means of a little exercise, his feet, hands and face were completely frozen; his lips became livid, and his eyes almost extinct; by-and-by he was not able to support himself on horseback. Our only remedy was to wrap him in blankets, to pack him upon a camel, and to leave the rest to the merciful goodness of Divine Providence.

One day, as we were following the sinuosities of a valley, our hearts oppressed with sad thoughts, all of a sudden we perceived two horsemen make their appearance on the ridge of an adjacent hill. At this time, we were travelling in the company of a small party of Thibetian merchants, who, like ourselves, had allowed the main body of the caravan to precede them, in order to save their camels the fatigue of too hurried a march. " Tsong-Kaba!" cried the Thibetians, " see, there are horsemen yonder, yet we are in the desert, and everyone knows that there are not even shepherds in this locality." They had scarcely uttered these words, when a number of other horsemen appeared at different points on the hills, and, to our extreme alarm, dashed down towards us at a gallop. What could these horsemen be doing in so barren a region ? What could they want with us ? The case was clear : we had fallen into the hands of thieves. Their appearance, as they approached, was anything but reassuring : a carbine slung at the saddle bow, two long sabres in the girdle, thick black hair falling in disorder over the shoulders, glaring eyes, and a wolf's skin ſtuck on the head by way of a cap ; such was the portrait of each of the gentlemen who now favoured us with their company. There were twenty-seven of them, while we numbered only eighteen, of which eighteen all were by no means practised warriors. However, both armies alighted, and a valorous Thibetian of our party advanced to parley with the chief of the brigands, who was distinguished from his men by two red pennants which floated from his saddle back. After a long and somewhat animated conversation : " Who is that man ? " asked the chief of the Kolo, pointing to M. Gabet, who, faſtened upon his camel, was the only person who had not alighted. " He is a Grand Lama of the weſtern sky," replied the Thibetian merchant; "the power of his prayers is infinite." The Kolo raised his clasped hands to his forehead, in token of respect, and looked at M. Gabet, who, with his frozen face, and his singular envelope of many-coloured wrappings, was by no means unlike those alarming idols that we see in pagan temples. After contemplating for awhile the famous Lama of the weſtern sky, the brigand addressed some further words, in an undertone, to the Thibetian merchant; then, making a sign to his companions, they all jumped into their saddles, set off at a gallop, and soon disappeared behind the mountains. " Do not let us go any further to-day," said the Thibetian merchant; " but set up our tents where we are; the Kolo are robbers, but they have lofty and generous souls; when they see that we place ourselves without fear in their hands, they will not attack us. Besides," added he, " I believe they hold in much awe the power of the Lamas of the weſtern sky." We adopted the counsel of the Thibetian merchants, and proceeded to encamp.

The tents were scarcely set up, when the Kolo reappeared on the creſt of the mountain, and once more galloped down upon us with their habitual impetuosity. The chief alone entered the encampment, his men awaiting him a short diſtance outside. The Kolo addressed the Thibetian who had previously conversed with him. " I have come," said he, " for an explanation of a point that I don't at all underſtand. You know that we are encamped on the other side of the mountain, yet you venture to set up your tents here, close by us. How many men, then, have you in your company?" " We are only eighteen; you, I believe, are twenty-seven in number; but brave men never run away." " You'll fight, then?" " If there were not several invalids amongſt us, I would answer yes; for I have already shown the Kolo that I am not afraid of them." " Have you fought with the Kolo? When was it? What's your name?" " It's five years ago, at the affair of the Tchanak-Kampo, and here's a little reminiscence of it "; and throwing back the sleeve of his right arm, he showed the cicatrice of a great sabre cut. The brigand laughed, and again requested his interlocutor's name. "I am called Rala-Tchembe [Rala-chembe]," said the merchant; "you ought to know the name." "Yes, all the Kolos know it; it is the name of a brave man." So saying, he dismounted, and taking a sabre from his girdle, presented it to the Thibetian. "Here," said he, " accept this sabre; 'tis the best I have; we have fought one another before; in future, when we meet, it shall be as brothers." The Thibetian received the brigand's present, and gave him, in return, a handsome bow and quiver which he had bought at Peking.

The Kolo, who had remained outside the camp upon seeing their chief fraternize with the chief of the caravan, dismounted, fastened their horses to each other, two and two, by the bridles, and came to drink a friendly cup of tea with the travellers, who now, at length, began to breathe freely. All these brigands were extremely affable, and they asked us various questions about the Tartar-Khalkhas, whom, they said, they were particularly anxious to see, by reason that, in the preceding year, these warriors had killed three of their companions, whom they were eager to avenge. We had a little chat about politics too. The brigands affirmed that they were warm friends of the Talé-Lama, and irreconcilable enemies to the Emperor of China; on which account they seldom failed to pillage the embassy on its way to Peking, because the Emperor was unworthy to receive gifts from the Talé-Lama, but that they ordinarily respected it on its return, because it was altogether fitting that the Emperor should send gifts to the Talé-Lama. After having done honour to the tea and *tsamba* of the caravan, the brigands wished us a good journey, and returned to their own encampment. All these fraternal manifestations did not prevent our sleeping with one eye open; our repose, however, was not disturbed, and in the morning we resumed our way in peace. Of the many thousands of pilgrims who have performed the journey to Lha-Ssa, there are very few who can boaſt of having had so close a view of the robbers, at so small a coſt.

We had escaped one great danger; but another awaited us, we were informed, far more formidable in its chara&ter, though different in kind. We were beginning to ascend the vaſt chain of the Tant-La [Dang-la] mountains, on the plateau of which, our travelling companions assured us, the invalids would die and those who were now well would become invalids, with but a small chance of living. The death of M. Gabet was considered quite a matter of certainty. After six days' laborious ascent of several mountains, placed amphitheatrically, one above another, we at length reached the famous plateau, the moſt elevated point, perhaps, on the earth's surface. The snow there appeared an incruſtation, an ordinary portion of the soil. It cracked beneath our feet, but the feet left scarcely any impression upon it. The entire vegetation consiſted of an occasional tuft of a low, sharp-pointed, smooth grass, ligneous within, and as hard as iron, but not brittle; so that it might very well be converted into mattress needles. The animals were, however, so famishing that they were fain to attack even this atrocious forage, which absolutely cracked between their teeth, and could be realized at all only by vigorous efforts and at the coſt of infinite lip bleeding.

From the brow of this magnificent plateau we could see below us the peaks and needles of numerous ridges, the ramifications of which were loſt in the horizon. We had never witnessed anything at all comparable with this grand, this gigantic spe&acle. During the twelve days that we were journeying along the heights of Tant-La, we enjoyed fine weather; the air was calm, and it pleased God to bless us each day with a warm, genial sunshine, that materially modified the ordinary coldness of the atmosphere. Still the air, excessively rarified at that enormous altitude, was still piercing, and monstrous eagles, which followed the track of the caravan, were daily provided with a number of dead bodies. The small caravan of the French mission itself paid its tribute to death; but, happily, that tribute was only in the shape of our little black mule, which we abandoned at once with regret and with resignation. The dismal prophecy that had been announced with reference to M. Gabet was falsified. The mountains, which were to have been fatal to him, proved, on the contrary, highly favourable, restoring to him, by degrees, health and strength. This blessing, almost unexpected by us, even at the hands of the God of Mercy, made us forget all our past miseries. We resumed all our courage, and firmly entertained the hope that the Almighty would permit us to accomplish our journey.

The descent of Tant-La, though long in duration, was rapid in itself. Throughout four whole days, we were going down, as it seemed, a gigantic staircase, each step of which consisted of a mountain. At the bottom we found some hot springs, of an extremely magnificent description. Amongst huge rocks, you see a great number of reservoirs, hollowed out by the hand of nature, in which the water boils and bubbles, as in a vast cauldron over a fierce fire. Sometimes the active fluid escapes through the fissures of the rocks, and leaps, in all directions, by a thousand capricious jets. Every now and then the ebullition, in particular reservoirs, grows so furious that tall columns of water rise into the air, as though impelled by some tremendous pumping machinery. Above these springs, thick vapours, collecting in the air, condense into white clouds. The water is sulphureous. After bubbling and dashing about in its huge granite reservoirs, it boils over, and quitting the rocks, which had seemed to wish to keep it captive, pours down by various currents into a small valley below, where it forms a large stream, flowing over a bed of flints, yellow as gold. These boiling waters do not long preserve their fluidity. The extreme rigour of the atmosphere cools them so rapidly, that within a mile and a half from its source, the stream they have thus formed is almost frozen through. These hot springs are of frequent occurrence in the mountains of Thibet, and the Lama physicians, who attribute to them considerable medicinal value, constantly prescribe their use, both internally and externally.

From the Tant-La mountains to Lha-Ssa, the ground constantly declines. As you descend, the intensity of the cold diminishes, and the earth becomes clothed with more vigorous and more varied vegetation. One evening we encamped in a large plain, where the pasturage was marvellously abundant, and as our cattle had been for some time past on very short commons indeed, we determined to give them the full benefit of the present opportunity, and to remain where we were for two days.

Next morning, as we were quietly preparing our tea, we perceived in the distance a troop of horsemen galloping towards our encampment at full speed. The sight seemed to freeze the very blood in our veins; we stood for a moment perfectly petrified. After the first moment of stupor, we rushed out of our tent, and made to Rala-Tchembe. "The Kolo! the Kolo!" cried we; "here's a great body of Kolo advancing against us." The Thibetian merchants, who were boiling their tea and mixing their *tsamba*, laughed at our alarm, and told us to sit down quite at our ease. "Take breakfast with us," said they; "there are no Kolo to fear here; the horsemen you see yonder are friends. We are now entering upon an inhabited country; behind the hill there, to the right, are a number of black tents, and the horsemen, whom you take to be Kolo, are shepherds." These words reſtored our equanimity, and with our equanimity returned our appetite, so that we were very happy to accept the invitation to breakfaſt with which we had been favoured. We had scarcely taken up a cup of buttered tea before the horsemen made their appearance at the door of the tent. So far from being brigands, they were worthy fellows who came to sell us butter and fresh meat; their saddles were regular butchers' ſtalls hung with joints of mutton and venison, which reſted on the sides of their horses. We purchased eight legs of mutton, which, being frozen, were easily susceptible of transport. They coſt us an old pair of Peking boots, a Peking ſteel, and the saddle of our defunct mule, which luckily could also boaſt of Peking origin. Everything coming from Peking is highly prized by the Thibetians, more especially by that portion of the population which has not advanced beyond the paſtoral and nomadic life. The merchants who accompany the caravan take care, accordingly, to label every package "Goods from Peking." Snuff is especially an object of earneſt competition among the Thibetians. All the shepherds asked us whether we had not snuff from Peking. M. Huc, who was the only snuff-taker of our party, had formerly possessed a quantity of the precious commodity, but it had all departed, and for the laſt eight days he had been reduced to the necessity of filling his snuff-box and his nose with a frightful mixture of duſt and ashes. Those who are devotees of snuff will at once comprehend all the horrors to poor M. Huc of this deplorable position.

Condemned for the laſt two months to live upon barley-meal, moiſtened with tea, the mere sight of our legs of mutton seemed to fortify our ſtomachs and invigorate our emaciated limbs. The remainder of the day was occupied in culinary preparations. By way of condiment and seasoning, we had only a little garlic, and that little so frozen and dried that it was almoſt imperceptible in its shell. We peeled, however, all we had, and ſtuck it into two legs of mutton, which we set to boil in our great cauldron. The *argols*, which abounded in this blessed plain, supplied ample materials for cooking our ineſtimable supper. The sun was juſt setting, and Samdadchiemba, who had been inspecting one of the legs of mutton with his thumb-nail, had triumphantly announced that the mutton was boiled to a bubble, when we heard in all directions, the disaſtrous cry, " Fire ! fire ! " (*Mi yon ! mi yon !* [*me-yod*]). At one bound we were outside our tent, where we found that the flame, which had caught some dry grass in the interior of the encampment, and menaced to assail also our linen tents, was spreading about in all directions with fearful rapidity. All the travellers, armed with their felt carpets, were endeavouring to ſtifle the flame, or at all events to keep it from reaching the tents, and in this latter effort they were quite successful. The fire, repulsed on all sides, forced an issue from the encampment, and rushed out into the desert, where, driven by the wind, it spread over the paſturages, which it devoured as it went. We thought, however, that we had nothing further to fear ; but the cry, " Save the camels ! save the camels ! " at once reminded us how little we knew of a conflagration in the desert. We soon perceived that the camels ſtolidly awaited the flame, inſtead of fleeing from it, as the horses and oxen did We thereupon haſtened to the succour of our beaſts, which, at the moment, seemed tolerably remote from the flame. The flame, however, reached them as soon as we did, and at once surrounded us and them. It was to no purpose we pushed and beat the ſtupid brutes; not an inch would they ſtir; but there they ſtood phlegmatically gaping at us with an air that seemed to ask us what right we had to come and interrupt them at their meals. We really felt as if we could have killed the impracticable beaſts. The fire consumed so rapidly the grass it encountered, that it soon assailed the camels, and caught their long, thick hair; and it was with the utmoſt exertion that, by the aid of the felt carpets we had brought with us, we extinguished the flame upon their bodies. We got three of them out of the fire, with only the end of their hair singed, but the fourth was reduced to a deplorable condition; not a briſtle remained on its entire body; the whole syſtem of hair was burned down to the skin, and the skin itself was terribly charred.

The extent of paſturage consumed by the flame might be about a mile and a quarter long by three quarters of a mile broad. The Thibetians were in ecstacies at their good fortune in having the progress of conflagration so soon ſtayed, and we fully participated in their joy, when we learned the full extent of the evil with which we had been menaced. We were informed that if the fire had continued much longer it would have reached the black tents, in which case the shepherds would have pursued and infallibly massacred us. Nothing can equal the fury of these poor children of the desert when they find the paſtures, which are their only resource, reduced to ashes, no matter whether by malice or by mischance. It is much the same thing to them as deſtroying their herds.

When we resumed our journey the broiled camel was not yet dead, but it was altogether incapable of service; the three others were fain to yield to circumſtances, and to share among them the portion of baggage which their unlucky travelling companion had

THIBET, AND CHINA

hitherto borne. However, the burdens of all of them had very materially diminished in weight since our departure from Koukou-Noor; our sacks of meal had become little better than sacks of emptiness; so that, after descending the Tant-La mountains we had been compelled to put ourselves upon an allowance of two cups of *tsamba* per man, per diem. Before our departure, we had made a fair calculation of our reasonable wants, *in prospectu*; but no such calculation could cover the waste committed upon our provender by our two cameleers; by the one through indifference and stupidity, by the other through malice and knavery.

Fortunately, we were now approaching a large Thibetian station, where we should find the means of renewing our stores.

After following, for several days, a long series of valleys, where we saw, from time to time, black tents and great herds of yaks, we at last encamped beside a large Thibetian village. It stands on the banks of the river Na-Ptchu [Nag-ch'u], indicated on M. Andriveau-Goujon's map, by the Mongol name of Khara-Oussou [Khara-usu], both denominations equally signifying black waters. The village of Na-Ptchu is the first Thibetian station of any importance that you pass on this route to Lha-Ssa. The village consists of mud-houses and a number of black tents. The inhabitants do not cultivate the ground. Although they always live on the same spot, they are shepherds like the nomadic tribes, and occupy themselves solely with the breeding of cattle. We were informed that at some very remote period, a king of Koukou-Noor made war upon the Thibetians, and having subjugated them to a large extent, gave the district of Na-Ptchu to the soldiers whom he had brought with him. Though these Tartars are now fused with the Thibetians, one may still observe among the black tents, a certain number of Mongol huts. This event may also serve to explain the origin of a number of Mongol expressions which are used in the country, having passed within the domain of the Thibetian idiom.

The caravans which repair to Lha-Ssa, are necessitated to remain several days at Na-Ptchu, in order to arrange a fresh syſtem of conveyance; for the difficulties of an awfully rocky road do not permit camels to proceed further. Our firſt business, therefore, was to sell our animals; but they were so wretchedly worn that no one would look at them. At laſt, a sort of veterinary surgeon, who, doubtless, had some recipe for reſtoring their ſtrength and appearances, made us an offer, and we sold him the three for fifteen ounces of silver, throwing in the grilled one into the bargain. These fifteen ounces of silver juſt sufficed to pay the hire of six long-haired oxen, to carry our baggage to Lha-Ssa.

A second operation was to discharge the Lama of the Ratchico mountains. After having settled with him on very liberal terms, we told him that if he proposed to visit Lha-Ssa, he muſt find some other companions, for that he might consider himself wholly freed from the engagements which he had contraćted with us; and so, at laſt, we got rid of this rascal, whose miscondućt had fully doubled the trouble and misery that we had experienced on the way in his company.

Our conscience imposes upon us the duty of here warning persons whom any circumſtances may lead to Na-Ptchu, to be carefully on their guard there againſt thieves. The inhabitants of this Thibetian village are remarkable for their peculations, robbing every Mongol or other caravan that comes to the place, in the moſt shameful manner. At night, they creep into the travellers' tents, and carry off whatever they can lay hands upon; and in broad day itself they exercise their deplorable ingenuity in this line with a coolness, a presence of mind, and an ability which might arouse envy in the moſt diſtinguished Parisian thieves.

After having laid in a supply of butter, *tsamba*, and legs of mutton, we proceeded on our way to Lha-Ssa, from which we were now only diſtant fifteen days' march. Our travelling companions were some Mongols of the kingdom of Khartchin [Kharachin], who were repairing in pilgrimage to Monhe-Dchot "the Eternal Sanctuary" as the Tartars call Lha-Ssa, and who had with them their grand *Chaberon*: that is to say, a Living Buddha, the superior of their Lamasery. This *Chaberon* was a young man of eighteen, whose manners were agreeable and gentlemanly, and whose face, full of ingenuous candour, contraſted singularly with the part which he was conſtrained habitually to enact. At the age of five he had been declared Buddha and Grand Lama of the Buddhiſts of Khartchin, and he was now about to pass a few years in one of the Grand Lamaseries of Lha-Ssa, in the ſtudy of prayers and of the other knowledge befitting his dignity. A brother of the King of Khartchin and several Lamas of quality were in attendance to escort and wait upon him. The title of Living Buddha seemed to be a dead weight upon this poor young man. It was quite manifeſt that he would very much have liked to laugh and chat and frolic about at his ease; and that, *en route*, it would have been far more agreeable to him to have dashed about on his horse, whither he fancied, than to ride, as he did, solemnly between two horsemen, who, out of their extreme respect, never once quitted his sides. Again, when they had reached an encampment, inſtead of remaining eternally squatted on cushions, in a corner of his tent, apeing the idols in the Lamasery, he would have liked to have rambled about the desert, taking part in the occupations of nomadic life; but he was permitted to do nothing of the sort. His business was to be Buddha, and to concern himself in no degree with matters which appertained to mere mortals.

The young *Chaberon* derived no small pleasure from an occasional chat in our tent; there, at all events, he was able to lay aside, for a time, his official divinity, and to belong to mankind. He heard with great interest what we told him about the men and things of Europe; and questioned us, with much ingenuity, respecting our religion, which evidently appeared to him a very fine one. When we asked him, whether it would not be better to be a worshipper of Jehovah than a *Chaberon*, he replied that he could not say. He did not at all like us to interrogate him respecting his anterior life, and his continual incarnations; he would blush when any such questions were put to him, and would always put an end to the conversation by saying that the subject was painful to him. The simple fact was that the poor lad found himself involved in a sort of religious labyrinth, the meanderings of which were perfectly unknown to him.

The road which leads from Na-Ptchu to Lha-Ssa is, in general, rocky and very laborious, and when it attains the chain of the Koiran mountains it becomes fatiguing in the highest degree. Yet, as you advance, your heart grows lighter and lighter, at finding yourself in a more and more populous country. The black tents that speckle the background of the landscape, the numerous parties of pilgrims repairing to Lha-Ssa, the infinite inscriptions engraved on the stones erected on each side of the way, the small caravans of long-tailed oxen that you meet at interval —all this contributes to alleviate the fatigues of the journey.

When you come within a few days' march of Lha-Ssa, the exclusively nomadic character of the Thibetians gradually disappears. Already, a few cultivated fields adorn the desert; houses insensibly take the place of black tents. At length, the shepherds vanish altogether, and you find yourself amidst an agricultural people.

On the fifteenth day after our departure, from Na-Ptchu, we arrived at Pampou [Pampu], which on account of its proximity to Lha-Ssa is regarded by the pilgrims as the vestibule of the holy city. Pampou, erroneously designated "Panctou" on the map, is a fine plain watered by a broad river, a portion of whose stream, distributed in canals, diffuses fertility all around. There is no village, properly so called; but you see, in all directions, large farm-houses with handsome terraces in front, and beautifully white with lime-wash. Each is surrounded with tall trees, and surmounted with a little tower, in the form of a pigeon-house, whence float banners of various colours, covered with Thibetian inscriptions. After travelling for more then three months through hideous deserts, where the only living creatures you meet are brigands and wild beasts, the plain of Pampou seemed to us the most delicious spot in the world. Our long and painful journey had so nearly reduced us to the savage state, that anything in the shape of civilization struck us as absolutely marvellous. We were in ecstacies with everything: a house, a tree, a plough, a furrow in the ploughed field, the slightest object seemed to us worthy of attention. That, however, which most forcibly impressed us, was the prodigious elevation of the temperature which we remarked in this cultivated plain. Although it was now the end of January, the river and its canals were merely edged with a thin coat of ice, and scarcely any of the people wore furs.

At Pampou, our caravan had to undergo another transformation. Generally speaking, the long-haired oxen are here replaced by donkies, small in size, but very robuſt, and accuſtomed to carry baggage. The difficulty of procuring a sufficient number of these donkies to convey the baggage of the Khartchin-Lamas, rendered it necessary for us to remain two days at Pampou. We availed ourselves of the opportunity to arrange our toilet, as well as we could. Our hair and beards were so thick, our faces so blackened with the smoke of the tent, so ploughed up with the cold, so worn, so deplorable, that, when we had here the means of looking at ourselves in a glass, we were ready to weep with compassion at our melancholy appearance. Our coſtume was perfectly in unison with our persons.

The people of Pampou are for the moſt part in very easy circumſtances, and they are always gay and frolicsome accordingly. Every evening they assemble, in front of the different farms, where men, women and children dance to the accompaniment of their own voices. On the termination of the *bal champêtre*, the farmer regales the company with a sort of sharp drink, made with fermented barley, and which, with the addition of hops, would be very like our beer.

After a two days' hunt through all the farms of the neighbourhood, the donkey-caravan was organized, and we went on our way. Between us and Lha-Ssa there was only a mountain, but this mountain was, paſt contradiction, the moſt rugged and toilsome that we had as yet encountered. The Thibetians and Mongols ascend it with great unction, for it is underſtood amongſt them that whoever attains its summit, attains, *ipso facto*, a remission of all his or her sins. This is certain, at all events, that whoever attains the summit has undergone on the way a moſt severe penance; whether that penance is adequate to the remission of sins, is another queſtion altogether. We had departed at one o'clock in the morning, yet it was not till ten in the forenoon that we reached this so beneficial summit. We were fain to walk nearly the whole distance, so impracticable is it to retain one's seat on horseback along the rugged and rocky path.

The sun was nearly setting when, issuing from the last of the infinite sinuosities of the mountain, we found ourselves in a vast plain, and saw on our right Lha-Ssa, the famous metropolis of the Buddhic world. The multitude of aged trees which surround the city with a verdant wall ; the tall white houses, with their flat roofs and their towers : the numerous temples with their gilt roofs, the Buddha-La [Potala], above which rises the palace of the Talé-Lama—all these features communicate to Lha-Ssa a majestic and imposing aspect.

At the entrance of the town some Mongols with whom we had formed an acquaintance on the road, and who had preceded us by several days, met us, and invited us to accompany them to lodgings which they had been friendly enough to prepare for us. It was now the 29th January, 1846 ; and it was eighteen months since we had parted from the Valley of Black Waters.

CHAPTER V

AFTER eighteen months' struggle with sufferings and obstacles of infinite number and variety, we were at length arrived at the termination of our journey, though not at the close of our miseries. We had no longer, it is true, to fear death from famine or frost in this inhabited country; but trials and tribulations of a different character were no doubt about to assail us, amidst the infidel populations, to whom we desired to preach Christ crucified for the salvation of mankind. Physical troubles over, we had now to undergo moral sufferings; but we relied, as before, on the infinite goodness of the Lord to aid us in the fight, trusting that He who had protected us in the desert against the inclemency of the seasons, would continue to us His divine assistance against the malice of man, in the very heart and capital of Buddhism.

The morning after our arrival at Lha-Ssa, we engaged a Thibetian guide, and visited the various quarters of the city, in search of a lodging. The houses at Lha-Ssa are for the most part several stories high, terminating in a terrace slightly sloped, in order to carry off the water; they were whitewashed all over, except the bordering round the doors and windows, which are painted red or yellow. The reformed Buddhists are so fond of these two colours, which are, so to speak, sacred in their eyes, that they especially name them Lamanesque colours. The people of Lha-Ssa are in the habit of painting their houses once a year, so that they are always perfectly clean, and seem, in fact, just built; but the interior is by no means in harmony with the fine outside. The rooms are dirty, smoky, stinking, and encumbered with all sorts of utensils and furniture, thrown about in a most disgusting confusion. In a word, the Thibetian habitations are literally whited sepulchres; a perfect picture of Buddhism and all other false religions, which carefully cover, with certain general truths and certain moral principles, the corruption and falsehood within.

After a long search, we selected two rooms, in a large house, that contained in all fifty lodgers. Our humble abode was at the top of the house, and to reach it we had to ascend twenty-six wooden stairs, without railing, and so steep and narrow that in order to prevent the disagreeable incident of breaking our necks, we always found it prudent to use our hands as well as our feet. Our suite of apartments consisted of one great square room and one small closet, which we honoured with the appellation of cabinet. The larger room was lighted, north-east by a narrow window, provided with three thick wooden bars, and, above, by a small round skylight, which latter aperture served for a variety of purposes; first, it gave entrance to the light, the wind, the rain, and the snow; and secondly it gave issue to the smoke from our fire. To protect themselves from the winter's cold, the Thibetians place in the centre of their rooms a small vessel of glazed earth, in which they burn *argols*. As this combustible is extremely addicted to diffuse considerably more smoke than heat, those who desire to warm themselves find it of infinite advantage to have a hole in the ceiling, which enables them to light a fire without incurring the risk of being stifled by the smoke. You do, indeed, undergo the small inconvenience of receiving, from time to time, a fall of snow, or rain on your back: but those who have followed the nomadic life are not deterred by such trifles. The furniture of our larger apartment

TRAVELS IN TARTARY,

consisted of two goat-skins spread on the floor, right and left of the fire dish; of two saddles, our travelling, tent, some old pairs of boots, two dilapidated trunks, three ragged robes, hanging from nails in the wall, our night things rolled together in a bundle, and a supply of *argols* in the corner. We were thus placed at once on the full level of Thibetian civilization. The closet, in which stood a large brick stove, served us for kitchen and pantry, and there we installed Samdadchiemba, who, having resigned his office of cameleer, now concentrated the functions of cook, steward and groom. Our two white steeds were accommodated in a corner of the court, where they reposed after their laborious but glorious campaign, until an opportunity should present itself of securing new masters; at present the poor beasts were so thoroughly worn down that we could not think of offering them for sale, until they had developed some little flesh between the bone and the skin.

As soon as we were settled in our new abode, we occupied ourselves with inspecting the capital of Thibet, and its population. Lha-Ssa is not a large town, its circuit being at the utmost two leagues. It is not surrounded like the Chinese towns with ramparts; formerly, indeed, we were told it had walls, but these were entirely destroyed in a war which the Thibetians had to sustain against the Indians of Boutan [Bhutan]. At present not a trace of wall remains. Around the suburbs, however, are a great number of gardens, the large trees in which form, for the town, a magnificent wall of verdure. The principal streets of Lha-Ssa are broad, well laid out, and tolerably clean, at least when it does not rain: but the suburbs are revoltingly filthy. The houses, as we have already stated, are in general large, lofty and handsome; they are built some with stone, some with brick and some with mud, but they are all so

THIBET, AND CHINA

elaborately covered with lime-wash that you can distinguish externally no difference in the material. In one of the suburban districts there is a locality where the houses are built with the horns of oxen and sheep. These singular constructions are of extreme solidity and look very well. The horns of the oxen being smooth and white, and those of the sheep, on the contrary, rough and black, these various materials are susceptible of infinite combinations, and are arranged accordingly, in all sorts of fantastic designs; the interstices are filled up with mortar. These houses are the only buildings that are not lime-washed; the Thibetians having taste enough to leave the materials in their natural aspect, without seeking to improve upon their wild and fantastic beauty. It is superfluous to add, that the inhabitants of Lha-Ssa consume an immense quantity of beef and mutton; their horn-houses incontestably demonstrate this fact.

The Buddhist temples are the most remarkable edifices in Lha-Ssa. We need not here describe them, for they all closely resemble those which we have already had cause to pourtray. We will only remark, therefore, that the temples of Lha-Ssa are larger, richer, and more profusely gilt than those of other towns.

The palace of the Talé-Lama merits, in every respect, the celebrity which it enjoys throughout the world. North of the town, at the distance of about a mile, there rises a rugged mountain, of slight elevation and of conical form, which, amid the plain, resembles an islet on the bosom of a lake. This mountain is entitled Buddha-La (mountain of Buddha, divine mountain), and upon this grand pedestal, the work of nature, the adorers of the Talé-Lama have raised the magnificent palace wherein their Living Divinity resides in the flesh. This palace is an aggregation of several temples, of various size and decoration; that which occupies the centre is four stories high, and overlooks all the rest; it terminates in a dome, entirely covered with plates of gold, and surrounded with a peristyle, the columns of which are, in like manner, all covered with gold. It is here that the Talé-Lama has set up his abode. From the summit of this lofty sanctuary he can contemplate, at the great solemnities, his innumerable adorers advancing along the plain or prostrate at the foot of the divine mountain. The secondary palaces, grouped round the great temple, serve as residences for numerous Lamas, of every order, whose continual occupation it is to serve and do honour to the Living Buddha. Two fine avenues of magnificent trees lead from Lha-Ssa to the Buddha-La, and there you always find crowds of foreign pilgrims, telling the beads of their long Buddhist chaplets, and Lamas of the court, attired in rich costume, and mounted on horses splendidly caparisoned. Around the Buddha-La there is constant motion; but there is, at the same time, almost uninterrupted silence, religious meditations appearing to occupy all men's minds.

In the town itself the aspect of the population is quite different; there all is excitement, and noise, and pushing, and competition, every single soul in the place being ardently occupied in the grand business of buying and selling. Commerce and devotion incessantly attracting to Lha-Ssa an infinite number of strangers, render the place a rendezvous of all the Asiatic peoples; so that the streets, always crowded with pilgrims and traders, present a marvellous variety of physiognomies, costumes, and languages. This immense multitude is for the most part transitory; the fixed population of Lha-Ssa consists of Thibetians, Pebouns, Katchis [K'a-chê] and Chinese.

The Thibetians belong to the great family which we are accustomed to designate by the term Mongol race; they have black eyes, a thin beard, small, contracted eyes, high cheek-bones, pug noses, wide mouths and thin lips; the ordinary complexion is tawny, though, in the upper class, you find skins as white as those of Europeans. The Thibetians are of the middle height; and combine, with the agility and suppleness of the Chinese, the force and vigour of the Tartars. Gymnastic exercises of all sorts and dancing are very popular with them, and their movements are cadenced and easy. As they walk about, they are always humming some psalm or popular song; generosity and frankness enter largely into their character; brave in war, they face death fearlessly; they are as religious as the Tartars, but not so credulous. Cleanliness is of small estimation among them; but this does not prevent them from being very fond of display and rich sumptuous clothing.

The Thibetians do not shave the head, but let the hair flow over their shoulders, contenting themselves with clipping it, every now and then, with the scissors. The dandies of Lha-Ssa, indeed, have of late years adopted the custom of braiding their hair in the Chinese fashion, decorating the tresses with jewellery, precious stones and coral. The ordinary head-dress is a blue cap, with a broad border of black velvet surmounted with a red tuft; on high days and holidays they wear a great red hat, in form not unlike the Basquebarret cap, only larger and decorated at the rim with long, thick fringe. A full robe, fastened on the right side with four hooks, and girded round the waist by a red sash, red or purple cloth boots, complete the simple, yet graceful costume of the Thibetian men. Suspended from the sash is a green taffeta bag, containing their inseparable wooden cups, and two small purses, of an oval form and richly embroidered, which contain nothing at all, being designed merely for ornament.

TRAVELS IN TARTARY,

The dress of the Thibetian women closely resembles that of the men; the main difference is, that over the robe, they add a short, many-coloured tunic, and that they divide their hair into two braids, one hanging down each shoulder. The women of the humbler classes wear a small yellow cap, like the cap of liberty that was in fashion in France at the time of our first republic. The head decoration of the ladies is a graceful crown composed of pearls. The Thibetian women submit, in their toilet, to a custom, or rather rule, doubtless quite unique, and altogether incredible to those who have not actually witnessed its operation: before going out of doors, they always rub their faces over with a sort of black, glutinous varnish, not unlike currant jelly; and the object being to render themselves as ugly and hideous as possible, they daub this disgusting composition over every feature, in such a manner as no longer to resemble human creatures. The origin of this monstrous practice was thus related to us: Nearly 200 years ago, the Nomekhan [Nomun-khan], a Lama king, who ruled over Hither Thibet, was a man of rigid and austere manners. At that period, the Thibetian women had no greater fancy for making themselves ugly than other women; on the contrary they were perfectly mad after all sorts of luxury and finery, whence arose fearful disorders, and immorality that knew no bounds. The contagion, by degrees, seized upon the holy family of the Lamas; the Buddhist monasteries relaxed their ancient and severe discipline, and were a prey to evils which menaced them with complete and rapid dissolution. In order to stay the progress of a libertinism which had become almost general, the Nomekhan published an edict, prohibiting women from appearing in public otherwise than with their faces bedaubed, in the manner we have described. Lofty moral and religious considerations were adduced in support of this strange law, and the refractory were menaced with the severest penalties, and, above all, with the wrath of Buddha. There needed, assuredly, more than ordinary courage to publish such an edict as this; but the most extraordinary circumstance of all is, that the women were perfectly resigned and obedient. Tradition has handed down not the least hint of any insurrection, or the slightest disturbance even, on the subject, and conformably with the law, the women have blackened themselves furiously and uglified themselves furiously, down to the present time. In fact, the thing has now come to be considered a point of dogma, an article of devotion; the women who daub themselves most disgustingly being reputed the most pious. In the country places the edict is observed with scrupulous exactitude, and to the entire approbation of the censors; but at Lha-Ssa, it is not unusual to meet in the streets women, who, setting law and decency at defiance, actually have the impudence to show themselves in public with their faces unvarnished, and such as nature made them. Those, however, who permit themselves this license, are in very ill odour, and always take care to get out of the way of the police.

It is said that the edict of the Nomekhan has been greatly promotive of the public morality. We are not in a position to affirm the contrary, with decision, but we can affirm that the Thibetians are far indeed from being exemplary in the matter of morality. There is lamentable licentiousness amongst them, and we are disposed to believe that the blackest and ugliest varnish is powerless to make corrupt people virtuous. Christianity can alone redeem the pagan nations from the shameful vices in which they wallow.

At the same time, there is one circumstance which may induce us to believe that in Thibet there is less corruption than in certain other pagan countries.

The women there enjoy very great liberty. Instead of vegetating, prisoners in the depths of their houses, they lead an active and laborious life. Besides fulfilling the various duties of the household, they concentrate in their own hands all the petty trade of the country, whether as hawkers, as stall-keepers in the streets, or in shops. In the rural districts, it is the women who perform most of the labours of agriculture.

The men, though less laborious and less active than the women, are still far from passing their lives in idleness. They occupy themselves especially with spinning and weaving wool. The stuffs they manufacture, which are called *poulou* [*p'u-lu*], are of a very close and solid fabric; astonishingly various in quality, from the coarsest cloths to the finest possible merino. By a rule of reformed Buddhism, every Lama must be attired in red *poulou*. The consumption of the article in Thibet itself is very large, and the caravans export considerable quantities of it to Northern China and Tartary. The coarser *poulou* is cheap, but the superior qualities are excessively dear.

The pastile-sticks, so celebrated in China under the name of *Tsan-Hiang* [*tsang-hsiang*] "perfumes of Thibet" are an article of leading commerce with the people of Lha-Ssa, who manufacture them with the ash of various aromatic trees mixed with musk and gold dust. Of these various ingredients, they elaborate a pink paste, which is then moulded into small cylindrical sticks, three or four feet long. These are burned in the Lamaseries, and before the idols which are worshipped in private houses. When these pastile-sticks are once lighted, they burn slowly, without intermission, until they are completely consumed, diffusing all around a perfume of the most exquisite sweetness. The Thibetian merchants, who repair every year to Peking in the train of the embassy, export considerable quantities of it, which they sell at an

THIBET, AND CHINA

exorbitant price. The Northern Chinese manufacture pastile-sticks of their own, which they sell equally under the name of *Tsan-Hiang*; but they will sustain no comparisons with those which come from Thibet.

The Thibetians have no porcelain, but they manufacture pottery of all sorts in great perfection. As we have already observed, their own breakfast, dinner, and tea-service consists simply and entirely of a wooden cup, which each person carries either in his bosom, or suspended from his girdle in an ornamental purse. These cups are made of the roots of certain fine trees that grow on the mountains of Thibet. They are graceful in form, but simple and without any sort of decoration, other than a slight varnish which conceals neither their natural colour nor the veins of the wood. Throughout Thibet, everyone, from the poorest mendicant up to the Talé-Lama, takes his meals out of a wooden cup. The Thibetians, indeed, make a distinction of their own, unintelligible to Europeans, between these cups, some of which are bought for a few small coins, while others cost up to a hundred ounces of silver, or nearly £40. If we were asked what difference we had discerned between these various qualities of cups, we should reply, most conscientiously, that they all appeared to us pretty nearly of the same value, and that with the best disposition in the world to be convinced, we had utterly failed to perceive any distinction of moment between them. The first-quality cups, however, according to the Thibetians, have the property of neutralizing poisons.

Some days after our arrival at Lha-Ssa, desirous of renewing our meal-service, which had become somewhat worn, we went into a cup-shop. A Thibetian dame, her face elaborately varnished with black, sat behind the counter. The lady, judging from our exotic appearance, probably, that we were personages of diſtinƈtion, opened a drawer and took out two small boxes, artiſtically executed, each of which contained a cup, thrice enveloped in soft paper. After examining the goods with a certain degree of suspense, we asked the price; " *Tchik-la, gatse resi* [g *Chig-la ga-ts'od red-pa*]?" (How much a-piece?) " Excellency, fifty ounces of silver each." The words came upon us like a thunder-clap, that filled our ears with a buzzing noise, and our eyes with the conviƈtion that the shop was turning round. Our entire fortune would scarcely have purchased four of these wooden cups. Upon coming somewhat to ourselves, we respeƈtfully reſtored the two precious bowls to their respeƈtive boxes, and passed in review the numerous colleƈtion that was unceremoniously displayed on the shelves of the shop. " And these, how much are these each?" " Excellency, two for an ounce of silver." We forthwith disbursed the ounce of silver, and carried off, in triumph, the two wooden cups, which appeared to us precisely the same as those for which we had been asked £20 a-piece. On our return home, the maſter of the house, to whom we showed our purchase, gratified us with the information that for an ounce of silver we ought to have had at leaſt four such cups as the two we had received.

Poulou, paſtile-ſticks, and wooden-cups, are the three principle branches of induſtry which the Thibetians successfully prosecute. Their other manufaƈtures are so poor and coarse as to be unworthy of any special mention. Their agricultural produƈtions scarcely merit notice. Thibet, almoſt entirely covered with mountains, or cut up with impetuous torrents, affords to its population very little cultivable space. It is only in the valleys that anything like an harveſt can be expeƈted. The Thibetians cultivate little wheat, and ſtill less rice.

THIBET, AND CHINA

The chief production is *Tsing-Kou* '[*ching-k'uo*] or black barley, of which is made the *tsamba*, that basis of the aliment of the entire Thibetian population, rich and poor. The town of Lha-Ssa itself is abundantly supplied with sheep, horses, and oxen. There is excellent fish, also, sold there, and pork, of most exquisite flavour; but for the most part so dear as to be quite out of reach of the humbler classes. In fact, the Thibetians, as a rule, live very poorly. Their ordinary repast is buttered tea and *tsamba*, mixed coarsely together with the finger. The richest people observe the same diet; it is quite pitiable to see them swallowing such miserable provender out of cups, some of which have cost £40. Meat, when eaten at all, is not eaten with the ordinary repasts, but apart, as a luxurious speciality, in the same way that elsewhere people eat costly fruit, or extra fine pastry on these occasions. There are usually served up two plates, one with boiled meat, the other with raw meat, which the Thibetians devour with equal appetite, unassisted by any seasoning whatever. They have, however, wit enough not to eat without drinking. From time to time they fill their dear wooden cups with a sort of acid liquor, made of fermented barley, not at all disagreeable to the palate.

Thibet, so poor in agricultural and manufacturing products, is rich, beyond all imagination, in metals. Gold and silver are collected there so readily that the common shepherds have become acquainted with the art of purifying these precious metals. You often see them, in the ravines, or in the hollows of the mountains, seated round a fire of *argols*, amusing themselves with purifying in a rude crucible the gold-dust they have found while tending their herds. The result of this abundance of the precious metals is, that specie is of low value, and that, consequently, goods always maintain a very high price. The monetary system of the Thibetians consists entirely of silver coins, which are somewhat larger, but not so thick as our francs. On one side, they bear inscriptions in Thibetian, Parsee, or Indian characters; on the other, a crown composed of eight small, round flowers. To facilitate commerce, these coins are cut into pieces, the number of flowers remaining on each piece determining its value. The entire coin is called *Tchan-Ka* [*tang-ka*]. A *Tche-Ptche* [*khapch'e (kha-phyed)*] is one half of the *Tchan-Ka*; or, in other words, is a piece of four flowers only. The *Cho-Kan* [*sho-gang*] has five flowers, the *Ka-Gan* [*ka'-gang*] three. In the larger commercial operations, they employ silver ingots, which are weighed in a Roman balance, upon the decimal system. Generally speaking, the Thibetians reckon up accounts upon their beads; some people, however, and especially the merchants, use the Chinese *souan-pan*, while the learned employ the numerals which the Europeans call Arabic, and which appear to have been of very ancient date in Thibet. We have seen several Lamanesque manuscripts, illustrated with astronomical figures and diagrams, all of them represented by Arabic numerals, which were also used in the paging of the volumes. Some of these figures differed slightly from the Arabic numerals used in Europe; the most marked difference we noticed was that of the 5, which, in these manuscripts, was turned upside down, thus: ⸺.

From the few details we have thus given as to the productions of Thibet, it may be concluded that this country is perhaps the richest, and, at the same time, the poorest in the world; rich in gold and silver, poor in all that constitutes the well-being of the masses. The gold and silver collected by the people is absorbed by the great people, and especially by the Lamaseries, those immense reservoirs, into which flow, by a thousand channels, all the wealth of these vast regions.

THIBET, AND CHINA

The Lamas, invested with the major part of the currency, by the voluntary donations of the faithful, centruple their fortunes by usury that puts even Chinese knavery to the blush. The offerings they receive are converted, as it were, into hooks, with which they catch the purses out of everyone's pocket. Money being thus accumulated in the coffers of the privileged classes, and, on the other hand, the necessaries of life being only procurable at a very high price, it results from this capital disorder that a great proportion of the population is constantly plunged in the most frightful destitution. At Lha-Ssa the number of mendicants is very considerable. They go from door to to door, soliciting a handful of *tsamba*, and enter any one's house without the least ceremony. Their manner of asking charity is to hold out the closed hand, with the thumb raised. We must add, in commendation of the Thibetians, that they are generally very kind and compassionate, rarely sending away the poor unassisted.

Among the foreigners settled at Lha-Ssa, the Pebouns are the most numerous. These are Indians from the vicinity of Boutan, on the other side of the Himalaya mountains. They are of slight frame, but very vigorous, active and animated; their features are rounder than those of the Thibetians: the complexion very dark, the eyes small, black, and roguish : the forehead is marked with a dark, cherry-coloured spot, which they renew every morning. They are all attired in a uniform robe of pink *poulou*, with a small felt cap of the same colour, but of a somewhat darker tint. When they go out, they add to their costume a long red scarf, which twice encircles the neck like a great collar, and the two ends of which are thrown back over the shoulders.

The Pebouns are the only workers in metals at Lha-Ssa. It is in their quarter that you must seek the iron-smiths, the braziers, the plumbers, the tinmen, the founders, the goldsmiths, the jewellers, the machinists, and even the physicians and the chemists. Their workshops and laboratories are nearly underground. You enter them by a long, narrow opening, down three or four steps. Over the doors of all their houses, you see a painting representing a red globe, and below it a white crescent. These manifestly signify the sun and the moon; but the particular allusions conveyed we omitted to ascertain.

You find, among the Pebouns, artists very distinguished in metallurgy. They manufacture all sorts of vases, in gold and silver, for the use of the Lamaseries, and jewellery of every description that certainly would reflect no discredit upon European artists. It is they who construct for the Buddhist temples those fine roofs of gilt plates, which resist all the inclemencies of the seasons, and always retain a marvellous freshness and glitter. They are so skilful at this class of work that they are sent to the very interior of Tartary to decorate the great Lamaseries. The Pebouns are also the dyers of Lha-Ssa. Their colours are vivid and enduring; stuffs upon which they have operated may wear out, but they never lose their colour. They are only permitted, however, to dye the *poulou*. All stuffs coming from foreign countries must be worn as they are, the government absolutely prohibiting the dyers from at all exercising their industry upon them. The object of this prohibition is probably the encouragement of the stuffs manufactured at Lha-Ssa.

The Pebouns are in disposition extremely jovial and child-like. In their hours of relaxation they are full of laughter and frolic; and even while at work they are constantly singing. Their religion is Indian Buddhism. Although they have not adopted the reformation of Tsong-Kaba, they respect the Lamanesque ceremonies and rites. They never fail, on all the more solemn occasions, to proſtrate themselves at the feet of the Buddha-La, and to offer their adorations to the Talé-Lama.

Next to the Peboun, you remark at Lha-Ssa, the Katchi, or Mussulmen, from Cashmere—their turban, their large beard, their grave, solemn ſtep, their physiognomy full of intelligence and majeſty, the neatness and richness of their attire—everything about them presents an emphatic contraſt with the peoples of inferior race, by whom they are surrounded. They have at Lha-Ssa a governor, to whom they are immediately subjeƈt, and whose authority is recognized by the Thibetian government. This officer is, at the same time, the local head of the Mussulman religion ; so that his countrymen consider him, in this foreign land, at once their *pacha* [*pasha*] and their mufti. The Katchi have been eſtablished at Lha-Ssa for several centuries, having originally abandoned their own country, in order to escape the persecutions of a certain *pacha* of Cashmere, whose despotism had become intolerable to them ; and the children of these firſt emigrants found themselves so well off in Thibet, that they never thought of returning to their own country. The descendants ſtill keep up a correspondence with Cashmere, but the intelligence they receive thence is little calculated to give them any desire to renounce their adopted country. The Katchi governor, with whom we got upon very intimate terms, told us that the Pelings of Calcutta (the English), were now the real maſters of Cashmere. " The Pelings," said he, " are the moſt cunning people in the world. Little by little they are acquiring possession of all the countries of India, but it is always rather by ſtratagem than by open force. Inſtead of overthrowing the authorities, they cleverly manage to get them on their side, to enliſt them in their interest. Hence it is that, in Cashmere, the saying is: The world is Allah's, the land the Pacha's; it is the [East India] Company that rules."

The Katchi are the richest merchants at Lha-Ssa. All the establishments for the sale of linen, and other goods for personal and other use, belong to them. They are also money-changers, and traffic in gold and silver: hence it is that you almost always find Parsee characters on the Thibetian coinage. Every year some of their number proceed to Calcutta for commercial operations, they being the only class who are permitted to pass the frontiers to visit the English. On these occasions they are furnished with a passport from the Talé-Lama, and a Thibetian escort accompanies them to the foot of the Himalaya mountains. The goods, however, which they bring from Calcutta, are of very limited extent, consisting merely of ribands, galloons, knives, scissors, and some other articles of cutlery and ironmongery, and a small assortment of cotton goods. The silks and linens in their warehouses, and of which they have a large sale at Lha-Ssa, come from Peking by the medium of the caravans; the linen goods, being Russian, come to them much cheaper than they buy them at Calcutta.

The Katchi have a mosque at Lha-Ssa, and are rigid observers of the law of Mahomet—openly and even ostentatiously expressing their contempt for all the superstitious practices of the Buddhists. The first Katchi who arrived at Lha-Ssa married Thibetian wives, whom they compelled to renounce their own religion, and to embrace Mahometanism. But now, the rule with them is only to contract marriage alliances amongst themselves; so that there has imperceptibly become formed, in the heart of Thibet, a small nation apart, having neither the costume, nor the manners, nor the language, nor the religion of the natives. As they do not prostrate themselves before the Talé-Lama, and do not pray in the Lamaseries, everybody says they are infidels ; but as, for the most part, they are rich and powerful, people stand aside in the streets to let them pass, and put out their tongues to them in token of respect. In Thibet, when you desire to salute anyone, you take off your hat, put out your tongue, and scratch the right ear, all three operations being performed simultaneously.

The Chinese you find at Lha-Ssa are for the most part soldiers or officers of the tribunal ; those who fix their residence in this town are very few in number. At all times the Chinese and the Thibetians have had relations more or less important : they frequently have waged war against each other, and have tried to encroach upon one another's rights. The Tartar-Mantchou dynasty, as we have already remarked elsewhere, saw from the commencement of their elevation the great importance of conciliating the friendship of the Talé-Lama, whose influence is all-powerful over the Mongol tribes ; consequently, they have never failed to retain at the court of Lha-Ssa two Grand Mandarins invested with the title of *Kin-Tchai* [*Ch'in-ch'ai*], which signifies ambassador, or envoy-extraordinary. The ostensible mission of these individuals is to present, under certain fixed circumstances, the homage of the Chinese Emperor to the Talé-Lama, and to lend him the aid of China in any difficulties he may have with his neighbours. Such, to all appearance, is the purport of this permanent embassy ; but in reality they are only in attendance to flatter the religious belief of the Mongols, and to bind them to the reigning dynasty, by making them believe that the government of Peking has great veneration for the divinity of the Buddha-La. Another advantage of this embassy is, that the two *Kin-Tchais* can easily, at Lha-Ssa, watch the movements of the people on the confines of the empire, and send information of them to their government.

In the thirty-fifth year of the reign of Kien-Long, the court of Peking had at Lha-Ssa two *Kin-Tchai*, or ambassadors, the one named Lo, the other Pou ; by a combination of the two names, these men were called the *Kin-Tchais (Lo-Pou)*. The word *Lo-Pou (la-p'ug]* signifying in Thibetian " radish." This term was, to a certain extent, an insult, and the people of Lha-Ssa, who had never regarded with a pleased eye the presence of the Chinese in the country, were delighted to take up this denomination. Besides, for some time paſt, the two Chinese Mandarins had given, by their behaviour, umbrage to the Thibetians ; they interfered every day more and more in the affairs of the ſtate, and openly encroached on the rights of the Talé-Lama. At laſt, as a climax of annoyance, they ordered numerous Chinese troops into Thibet, under the pretext of protecting the Talé-Lama from certain Nepaulese tribes who were giving him uneasiness. It was easy to see that China sought to extend its empire and dominion into Thibet. The opposition of the Thibetian government was, they say, terrible, and the Nomekhan exerted all his authority to check the usurpation of the two *Kin-Tchai*. One day, as he was going to the palace of the Chinese ambassadors, a young Lama threw a note into his litter, on which were written the words, *Lo Pou, ma, sa* [*la-p'ug maza*], which signifies, Do not eat radishes—abſtain from radishes. The Nomekhan clearly saw, that by this play upon words, someone wished to advise him to be on his guard againſt the *Kin-Tchais (Lo-Pou)* ; but as the warning was not clear or precise, he went on. Whilſt he was in secret conversation with the two delegates of the court of Peking, some satellites suddenly entered the apartment, poniarded the Nomekhan, and cut off his head. A Thibetian cook, who was in an adjoining room, ran, on hearing the victim's cries, took possession of the bleeding head, stuck it on a pike, and ran through the streets of Lha-Ssa, crying, "Vengeance—death to the Chinese!" The whole town was raised; all rushed to arms, and went tumultuously to the palace of the *Kin-Tchai*, who were cut in pieces. The fury of the people was so great that they attacked, indiscriminately, all the Chinese, and hunted them down like wild beasts—not only at Lha-Ssa, but also at the other places in Thibet, where they had established military stations, making a ruthless butchery of them. The Thibetians, it is said, did not lay down their arms till they had pitilessly pursued and massacred all the Chinese to the very frontiers of Sse-Tchouan and Yun-Nan.

The news of this frightful catastrophe having reached the court of Peking, the Emperor Kien-Long immediately ordered large levies of troops throughout the empire, and had them marched against Thibet. The Chinese, as in almost all the wars they have waged with their neighbours, were worsted, but they were successful in negociation. Matters were replaced on their former footing, and since then, peace has never been seriously disturbed between the two governments.

The military force which the Chinese keep up in Thibet is inconsiderable. From Sse-Tchouan to Lha-Ssa, they have, at each stage, miserable barracks, designed to facilitate the journeys of the imperial couriers. In the town of Lha-Ssa, their garrison consists of a few hundred soldiers, whose presence contributes to adorn and protect the position of the ambassadors. From Lha-Ssa, going towards the south as far as Boutan, they have also a line of barracks, very badly kept. On the frontiers, they guard, conjointly with the Thibetian troops, the high mountains which separate Thibet from the first English stations. In the other parts of Thibet there are no Chinese, their entrance thither being strictly forbidden.

The soldiers and the Chinese Mandarins established in Thibet are in the pay of the government of Peking; they generally remain three years in the country. When this time has elapsed others are sent to replace them, and they return to their respective provinces. There are some of them, however, who, on the termination of their service, obtain leave to settle at Lha-Ssa, or in the towns on the road to Sse-Tchouan. The Chinese at Lha-Ssa are very few in number; and it would be rather difficult to say to what profession they attach themselves to make their living. Generally speaking, they are jacks-of-all-trades, having a thousand ways of transferring to their own purses the *tchan-kas* of the Thibetians. Many of them take a wife in the country; but the bonds of marriage are inadequate to fix them for life in their adopted country. After a certain number of years, when they consider they have accumulated enough, they return to China, and leave behind them wife and children, excepting the sons, whom they would scruple to abandon. The Thibetians fear the Chinese, the Katchi despise them, the Peboun laugh at them.

Of the several classes of strangers sojourning at, or merely visiting Lha-Ssa, there was no one to which we seemed to belong: we resembled no one. Accordingly, from the first day of our arrival, we observed that the strangeness of our physiognomy attracted general attention. When we passed along the streets the people looked at us with astonishment, and then advanced, in an undertone, various hypotheses as to our nation. At one time they took us for two Muftis lately come from Cashmere; at another time for two Indian Brahmins; some said we were Lamas from the north of Tartary; others maintained that we

THIBET, AND CHINA

were merchants from Peking, and that we had disguised ourselves in order to accompany the Thibetian embassy. But all these suppositions soon vanished, for we formally declared to the Katchi that we were neither Mufti nor Cashmerians; to the Peboun, that we were neither Indians nor Brahmins: to the Mongols, that we were neither Lamas nor Tartars; to the Chinese, that we were neither merchants, nor from the Central Kingdom. When all were convinced that we did not belong to any of these categories they began to call us White Azaras [Hazara]. The denomination was very picturesque, and rather pleased us; we were not, however, inclined to adopt it before getting some information on the point. We therefore asked what they meant by White Azaras. The answer we got was that the Azaras were the most fervent of all the adorers of Buddha, that they were a large tribe of Indians, and that out of devotion they often made a pilgrimage to Lha-Ssa. It was added, that as we were neither Thibetians, nor Katchi, nor Peboun, nor Tartars, nor Chinese, we must certainly be Azaras. There was only this little difficulty in the way, that the Azaras who had previously been at Lha-Ssa, were black; it had become necessary, therefore, in order to solve the difficulty, to call us White Azaras. We again rendered homage to the truth, and declared that we were not Azaras of any kind, white or black. All these doubts about our origin were at first amusing enough; but they soon became serious. Some ill-disposed persons went on to consider that we must be Russians or English, and ultimately almost everybody honoured us with the latter qualification. It was set forth, without further hesitation, that we were Pelings from Calcutta, that we had come to investigate the strength of Thibet, to make maps, and to devise means to get possession of the country. All national prejudice apart, it was very annoying to us to be taken for the subjects of her Britannic Majesty. Such a *quid-pro-quo* could not but render us very unpopular, and, perhaps, end in our being cut to pieces; for the Thibetians, why, we know not, have taken it into their heads that the English are an encroaching people, who are not to be trusted.

To cut short the various chatter circulated about us, we resolved to conform to a regulation in force at Lha-Ssa, and which commands all strangers, who are desirous of staying in the town, to present themselves to the authorities. We went accordingly to the chief of police, and declared to him that we belonged to the Western Heaven, to a great kingdom called France, and that we had come to Thibet to preach the Christian religion, of which we were the ministers. The person to whom we made this declaration was cold and impenetrable as became a bureaucrat. He phlegmatically drew his bamboo quill from behind his ear, and began to write, without the slightest observation, what we had told him. He contented himself with repeating twice or thrice, between his teeth, the words "France," and "Christian religion," like a man who does not know what you mean. When he had done writing, he wiped his pen, still wet with ink, in his hair, and replaced it behind his right ear, saying, "*Yak pore* [*Yak pore* (*yag-po-re,*)]" (very well); "*Temou chu* [*temu shu* (*bde-mo-bshugs*)]" (dwell in peace), we replied, and putting out our tongues at him, we left him, delighted at having placed ourselves on a proper footing with the police. We then walked about the streets of Lha-Ssa with a firmer and more assured step, and regardless of the remarks that continually assailed our ears. The lawful position we had established raised us in our own eyes, and restored our courage. What a happiness at length to find ourselves in an hospitable land, and to be able to breathe a free air, after living so long in China; always in conſtraint, always outside the law, always occupied with plans for tricking the government of his Imperial Majeſty.

The sort of indifference with which our declaration was received by the Thibetian authorities did not surprise us in the leaſt. From the information we had received of the position of ſtrangers at Lha-Ssa, we were convinced we should have no difficulty in the matter. The Thibetians do not profess, in regard to other people, those principles of exclusion which conſtitute the diſtinctive character of the Chinese nation. Everyone is allowed to enter Lha-Ssa; everyone can go and come, and engage in commerce and induſtrial pursuits without the leaſt reſtraint. If entrance into Thibet is forbidden to the Chinese, this prohibition muſt be attributed to the government of Peking, which, to show its complete adherence to its narrow and suspicious policy, forbids its subjects to penetrate among other nations. It is probable that the English would not be excluded more than any other nation, had not their invasive march into Hindoſtan inspired the Talé-Lama with a natural terror.

We have already mentioned the many and striking analogies between the Lamanesque worship and the Catholic rites—Rome and Lha-Ssa—the pope and the Talé-Lama,[1] might furnish further analogies. The Thibetian government, being purely Lamanesque, seems in some sort framed upon the ecclesiaſtical government of the Pontifical ſtates. The Talé-Lama is the political and religious head of all the Thibetian

---

[1] Dalae-Lama is altogether an erroneous form of this designation; the words are Talé-Lama. Talé, in Thibetian, means sea, and the appellation has been applied to the Grand Lama of Thibet, because this personage is locally supposed to be a sea of wisdom and power.

countries; in his hands is all the legislative, executive, and administrative power. The common law and some rules left by Tsong-Kaba, serve to direct him in the exercise of his immense authority. When the Talé-Lama dies, or, in the language of the Buddhists, when he transmigrates, a child is selected who is to continue the imperishable personification of the Living Buddha. This election is made by the Grand assembly of the Houtouktou Lamas, whose sacerdotal dignity is only inferior to that of the Talé-Lama. By-and-by we will enter more fully into the form and rules of this singular election. As the Talé-Lama is not only a religious and political sovereign of the Thibetians, but also their visible deity, it is obvious that he cannot, without seriously compromising his divinity, descend from the height of his sanctuary, to meddle, on all occasions, with human affairs. He has, therefore, reserved to himself the matters of primary importance, content to reign much, and to govern very little. The exercise of his authority wholly depends on his will and pleasure. There is no charter or constitution to regulate his conduct.

After the Talé-Lama, whom the Thibetians also call Kian-Ngan-Remboutchi [rGyal-ba-Rin-po-ch'e] "sovereign treasure," comes the Nomekhan, or Spiritual Emperor. The Chinese give him the name of Tsan-Wang [Tsang-wang], "king of Thibet." This personage is nominated by the Talé-Lama, and must be selected from the class of *Chaberon* Lamas. He retains office for life, and can only be overthrown by some state stroke. All the affairs of the government are managed by the Nomekhan, and four ministers called *Kalons*. The *Kalons* are chosen by the Talé-Lama, from a list of candidates made out by the Nomekhan; they do not belong to the sacerdotal tribe, and may marry: the duration of their power is unlimited. When they render themselves unworthy of their office, the

THIBET, AND CHINA

Nomekhan sends a report to the Talé-Lama, who dismisses them, if he thinks proper. The subaltern funćtionaries are selećted by the *Kalons*, and moſt frequently belong to the class of Lamas.

The provinces are divided into several principalities, which are governed by Houtouktou Lamas. These petty ecclesiaſtical sovereigns receive their inveſtiture from the Talé-Lama, and recognize his sovereign authority. Generally they are of a warlike turn, and frequently engage with their neighbours in hoſtile skirmishes, which are always accompanied by pillage and conflagration.

The moſt potent of these Lama sovereigns is the Bandchan-Remboutchi. He resides at Djachi-Loumbo "mountain of oracles," capital of Further Thibet. This town is situate south of Lha-Ssa, and is only eight days' journey from it. The celebrity of the present Bandchan is prodigious; his partisans assert that his spiritual power is as great is that of the Talé-Lama, and that the sanćtuary of Djachi-Loumbo does not yield in sanćtity to that of the Buddha-La. It is generally, however, admitted, that the temporal power of the Talé-Lama is superior to that of the Bandchan-Remboutchi. Great rivalry will not fail to manifeſt itself, sooner or later, between Lha-Ssa and Djachi-Loumbo, and occasion dismal dissensions among the Thibetians.

The present Bandchan-Remboutchi is sixty years of age; he is, they say, of a fine and majeſtic frame, and aſtonishingly vigorous for his advanced age. This singular personage ſtates himself to be of Indian origin, and that it is already some thousands of years since his firſt incarnation took place in the celebrated country of the Azaras. The physiognomiſts who, at our firſt coming to Lha-Ssa, took us for white Azaras, failed not to urge us to go and offer our devotions to the Djachi-Loumbo, assuring us that in our quality of countrymen of the Bandchan-Remboutchi, we should have a very good reception. The learned Lamas, who occupy themselves with Buddhic genealogies, explain how the Bandchan, after numerous and marvellous incarnations in Hindoſtan, ended by appearing in Further Thibet, and fixing his residence at Djachi-Loumbo. Whatever may be his biography, which, fortunately, we are not bound to believe in, it is certain that this able Lama has managed to eſtablish an aſtonishing reputation. The Thibetians, the Tartars, and the other Buddhiſts call him by no other name than the Great Saint, and never pronounce his name without clasping their hands and raising their eyes to heaven. They pretend that his knowledge is universal. He knows how to speak, they say, all the languages of the universe without having ever ſtudied them, and can converse with pilgrims from all parts of the world. The Tartars have so ſtrong a faith in his power, that they invoke him continually. In dangers, in afflictions, in all matters of difficulty, they have in their mouths the magic word *bokte* (saint).

The pilgrims who come to Thibet never fail to visit the Djachi-Loumbo, to proſtrate themselves at the feet of the Saint of Saints, and to present to him their offerings. No one can form a notion of the enormous sums which the Tartar caravans bring him every year. In return for the ingots of gold and silver which he shuts up in his coffers, the Bandchan distributes among his adorers shreds of his old clothes, bits of paper printed with Mongol or Thibetian sentences, earthen ſtatuettes, and red pills of infallible efficaciousness againſt all sorts of maladies. The pilgrims receive with veneration these trifles, and deposit them religiously in a bag which they have always hanging from their necks.

Those who make the pilgrimage to Djachi-Loumbo, seculars or Lamas, men or women, all enrol themselves in the society of *Kalons*, inſtituted by the

THIBET, AND CHINA

Bandchan-Remboutchi. Almost all the Buddhists aspire to the happiness of becoming members of this association, which will give rise, some day, to some important event in Upper Asia. All minds, even now, are vividly occupied with the presentiment of a grand catastrophe. Here are some of the strange prophecies that are current on this subject.

When the saint of Djachi-Loumbo, when the Bandchan-Remboutchi dies, he will not transmigrate, as heretofore, in Further Thibet. His new incarnation will take place to the north of Lha-Ssa, in the steppes inhabited by the Ourianghai, in the country called Thien-Chan-Pé-Lou [T'ien-shan-pei-lu], between the Celestial Mountains and the chains of the Altai. While he remains there, a few years, incognito, preparing himself by retirement, prayer, and good works, for the great events of the future, the religion of Buddha will continue to grow weaker and weaker in all men's hearts; it will only exist in the bosoms of the brotherhood of the *Kalons*. At this disastrous epoch the Chinese will gain influence in Thibet; they will spread themselves over the mountains and through the valleys, and will seek to possess themselves of the empire of the Talé-Lama. But this state of things will soon pass away; there will be a general rise of the people; the Thibetians will take up arms and will massacre in one day all the Chinese, young and old, and not one of them shall pass the frontiers.

A year after this sanguinary day, the Chinese Emperor will raise innumerable battalions, and will lead them against the Thibetians. There will be a terrible reaction; blood will flow in torrents, the streams will be red with gore, and the Chinese will gain possession of Thibet. But this triumph will not be of long duration. Then it will be that the Bandchan-Remboutchi will manifest his power. He will summon all the *Kalons* of the holy society. Those who shall have already died will return to life, and they will all assemble in a vaſt plain of Thien-Chan-Pé-Lou. There the Bandchan will diſtribute arrows and fusils to all of them, and will form of this multitude a formidable army of which he himself will take the command. The society of *Kalons* will march with the Saint of Saints, and will throw themselves on the Chinese, who will be cut to pieces. Thibet will be conquered, then China, then Tartary, and finally, the vaſt empire of the Oros. The Bandchan will be proclaimed universal sovereign, and under his holy influence Lamanism will be soon reſtored to its priſtine vigour, superb Lamaseries will rise everywhere, and the whole world will recognize the infinite power of Buddhic prayers.

These predictions, of which we content ourselves with giving a mere summary, are related by everyone in moſt minute detail; but what is moſt surprising is, that no one seems to entertain the leaſt doubt of the full accomplishment of the events they foretell. Everyone speaks of them as of things certain and infallible. The Chinese residing at Lha-Ssa seem likewise to attach credit to the prediction, but they take good care not to trouble their heads much about it; they hope that the crisis will not come for a long while, that by that time they may be dead, or at leaſt be able to anticipate it. As for the Bandchan-Remboutchi, they say he is preparing himself vigorously for the grand revolution of which he is deſtined to be the soul. Although already advanced in years he often practices military exercises; every moment which is not absorbed by his high functions as Living Buddha he employs in making himself familiar with his future position of generalissimo of the *Kalons*. They affirm that he shoots an arrow very skilfully, and that he handles with great dexterity the lance and the

THIBET, AND CHINA

matchlock. He breeds large herds of horses for his future cavalry, and packs of enormous dogs, which, combining prodigious strength with superior intelligence, are destined to play an important part in the grand army of the *Kalons*.

These absurd and extravagant ideas have so made their way with the masses, and particularly those who belong to the society of the *Kalons*, that they are very likely, at some future day, to cause a revolution in Thibet. It is never without result that people thus preoccupy their minds with the future. After the death of the Grand Lama of Djachi-Loumbo, a reckless adventurer will only have to proceed to Thien-Chan-Pé-Lou, boldly proclaim himself Bandchan-Remboutchi, and summon the *Kalons* together—nothing more will, probably, be required to raise these fanatical people.

An actual and immediate result of this society of the *Kalons* is to give the Bandchan-Remboutchi an importance which seems by slow degrees to be compromising the supremacy of the Talé-Lama. This result is the more feasible that the sovereign of Lha-Ssa is a child of nine years old and that his three predecessors have fallen victims to a violent death before attaining their majority, which is fixed by the laws at twenty years of age. The Bandchan-Remboutchi, who seems to be an able and ambitious man, will not have failed to take advantage of these four minorities to confiscate to his own advantage a portion of the spiritual and temporal power of the Talé-Lama.

The violent deaths of the three Talé-Lamas, the immediate predecessors of the reigning sovereign, gave rise, in the year 1844, to an event which occupied the attention of all Thibet, Tartary, and even China, and which, on account of its importance, deserves, perhaps, a brief notice here. The unprecedented phenomenon of three Talé-Lamas dying successively in the flower of their age, had plunged the inhabitants of Lha-Ssa into a ſtate of mournful conſternation. Gradually, dark rumours began to circulate, and soon the words " crime," " assassination," were heard. The thing went so far that they related in the ſtreets of the town and all the Lamaseries all the circumſtances of these dismal events. It was said that the firſt Talé-Lama had been ſtrangled, the second crushed by the roof of his sleeping apartment, and the third poisoned with his numerous relations, who had come to settle at Lha-Ssa. The superior Lama of the Grand Lamasery of Kaldan, who was very much attached to the Talé-Lama, had suffered the same fate. The public voice denounced the Nomekhan as the author of all these crimes. The four miniſters had no doubt about the matter, knowing the whole truth ; but they found themselves unable to avenge the death of their sovereign ; they were too weak to ſtruggle with the Nomekhan, who was supported by numerous and powerful friends.

This Nomekhan was a Si-Fan, a native of the principality of Yang-Tou-Sse, in the province of Kan-Sou. The supreme dignity of Tou-Sse was hereditary in his family, and a great number of his relations, settled at Lha-Ssa for several generations, exercised great influence over the affairs of Thibet. The Nomekhan of Yang-Tou-Sse was ſtill very young when he was inveſted with an authority inferior only to that of the Talé-Lama. They say that a few years after his elevation to power, he manifeſted his ambitious sentiments and a boundless desire for domination. He used his own great wealth and the influence of his relations, to surround himself with dependents wholly devoted to his intereſt. He took particular care to secure partisans among the Lamas ; and, to this end, he took under his immediate proteƈtion the famous Lamasery of Sera, situated half a league from Lha-Ssa, and containing upwards of 15,000 Buddhiſt monks. He loaded it with presents, granted it infinite privileges and revenues, and placed, in its different departments, a great number of his creatures. The Lamas of Sera failed not to acquire great enthusiasm for the Nomekhan; they regarded him as a saint of the firſt degree, and compiled an enumeration of his perfeƈtions as extensive and pompous as that of the perfeƈtions of Buddha. Supported by the powerful party he had got together, the Nomekhan withdrew all bounds from his projeƈt of usurpation. It was then that he caused the three young Lamas to be murdered in succession, in order to keep for himself the position of Regent. Such was the Nomekhan of Yang-Tou-Tse, or rather, such was he represented to us during our ſtay at Lha-Ssa.

It was not easy, as may be seen, to overthrow a personage whose power was so solidly based. The *Kalon* miniſters, unequal to an open ſtruggle with the Nomekhan, resolved to dissimulate, and to work, meanwhile, in secret, at the downfall of this execrable man. The assembly of the Houtouktou eleƈted a new Talé-Lama, or rather indicated the child into whose body the soul of the Living Buddha had transmigrated. He was enthroned at the summit of the Buddha-La. The Nomekhan, like the other dignitaries, proceeded to throw himself at his feet, worshipped him with all devotion, but with the full resolution, doubtless, to make him undergo a fourth transmigration, when he should think proper.

The *Kalons* secretly adopted measures to prevent a new cataſtrophe. They consulted with the Bandchan-Remboutchi of Djachi-Loumbo, and it was determined that, to check the infamous projeƈts of the Nomekhan, they should call to their aid the irresiſtible power of the Emperor of China. A requeſt was accordingly drawn up and signed by the Bandchan and the four

TRAVELS IN TARTARY,

Kalons, and privately sent to Peking by the embassy of 1844. For three special reasons the government of Peking could not dispense with granting to the Thibetians the protection they demanded under these grave circumstances. In the first place the Tartaro-Mantchou dynasty had solemnly declared itself protector of the Talé-Lama; in the second place, the Nomekhan, as being a native of Yang-Tou-Sse, in the province of Kan-Sou, was in some degree amenable to the Chinese Emperor; finally, politically speaking, it was an excellent opportunity for the court of Peking to establish its influence in Thibet, with a view to the realization of its projects of usurpation.

The request sent to Peking by the Bandchan-Remboutchi and the four *Kalons*, was received with all the favour that could be desired, and the Government there determined to send to Lha-Ssa an ambassador of energy and prudence, capable of overthrowing the power of the Nomekhan. The Emperor thought of the Mandarin Ki-Chan [Ch'i-shan], and charged him with this difficult mission.

Before proceeding further, it will not, perhaps, be superfluous to give a sketch of this Ki-Chan, a very celebrated personage in China, who has played an important part in the affair of the English at Canton. Ki-Chan is of Tartaro-Mantchou origin; he commenced his career as a scrivener in one of the six grand tribunals of Peking. His rare capacity was soon remarked, and although he was still very young, he rapidly mounted all the steps of the magistracy. At the age of twenty-two he was governor of the province of Ho-Nan; at the age of twenty-five he was its viceroy, but he was dismissed from this charge for not having been able to foresee an overflow of the Yellow River, which caused great disasters in the province that was entrusted to him. His disgrace did not last long; he was reinstated in his former dignity,

THIBET, AND CHINA

and sent, successively, in quality of viceroy, to the provinces of Chan-Toung, Sse-Tchouan, and Pe-Tche-Li. He was decorated with the red button, the peacock's feather, and the yellow tunic, with the title of *Heou-Ye* [*hou-ye*] "imperial prince." At length he was nominated *Tchoung-Tang* [*chung-t'ang*], the highest dignity to which a Mandarin can ever aspire. They have only eight *Tchoung-Tangs* in the empire; four Mantchous and four Chinese; these compose the privy council of the Emperor, and have the right of direct correspondence with him.

Towards the close of the year 1839, Ki-Chan was sent to Canton, as viceroy of the province, and with the title of imperial commissioner he had full powers to treat, in the name of his government, with the English, and to re-establish the peace which had been disturbed by the foolish and violent proceedings of his predecessor Lin. That which most emphatically proves the capacity of Ki-Chan is, that on his arrival at Canton, he recognized the infinite superiority of the Europeans over the Chinese, and saw that war was impossible. He, accordingly, forthwith commenced negociations with Mr. Elliott, the English plenipotentiary, and peace was concluded, on the consideration of the cession of the small island of Hong-Kong. To cement the good understanding that had been established between the Emperor Tao-Kouang and Queen Victoria, Ki-Chan gave the English authorities a magnificent banquet, at which was present M. de Rosamel, the commander of the corvette *Danaide*, which had arrived a few days before in the roads of Macao. Everyone was enchanted with the graceful and affable manners of the commissioner-general.

A few days only elapsed before the intrigues worked at Peking by the former imperial commissioner, Lin, occasioned the disallowance by the Emperor of the treaty that had just been concluded at Canton.

TRAVELS IN TARTARY,

Ki-Chan was accused of having allowed himself to be corrupted by English gold, and of having sold to the "sea devils" the territory of the Celestial Empire. The Emperor sent him a furious letter, declaring him worthy of death, and ordering him to repair to Peking forthwith. The poor imperial commissioner had not his head cut off, as everyone expected. The Emperor, in his paternal mildness, gave him his life, and merely degraded him from all his titles, withdrew all his decorations, confiscated his property, razed his house, sold his wives by public auction, and banished him to the depths of Tartary. The numerous and influential friends whom Ki-Chan had at court, did not desert him in his reverses; they laboured with courage and perseverance to reinstate him in the good graces of the Emperor. In 1844, he was, at length, recalled, and sent to Lha-Ssa as envoy-extraordinary in the matter of the Nomekhan. He departed, decorated with the blue button, instead of the red one, which he wore before his fall; they restored to him the peacock's feather, but the privilege of wearing the yellow tunic was still withheld. His friends at Peking clubbed together and built for him a magnificent house. The post of *Kin-Tchai*, amid the mountains of Thibet, was still considered banishment; but it was a step towards a glorious and complete reinstatement. Immediately upon his arrival at Lha-Ssa, Ki-Chan concerted with the Bandchan-Remboutchi, and had the Nomekhan arrested. He then proceeded to examine all the persons attached to the service of the accused, and in order to facilitate their declaration of the truth, he had long bamboo needles thrust under their nails; by this means, as the Chinese phrase it, "truth was separated from falsehood," and the conduct of the Nomekhan was brought to light. The wretched man avowed his crimes voluntarily, in order to avoid the torture. He acknowledged himself guilty of taking

THIBET, AND CHINA

away three lives from the Talé-Lama, of having used violent means to make him transmigrate, the first time by strangulation, the second time by suffocation, and the third by poison. A confession was drawn up in the Tartar, Chinese, and Thibetian languages; the Nomekhan and his accomplices signed it; the Bandchan-Remboutchi, the four *Kalons*, and the Chinese ambassador set their seals to it; and it was immediately forwarded to Peking by a courier-extraordinary. All this was done in secret. Three months afterwards, the capital of Thibet was thrown into a state of the greatest agitation; there was seen placarded on the great gate of the Nomekhan's palace an imperial edict in three languages, on yellow paper, and with borders representing winged dragons. After a long flourish about the duties of kings, and of sovereigns, great and small, and an exhortation to the potentates, monarchs, princes, magistrates and people of the four seas, to walk in the path of justice and virtue, under pain of incurring the wrath of heaven and the indignation of the Grand Khan, the Emperor recounted the crime of the Nomekhan, and condemned him to perpetual banishment on the banks of the Sakhalien-Oula, in the depths of Mantchouria. At the end was the usual formula: " Tremble and obey."

The inhabitants of Lha-Ssa collected round these strange placards, which they were unused to see on the walls of their town. The report of the condemnation of the Nomekhan spread rapidly among the people. Numerous groups began to form, who discussed the point with vehemence, but in whispers. All faces were animated, and from every quarter there rose a deep murmur. This agitation among the Thibetian people arose not so much from the merited downfall of the Nomekhan as from the interference of the Chinese authorities, an interference which everyone felt to be very humiliating.

TRAVELS IN TARTARY,

At the Lamasery of Sera opposition manifested itself with an altogether different sort of energy. As soon as they had notice there of the imperial edict, the insurrection was spontaneous and general. Those 15,000 Lamas, who were all devoted to the cause of the Nomekhan, armed themselves hastily with lances, fusils, sticks, whatever came first to hand, and threw themselves into Lha-Ssa, which was only half a league distant. The thick clouds of dust which they raised in their disorderly course, and the terrible shouts they sent forth, announced their arrival to the inhabitants of Lha-Ssa—" The Lamas of Sera! Here are the Lamas of Sera!" Such was the cry which resounded through the town, and inspired all hearts with fear. The Lamas burst like an avalanche upon the house of the Chinese ambassador, and dashed in the door with shouts of " Death to Ki-Chan! death to the Chinese!" But they found no one upon whom they could vent their rage. The ambassador, forewarned in time of their arrival, had run and concealed himself in the house of a *Kalon*, and the people of his train were dispersed over the town. The multitude of Lamas then divided itself into several bands, some took their way to the palace of the Nomekhan, and others besieged the dwellings of the *Kalons*, demanding loudly that they should give up to them the Chinese ambassador. There was, on this point, a long and fierce contest, in which one of the four Thibetians was torn to pieces, and the others received wounds more or less dangerous.

Whilst they were contending with the *Kalons* for possession of the person of Ki-Chan, the most numerous party of the Lamas had broken into the prison where the Nomekhan was confined, and wanted to bear him in triumph to the Lamasery of Sera. The Nomekhan, however, strongly opposed this intention, and exerted all his influence to calm the excitement of the Lamas.

He told them that their inconsiderate revolt aggravated his position inſtead of ameliorating it. " I am," said he, "the victim of a conspiracy. I will go to Peking; I will explain the whole affair to the Emperor, and will return in triumph amongſt you. At present we have only to obey the imperial decree. I will depart, as I have been commanded. Do you go back quietly to your Lamasery." These words did not shake the resolution of the Lamas, but, night falling, they returned tumultuously to Sera, promising themselves a better plan for the morrow. When day broke, the Lamas began to move about in their vaſt monaſtery, and to prepare themselves for a fresh invasion of the town of Lha-Ssa, but, to their great aſtonishment, they perceived in the plain, round about the Lamasery, numerous tents and a multitude of Chinese and Thibetian soldiers, armed to the teeth, and prepared to bar their passage. At this sight, all their valour evaporated: the marine conch was sounded, and these extempore soldiers, throwing aside their arms, re-entered their cells, took their books under their arms, and quietly proceeded to the choir, to recite, as usual, their matins.

A few days afterwards, the Nomekhan, accompanied by a ſtrong escort, took the road to Sse-Tchouan, and proceeded like a sheep, to the place of exile that had been assigned him. They could never underſtand at Lha-Ssa how the man, who had not hesitated to murder three Talé-Lamas, had not chosen to take advantage of the insurrection of the Lamas of Sera. Certain it is, that, with a single word, he might have annihilated all the Chinese at Lha-Ssa, and moſt probably set all Thibet in a blaze; but the Nomekhan was not formed to play such a part; he had the cowardly energy of an assassin, but not the audacity of a revolutioniſt.

Ki-Chan, encouraged by his triumph, wanted to extend his power to the Thibetian accomplices of the

Nomekhan. This claim, however, did not suit the *Kalons*, who told him that to them alone belonged the right of judging men who in no wise were subject to China, and against whom they had not asked for the protection of the Emperor. The *Kin-Tchai* did not press the point; but, not to appear to yield to the Thibetian authorities, he replied to them officially, "that he left to them these inferior assassins, who were below the notice of the representative of the Emperor."

A new Nomekhan was elected in the place of the exile. The person selected for this important charge was the *Chaberon* of the Lamasery of Ran-Tchan, a young man of eighteen years of age. The Tlé-Lama and the new Nomekhan being minors, at the time that we arrived at Lha-Ssa the regency was entrusted to the First *Kalon*. All the solicitude of the Regent was applied to the erection of barriers against the encroachments and usurpation of the Chinese ambassador, who sought, by all possible means, to avail himself of the present feebleness of the Thibetian government.

CHAPTER VI

As soon as we had presented ourselves to the Thibetian authorities, declaring our characters and the object which had brought us to Lha-Ssa, we availed ourselves of the semi-official position we had thus taken, to enter into communication with the Thibetian and Tartar Lamas, and thus, at last, to begin our work as missionaries. One day, when we were sitting beside our modest hearth, talking of religious questions with a Lama who was well versed in Buddhist learning, a Chinese dressed in exquisite style suddenly appeared before us, saying that he was a merchant and very desirous of buying our goods. We told him we had nothing to sell. "How, nothing to sell?" "Not anything, except indeed those two old saddles, which we do not want any longer." "Ah, exactly; that is just what I am looking for; I want saddles." Then, while he examined our poor merchandise, he addressed to us a thousand questions about our country and the places we had visited before we came to Lha-Ssa. Shortly afterwards there arrives a second Chinese, then a third, and at last two Lamas, in costly silk scarves. All these visitors insisted upon buying something from us; they overwhelmed us with questions, and seemed, at the same time, to scrutinize with distrust all the corners of our chamber.

We might say, as often as we liked, that we were not merchants—they insisted. In default of silk, drapery, or hardware, they would like our saddles; they turned them round and round in every way, finding them now perfectly magnificent, now abominable. At last, after long haggling and cross-questioning, they went off, promising to return.

The visit of these five individuals occasioned much serious reflection; their manner of acting and speaking was not at all natural. Although they came one after the other, yet they seemed perfectly to understand each other, and to aim at the same end by the same means. Their desire of buying something from us was evidently a mere pretext for disguising their intentions: These people were rather swindlers or spies, than real merchants. "Well," we said, "let us wait quietly; sooner or later we shall see clearly into this affair."

As it was dinner time, we sat down to table, or rather, we remained at the fireside, contemplating the pot, in which a good cut of beef had been boiling for some hours. Samdadchiemba, in his quality of steward, brought this to the surface of the liquid by means of a large wooden spoon, seized it with his nails, and threw it on the end of a board, where he cut it into three equal pieces; each then took his portion in his cup, and with the aid of a few rolls baked in the ashes, we tranquilly commenced our dinner without troubling ourselves very much about swindlers or spies. We were at our dessert—that is to say, we were about to rinse our cups with some buttered tea, when the two Lamas, the pretended merchants, made their re-appearance. "The Regent," they said "awaits you in his palace; he wants to speak to you." "But," cried we, "does the Regent, perchance, also want to buy our old saddles?" "It is not a question about either saddles or merchandise. Rise at once, and follow us to the Regent." The matter was now beyond a doubt; the government was desirous of meddling with us—to what end? Was it to do us good or ill, to give us liberty, or to shackle us, to let us live or to make us die? This we could not tell. "Let us go to the Regent," we said, "and trust for the rest to the will of our heavenly Father."

After having dressed ourselves in our best, and put

on our majestic caps of fox-skin, we said to our apparitor, " We are ready." " And this young man ? " he said, pointing to Samdadchiemba, who had turned his eyes upon him with no very affectionate expression. " This young man, he is our servant, he will take care of the house in our absence." " No, no, he must come too ; the Regent wishes to see all three of you." Samdadchiemba shook, by way of making his toilet, his great robe of sheepskin, placed, in a very insolent manner, a small black cap over his ear, and we departed all together, after padlocking the door of our lodging,

We went at a rapid pace for about five or six minutes, and then arrived at the palace of the First *Kalon*, the Regent of Thibet. After having crossed a large courtyard, where were assembled a great number of Lamas and Chinese, who began to whisper when they saw us appear, we were stopped before a gilt door, the folds of which stood ajar ; our leader passed through a small corridor on the left, and an instant after the door was opened. At the farther end of an apartment, simply furnished, we perceived a personage sitting with crossed legs on a thick cushion covered with a tiger's skin : it was the Regent. With his right hand he made us a sign to approach. We went close up to him, and saluted him by placing our caps under our arms. A bench covered with a red carpet stood on our right ; on this we were invited to sit down—we complied immediately. Meantime the gilt door was closed, and there remained in the saloon only the Regent and seven individuals, who stood behind him—namely, four Lamas of a modest and composed bearing, two sly-looking, mischievous-eyed Chinese, and a person whom, by his long beard, his turban and grave countenance, we recognized to be a Mussulman. The Regent was a man of fifty years of age ; his large features, mild and remarkably pallid, breathed a truly royal majesty ; his dark eyes, shaded by long lashes, were intelligent and gentle. He was dressed in a yellow robe, edged with sable; a ring, adorned with diamonds, hung from his left ear, and his long, jet black hair was collected altogether at the top of his head and fastened by three small gold combs. His large red cap, set with pearls and surmounted by a coral ball, lay at his side on a green cushion.

When we were seated, the Regent gazed at us for a long while in silence, and with a minute attention. He turned his head alternately to the right and left, and smiled at us in a half mocking, half friendly manner. This sort of pantomime appeared to us at last so droll that we could not help laughing. "Come," we said in French in an undertone; "this gentleman seems a good fellow enough; our affair will go on very well." "Ah!" said the Regent, in a very affable tone, "what language is that you speak? I did not understand what you said?" "We spoke the language of our country." "Well, repeat aloud what you said just now." "We said, 'This gentleman seems a good-natured fellow enough.'" The Regent, turning to those who were standing behind him, said, "Do you understand this language?" They all bowed together, and answered that they did not understand it. "You see, nobody here understands the language of your country. Translate your words into the Thibetian." "We said, that in the physiognomy of the First *Kalon* there was expressed much kindliness." "Ah! you think I have much kindliness; yet I am very ill-natured. Is it not true that I am very ill-natured?" he asked his attendants. They answered merely by smiling. "You are right," continued the Regent; "I am kind, for kindness is the duty of a *Kalon*. I must be kind towards my people, and also towards strangers." He then addressed to us a long harangue, of which we could comprehend only a few sentences. When he had finished, we told him that, not being much accustomed to the Thibetian language, we had not fully penetrated the sense of his words. The Regent signed to a Chinese, who, stepping forward, translated to us his harangue, of which the following is the outline. We had been summoned without the slightest idea of being molested. The contradictory reports that had circulated respecting us since our arrival at Lha-Ssa had induced the Regent to question us himself, in order to know where we came from. " We are from the western sky," we said to the Regent. " From Calcutta ? " " No ; our country is called France." " You are, doubtless, Peling ? " " No, we are Frenchmen." " Can you write ? " " Better than speak." The Regent, turning round, addressed some words to a Lama, who disappearing, returned in a moment with paper, ink, and a bamboo point. " Here is paper," said the Regent ; " write something." " In what language— in Thibetian ? " " No, write some letters in your own country's language." One of us took the paper on his knees and wrote this sentence : " What avails it to man to conquer the whole world, if he lose his soul ? " " Ah, here are characters of your country ! I never saw any like them ; and what is the meaning of that ? " We wrote the translation in Thibetian, Tartar, and Chinese, and handed it to him. " I have not been deceived," he said ; " you are men of great knowledge. You can write in all languages, and you express thoughts as profound as those we find in the prayer-books." He then repeated, slowly moving his head to and fro, " what avails it to man to conquer the whole world if he lose his own soul."

While the Regent and his attendants were indulging in their raptures at our wonderful knowledge, we heard on a sudden, in the courtyard of the palace, the cries of the crowd and the sonorous noise of the Chinese tamtam. "Here is the ambassador of Peking," said the Regent, "he wishes to examine you himself. Tell him frankly what concerns you, and rely on my protection; it is I who govern the country." This said he quitted the saloon with his retinue through a small secret door, and left us alone in the judgment-hall.

The idea of falling into the hands of the Chinese made at first a disagreeable impression upon us; and the picture of those horrible persecutions which at different times have afflicted the christendoms of China, seized upon our imagination; but we soon recovered our spirits in the reflection that we were alone, and isolated as we were in the midst of Thibet, could not compromise anyone. This thought gave us courage. "Samdadchiemba," we said to our young neophyte, "now must we show that we are brave men, that we are Christians. This affair will perhaps proceed to great lengths; but let us never lose sight of eternity. If we are treated well, we shall thank God for it; if we are maltreated, we shall thank Him nevertheless, for we shall have the happiness of suffering for the faith. If we are killed, the martyrdom will be a splendid crowning of all our labours. To arrive, after a journey of only eighteen months, in heaven, were not that a good journey? were not that happiness? What do you say, Samdadchiemba?" "I have never been in fear of death; if I am asked whether I am a Christian, you will see if I tremble."

This excellent frame of mind in Samdadchiemba filled our hearts with joy, and completely dissipated the unpleasant impressions which this misadventure had occasioned. We thought for a moment of considering the questions that would probably be put to us, and the answers we should give; but we rejected this counsel of mere human prudence, reflecting that the moment had come for us to keep strictly to the injunction which our Saviour addressed to his disciples, that " when they were brought before the synagogues, governors, and kings, they should take no thought how or what they should speak"; only it was agreed that we should salute the Mandarin in the French way, and that we should not kneel before him. We thought that, having the honour to be Chriftians, missionaries and Frenchmen, we might very fairly insift on ftanding erect before any Chinese whatsoever.

After waiting a few moments, a young Chinese, elegantly dressed, and of very graceful manners, came to inform us that Ki-Chan, grand ambassador of the grand Emperor of China, wished to examine us. We followed our amiable apparitor, and were ushered into a saloon decorated in the Chinese ftyle, where Ki-Chan was seated upon a sort of throne, about three feet high, and covered with red cloth. Before him was a small table of black laque, upon which were an inkftand, some pens, some sheets of paper, and a silver vase filled with snuff. Below the throne were four scribes, two on the right and two on the left; the reft of the saloon was occupied by a great number of Chinese and Thibetians, who had put on their holiday dresses to attend the inquiry.

Ki-Chan, although sixty years old, seemed to us full of ftrength and vigour. His face is, without contradiction, the moft noble, elegant, and intellectual that we have seen amongft the Chinese. When we took off our caps to him, and made him one of our beft bows, " 'Tis well, 'tis well," he said; " follow your own cuftoms. I have been told you speak correctly the language of Peking. I want to talk with you for a moment." " We make many blunders in speaking, but your marvellous underftanding will know how to remedy the obscurity of our words." " Why, this is pure Pekinese. You Frenchmen possess a great facility for all learning. You are Frenchmen, are you not?" " Yes, we are Frenchmen." " Oh, I know the French; there were formerly a great many of them at Peking; I used to see some of them." "You must have known them, too, at Canton, when you were imperial commissioner?" This reminiscence furrowed the forehead of our judge; he took an abundant pinch of snuff out of his box, and threw it up his nose in a very bad humour. "Yes, that is true; I have seen many Europeans at Canton. You are of the religion of the Lord of Heaven, are you not?" "Certainly we are; moreover, preachers of that religion." "I know, I know; you have come hither, doubtless, to preach that religion?" "We have no other object." "Have you already travelled over a great number of countries?" "We have travelled over all China, Tartary, and now we are in the capital of Thibet." "With whom did you live when you were in China?" "We do not answer questions of that sort." "And if I command you to do so?" "We should not obey." Here the irritated judge struck the table with his fist. "You know," we said, "that Christians have no fear; why, then, seek to intimidate us?" "Where did you learn Chinese?" "In China." "In what place?" "A little everywhere." "And the Tartar, you know it? where did you learn it?" "In Mongolia, in the Land of Grass."

After some other trifling questions, Ki-Chan, telling us that we must be tired, invited us to seat ourselves. Then suddenly changing his tone and manner, he addressed Samdadchiemba, who, with his hand on his hip, had been standing a little behind us. "And you," he said in a dry and angry voice, "whence are you?" "I am from Ki-Tou-Sse?" "What is Ki-Tou-Sse? who knows that?" "Ki-Tou-Sse is in San-Tchouan." "Ah, you are from San-Tchouan, in the province of Kan-Sou. Son of the central nation, on your knees!" Samdadchiemba turned pale, his hand left his hip, and his arm modestly glided down along his leg. " On your knees," repeated the Mandarin, in a thundering voice. Samdadchiemba fell on his knees, saying: " On my knees, standing or sitting, 'tis all the same to me: a man of labour and fatigue, as I am, is not accustomed to take his ease." " Ah, you are from Kan-Sou," said the judge, taking large pinches of snuff; " ah! you are from Kan-Sou; you are a child of the central nation! Very well; in that case it is within my province to deal with you. Son of the central nation, answer your father and mother, and take heed how you tell lies. Where did you meet with these two foreigners? How did you become attached to their service?" Samdadchiemba gave, with perfect self-confidence, a long history of his life, which seemed to interest the auditory; he then related how he had made our acquaintance in Tartary, and the reasons that had induced him to follow us. Our young neophyte spoke with dignity, and, moreover, with a prudence which we had not expected. " Why did you adopt the religion of the Lord of Heaven? Don't you know that this is forbidden by the grand Emperor?" "The *entirely humble*[1] adopted that religion, because it is the only true religion. How could I suppose that the grand Emperor proscribed a religion which orders men to do good and to avoid evil?" " That is true, the religion of the Lord of Heaven is holy; I know it. Why did you enter the service of these foreigners? Don't you know that the laws forbid that?" " How should an ignorant man, as I am, know who is a foreigner, and who is not? These men always showed kindness to me, always exhorted me to practise virtue; why was I not to follow them?" " How much wages do they pay you?" " If I accompany them, it is to save my

[1] *Siao-ti* [*hsiao-ti*], an expression used by the Chinese when they speak of themselves in the presence of Mandarins.

soul, and not to get money. My maſters have never let me want rice and clothes, and with that I am satisfied." "Are you married?" "As I was a Lama, before entering the religion of the Lord of Heaven, I have never been married." The judge then laughingly addressed an indelicate question to Samdadchiemba, who lowered his eyes and remained silent. One of us rising, said to Ki-Chan: "Our religion not only prohibits the commission of impure actions, but also the thinking or speaking of them; it is even not permitted to us to liſten to indecent expressions." These words pronounced with calmness and solemnity, raised a slight blush on the face of his excellency the ambassador of China. "I know," he said, "I know the religion of the Lord of Heaven is holy; I know it, for I have read its books of doctrine; he who should ſtrictly keep all its precepts would be a man without reproach." He made a sign to Samdadchiemba to rise; then, turning to us, he said: "It is night, you muſt be tired; it is time to take supper; you may go; to-morrow, if I want you, I will send for you."

The ambassador Ki-Chan was quite right, it was very late, and the various emotions which had been furnished to us in the course of the evening had not by any means supplied the place of supper. On leaving the Sinico-Thibetian pretorium, we were accoſted by a venerable Lama, who informed us that the Firſt *Kalon* awaited us. We crossed the court, illuminated by some red lanterns; turned on the right, to a perilous ſtaircase, which we ascended, prudently holding on by our conductor's robe; then, after traversing a long terrace, in the dubious light of the ſtars, we were introduced to the Regent. The large and lofty room was splendidly lighted by butter-oil lamps, the walls, the ceiling, even the floor, were all covered with gilding and brilliant colours. The

Regent was alone; he bad us sit down near himself on a rich carpet, and endeavoured to express by his words, and still more by his gestures, how deep an interest he felt in us. Above all, we clearly understood that he was making arrangements to keep us from starving. Our pantomime was interrupted by the arrival of a person, who left, upon entering, his slippers at the door; it was the governor of the Cashmerian Mussulmen. After having saluted the company, by raising his hand to his forehead, and pronouncing the formula "Salamalek" he leant against a column in the centre of the room, which supported the ceiling. The Mussulman governor spoke Chinese very well; and the Regent had accordingly sent for him to act as interpreter. Immediately upon his arrival, a servant placed before us a small table, and supper was served up to us at the expense of the Thibetian government. We shall not say anything here as to the Regent's *cuisine*; firstly, because our keen appetite did not permit us to pay sufficient attention to the quality of the dishes; secondly, because that day our minds were more occupied with politics than with gastronomy. All of a sudden we missed Samdadchiemba; we asked what had become of him: "He is with my servants," answered the Regent; "do not trouble yourself on his account, he shall not want for anything."

During, and after the repast, there was much inquiry about France and the countries we had visited. Then the Regent, pointing to the pictures that adorned his room, asked whether we could ourselves paint any such. "We cannot paint," was our answer; "study, and the preaching of the doctrine of Jehovah are our only occupations." "Oh, don't tell me you cannot paint; I know that the people of your country are very skilful in that art." "Yes, those who make it their employment; but our clergymen are not in the habit of exercising it." "Though you may not follow this art specially, yet you are not unacquainted with it; you can, doubtless, draw geographical maps?" "No, we cannot." "How! on your journey did you never sketch, did you never make a map?" "Never." "Oh, that is impossible!" The pertinacity of the Regent in questioning us on this subject, made us pause to reflect; presently we expressed the surprise we felt at all these inquiries. "I see," he said, "that you are straightforward, honest men; I will speak frankly to you. The Chinese are very suspicious, you are aware of that: you have been long enough in China to know it as well as I do; well, they believe that you are travelling through foreign kingdoms on purpose to draw maps of them and to explore them. If you do draw, if you do make geographical maps, admit it without fear; rely on my protection." Evidently the Regent was afraid of an invasion; he fancied, perhaps, that we were charged with laying down the route for some formidable army, ready to overwhelm Thibet. We endeavoured to dissipate his fears, and to assure him of the extremely peaceful views of the French government. We admitted, however, that amongst our effects there was a great number of drawings and geographical maps, and that we had even a map of Thibet. At these words, the face of the Regent was suddenly contracted; but we hastened to add, in order to quiet him, that all our drawings and maps were printed, and that we were not their authors. We took the opportunity to speak to the Regent and the Cashmerian governor, of the geographical knowledge of the Europeans. They were greatly astonished when we told them that, with us, children of ten and twelve years old possessed an exact and complete idea of all the kingdoms of the world.

    The conversation extended far into the night. At last the Regent rose, and asked us whether we did not feel in want of a little repose. "We only awaited," we answered, "for the permission of the *Kalon*, to return to our lodgings." "Your lodgings! I have ordered an apartment to be prepared for you in my palace; you will sleep here to-night: to-morrow, you can return to your house." We sought to excuse ourselves from accepting the kind offer of the Regent; but soon became aware that we were not at liberty to refuse what we had been simple enough to consider a compliment. We were regular prisoners. We took leave of the Regent rather coolly, and followed an individual, who, after crossing a great many rooms and corridors, ushered us into a sort of closet, which we might fairly call a prison, as we were not permitted to leave it for any other place.

There had been prepared for us two couches, which, no doubt, were infinitely superior to our own beds; nevertheless, we regretted our poor pallets whereon we had so long enjoyed a free and independent sleep throughout our travels in the desert. Lamas and attendants of the Regent came in great numbers to see us. Those who had gone to bed got up, and soon we heard, in this vaſt palace, lately so calm and silent, doors opened and shut, and the rapid ſteps of the curious sounding in the passages. Crowds thronged around us and examined us with insupportable avidity. In all those eyes ſtaring at us there was neither sympathy nor ill-will; they simply expressed vapid curiosity. To all these individuals around us, we represented merely a kind of zoological phenomenon. Oh, how hard it is to be exposed thus to an indifferent multitude! When we thought that these troublesome people had sufficiently ſtared and whispered, and ought now to be satisfied, we informed them that we were going to bed, and that we should feel extremely obliged if they would be kind enough to retire. Everyone bowed: some of them even were polite enough to put out their tongues at us; but nobody ſtirred. It was evident that they had a mind to know how we should behave on going to bed. This desire seemed to us somewhat misplaced; but we thought we would submit to it up to a certain point. Accordingly, we knelt down, made the sign of the cross, and recited, aloud, our evening prayer. As soon as we commenced, the whispering ceased, and a religious silence prevailed. When the prayer was finished, we once more invited the crowd to leave us, and, in order to add efficacy to our words, we extinguished the light. The crowd, thus plunged into deep darkness, adopted the course of firſt having a hearty laugh, and then retiring gropingly. We closed the door of our prison and laid down to reſt.

When ſtretched on the beds of the Firſt *Kalon*, we felt much more disposed to talk than to sleep. We experienced a certain pleasure in recapitulating the adventures of the day. The feigned merchants who wanted to purchase our saddles, our appearance before the Regent, the examination we had undergone by the ambassador, Ki-Chan, our supper at the expense of the public treasury, our long conversation with the Regent: all this appeared to us a phantasmagoria. It seemed as though our whole day had been a long nightmare. Our journey itself, our arrival at Lha-Ssa, everything seemed incredible. We asked one another whether it was true, that we, missionaries, Frenchmen, were really in the ſtates of the Talé-Lama, in the capital of Thibet, sleeping in the very palace of the Regent. All these events, paſt and present, clashed in our heads. The future, especially, appeared to us enveloped in dark, thick clouds. How was all this to end? Would they say to us, "You are free; go wherever you please?" Would they keep us in this prison? or would they ſtrangle us? These refleƈtions were well calculated to chill the heart and to cause a head-ache. But truſt in God is a grand thing in such trials ! How happy is one in feeling one's self supported by Providence, when one is thus left alone, abandoned, and destitute of succour. "Oh," said we to each other, "let us be prepared for the worst relying upon the protection of our Heavenly Father! Not a single hair will fall from our heads without his permission."

We went to sleep amid these considerations, but our slumber was light and disturbed. As soon as dawn appeared, the door of our cell was gently opened, and the governor of the Katchi entered. He took a seat at our side, between the two couches, and asked us in kind, affectionate tones, whether we had spent a good night. He then presented to us a basket of cakes, made by his family, and some dried fruits from Ladak. We were deeply touched by this attention, which seemed to announce that we had met with a sincere and devoted friend.

The governor of the Katchi was thirty-two years old : his face, full of nobleness and majesty, breathed at the same time a kindness and candour well calculated to arouse our confidence. His looks, his words, his deportment, everything about him, seemed to express that he felt a very lively interest in us. He had come to acquaint us with what would be done during the day, with reference to us. "In the morning," he said, "the Thibetian authorities will go with you to your lodgings. They will put a seal upon all your effects, which will then be brought before the tribunal, and be examined by the Regent and the Chinese ambassador, in your presence. If you have no manuscript maps in your baggage you need fear nothing ; you will not be molested in any way. If, on the contrary, you have any such maps, you would do well to let me know beforehand, as in this case, we may perhaps find some way to arrange the affair. I am very intimate with the Regent,(this we had, indeed, observed the night before during our supper); and it is he himself who directed me to make to you this confidential communication." He then added, in an under voice, that all these difficulties were got up against us by the Chinese, against the will of the Thibetian government. We answered the governor of Katchi, that we had not a single manuscript map; and we then gave him, in detail, a statement of all the articles that were in our trunks. " Since they are to be examined to-day, you will judge for yourself whether we are people to be believed." The countenance of the Mussulman brightened. " Your words," he said, " quite reassure me. None of the articles you have described can at all compromise you. Maps are feared in this country—extremely feared, indeed; especially since the affair of a certain Englishman named Moorcroft, who introduced himself into Lha-Ssa, under the pretence of being a Cashmerian. After a sojourn there of twelve years, he departed; but he was murdered on his way to Ladak. Amongst his effects they found a numerous collection of maps and plans, which he had drawn during his stay at Lha-Ssa. This circumstance has made the Chinese authorities very suspicious on this subject. As you do not draw maps, that is all right; I will now go and tell the Regent what I have heard from you."

When the governor of Katchi had left us, we rose, for we had remained in bed, without ceremony, during his long visit. After having offered up our morning prayer, and prepared our hearts to patience and resignation, we ate the breakfast which had been sent to us by order of the Regent. It consisted of a plate of rolls stuffed with sugar and minced meat, and a pot of richly-buttered tea. But we gave the preference to the cakes and dried fruit which the governor of Katchi had presented to us.

Three Lama ushers soon came and announced to us

the order of the day ; viz., that our luggage was to be inspected. We submitted respectfully to the orders of the Thibetian authority, and proceeded to our lodgings, accompanied by a numerous escort all the way. From the palace of the Regent to our habitation we observed great excitement ; they were sweeping the streets, removing the dirt, and decorating the fronts of the houses with large strips of *poulou*, yellow and red. We asked ourselves what all this meant ? for whom were all these demonstrations of honour and respect ? Suddenly we heard behind us loud acclamations, and turning round we saw the Regent, who was advancing, mounted on a magnificent white charger, and surrounded by numerous horsemen. We arrived at our lodgings nearly at the same time with him. We opened the padlock by which the door was fastened, and requested the Regent to honour us by entering the apartments of the French missionaries.

Samdadchiemba, whom we had not seen since our audience with the Chinese ambassador, was there too. He was quite stupified, for he could not comprehend these proceedings. The servants of the Regent, with whom he had passed the night, could not give him any information. We said to him some words of encouragement, giving him to understand that we were not yet quite on the eve of martyrdom.

The Regent took a seat in the middle of our room on a gilded chair, which had been brought from the palace for this purpose, and asked whether what he saw in our room was all we possessed ? " Yes ; that is all we possess ; neither more nor less. These are all our resources for invading Thibet." " There is satire in your words," said the Regent ; " I never fancied you such dangerous people. What is that ? " he added, pointing to a crucifix we had fixed against the wall. " Ah, if you really knew what that was, you would not say that we were not formidable; for by that we design to conquer China, Tartary, and Thibet." The Regent laughed, for he only saw a joke in our words, which yet were so real and serious.

A scribe sat down at the feet of the Regent, and made an inventory of our trunks, clothes and kitchen implements. A lighted lamp was brought, and the Regent took from a small purse which hung from his neck, a golden seal, which was applied to all our baggage. Nothing was omitted; our old boots, the very pins of our travelling tent, were all daubed with red wax and solemnly marked with the seal of the Talé-Lama.

When this long ceremony was completed, the Regent informed us that we muſt now proceed to the tribunal. Some porters were sent for, and found in very brief time. A Lama of the police had only to present himself in the ſtreet and summon, in the name of the law, all the passers by, men, women, and children, to come into the house immediately and assiſt the government. At Lha-Ssa the syſtem of enforced labour is in a most prosperous and flourishing ſtate; the Thibetians coming into it with entire willingness and good grace.

When enough labourers were collected, all our goods were diſtributed among them, and the room was completely cleared, and the procession to the tribunal set out with great pomp. A Thibetian horse soldier, his drawn sword in hand, and his fusil at his side, opened the procession; after him came the troop of porters, marching between two lines of Lama satellites; the Regent, on his white charger, surrounded by a mounted guard of honour, followed our baggage; and laſt, behind the Regent, marched the two poor French missionaries, who had, by way of suite, a no very agreeable crowd of gapers. Our mien was not particularly imposing. Led like malefactors, or, at least, like suspected persons, we could only lower our eyes, and modestly pass through the numerous crowd that thronged on our way. Such a position was, indeed, very painful and humiliating; but the remembrance of our holy Saviour, dragged to the pretorium, through the streets of Jerusalem, was sufficient to mitigate the bitterness with which we were afflicted. We prayed to him to sanctify our humiliations by his own, and to accept them in remembrance of his Passion.

When we arrived at the tribunal, the Chinese ambassador attended by his staff, was already in his place. The Regent addressed him: "You want to examine the effects of these strangers; here they are; examine them. These men are neither rich, nor powerful, as you suppose." There was vexation in the tone of the Regent, and, at bottom, he was naturally enough annoyed at this part of policeman which he had to play. Ki-Chan asked us if we had no more than two trunks. "Only two; everything has been brought here; there remains in our house not a rag, not a bit of paper." "What have you got in your two trunks?" "Here are the keys; open them, empty them, and examine them at your pleasure." Ki-Chan blushed, and moved back. His Chinese delicacy was touched. "Do these trunks belong to me?" he said with emotion. "Have I the right to open them? If anything should be missed afterwards, what would you say?" "You need not be afraid; our religion forbids us rashly to judge our neighbour." "Open your trunks yourselves; I want to know what they contain; it is my duty to do so; but you alone have the right to touch what belongs to you."

We broke the seal of the Talé-Lama, the padlock was removed, and these two trunks, which had been pierced by all eyes for a long time past, were at last opened to the general gaze. We took out the contents, one after another, and displayed them on a large table. First came some French and Latin volumes, then some Chinese and Tartar books, church linen, ornaments, sacred vases, rosaries, crosses, medals, and a magnificent collection of lithographs. All the spectators were lost in contemplation of this small European museum. They opened large eyes, touched each other with the elbow, and smacked their tongues in token of admiration. None of them had ever seen anything so beautiful, so rich, so marvellous. Everything white they considered silver, everything yellow, gold. The faces of all brightened up, and they seemed entirely to forget that we were suspected and dangerous people. The Thibetians put out their tongues and scratched their ears at us; and the Chinese made us the most sentimental bows. Our bags of medals, especially, attracted attention, and it seemed to be anticipated that, before we left the court, we should make a large distribution of these dazzling gold pieces.

The Regent and Ki-Chan, whose minds were elevated above those of the vulgar, and who certainly did not covet our treasure, nevertheless forgot their character as judges. The sight of our beautiful coloured pictures transported them quite out of themselves. The Regent kept his hands joined, and preserved a continuous stare with his mouth open, whilst Ki-Chan, showing off his knowledge, explained how the French were the most distinguished artists in the world. At one time, he said, he knew, at Peking, a French missionary who painted portraits that were quite alarmingly like. He kept his paper concealed in the sleeve of his robe, took the likeness as it were by stealth, and, in a whiff, all was done. Ki-Chan asked us if we had not watches, telescopes, magic-lanterns, etc. etc. We thereupon opened a small box which no one had hitherto remarked, and which contained a microscope. We adjusted its various parts, and no one had eyes but for this singular machine, in pure gold, as they took it to be, and which, certainly, was about to perform wondrous things. Ki-Chan alone knew what a microscope was. He gave an explanation of it to the public, with great pretension and vanity. He then asked us to put some animalculæ on the glass. We looked at his excellency out of the corner of the eye, and then took the microscope to pieces, joint by joint, and put it in the box. "We thought," said we to Ki-Chan, with a formal air, "we thought that we came here to undergo judgment, and not to play a comedy." "What judgment!" exclaimed he, abruptly; "we wished to examine your effects, ascertain really who you were, and that is all." "And the maps: you do not mention them." "Oh, yes—yes! that is the great point; where are your maps?" "Here they are," and we displayed the three maps we had: a map of the world, the two hemispheres upon the projection of Mercator, and a Chinese empire.

The appearance of these maps seemed to the Regent a clap of thunder; the poor man changed colour three or four times in the course of a minute, as if we had shown our death warrant. "It is fortunate for us," said we to Ki-Chan, " that we have met with you in this country. If, by ill luck, you had not been here, we should have been utterly unable to convince the Thibetian authorities that these maps are not our own drawing. But an instructed man like yourself, conversant with European matters, will at once see that these maps are not our own work." Ki-Chan was evidently much flattered by the compliment. "Oh, it is evident," said he, at the first glance, "that these maps are printed. Look here," said he to the Regent; "these maps are not drawn by these men; they were printed in the kingdom of France. You cannot distinguish that, but I have been long used to objects, the productions of the Western Heaven." These words produced a magical effect on the Regent. His face became radiant, and he looked at us with a look of satisfaction, and made a gracious movement with his head, as much as to say, " It is well; you are honest people."

We could not get off without a little geographical lecture. We yielded charitably to the wishes of the Regent and the Chinese ambassador. We indicated with our fingers on the map of Mercator, China, Tartary, and Thibet, and all the other countries of the globe. The Regent was amazed at seeing how far we were from our native land, and what a long journey we had been obliged to make, by land and water, to come and pay him a visit in the capital of Thibet. He regarded us with astonishment, and then raised the thumb of his right hand, saying, " You are men like that," signifying, in the figurative language of the Thibetians : you are men of a superlative stamp. After recognizing the principal points of Thibet, the Regent inquired whereabouts was Calcutta ? "Here," we said, pointing to a little round speck on the borders of the sea. " And Lha-Ssa : where then is Lha-Ssa ? " " Here it is." The eyes and finger of the Regent went from Lha-Ssa to Calcutta, and from Calcutta to Lha-Ssa. " The Pelings of Calcutta are very near our frontiers," said he, making a grimace, and shaking his head. " No matter," he added, " here are the Himalaya mountains."

The course of geography being ended, the maps were folded up again, placed in their respective cases, and we passed on to religious subjects. Ki-Chan had long since become acquainted with these matters. When he was viceroy of the province of Pe-Tche-Li, he had sufficiently persecuted the Christians to have numerous opportunities of making himself familiar with everything connected with the Catholic worship ; and he accordingly now displayed his knowledge. He explained the images, the sacred vases, the ornaments. He even informed the company that in the box of holy oils there was a famous remedy for people at death's door. During all these explanations the Regent was thoughtful and abstracted; his eyes were constantly turned towards a large host-iron. These long pincers, terminating in two large lips, seemed to act powerfully on his imagination. He gave us an inquiring look, seeming to ask us if this frightful implement was not something like an infernal machine. He was only re-assured upon viewing some wafers that we kept in a box, for he then comprehended the use of this strange object.

The worthy Regent was all joyous and triumphant, when he saw that we had nothing in our possession calculated to compromise us. "Well," said he to the Chinese ambassador with a sneer, "what do you think of these men? What must we do with them? These men are Frenchmen, they are ministers of the religion of the Lord of Heaven, they are honest men; we must leave them in peace." These flattering word were received in the saloon with a murmur of approbation, and the two missionaries, said, from the bottom of their hearts, *Deo gratias*.

The porters shouldered our luggage, and we returned to our lodging with undoubtedly greater alacrity and lighter hearts than when we had left it. The news of our reinstatement soon spread through the town, and the Thibetian people hastened from all quarters to congratulate us. They saluted us heartily, and the French name was in everyone's mouth. Thenceforward the white Azaras were entirely forgotten.

When we had refurnished our apartments we gave some *Tchang-Ka* to the porters, in order that they might drink our health in a pot of Thibetian small beer, and appreciate the magnanimity of the French, in not making people work for nothing.

Everyone having gone away, we resumed our accuſtomed solitude, and solitude inducing reflection, we discovered two important things. In the firſt place, that we had not yet dined, and in the second, that our horses were no longer in the ſtable. Whilſt we were considering how to get something quickly cooked, and how to find where our horses were, we saw at the threshold of our door the governor of the Katchi, who relieved us from the double embarrassment. This excellent man, having forseen that our attendance at the court of inquiry would not allow us time to make our pot boil, came, followed by two servants carrying a basket of provisions, with an ovation he had prepared for us. "And our horses—can you give us any information about them? We no longer see them in the court?" "I was going to tell you about them; they have been since yeſterday evening in the Regent's ſtables. During your absence they have felt neither hunger nor thirſt. I heard you say you intended to sell them—is that so?" "Oh, quite so, these animals ruin us; and yet they are so thin, no one will buy them." "The Regent wants to buy them." "The Regent!" "Yes, the Regent himself. Do not smile, it is no jeſt." "How much do you want for them?" "Oh, whatever he likes to give." "Well, then, your horses are purchased," and so saying, the Cashmerian unrolled a small packet he had under his arm, and laid upon the table two silver ingots, weighing ten ounces each." "Here," said he, "is the price of your two horses." We thought our beaſts, worn and attenuated as they were, not worth the money, and we conscientiously said so to the governor of the Katchi; but it was impossible to modify the transaction which had been all settled and concluded beforehand. The Regent made out that our horses, although thin, were of an excellent breed, since they had not succumbed beneath the fatigues of our long journey. Besides, they had, in his eyes, a special value, because they had passed through many countries, and particularly because they had fed on the paſtures of Kounboum, the native place of Tsong-Kaba. Twenty extra ounces of silver in our low purse was almoſt a fortune. We could be generous with it; so, on the spot, we took one of the ingots and placed it on Samdadchiemba's knees. "This is for you," we said, "you will be able with it to clothe yourself in holiday dress from head to foot." Samdadchiemba thanked us coldly and awkwardly; then the muscles of his face became distended, his noſtrils swelled, and his large mouth assumed a smile. At laſt he could not reſtrain his joy; he rose and made his ingot leap in the air twice or thrice, crying, "This is a famous day!" And Samdadchiemba was right. This day, so sadly begun, had been fortunate beyond anything we could have expected. We had now, at Lha-Ssa, an honourable position, and we were to be allowed to labour freely in the propagation of the gospel.

The next day was ſtill more lucky for us than its predecessor; putting, as it were, a climax to our prosperity. In the morning we proceeded, accompanied by the Cashmerian governor, to the palace of the Regent, to whom we desired to express our gratitude for the manifeſtations of intereſt with which he had honoured us. We were received with kindness and cordiality. He told us, in confidence, that the Chinese were jealous of our being at Lha-Ssa; but that we might count on his protection, and reside freely in the country, without any one having a right to interfere with us. "You are very badly lodged," added he; "your room seemed to me dirty, small, and uncomfortable. I would have ſtrangers like you, men come from so great a diſtance, well treated at

Lha-Ssa. In your country of France, do they not treat strangers well?" "They treat them excellently. Oh, if you could but go there some day, you would see how our Emperor would receive you." " Strangers are guests; you must leave your present abode ; I have ordered a suitable lodging to be prepared for you in one of my houses." We accepted this generous offer with grateful thanks. To be lodged comfortably and free of expense was not a thing for men in our position to despise ; but we appreciated, above all, the advantage of residing in one of the Regent's own houses. So signal a favour, such emphatic protection, on the part of the Thibetian authorities, could not but give us with the inhabitants of Lha-Ssa great moral influence, and facilitate our apostolic mission.

On leaving the palace, we proceeded, without loss of time, to visit the house which had been assigned to us ; it was superb—charming. The same evening we effected our removal, and took possession of our new dwelling.

Our first care was to erect in our house a small chapel. We selected the largest and best apartment ; we papered it as neatly as possible, and we then adorned it with holy images. Oh ! how our hearts flowed with joy, when we were at length allowed to pray publicly at the foot of the cross, in the very heart of the capital of Buddhism, which perhaps had never before beheld the sign of our redemption. What a comfort to us to be able, at length, to announce the words of life to the ears of these poor people, sitting for so many ages in the shadow of death. This little chapel was certainly poor, but it was to our minds that hundredfold which God has promised to those who renounce all things for his service. Our hearts were so full, that we thought we had cheaply bought the happiness we now enjoyed, by two years of suffering and tribulation in the desert.

THIBET, AND CHINA

Everyone at Lha-Ssa visited the chapel of the French Lamas ; many, after satisfying themselves with asking us a few explanations as to the meaning of the images they beheld, went away, putting off till some other time further inſtruction in the holy doctrine of Jehovah; but several felt inwardly ſtruck, and seemed to attach a great importance to the ſtudy of the truths we had come to announce. Every day they came to us regularly, they read with attention the summary of the Chriſtian religion, which we had composed at the Lamasery of Kounboum, and entreated us to tell them the " true prayers."

The Thibetians were not the only persons who seemed zealous to ſtudy our holy religion. Among the Chinese, the secretaries of the ambassador Ki-Chan often came to visit us, to hear about the great doctrine of the weſt; one of them, to whom we lent some works written in Tartaro-Mantchou, was convinced of the truth of Chriſtianity and of the necessity of embracing it, but he had not courage enough to make an open profession of faith whilſt he was attached to the embassy ; he wished to wait until he should be free to return to his country. God grant that his good intentions may not vanish.

A physician, a native of the province of Yun-Nan, displayed more courage. This young man, since his arrival at Lha-Ssa, had led so ſtrange a life, that everyone called him the Chinese hermit. He never went out, except to visit his patients, and ordinarily he only visited the poor. The wealthy in vain solicited his attendance ; he disdained to notice their invitations, unless compelled by necessity to obtain some aid, for he never took anything from the poor, to whose service he had devoted himself. The time not absorbed in visiting his patients, he consecrated to ſtudy; he passed, indeed, the greater part of the night over his books. He slept little, and only took, throughout the day, one single meal of barley-meal, never eating meat. You needed, indeed, only to see him to be convinced that he led a hard and self-denying life; his face was extremely pale and thin, and although he was not more than thirty years old, his hair was almoſt entirely white.

One day, he paid us a visit while we were repeating our breviary in our little chapel; he ſtopped short a few ſteps from the door, and awaited in grave silence. A large coloured image, representing the Crucifixion, had no doubt fixed his attention; for, as soon as we had finished our prayers, he asked us abruptly and without ſtaying to make the usual salutations, to explain to him the meaning of that image. When we had answered his queſtion, he crossed his arms upon his cheſt, and without uttering a single word, remained motionless, his eyes fixed upon the image of the Crucifixion; he retained this position for nearly half-an-hour; at length his eyes were filled with tears. He extended his arms towards the Chriſt, fell on his knees, ſtruck the earth thrice with his forehead, and rose, exclaiming, " That is the only Buddha that men ought to worship." He then turned to us, and after making a profound bow, added, " You are my maſters, accept me as your disciple."

All this surprised us greatly. We could not help believing that a powerful impulse of grace had moved his heart. We briefly explained to him the principal points of the Chriſtian religion, and to all we told him, he simply replied with an expression of faith truly aſtonishing, " I believe ! " We presented to him a small crucifix of gilt copper, and asked him if he would accept it. His only answer was an earneſt inclination of the head. As soon as he had the crucifix in his hand, he solicited us to give him a cord, and he immediately hung the cross round his neck; he then asked what prayer he ought to recite before the cross ? "We will lend you," we said, "some Chinese books, wherein you will find explanations of the doctrine, and numerous forms of prayer." "My masters, that is well, but I wish to have a short and easy prayer, which I can learn immediately, and repeat often and everywhere." We taught him to say, "Jesus, Saviour of the world, have mercy on me." For fear of forgetting these words, he wrote them on a piece of paper, which he placed in a small purse, suspended from his girdle; he then went away, assuring us that the recollection of this day would never be effaced from his memory.

This young physician applied himself with ardour to learn the truths of the Christian religion; but the most remarkable circumstance was, that he took no pains to hide the faith he had in his heart. When he came to visit us, or when we met him in the streets, he always had the crucifix glittering on his breast, and he never failed to approach us with the words, "Jesus, Saviour of the world, have mercy on me." It was the form of saluting us which he had adopted.

Whilst we were making efforts to spread the evangelical seed amongst the population of Lha-Ssa, we did not neglect the endeavour to sow the divine seed also in the very palace of the Regent, and this not without the hope of reaping there one day a precious harvest. Since our trial, so to speak, our intercourse with the Regent had become frequent, and even intimate. Almost every evening, when he had finished his labours of ministry, he invited us to partake with him his Thibetian repast, to which he always added for ourselves some dishes cooked in the Chinese fashion. Our conversations generally extended far into the night.

The Regent was a man of extraordinary capacity; of humble extraction, he had raised himself gradually, and by his own merits, to the dignity of First *Kalon*.

This had occurred three years before. Up to that time he had always fulfilled arduous and laborious funcions; he had frequently traversed, in all direcions, the immense regions of Thibet, either to make war or to negociate with the neighbouring ſtates, or to inspec the conduc of the Houtouktou governors of the various provinces. So acive, so busy a life, so apparently incompatible with ſtudy, had not prevented him from acquiring a profound knowledge of Lamanesque works. Everyone concurred in saying that the knowledge of the moſt renowned Lamas was inferior to that of the Regent. The facility with which he conduced public business was matter of especial admiration. One day we were with him when they brought him a great many rolls of paper, dispatches from the provinces; a sort of secretary unrolled them one after the other, and gave them to him to read, bending on one knee. The Regent haſtily ran his eye over them without interrupting the conversation with us. As soon as he had gathered the contents of a dispatch, he took his bamboo ſtyle, and wrote his orders at the bottom of the roll, and thus transaced all his affairs with promptitude, and as if for amusement. We are not competent to judge of the literary merit that was attributed to the Firſt *Kalon*. We can only say that we never saw Thibetian writing as beautiful as his.

The Regent was very fond of engaging in religious discussions, and they moſt frequently formed the subjec of our conversations. At the commencement, he said to us these remarkable words: " All your long journeys you have undertaken solely with a religious objec. You are quite right, for religion is the thing moſt essential to man. I see that the French and the Thibetians have the same view on that subjec. We do not at all resemble the Chinese, who hold the soul of no account; yet your religion is not the same as ours. It is important we should ascertain which is the true one. Let us, then, examine both carefully and sincerely; if yours is right, we will adopt it; how could we refuse to do so? If, on the contrary, ours is the true religion, I believe you will have the good sense to follow it." This arrangement seemed to us excellent; we could not at the time desire better.

We commenced with Christianity. The Regent, always amiable and polished in his conversation with us, said that, as we were his guests, our belief ought to have the honour of priority. We successively reviewed the dogmatical and moral truths. To our great astonishment, the Regent did not seem surprised at anything we said. "Your religion," he incessantly repeated, " is conformable with ours; the truths are the same; we only differ in the explanations. Of what you have seen and heard in Tartary and Thibet, there is, doubtless, much to blame; but you must not forget that the numerous errors and superstitions you may have observed were introduced by ignorant Lamas, and that they are rejected by well-informed Buddhists." He only admitted, between him and us, two points of difference—the origin of the world, and the transmigration of souls. The belief of the Regent, though it here and there seemed to approximate to the Catholic doctrine, nevertheless resulted in a vast pantheism; but he affirmed that we also arrived at the same result, and he did his best to convince us of this.

The Thibetian language, essentially religious and mystic, conveys with much clearness and precision all the ideas respecting the human soul and divinity. Unfortunately we were not sufficiently versed in this language and were compelled, in our conversations with the Regent, to have recourse to the Cashmerian governor to interpret for us; but, as he himself was not very skilful in rendering metaphysical ideas into Chinese, it was often difficult to understand each other. One day, the Regent said to us, " The truth is clear in itself, but if you envelope it in obscure words, one cannot perceive it. So long as we are obliged to communicate in Chinese, it will be impossible to make ourselves intelligible to each other. We shall never be able to discuss the matter to advantage till you speak the Thibetian language fluently." We quite concurred in the justice of this observation. We replied to the Regent, that the study of the Thibetian tongue was a great object of solicitude with us, and that we laboured hard at it every day. " If you like," said he, " I will facilitate your acquisition of it." And thereupon he called a servant and said to him a few words which we did not understand.

A youth, elegantly dressed, immediately came, and saluted us with much grace. " This is my nephew," said the Regent ; " I present him to you as at once tutor and pupil ; he will pass the whole day with you, and you will thus have the opportunity of practising the Thibetian language ; in return, you will give him some lessons in Chinese and Mantchou." We gratefully adopted the proposition, and were enabled, by this means, to make rapid progress in the language of the country. The Regent was very fond of talking about France, during our long visits; he asked us a number of questions about the manners, customs, and productions of our country. All we told him of the steam-boats, the railways, the balloons, gas, telegraphs, the daguerreotype, our industrial productions, completely amazed him, and gave him an immense idea of the grandeur and power of France. One day when we were talking to him of observatories and astronomical instruments, he asked if we would allow him to examine closely the strange and curious machine which we kept in a box : he meant the microscope. As we were in a better humour and infinitely more amiable than when the officers inspected our property, we readily satisfied the curiosity of the Regent. One of us ran to our residence, and returned immediately with the wonderful instrument. While adjusting, we tried to give our auditor, as well as we could, some notions of optics, but seeing that the theory did not excite much enthusiasm, we proceeded at once to the practice. We asked if one of the company would be so good as to procure us a louse. The article was easier to find than a butterfly. A noble Lama, secretary to his excellency the First *Kalon*, had merely to put his hand under his silk dress to his armpit, and an extremely vigorous louse was at our disposition. We seized it by the sides with our nippers, but the Lama forthwith opposed this proceeding, and insisted upon putting a stop to the experiment, on the ground that we were going to cause the death of a living being. "Do not be afraid," we said, " your louse is only taken by the skin; besides, he seems strong enough to get over the pressure, even were it greater." The Regent, who, as we have before mentioned, had religious theories superior to those of the common herd, told the Lama to be silent, and to allow us to proceed. We continued the experiment, and fixed in the glass the poor little beast, that struggled, with all its might, at the extremity of the nippers. We then requested the Regent to apply his right eye, shutting his left, to the glass at the top of the machine. " Tsong-Kaba ! " exclaimed the Regent, " the louse is as big as a rat." After looking at it for a moment, he raised his head and hid his face with both hands, saying, it was horrible to look at. He tried to dissuade the others from examining it; but his influence failed to make any impression. Everyone, in his turn, looked through the microscope, and started back with cries of horror. The Lama secretary, seeing that his little animal scarcely moved, advanced a claim in its favour. We removed the nippers, and let the louse fall into the hands of its owner. But, alas! the poor victim did not move. The Regent said, laughingly, to his secretary, "I think your louse is unwell; go and see if you can get it to take some physic, otherwise it will not recover."

No one wishing to see other living creatures, we continued the entertainment by passing a small collection of microscopical pictures before the eyes of the spectators. Everyone was charmed, and exclaimed with admiration, "What prodigious capacity the French have!" The Regent told us, "Your railways and your aerial ships no longer astonish me so much; men who can invent such a machine as that, are capable of anything."

The First *Kalon* was so delighted with the productions of our country, that he took a fancy to study the French language. One evening we brought him, in accordance with his wish, a French alphabet, each letter of which had the pronunciation written beneath it in Thibetian characters. He ran his eye over it, and when we proposed to give him some explanations, he replied, that they were not necessary, as what we had written was quite clear.

The next day, as soon as we appeared in his presence, he asked us what was the name of our emperor. "Our emperor is called Louis Philippe." "Louis Philippe! Louis Philippe! very well." He then took his style, and began to write. An instant afterwards, he gave us a piece of paper, on which was written, in very well formed characters, Louy-Filipe.

During the brief period of our prosperity at Lha-Ssa, we had also tolerably intimate communication with the Chinese ambassador Ki-Chan. He sent for us twice or thrice, to talk politics, or, as the Chinese phrase it, to speak idle words. We were much surprised to find him so intimately acquainted with the affairs of Europe. He spoke a good deal about the English and Queen Victoria. "It appears," said he, "that this woman has great abilities; but her husband, in my opinion, plays a very ridiculous part; she does not let him meddle with anything. She laid out for him a magnificent garden full of fruit-trees and flowers of all sorts, and there he is always shut up, passing his time walking about. They say that in Europe there are other countries where women rule. Is it so? Are their husbands also shut up in gardens? Have you in the kingdom of France any such usage?" "No, in France the women are in the gardens, and the men in the State." "That is right, otherwise all is disorder."

Ki-Chan inquired about Palmerston, and whether he was still at the head of foreign affairs. "And Ilu [Ilü],[1] what has become of him? Do you know him?" "He was recalled; your fall involved his." "That is a pity. Ilu had an excellent heart, but he was devoid of prompt resolution. Has he been put to death or banished?" "Neither the one nor the other. In Europe they do not proceed to such extremities as you at Peking." "Ay, truly; your Mandarins are more fortunate than we: your government is better than ours; our Emperor cannot know everything, and yet he judges everything, and no one may presume to object. Our Emperor tells us, That is white; we prostrate ourselves and answer, Yes, that is white; he then points to the same thing, and says, That is black; we again prostrate ourselves and reply, Yes, that is black." "But if you were to say that a thing cannot be at once white and black?" "The Emperor would perhaps say to a person who exhibited such courage, You are right; but, at the same time, he would have him strangled or beheaded.

[1] The Chinese name for Mr. Elliot, the English Plenipotentiary at Canton, at the commencement of the Anglo-Chinese war.

Oh, we have not like you a general assembly of the chiefs (Tchoung-Teou-Y [Chung-t'ou-i]; so Ki-Chan designated the Chamber of Deputies). If your Emperor wished to act contrary to justice, your Tchoung-Teou-Y would be there to stop him."

Ki-Chan related to us the strange manner in which the great affair of the English in 1839 had been managed at Peking. The Emperor convoked the eight *Tchoung-Tang* who constituted his privy council, and spoke to them of the events that had occurred in the south. He told them that some adventurers from the western seas had manifested themselves rebellious and insubordinate; that they must be taken and punished severely, in order to give an example to all who might be tempted to imitate their misconduct. After thus stating his opinion, the Emperor asked the advice of his council. The four Mantchou *Tchoung-Tang* prostrated themselves and said, " *Tché, tché, tché, Tchou-Dze-Ti, Fan-Fou*" [*Ché, ché, chu-tzu-ti, fen-fu*]. (Yes, yes, yes: such is the command of the master.) The four Chinese *Tchoung-Tang* prostrated themselves in their turn, and said, " *Ché, ché, ché, Hoang-Chang-Ti, Tien-Ngen*" [*Shih, shih, shih, Hoang-shang-ti t'ien-ên*]. (Yes, yes, yes; it is the celestial benefit of the Emperor.) After this, nothing further had to be said, and the council was dismissed. This anecdote is perfectly authentic, for Ki-Chan is one of the eight *Tchoung-Tang* of the empire. He added that, for his part, he was persuaded that the Chinese were incapable of contending against the Europeans, unless they altered their weapons and changed their old habits; but that he should take care not to say so to the Emperor, because, besides that the suggestion would be futile in itself, it would perhaps cost him his life.

Our frequent conferences with the Chinese ambassador, the Regent, and the Cashmerian governor,

THIBET, AND CHINA

contributed not a little to secure for us the confidence and consideration of the inhabitants of Lha-Ssa. On seeing the number of those who came to visit us, and to be inſtruᶜted in our holy religion, augment from day to day, we felt our hopes enlarge and our courage increase. Yet, amidſt these consolations, one thought conſtantly vexed us ; it was that we could not present to the Thibetians the inspiring speᶜtacle of the pompous and touching feſtivals of Catholicism. We were convinced that the beauty of our ceremonies would have a powerful influence over the minds of these people, so eager after all that appertains to external worship.

The Thibetians, as we have already observed, are eminently religious ; but, with the exception of a few contemplative Lamas, who withdraw to the summits of mountains and pass their lives in the hollows of rocks, they are very little disposed to myſticism. Inſtead of confining their devotion within their inner hearts, they like, on the contrary, display by outward aᶜts ; and accordingly pilgrimages, noisy ceremonies in the Lamaseries, proſtrations on the tops of their houses, are praᶜtices extremely to their taſte. They always have in their hands the Buddhiſt rosary, turning and twiſting it, and incessantly murmur prayers, even when they are engaged in business.

There exiſts at Lha-Ssa a very touching cuſtom, and which we felt a sort of jealousy at finding among infidels. In the evening, juſt as the day is verging on its decline, all the Thibetians ſtay business, and meet together, men, women and children, according to their sex and age, in the principal parts of the town, and in the public squares. As soon as groups are formed, everyone kneels down, and they begin slowly and in undertones to chant prayers.

The religious concerts produced by these numerous assemblages create throughout the town an immense solemn harmony, which operates forcibly on the soul. The first time we witnessed this spectacle, we could not help drawing a painful comparison between this pagan town, where all prayed together, and the cities of Europe, where people would blush to make the sign of the cross in public. The prayer which the Thibetans chant in these evening assemblies, varies according to the seasons of the year; that, on the contrary, which they repeat on their rosary, is always the same and only consists of six syllables—*Om mani padme houm* [*Om mani padme hûm*]. This formula, which the Buddhists call, by abbreviation, the *mani*, is not only in everyone's mouth, but you see it written everywhere about, in the streets, in the squares, and in houses. On all the flags that float above the doors, or from the summit of the public edifices, there is always a *mani* printed in Landza [Lantsa], Tartar and Thibetian characters. Certain rich and zealous Buddhists maintain, at their own expense, companies of Lama sculptors, whose business it is to diffuse the *mani*. These singular missionaries, travel, chisel and mallet in hand, over hill, dale and desert, engraving the sacred formula upon the stones and rocks.

According to the opinion of the celebrated orientalist Klaproth, *Om mani padme houm* is merely the Thibetian transcription of a Sanscrit formula brought from India to Thibet. Towards the middle of the seventh century of our era, the famous Hindoo Tonmi-Sambhodha [Tonmi-Sambhota] introduced writing into Thibet; but as the Landza alphabet, which he had at first adopted, seemed to King Srong-Bdzan-Gombo [Srong-btsan-sgam-po] too complex and too difficult to learn, he invited the learned personage to draw up an easier writing, better adapted to the Thibetian tongue. Accordingly, Tonmi-Sambhodha shut himself up for awhile, and composed the Thibetian writing now in use, and which is merely a modification of Sanscrit characters. He also initiated the king into the mysteries of Buddhism, and communicated to him the sacred formula *Om mani padme houm*, which spread rapidly through all the countries of Thibet and Mongolia.

This formula has, in the Sanscrit language, a distinct and complete meaning, which cannot be traced in the Thibetian idiom. *Om* is, among the Hindoos, the mystic name of the Divinity, with which all their prayers begin. It is composed of A, the name of Vishnu; of O, that of Siva; and of M, that of Brahma. This mystic particle is also equivalent to the interjection O, and expresses a profound religious conviction; it is, as it were, a formula of the act of faith; *mani* signifies a gem, a precious thing; *padma* the lotus; *padme*, the vocative of the same word. Lastly, *houm* is a particle expressing a wish, a desire, and is equivalent to our Amen. The literal sense, then, of this phrase is this:

> Om mani padme houm
> O the gem in the lotus, Amen.

The Buddhists of Thibet and Mongolia have not been content with this clear and precise meaning, and have tortured their imaginations in their endeavours to find a mystic interpretation of each of the six syllables composing the sentence.

They have written an infinity of voluminous books, wherein they have piled one extravagance on another, to explain their famous *mani*. The Lamas are wont to say that the doctrine contained in these marvellous words is immense, and that the whole life of a man is insufficient to measure its breadth and depth. We were anxious to know what the Regent thought of this formula. This is what he said on the subject: " Living beings, in Thibetian *semdchan* [*sems-chan*] and in Mongol *amitan,* are divided into six classes—angels, demons, men, quadrupeds, birds, and reptiles.[1] These six classes of living beings correspond to the six syllables of the formula *Om mani padme houm.* Living beings, by continual transformations, and according to their merit or demerit, pass about in these six classes until they have attained the apex of perfection, when they are absorbed and lost in the grand essence of Buddha ; that is to say, in the eternal and universal soul, whence emanate all souls, and wherein all souls, after their temporary evolutions, are destined to meet and become fused.

" Living beings have, according to the class to which they belong, particular means of sanctifying themselves, of rising to a superior class, of obtaining perfection, and arriving, in process of time, at the period of their absorption. Men who repeat very frequently and devotedly *Om mani padme houm,* escape falling, after death, into the six classes of animate creatures corresponding to the six syllables of the formula, and obtain the plenitude of being by their absorption into the eternal and universal soul of Buddha."

We know not whether this explanation, which was given to us by the Regent himself, is generally adopted by the learned Buddhists of Thibet and Mongolia. We may, however, observe, as it appears to us, that it bears some analogy with the literal meaning : Oh, the gem in the lotus, Amen. The gem being the emblem of perfection, and the lotus of Buddha, it may perhaps be considered that these words express the desire to acquire perfection in order to be united with Buddha, to be absorbed in the universal soul. The symbolic formula, Oh, the gem in the lotus, Amen, might then be paraphrased thus : Oh, may I obtain perfection, and be absorbed in Buddha, Amen.

[1] The class of reptiles comprehends fish, mollusks, and all animals that are neither quadrupeds nor birds.

THIBET, AND CHINA

According to the explanation of the Regent, the *mani* would be, as it were, the summary of a vaſt pantheism, the basis of the whole belief of the Buddhiſts. The learned Lamas say that Buddha is the necessary, the independent Being, the Beginning and End of all things. The earth, the ſtars, mankind, everything that exiſts is a partial and temporary manifeſtation of Buddha. Everything was created by Buddha; in this sense, that everything proceeds from him, as light proceeds from the sun. All creatures sprung from Buddha have had a beginning, and will have an end; but in the same way that they have necessarily sprung from the universal essence, they will necessarily return to it. It is as the rivers and the torrents produced by the waters of the sea, and which, after a course, more or less long, proceed again to lose themselves in its immensity. So Buddha is eternal; his manifeſtations also are eternal; but in this sense, that there have been manifeſtations, and that there always will be manifeſtations, though taken separately, they have a beginning and an end.

Without inquiring too nicely whether this agrees or not with what precedes, the Buddhiſts admit, besides, an unlimited number of divine incarnations. They say that Buddha assumes a human body, and comes to dwell among men, in order to aid them in acquiring perfeċtion and to facilitate for them their reunion with the universal soul. These Living Buddhas conſtitute the numerous class of *Chaberons*, whom we have frequently noticed before. The moſt celebrated Living Buddhas are—at Lha-Ssa, the Talé-Lama; at Djachi-Loumbo, the Bandchan-Remboutchi; at the Grand Kouren, the Guison-Tamba; at Peking, the Tchang-Kia-Fo [Chang-chia-Fo (Chang skya)], a sort of grand almoner of the imperial court; and in the country of the Ssamba [Samba], at the foot of the Himalaya mountains, the Sa-Dcha-Fo

[Sa-skya-Fo]. This last has, they say, a somewhat singular mission. He prays night and day, in order to get the snow to fall continuously on the summit of the Himalaya; for, according to a Thibetian tradition, there exists behind these lofty mountains a savage and cruel people, who only await the subsidence of the snow to come over and massacre the Thibetian tribes, and to take possession of the country.

Although all the *Chaberons* are, without distinction, Living Buddhas, there is, nevertheless, among them, a hierarchy, of which the Talé-Lama is the head. All the rest acknowledge, or ought to acknowledge his supremacy. The present Talé-Lama, as we have said, is a child of nine years old, and he has now for six years occupied the palace of the Buddha-La. He is a Si-Fan by birth, and was taken from a poor and obscure family of the principality of Ming-Tchen-Tou-Sse [Ming-chen-t'u-ssü].

When the Talé-Lama dies, or to speak Buddhickly, when he has laid aside his human envelope, they proceed to the election of his successor, in the following manner: Prayers are directed to be offered up, and fasts to be performed in all the Lamaseries. The inhabitants of Lha-Ssa especially, as being the most interested in the affair, redouble their zeal and devotion. Everyone goes a pilgrimage round the Buddha-La and the *City of Spirits*. The *Tchu-Kors* are perpetually turning in everybody's hands, the sacred formula of the *mani* re-echoes day and night in all the streets of the town and perfumes are burnt in profusion everywhere. Those who think they possess the Talé-Lama in their family give information of the belief to the authorities at Lha-Ssa, in order that there may be established, in the children so indicated, their quality of *Chaberons*. In order to be able to proceed to the election of the Talé-Lama, there must

THIBET, AND CHINA

be discovered three *Chaberons*, authentically recognized as such. The candidates come to Lha-Ssa, and the Houtouktous of the Lamanesque states meet in assembly. They shut themselves up in a temple of the Buddha-La, and pass six days in retirement, fasting and praying. On the seventh day, they take a golden urn, containing three fish, likewise of gold, upon which are engraved the names of the three little candidates for the functions of the divinity of the Buddha-La. They shake the urn, the eldest of the Houtouktous draws out a fish, and the child whose name is thus designated by lot is immediately proclaimed Talé-Lama. He is then conducted, in great pomp, to [through] the street[s] of the City of Spirits, everyone devoutly prostrating himself on his passage, and is placed in his sanctuary.

The two *Chaberons* in swaddling clothes, who have contested for the place of Talé-Lama, are carried back by their nurses to their respective families; but to compensate them for not having succeeded, government makes them a present of 500 ounces of silver.

The Talé-Lama is venerated by the Thibetians and the Mongols like a divinity. The influence he exercises over the Buddhist population is truly astonishing; but still it is going too far to say that his excrements are respectfully collected, and made into amulets which devotees enclose in pouches and carry round their necks. It is equally untrue that the Talé-Lama has his arms and head encircled with serpents, in order to strike the imagination of his worshippers. These assertions, which we read in some geographies, are entirely without foundation. During our stay at Lha-Ssa, we asked a good many question on this point, and everyone laughed in our faces. Unless it could be made out that, from the Regent to our *argol* merchant, all conspired to hide the truth from us, it must be admitted that the narratives, which have given circulation to such fables, were written with but very little caution.

It was not possible for us to get a sight of the Talé-Lama; not that there is any great difficulty made in admitting the curious, or devotees, to see him, but we were prevented by a rather singular circumstance. The Regent had promised to take us to the Buddha-La, and we were upon the point of fulfilling this noble visit, when all of a sudden an alarm was started that we should give the Talé-Lama the small-pox. This malady had, in fact, just manifested itself at Lha-Ssa, and the people declared that it had been brought from Peking by the great caravan which arrived a few days before. As we had formed part of that caravan, we were asked whether it would not be better to postpone our visit, in order that we might not expose the Talé-Lama to the risk of catching the disease. The proposition was too reasonable to admit of our making any objection.

The fear which the Thibetians have of the small-pox is something inconceivable. They never mention its name, even, without a sort of stupor, as though they were speaking of the greatest scourge that could by possibility desolate mankind. And, indeed, there is no year in which this malady does not make fearful ravages at Lha-Ssa, and the only remedy which has hitherto suggested itself to the government as a preservative for the population against this fearful epidemic, is to proscribe the wretched families who are seized with it. As soon as the small-pox has declared itself in a house, all the inhabitants must dislodge, and repair, whether they will or not, far from the city to the summits of the mountains, or the depths of the valleys. No one may hold any communication whatever with the poor wretches, who soon die of hunger and privation, or become the prey of wild beasts. We did not fail to make the Regent acquainted with the

THIBET, AND CHINA

precious means used by the European nations to preserve themselves from the disorder; and one of the chief circumstances which procured for us the goodwill and protection of the Regent was his hope that we might one day introduce vaccination into Thibet. The missionary who should be fortunate enough to endow the Thibetians with so invaluable a blessing, would assuredly acquire over their minds an influence capable of competing with that of the Talé-Lama itself. The introduction of vaccination into Thibet by the missionaries would, not improbably, be the signal of the downfall of Lamanism, and of the establishment of the Christian religion among these infidel tribes.

People afflicted with the itch and leprosy are numerous at Lha-Ssa. These cutaneous diseases are engendered by the want of cleanliness, more peculiarly prevalent among the lower classes of the population. Cases of hydrophobia are not unfrequent among the Thibetians; and one is only surprised that this horrible malady does not commit greater ravages, when one bears in mind the terrible multitudes of gaunt, famishing dogs that are always prowling about the streets of Lha-Ssa. These animals, in fact, are so numerous in that city that the Chinese contemptuously say that the three great products of the capital of Thibet, are Lamas, women, and dogs—*Lama, Ya-Teou [Ya-t'ou], Keou [kou]*.

This marvellous infinitude of dogs arises from the extreme respect which the Thibetians have for these animals, and the use to which they apply them in burying the dead. There are four different species of sepulture practised in Thibet; the first, combustion; the second, immersion in the rivers and lakes; the third, exposure on the summit of mountains; and the fourth, which is considered the most complimentary of all, consists in cutting the dead body in pieces and giving these to be eaten by the dogs. The laſt method is by far the moſt popular. The poor have only as their mausoleum the common vagabond dogs of the locality; but the more diſtinguished defunct are treated with greater ceremony. In all the Lamaseries a number of dogs are kept *ad hoc*, and within them the rich Thibetians are buried.[1]

---

[1] Strabo, speaking of the cuſtoms of the nomadic Scythians, as retained among the Sogdians and Bactrians, writes : " In the capital of Bactria they breed dogs to which they give a special name, which name, rendered into our language, means buriers. The business of these dogs is to eat up all persons who are beginning to fall into decay from old age or sickness. Hence it is that no tomb is visible in the suburbs of the town, while the town itself is all filled with human bones. It is said that Alexander abolished this cuſtom."

Cicero attributes the same cuſtom to the Hyrcanians, in his *Tusculan Queſtions*, (Lib, i. § 45): " In Hyrcania plebs publicos alit canes ; optimates, domesticos. Nobile autem genus canum illud scimus esse. Sed pro sua quisque facultate parat, à quibus lanietur : eamque optimam illi esse censent sepulturam."

Juſtin also says of the Parthians : " Sepultura vulgò aut avium aut canum aniatus eſt. Nuda demum ossa terrâ obruunt."

CHAPTER VII

WE have already referred to the travels of Moorcroft in Thibet, in noticing the excessive fear with which the designers and makers of geographical charts inspire the Thibetian government. One day, the governor of the Cashmerians brought to us one of his fellow countrymen, named Nisan, who had been for a long time the servant of Moorcroft at Lha-Ssa. He talked to us at some length about his old mafter, and the details he gave us confirmed all that had already been related to us. The adventures of this English traveller appearing to us too singular to be passed over wholly in silence, we have thought proper to give a short review of them.

According to the ftatements collected in the capital of Thibet itself, Moorcroft arrived from Ladak at Lha-Ssa in the year 1826; he wore the Mussulman dress, and spoke the Farsie [Persian] language expressing himself in that idiom with so much facility that the Cashmerians of Lha-Ssa took him for one of their countrymen. He hired a house in the town, where he lived for twelve years with his servant Nisan, whom he had brought from Ladak, and who himself thought that his mafter was a Cashmerian. Moorcroft had purchased a few herds of goats and oxen, which he had confided to the care of some Thibetian shepherds, who dwelt in the gorges of the mountains about Lha-Ssa. Under the pretext of inspecting his herds, the feigned Mussulman went freely about the country, making drawings and preparing his geographical charts. It is said that never having learnt the Thibetian language, he abstained from holding direct communication with the people of the country. At laſt, having dwelt for twelve years at Lha-Ssa, Moorcroft took his way back to Ladak, but whilſt he was in the province of Ngari, he was attacked by a troop of brigands who assassinated him. The perpetrators of this murder were pursued and arreſted by the Thibetian government, who recovered a portion of the property of the English traveller, among which was a collection of geographical designs and charts. It was only then, and upon sight of these objects, that the authorities of Lha-Ssa found out that Moorcroft was an Englishman.

Before separating from his servant, Moorcroft had given him a note, telling him to show it to the inhabitants of Calcutta if he ever went to that city, and that it would suffice to make his fortune. It was doubtless a letter of recommendation. The seizure of the effects of Moorcroft created such a diſturbance in Thibet, that Nisan, afraid of being compromised, deſtroyed his letter of recommendation. He told us himself that this note was written in characters exactly similar to ours.

The facts we have here related, we derive from the Regent, from the Cashmerian governor, from Nisan, and from several other inhabitants of Lha-Ssa. Before reaching this town, we had never heard of Moorcroft ; it was there we firſt learned the name of this English traveller. From what we have ſtated, it may be considered eſtablished that Moorcroft really went to Lha-Ssa in 1826, that he resided there for twelve years, and that he was afterwards assassinated on the road to Ladak from Lha-Ssa.

Let us turn now, however, to other information, extremely discrepant from that which was given us in the capital of Thibet. According to the *Universal Geography* of Charles Ritter,[1] Moorcroft made firſt a journey in 1812, which laſted two months ; he was

[1] *Asia*, vol. v. p. 800, German edition, 1833-1837.

THIBET, AND CHINA

afterwards directed by the Company to procure horses from Turkestan, wherewith to improve the breed of horses in India. For this purpose he undertook a second journey in November, 1819 ; he got as far as Ladak, where he remained two years. In the month of October, 1822, he left that town for Cashmere, and on the 25th of August, 1825, died at Andkou, on the way from Herat to Balk [Balkh]. The death of Moorcroft, at the date and place stated by Charles Ritter, was announced by his fellow-traveller, M. Tribeck, in a letter dated Balk, 6th September, 1825, and addressed to Captain Wade, the resident at Loudiana [Ludhiana].[1]

We confess that we cannot possibly reconcile such opposite statements. If Moorcroft was really not at Lha-Ssa, how is it that he was so well known there, and that the people there speak of his residence among them in terms so precise ? What interest could the Thibetians have in forging such a tale ? On the other hand, if Moorcroft was at Lha-Ssa, how can we explain that letter of M. Tribeck, which announces that his fellow-traveller died in 1825, exactly at the time, when, according to the other hypothesis, he was on his way to the capital of Thibet ?

Without pretending to reconcile these contradictions, we will cite a fact which concerns ourselves, and which will, perhaps, seem to bear some relation to the affair of Moorcroft. Some time after our arrival at Macao, we read the following article in the *Bengal Catholic Herald*,[2] a journal printed at Calcutta. " Canton, the 12th September. The French missionaries of our city have lately received the news of the deplorable death of two fathers of

---

[1] See *Asiatic Journal of London*, vol. xxi, p. 786, and vol. xxii, p. 596. A notice of Moorcroft's manuscripts was inserted in the *Journal of the Geographical Society of London*, 1831.

[2] Vol. xii, No. 9, p. 120.

their mission in Mongol-Tartary." After a cursory sketch of the Mongol-Chinese territory, the writer of the article proceeds thus :—" A French Lazarist, called Huc, arrived, about three years ago, amongst some Chinese families, who were established in the valley of Black Waters, about two hundred leagues journey from the Great Wall. Another Lazarist, whose name is unknown to me,[1] joined him in the plan of forming a mission among the Mongol Buddhists. They studied the Mongol language with the Lamas of the neighbouring Lamaseries. It seems that they were taken for foreign Lamas, and were treated in a friendly manner, particularly by the Buddhists, who are very ignorant, and who mistook the Latin of their breviaries for Sanscrit, which they do not understand, but for which they have a secret veneration, because the rites of their religious books, in Mongol, translated from the Sanscrit, are printed in red ink.

" When the missionaries thought themselves sufficiently learned in the language, they advanced into the interior, with the intention of commencing their work of conversion. From that time only uncertain rumours were heard about them, but in May last, from the interior of Mongol-Tartary, the news came that they had been tied to horses' tails and so dragged to death. The real causes of this event are not as yet known."

Whilst they were announcing our death so positively, we were approaching the termination of our long journey, and were close upon Canton, happily enjoying a health fully capable of refuting the news thus propagated concerning us. But if, by chance, we had perished among the mountains of Thibet, if we had been murdered there, the world would have remained convinced that we had been tied to horses' tails and had died in Mongolia. It would probably

[1] M. Gabet.

have never been believed that we had reached the capital of Thibet; and if, at some later time, some European traveller had visited Lha-Ssa and had been informed of our abode in that town, it would have been, perhaps, juſt as difficult to reconcile these ſtatements as those respecting Moorcroft. Although the death of the English traveller is a matter which we cannot clear up, we did not conceive that we could omit to say what we knew of it, without pretending to invalidate, by the accounts collected at Lha-Ssa, the documents set forth in the scientific London journals.

We were scarcely a month at Lha-Ssa before the numerous inhabitants of this town grew accuſtomed to speak with respect and admiration of the holy doctrine of Jehovah and of the great kingdom of France. The peace and tranquillity we enjoyed, the diſtinguished protection which the Thibetian government extended to us, the sympathy with which the people seemed to surround us, all inspired us with the hope, that, by the aid of God, we might lay in the very capital of Buddhism the foundation of a mission, the influence of which would soon extend itself among the nomad tribes of Mongolia. The moment seemed to have come when the Tartar pilgrims might at length learn, at Lha-Ssa, the only doctrine which can save men's souls, and civilize nations.

As soon as we considered our position at Lha-Ssa confirmed, we turned our thoughts to the means of renewing our communications with Europe in the speedieſt manner. The path of the desert was impracticable. We had, certainly, managed to cross once, and as it were by a miracle, these ſteppes infeſted by brigands and wild beaſts; but it was out of the queſtion to think of organizing a service of couriers along that frightful route. Supposing, besides, the fulleſt security that could be desired, the mere length of the journey was a thing to make one shudder. The road by India seemed alone practicable. From Lha-Ssa to the first English station is not quite a month's journey. By establishing one correspondent on the other side of the Himalaya mountains, and one at Calcutta, our communication with France would become, if not prompt and easy, at all events feasible. As this plan could only be put into execution with the consent of the Thibetian government, we communicated it to the Regent, who immediately entered into our views, and it was agreed that in the summer M. Gabet should undertake the journey to Calcutta, with a Thibetian escort, who were to accompany him as far as Boutan.

Such were the plans we were forming for the establishment of a mission at Lha-Ssa: but at this very moment the enemy to all good was hard at work to ruin our projects, and to remove us from a country which he seems to have chosen for the seat of his empire. Having heard here and there words of evil auspice, we comprehended that the Chinese ambassador was secretly plotting our expulsion from Thibet. The vague rumour of this persecution had, in fact, nothing about it to surprise us. From the outset, we had foreseen that if difficulties assailed us, they would emanate from the Chinese Mandarins. Ki-Chan, in fact, could not bear to see the Thibetian government receive with so much favour a religion and strangers whom the absurd prejudices of China have so long driven from her frontiers. Christianity and the French name excited too forcibly the sympathy of the people of Lha-Ssa, not to arouse Chinese jealousy. An agent of the court of Peking could not, without anger, reflect on the popularity which strangers enjoyed in Thibet, and on the influence which they might one day exercise in a country which China has every interest in keeping under her dominion. It was determined, therefore, that the preachers of the religion of the Lord of Heaven should be driven from Lha-Ssa.

One day, the ambassador, Ki-Chan, sent for us, and after sundry attempts at cajolery, ended by saying that Thibet was too cold, too poor a country for us, and that we had better think of returning to our kingdom of France. Ki-Chan addressed these words to us, with a sort of indifferent, careless manner, as though he supposed there could be no sort of objection to them. We asked him if, in speaking thus, he proposed to us advice or command. "Both the one and the other," he replied, coldly. "Since it is so, we have first to thank you for the interest which you seem to have in our welfare, in telling us that this country is cold and miserable. But you must know, that men such as we do not regard the goods and conveniences of this world; were it not so, we should have remained in our own kingdom of France. For know, there is not anywhere a country comparable with our own. As for the imperative portion of your words, this is our answer: 'Admitted into Thibet by the local authority, we recognize no right in you, or in any other person, to disturb our abode here.'" "How! you who are strangers, presume still to remain here?" "Yes, we are strangers, but we know that the laws of Thibet are not like those of China. The Peboun, the Katchi, the Mongols, are strangers like us, and yet they are permitted to live here in peace; no one disturbs them. What, then, is the meaning of this arbitrary proceeding of yours, in ordering Frenchmen from a country open to all people? If foreigners are to quit Lha-Ssa, why do you stay here? Does not your title of *Kin-Tchai* (ambassador) distinctly announce that you yourself are but a foreigner here?" At these words, Ki-Chan bounded on his velvet cushion. "I a foreigner!" cried he, "a foreigner! I, who bear the authority of the Grand Emperor, who, only a few months' since, condemned and exiled the Nomekhan." "We are acquainted with that affair. There is this difference between the Nomekhan and us, that the Nomekhan came from Kan-Sou, a province of the empire, and we come from France, where your Grand Emperor is nobody; and that the Nomekhan assassinated three Talé-Lamas, while we have done no injury to any man. Have we any other aim than to make known to men the true God, and to teach them the way to save their souls?" "Ay, as I have already said to you, I believe you to be honeſt people; but then the religion you preach has been declared wicked, and prohibited by our Grand Emperor." "To these words, we can only reply thus: The religion of the Lord of Heaven does not need the sanction of your Emperor to make it a holy religion, any more than we, of its mission, need it to come and preach in Thibet." The Chinese ambassador did not think it expedient to continue this discussion; he drily dismissed us, declaring that we might reſt assured he would make us quit Thibet. We haſtened to the Regent, in order to acquaint him with the melancholy interview we had had with Ki-Chan. The chief *Kalon* had been made aware of the projects of persecution which the Chinese Mandarins were hatching againſt us. He endeavoured to reassure us, and told us that, protecting in the country thousands of ſtrangers, he was powerful enough to give us the protection which the Thibetian government extended to all. "Besides," added he, "even though our laws did prohibit ſtrangers from entering our country, those laws could not affect you. Religious persons, men of prayer, belonging to all countries, are ſtrangers nowhere; such is the doctrine taught by our holy books. It is written: 'The yellow goat has no country, the Lama no family.' Lha-Ssa being the peculiar assembling-place and abode

THIBET, AND CHINA

of men of prayer, that title of itself should always secure for you liberty and protection." This opinion of the Buddhists, which constitutes a religious man a cosmopolite, is not merely a mystic idea written in books, but we have found it recognized in the manners and customs of the Lamaseries; when a man has had his head shaved, and assumes the religious habit, he renounces his former name to take a new one. If you ask a Lama of what country he is, he replies, " I have no country, but I pass my time in such a Lamasery." This manner of thinking and acting is even admitted in China, amongst the bonzes and other classes of religionists, who are called by the generic name of *Tchou-Kia-Jin* [*ch'u-chia-jen*], "a man who has left his family."

There was, respecting us, a controversy of several days' duration, between the Thibetian government and the Chinese ambassador. Ki-Chan, in order to insure better success to his aims, assumed the character of defender of the Talé-Lama. This was his argument: Sent to Lha-Ssa by his Emperor, to protect the Living Buddha, it was his duty to remove from him whatever was calculated to injure him. Certain preachers of the religion of the Lord of Heaven, animated, no doubt, by excellent intentions, were propagating a doctrine which, in the end, tended to destroy the authority and power of the Talé-Lama. Their avowed purpose was to substitute their religious belief for Buddhism, and to convert all the inhabitants of Thibet of every age, condition, and sex. What would become of the Talé-Lama when he had no worshippers? The introduction into the country of the religion of the Lord of Heaven, does it not lead directly to the destruction of the sanctuary of the Buddha-La, and consequently to the downfall of the Lamanesque hierarchy and of the Thibetian government? " I," said he, " who am here to protect the

Talé-Lama, can I permit, at Lha-Ssa, men who propagate such formidable doctrines ? When these doctrines have taken root, and it is no longer possible to extirpate them, who will be responsible for such a misfortune ? What shall I reply to the Grand Emperor, when he shall reproach me with my negligence and cowardice ? You Thibetians," said he to the Regent ; " you do not comprehend the gravity of this matter. Because these men are virtuous and irreproachable, you think they are harmless—it is a mistake. If they remain long at Lha-Ssa, they will spell-bind you. Among you, there is not a man capable of disputing with them upon religion. You will not be able to keep from adopting their belief, and then the Talé-Lama is undone."

The Regent did not enter at all into these apprehensions with which the Chinese ambassador endeavoured to inspire him. He maintained that our presence at Lha-Ssa could not in any way be prejudicial to the Thibetian government. " If the doctrine which these men hold," said he, " is a false doctrine, the Thibetians will not embrace it ; if, on the contrary, it is true, what have we to fear ? How can the truth be prejudicial to men ? These two Lamas of the kingdom of France," he added, " have not done any harm ; they are animated with the best intentions towards us. Can we, without good ground, deprive them of the liberty and protection which we extend here to all strangers, and particularly to men of prayer ? Can we make ourselves guilty of an actual and certain injustice, through an imaginary fear of some possible evil to come ? "

Ki-Chan reproached the Regent with neglecting the interests of the Talé-Lama, and the Regent on his part accused Ki-Chan of taking advantage of the minority of the sovereign to tyrannize over the Thibetian government. For our parts, in this unfortunate contest, we refused to acknowledge the authority of the Chinese Mandarin, and declared that we would not quit the country without a formal order from the Regent, who assured us that they should never extort from him any such thing.

The quarrel became more and more exacerbate every day. Ki-Chan resolved to take on himself to expel us from the country. Matters had come to such a crisis that prudence obliged us to yield to circumstances, and to oppose no further resistance, for fear of compromising the Regent, and of becoming, perhaps, the cause of lamentable dissensions between China and Thibet. By further opposing this unjust persecution, we might irritate too vehemently the Chinese, and furnish pretexts for their project of usurping the Thibetian government. If, on our account, a rupture unhappily broke out between Lha-Ssa and Peking, we should inevitably be held responsible for it; we should become odious in the eyes of the Thibetians, and the introduction of Christianity into these countries would be encountered hereafter with greater difficulties than ever. We therefore considered that it would be better to submit, and to accept with resignation the crown of persecution. Our conduct should prove to the Thibetians that at least we had come among them with peaceful intentions, and that we did not intend to establish ourselves there by violence.

Another consideration helped to confirm our resolution. It occurred to us that this very tyranny which the Chinese exercised against us might perhaps be the ultimate occasion of our missionaries establishing themselves in Thibet with security. In our simplicity, we imagined that the French government would not see with indifference this monstrous assumption of China, in daring to persecute Christianity and the French name even among foreign nations, and at a distance of more than a thousand leagues from

Peking. We were persuaded that the representative of France at Canton could not omit to make emphatic remonstrances to the Chinese authorities, and that he would obtain just reparation for the violence with which we had been treated. In thinking thus, we poor and obscure missionaries were far from wishing to give ourselves, in our own eyes, the least personal importance; but we do not disguise it, we were proud in the belief that our position as Frenchmen would be a sufficient title for our obtaining the protection of the government of our country.

After having maturely considered these points, we proceeded to the Regent. On learning that we had determined to leave Lha-Ssa, he seemed sad and embarrassed. He told us he greatly wished he had it in his power to secure for us a free and tranquil abode in Thibet; but that alone, and without the support of his sovereign, he had found himself too weak to resist the tyranny of the Chinese, who for several years past, taking advantage of the infancy of the Talé-Lama, had assumed unprecedented claims in the country. We thanked the Regent for his goodwill, and left him to wait upon the Chinese ambassador.

We told Ki-Chan that, at a distance from all protection, we had resolved to leave Lha-Ssa, since he was determined to compel us to do so; but that we protested against this violation of our rights. "Well, well," answered Ki-Chan, "you cannot do better; you must depart; it will be better for you, better for the Thibetians, better for me, better for everybody." He then told us that he had ordered all preparations to be made for our departure; that the Mandarin and escort who were to accompany us had been selected. It had even been arranged that we should depart in eight days, and that they should take us along the route which leads to the frontiers of China. This last

THIBET, AND CHINA

arrangement excited at once our indignation and surprise; it was inconceivable how they could have the cruelty to condemn us to a journey of eight months, whilst by proceeding towards India twenty-five days' march would suffice to carry us to the first European station, whence we could not fail to find means, both secure and easy, for reaching Calcutta. We forthwith and vehemently protested against the project, but our protest was disregarded, as was the request for some additional days rest, after the long journey we had just made, and to give time for the closing of the great wounds caused by the cold of the desert. All we could say to mollify the cruelty of the Chinese ambassador was unavailing.

We then laid aside our suppliant tone, and declared to the delegate of the court of Peking that we yielded to violence, but that we would denounce to our government: first, that the Chinese ambassador, installed at Lha-Ssa had arbitrarily and violently driven us thence, under the vain pretext that we were strangers and preachers of the Christian religion, which he called wicked and repudiated by his Emperor. In the second place, that in opposition to all right and all justice, he had prevented us from pursuing an easy and direct route of only twenty-five days' journey to drag us tyrannically into the interior of China, and make us undergo the hardships of an eight months' journey. Finally, that we would denounce to our government the barbarity with which they forced us to set out, without allowing us a little rest, a barbarity which, in our then state, we had a right to consider as an attempt upon our life. Ki-Chan replied that he had nothing to do with what the French government might think or do, that in his conduct he had only to regard the will of his Emperor. "If my master," he said, "knew that I had permitted two Europeans freely to preach the religion of the

TRAVELS IN TARTARY,

Lord of Heaven in Thibet, I should be lost. It would not be possible for me to escape death."

The next day, Ki-Chan sent for us in order to communicate to us a report he had drawn up on the subject of our affairs; and which he proposed to lay before the Emperor. "I did not wish," said he, "to let it go without reading it to you previously, for fear there should have escaped me in it any expressions inexact in themselves or distasteful to you." Having attained his chief object, Ki-Chan had resumed his amiable and conciliatory manner towards us. His report was unmeaning enough; what it said about us was neither good nor bad; it simply set forth a dry nomenclature of the countries we had passed through, since our departure from Macao. "Is this report as you like it?" said Ki-Chan; "do you see anything in it to alter?" M. Huc answered, that he had an observation to make of great importance. "Speak, I listen." "What I have to say to you does not interest us in the least: but it affects you very nearly." "Let us hear what it is." "My communication must be private: let your people withdraw." "These men are my servants; they all belong to my household; fear nothing." "Oh, it is not we who have anything to fear; all the danger is to you." "The danger to me! No matter, the officers of my suite may hear all." "If you will, you can repeat to them what I have to say; but I cannot speak in their presence." "Mandarins cannot hold secret conversation with strangers; it is forbidden by the laws." "In that case, I have nothing to tell you; send the report just as it is; but if it brings misfortune upon you, only blame yourself." The Chinese ambassador became pensive; he took infinite pinches of snuff, one after another, and then, as the result of long reflection, told his suite to retire, and to leave us alone with him.

THIBET, AND CHINA

When everyone had gone, M. Huc began : " Now," said he to Ki-Chan, " you will understand why I wished to speak to you in private, and how important it is to you that no one should hear what I have to tell you. You will judge if we are dangerous men, we who fear even to injure our persecutors." Ki-Chan was pale and disconcerted. " Let us hear," said he ; " explain yourself—let your words be candid and clear ; what would you say ? " " In your report, there is an inexactitude ; you make me set out from Macao with my brother Joseph Gabet, and yet I did not enter China till four years after him." " Oh, if that is all, it is easy to correct it." " Yes, very easy. This report, you say, is for your Emperor ; is it not so ? " " Certainly." " In that case, it is your duty to tell the Emperor the truth and nothing but the truth." " Oh, nothing but the truth ; let us correct the report. At what period did you enter China ? " " In the twentieth year of Tao-Kouang (1840)." Ki-Chan took his pencil and wrote in the margin—twentieth year of Tao-Kouang. " What moon ? " " The second moon." Ki-Chan hearing us speak of the second moon, laid down his pencil and looked at us with a fixed stare. " Yes, I entered the Chinese empire in the twentieth year of Tao-Kouang, in the second moon ; I passed through the province of Canton, of which you were at that time viceroy. Why do you not write ? are you not to tell all the truth to the Emperor ? " The face of Ki-Chan contracted. "Do you see now why I wished to talk to you in private ? " " Yes, I know the Christians are good people—does anyone here know of this matter ? " " No, not anyone." Ki-Chan took the report, tore it up : he wrote a fresh one, entirely different from the first. The dates of our first entry into China were not exactly set forth, and there was a pompous eulogium on our knowledge and sanctity. The poor man had been simple enough to believe that we attached a great importance to his Emperor's good opinion of us.

In accordance with the orders of Ki-Chan, we were to set out after the festivals of the Thibetian new year. We had only been at Lha-Ssa two months, and we had already passed the new year twice, first the European new year, and then the Chinese; it was now the turn of the Thibetian. Although at Lha-Ssa they reckon the year as in China, according to the lunar system, yet the calendars of these two countries do not agree: that of Lha-Ssa is always a month behind that of Peking. It is known that the Chinese, the Mongols, and most of the people of Eastern Asia, make use in their chronological calculations of a sexagenary cycle, composed of ten signs called trunks, and of twelve signs which bear the name of branches. Among the Tartars and Thibetians, the signs of the denary cycle are expressed by the names of the five elements repeated twice, or by the names of the five colours with their shades. The names of twelve animals denote the duodenary cycle.

DENARY CYCLE.

	Mongol.	Thibetian.	
1.	Moto [*modo*].	Cheng [*shing*].	Wood.
2.	Moto.	Cheng.	Wood.
3.	Gal [*gal*].	Mé [*me*].	Fire.
4.	Gal.	Mé.	Fire.
5.	Chéré [*shiroi*].	Sa [*sa*].	Earth.
6.	Chéré	Sa.	Earth.
7.	Témur [*temür*].	Dchak [*lchags*].	Iron.
8.	Témur	Dchak.	Iron.
9.	Oussou [*usu*].	Tchon [*ch'u*].	Water.
10.	Oussou.	Tchon.	Water.

DUODENARY CYCLE.

	Mongol.	Thibetian.	
1.	Khouloukhana [*khulugana*].	Chi-wa [*chi-va(byi-va)*]	Mouse.
2.	Oukhere [*üker*].	Lang [*glang*].	Ox.

THIBET, AND CHINA
DUODENARY CYCLE—continued.

MONGOL.	THIBETIAN.	
3. Bara [*bars*].	Tak [*stag*].	Tiger.
4. Tolé [*tôlai*].	Yen [*yos*].	Hare.
5. Lou [*luu*].	Dchouk [*'brug*].	Dragon.
6. Mokhé [*mogai*].	Phroul [*sbrul*].	Serpent.
7. Mori [*morin*].	Rta [*rta*].	Horse.
8. Khoui [*khonin*].	Lonk [*lug*].	Ram.
9. Betchi [*bechin*].	Preou [*spre'u*].	Monkey.
10. Takia [*takiya*].	Chia [*cha (bya)*]	Fowl.
11. Nokhé [*nokhai*].	Dchi [*khyi*].	Dog.
12. Khakhé [*gakhai*].	Phak [*phag*].	Pig.

To form the sexagenary cycle, the first two cycles are combined in the following manner:—

SEXAGENARY CYCLE.
MONGOL.

1. Moto khouloukhana [*modo khulugana*]. Wooden mouse.
2. Moto oukhere [*modo üker*]. Wooden ox.
3. Gal bara [*gal bars*]. Fire tiger.
4. Gal tolé [*gal tôlai*] Fire hare.
5. Chéré lou [*shiroi luu*]. Earth dragon.
6. Chéré Mokhé [*shiroi mogai*]. Earth serpent.
7. Temur mori [*temür morin*]. Iron horse.
8. Temur khoui [*temür khonin*]. Iron ram.
9. Oussou betchi [*usu bechin*]. Water monkey.
10. Oussou takia [*usu takiya*]. Water fowl.
11. Moto nokhé [*modo nokhai*]. Wooden dog.
12. Moto khakhé [*modo gahhai*]. Wooden pig.
13. Gal khouloukhana [*gal khulugana*]. Fire mouse.
14. Gal oukhere [*gal üker*]. Fire ox.
15. Chéré bara [*shiroi-bars*]. Earth tiger.
16. Chéré tolé [*shiroi tôlai*]. Earth hare.
17. Témur lou [*temür luu*]. Iron dragon.
18. Témur mokhé [*temür mogai*]. Iron serpent.
19. Oussou mori [*usu morin*]. Water horse.
20. Oussou khoui [*usu khonin*]. Water ram.
21. Moto betchi [*modo bechin*]. Wooden monkey.
22. Moto takia [*modo takiya*]. Wooden fowl.
23. Gal nokhé [*gal nokhai*]. Fire dog.
24. Gal khakhé [*gal gakhai*]. Fire pig.
25. Chéré khouloukhana [*shiroi khulugana*]. Earth mouse.
26. Chéré oukhéré [*shiroi üker*]. Earth ox.

TRAVELS IN TARTARY,

SEXAGENARY CYCLE—*continued.*

MONGOL.

27. Témur bara [*temür bars*].   Iron tiger.
28. Témur tolé [*temür tôlai*].   Iron hare.
29. Oussou lou [*usu luu*].   Water dragon.
30. Oussou makhé [*usu mogai*].   Water serpent.
31. Moto mori [*modo morin*].   Wooden horse.
32. Moto khoui [*modo khonin*].   Wooden ram.
33. Gal betchi [*gal bechin*].   Fire monkey.
34. Gal takia [*gal takiya*].   Fire chicken.
35. Chéré nokhé [*shiroi nokhai*].   Earth dog.
36. Chéré khakhé [*shiroi gakhai*].   Earth pig.
37. Témur khouloukhana [*temür khulugana*].   Iron mouse.
38. Témur oukhere [*temür üker*].   Iron ox.
39. Oussou bara [*usu bars*].   Water tiger.
40. Oussou tolé [*usu tôlai*]   Water hare.
41. Moto lou [*modo luu*].   Wooden dragon.
42. Moto mokhé [*modo mogai*].   Wooden serpent
43. Gal mori [*gal morin*].   Fire horse.
44. Gal khoui [*gal khonin*].   Fire ram.
45. Chéré betchi [*shiroi bechin*]   Earth monkey.
46. Chéré takia [*shiroi takiya*].   Earth fowl.
47. Témur nokhé [*temür nokhai*].   Iron dog.
48. Témur khakhé [*temür gakhai*].   Iron pig.
49. Oussou khouloukhana [*usu khulugana*].   Water mouse.
50. Oussou oukhere [*usu üker*].   Water ox.
51. Moto bara [*modo bars*]   Wooden tiger.
52. Moto tolé [*modo tôlai*]   Wooden hare.
53. Gal lou [*gal luu*].   Fire dragon.
54. Gal mokhé [*gal mogai*].   Fire serpent.
55. Chéré mori [*shiroi morin*].   Earth horse.
56. Chéré khoui [*shiroi takiya*].   Earth ram.
57. Témur betchi [*temür bechin*].   Iron monkey.
58. Témur takia [*temür takiya*].   Iron fowl.
59. Oussou nokhé [*usu nokhai*].   Water dog.
60. Oussou khakhé [*usu gakhai*].   Water pig.

As this cycle returns periodically every sixty years, it may be imagined that great confusion might occur in chronology if they had not a sure method of fixing the past sexagenary cycles. To obviate this inconvenience, the sovereigns give to each year of their reign a particular name, and by this means the cyclic epochs are fixed in a way to leave no doubt. Thus the Mongols say, " The twenty-eighth year Tao-Kouang, which is that of the fiery ram (1848 ".) In China the present sexagenary cycle commenced with the year 1805, and the years Tao-Kouang date from 1820, the epoch when the Emperor now reigning mounted the throne. It is to be observed that Chun-Tche Khang-Hi, Young-Tching [Yung-cheng] Kien-Loung, Kia-King, Tao-Kouang, are not at all the names of the six firſt Emperors of the Mantchou dynaſty, but special denominations to denote the years of their reign.

The Thibetians have adopted the use of the denary and duodenary cycles. But by making them undergo more numerous combinations than the Mongols, they obtain a cycle of 252 years. The twelve firſt years merely bear the names of twelve animals; then these same names are combined with those of the five elements, repeated twice up to the 72nd year of the cycle. They then add to these combinations the word *po* [*pho*] "male," which carries them up to the 132nd year; then the word *mo* "female," which takes it up to the 192nd year; finally they alternate the words *po* and *mo* to the end of the cycle.

This chronological syſtem, too complicated for the use of the lower classes, is confined to the Lamaseries, where it is studied and underſtood by the more learned Lamas. The masses live on from day to day, without an idea even of the exiſtence of this method of combining the cycles. Except the Regent, we found no one at Lha-Ssa who could tell us in what year we were. They seemed generally to be wholly unaware of the importance of denoting dates and years by particular names. One of the higheſt funétionaries of Lha-Ssa, a very celebrated Lama, told us that the Chinese method of counting the years was very embarrassing, and not at all comparable with the simplicity of the Thibetian method; he thought it more natural to say plainly, this year, last year, twenty or a hundred years ago, and so on. When we told him that this method would only serve to make history an inextricable confusion, "Provided we know," said he, "what occurred in times gone by, that is the essential point. What is the good of knowing the precise date of the occurrences? Of what use is that?"

This contempt, or rather this indifference for chronology, is observable, in fact, in most of the Lamanesque works; they are frequently without order or date, and merely present to the reader a hotchpotch of anecdotes piled one on another, without any precision, either about persons or events. Fortunately the history of the Thibetians being continually mixed up with that of the Chinese and the Tartars, one can apply the literature of these latter peoples to the introduction of a little order and precision into the Thibetian chronology.

During our stay at Lha-Ssa, we had occasion to remark that the Thibetians are very bad chronologists, not only with respect to leading dates, but even in the manner of reckoning each day the age of the moon. Their almanac is in a state of truly melancholy confusion, and this confusion entirely proceeds from the superstitious ideas of the Buddhists respecting lucky and unlucky days; all the days reputed unlucky, which occur in the course of the moon, are omitted, and do not count. Thus, for example, if the fifteenth day of the moon is a day of ill omen, they count the fourteenth twice over, and pass on direct to the sixteenth. Sometimes several days of ill-omen occur one after the other; but that is of no consequence; they cut them all off just the same, until they come to a lucky day. The Thibetians do not seem to find the least inconvenience in such a method.

THIBET, AND CHINA

The renewal of the year is, with the Thibetians, as with all people, a season of festivals and rejoicings. The last days of the twelfth moon are consecrated to the preparations for it; people lay in supplies of tea, butter, *tsamba,* barley wine, and some joints of beef and mutton. The holiday clothes are taken from the wardrobes; they remove the dust under which the furniture is generally hidden; they furbish up, clean, sweep, and try, in a word, to introduce into the interior of their houses a little order and neatness. The thing only happening once a year, all the households assume a new aspect; the domestic altars are the objects of especial care; they repaint the old idols, and they make, with fresh butter, pyramids, flowers and various ornaments designed to deck the little sanctuaries where the Buddhas of the family reside.

The first *Louk-So* [*lug-so*], or Rite of the Festival, commences at midnight, so that everyone sits up, impatiently awaiting this mystical and solemn hour, which is to close the old year and open the course of the new one. As we were not anxious to catch the exact point of intersection which separates the two Thibetian years, we went to sleep at our usual hour. We were in a deep slumber, when we were suddenly awakened by the cries of joy which issued from all sides, in all quarters of the town. Bells, cymbals, marine conches, tambourines, and all the instruments of Thibetian music, were set to work, and operated the most frightful uproar imaginable; it seemed as though they were receiving the new-born year with a charivari. We had once a good mind to get up, to witness the happiness of the merry inhabitants of Lha-Ssa, but the cold was so cutting, that after serious reflection, we opined that it would be better to remain under our thick woollen coverlets, and to unite ourselves in heart only with the public felicity.

TRAVELS IN TARTARY,

Repeated knocks on the door of our house, threatening to dash it into splinters, warned us that we muſt renounce our projeƈt. After several excuses, we were at laſt fain to leave our warm beds; we donned our clothes, and the door being opened, some Thibetians of our acquaintance rushed into our room, inviting us to the new year's banquet. They all bore in their hands a small vessel made of baked earth, in which floated on boiling water, balls composed of honey and flour. One of these visitors offered us a long silver needle, terminating in a hook, and invited us to fish in his basin. At firſt, we sought to excuse ourselves, objeƈting that we were not in the habit of taking food during the night, but they entreated us in so engaging a manner, they put out their tongues at us with so friendly a grace, that we were obliged to resign ourselves to the *Louk-So*. We each hooked a ball, which we then crushed between our teeth to ascertain its flavour. We looked at each other, making grimaces; however, for politeness sake, we had to swallow the dose. If we could only have got off with this firſt aƈt of devotion! but the *Louk-So* was inexorable; the numerous friends we had at Lha-Ssa succeeded each other almoſt without interruption, and we had perforce to munch Thibetian sweetmeats till daybreak.

The second *Louk-So* also consiſts in making visits, but with a different ceremony. As soon as the dawn appears, the Thibetians walk through the streets of the town, carrying in one hand a pot of buttered tea, and in the other a large gilt and varnished plate, filled with *tsamba*, piled up in the form of a pyramid, and surmounted by three ears of barley. On these occasions, it is not allowed to pay visits without the tsamba and the buttered tea. As soon as you have entered the house of a person to whom you propose to wish a happy year, you firſt of all make three proſtrations before the domeſtic altar, which is solemnly adorned and illuminated; then, after having burnt some leaves of cedar, or other aromatic tree, in a large copper censer, you offer to everyone present a cup of tea, and hand the plate, from which each takes a pinch of *tsamba*. The people of the house reciprocate the compliment to the visitors. The inhabitants of Lha-Ssa have a saying, the Thibetians celebrate the festival of the new year with *tsamba* and buttered tea; the Chinese with red paper and crackers; the Katchi with delicate meats and tobacco; the Peboun with songs and sports.

Although this popular saying is correct enough, the Pebouns do not altogether monopolize the gaiety of the period. The Thibetians also enliven their new years' fêtes with noisy rejoicings, in which the song and the dance always play a large part. Groups of children, with numerous bells hung from their green dresses, pervade the streets, giving, from house to house, concerts that are not wanting in harmony. The song, generally sweet and melancholy, is interspersed with animated choruses. During the strophe, all these little singers keep marking the time, by making, with their bodies, a slow and regular movement like the swinging of a pendulum; but when they come to the chorus, they vigorously stamp their feet on the ground in exact time. The noise of the bells, and of the nailed boots, produces a kind of wild accompaniment that strikes upon the ear not disagreeably, especially when it is heard at a certain distance. These youthful *dilettanti* having performed their concert, it is usual with those for whom they have sung to distribute among them cakes fried in nut-oil, and some balls of butter.

On the principal squares, and in front of the public monuments, you see, from morning till night, troops of comedians and tumblers amusing the people with their representations. The Thibetians have not, like the Chinese, collections of theatrical pieces; their comedians remain altogether and continuously on the ſtage, now singing and dancing, now exhibiting feats of ſtrength and agility. The *ballet* is the exercise in which they seem to excel the moſt. They waltz, they bound, they tumble, they pirouette with truly surprising agility. Their dress consiſts of a cap, surmounted by long pheasants' plumes, a black mask adorned with a white beard of prodigious length, large white pantaloons, and a green tunic coming down to the knees, and bound round the waiſt by a yellow girdle. To this tunic are attached, at equal diſtances, long cords, at the end of which are thick tufts of white wool. When the actor balances himself in time, these tufts gracefully accompany the movements of his body; and when he whirls round they ſtick out horizontally, form a wheel round the performer, and seem, as it were, to accelerate the rapidity of his pirouettes.

You also see at Lha-Ssa a sort of gymnaſtic exercise called the Dance of the Spirits. A long cord, made of leathern ſtraps, ſtrongly plaited together, is attached to the top of the Buddha-La, and descends to the foot of the mountain. The dancing sprites go up and down this cord, with an agility only to be compared with that of cats or monkeys. Sometimes, when they have reached the top, they fling out their arms as if about to swim, and let themselves slide down the rope with the velocity of an arrow. The inhabitants of the province of Ssang [Tsang] are reputed the moſt skilful in this kind of exercise.

The moſt singular thing we observed at Lha-Ssa, during the new year's feſtival, is what the Thibetians call the *Lha-Ssa-Morou* [*Lha-sa-Mo-ru*], that is, the total invasion of the town, and its environs, by innumerable bands of Lamas. The *Lha-Ssa-Morou* commences on the third day of the firſt moon. All

THIBET, AND CHINA

the Buddhist monasteries of the province of Oui open their doors to their numerous inhabitants, and you see great bodies of Lamas, on foot, on horseback, on asses, on oxen, and carrying their prayer-books and cooking utensils, arriving tumultuously by all the roads leading to Lha-Ssa. The town is soon overwhelmed at all points, by these avalanches of Lamas, pouring from all the surrounding mountains. Those who cannot get lodgings in private houses, or in public edifices, encamp in the streets and squares, or pitch their little travelling tents in the country. The *Lha-Ssa-Morou* lasts six entire days. During this time, the tribunals are closed, the ordinary course of justice is suspended, the ministers and public functionaries lose in some degree their authority, and all the power of the government is abandoned to this formidable army of Buddhist monks. There prevails in the town an inexpressible disorder and confusion. The Lamas run through the streets in disorderly bands, uttering frightful cries, chanting prayers, pushing one another about, quarrelling and sometimes having furious contests with their fists.

Although the Lamas generally show little reserve or modesty during these festive days, it is not to be supposed that they go to Lha-Ssa merely to indulge in amusements incompatible with their religious character; it is devotion, on the contrary, which is their chief motive. Their purpose is to implore the blessing of the Talé-Lama, and to make a pilgrimage to the celebrated Buddhist monastery called Morou, which occupies the centre of the town. Hence the name of *Lha-Ssa-Morou* given to these six festive days.

The monastery of Morou is remarkable for the splendour and wealth displayed in its temples. The order and neatness which always prevail here, make it, as it were, the model and example for the other monasteries of the province. West of the principal temple, there is a vast garden surrounded by a peristyle. In this is the printing establishment. Numerous workmen, belonging to the Lamasery, are daily occupied in engraving blocks, and printing Buddhist books. Their process being the same as that of the Chinese, which is sufficiently understood, we shall dispense with describing it. The Lamas who pay their annual visit to the festival of the *Lha-Ssa-Morou*, take the opportunity to purchase the books they require.

In the district of Lha-Ssa alone, they reckon more than thirty large Buddhist monasteries.[1] Those of Kaldan, of Preboung and Sera, are the most celebrated and the most populous. Each of them contains nearly 15,000 Lamas.

Kaldan, which means in Thibetian "celestial beatitude," is the name of a mountain situated east of Lha-Ssa about four leagues. It is on the summit of this mountain that the Lamasery of Kaldan stands. According to the Lamanesque books, it was founded in the year 1409 of our era by the famous Tsong-Kaba, reformer of Buddhism, and founder of the sect of the yellow cap. Tsong-Kaba fixed his residence there, and it was there he quitted his human envelope, when his soul was absorbed in the universal essence. The Thibetians pretend that they still see his marvellous body there, fresh, incorruptible, sometimes speaking, and, by a permanent prodigy, always holding itself in the air without any support. We have nothing to say about this belief of the Buddhists, because the too short stay we made at Lha-Ssa did not permit us to visit the monastery of Kaldan.

The Lamasery of Preboung [Prebung (?—Brasspungs)] "ten thousand fruits" is situate two leagues west of Lha-Ssa; it is built on the site of a lofty mountain. In the centre of the monastery, rises a

[1] In the province of Oui there are three thousand.

sort of kiosk, magnificently ornamented, and all shining with gold and paintings. It is reserved for the Talé-Lama, who repairs thither once a year, to explain to the monks the contents of the sacred volumes. The Mongol Lamas, who come to Thibet to perfect themselves in the science of prayer, and to obtain the degrees of the Lamanesque hierarchy, generally fix themselves at Preboung, which, on that account, is sometimes called in the country a Monastery of the Mongols.

Sera is situated north of Lha-Ssa, not more than half a league from the town. The Buddhist temples and the residences of the Lamas stand in the slope of a mountain planted with hollies and cypresses. The road followed by the pilgrims who come from Tartary passes by these houses. At a distance, these monuments, ranged in the form of an amphitheatre one above the other, and standing out upon the green base of the mountain, present an attractive and picturesque sight. Here and there, in the breaks of the mountain, and quite above the religious city, you see a great number of cells inhabited by contemplative Lamas, and which you can only reach with great difficulty. The monastery of Sera is remarkable for three large temples of several stories high, all the rooms of which are entirely gilt. Hence it is that the Lamasery has acquired the name of Sera, from the Thibetian word *ser*, which signifies gold. In the chief of these three temples, they religiously preserve the famous *tortché* [*dorje* (*mdo-rje*)], or sanctifying instrument, which, in the belief of the Buddhists, came from India through the air, to place itself, of its own accord, in the monastery of Sera. This instrument is of bronze, in form resembling a pestle; the middle, by which you hold it, is in one piece, and cylindrical; the two extremities swell out in oval form, and are covered with symbolical figures. Every Lama must possess a small *tortché*, made on the model of that which marvellously came from India. When they repeat their prayers, and during the religious ceremonies, this instrument is indispensable to them: they must sometimes hold it, sometimes lay it on their knees; then take hold of it again, and turn it in their hand, according to the rules of the ritual. The *tortché* of Sera is the object of great veneration. The pilgrims never fail to go and prostrate themselves before the niche, wherever it lies. At the new year's festival, it is carried in procession, with great pomp, to Lha-Ssa, to be presented to the adoration of the people of the town.

While the innumerable Lamas of *Lha-Ssa-Morou* were celebrating with transport their noisy festival, we, our hearts oppressed with sorrow, were occupied in the preparation for departure. We took down the little chapel wherein we had tasted such sweet, but alas, too short, consolation. After having essayed to plough and sow a poor little corner of this immense desert, we were obliged to abandon it, saying to ourselves that shortly, no doubt, the briar and the thorn would spring forth in abundance, and suffocate those precious germs of salvation which were already beginning to grow. Oh, how bitter and depressing were these thoughts! We felt our hearts breaking, and we had only strength enough to supplicate the Lord to send, to these poor children of darkness, missionaries more worthy of bearing to them the light of the faith.

The evening before our departure, one of the secretaries of the Regent entered our lodging, and presented to us, in his name, two great ingots of silver. This attention on the part of the First *Kalon* affected us deeply, but we considered we ought not to accept this sum. In the evening, in going to his palace to bid him adieu, we took back to him the two ingots.

We laid them before him on a small table, protesting to him that this proceeding resulted from no ill-feeling on our part; that, on the contrary, we should always remember, with gratitude, the good treatment we had received from the Thibetian government during the short stay we had made at Lha-Ssa; that we had no hesitation in expressing our belief that if it had depended on the Regent, we should throughout have enjoyed in Thibet the most tranquil and honourable repose; but that, as to this money, we could not receive it without compromising our conscience as missionaries and the honour of our nation. The Regent did not seem in any degree irritated by this proceeding. He told us that he understood our conduct, and could appreciate the objection we had expressed; that he would not insist on our accepting this money, but that still he should be very glad to make us some present upon separating. Then pointing to a dictionary in four languages, which he had often observed us turning over with interest, he asked us if this work would be agreeable to us. We thought we might receive this present without compromising in any way the dignity of our character, and we, on our parts, expressed to the Regent how happy we should be if he would deign to accept, as a reminiscence of France, the microscope, which had so excited his curiosity; our offer was kindly received.

At the moment of separation, the Regent rose and addressed to us these words :—" You are going away, but who can know future events? You are men of astonishing courage. Since you have been able to get thus far, I know you have in your hearts a great and holy resolve. I think you will never forget it; for my part, I shall always bear it in mind. You understand me: circumstances will not permit me to say more." " We understand," we replied to the Regent, " the full bearing of your words, and we will implore our God to realize one day the purpose they express." We then parted, our hearts bursting with grief, from this man who had been so kind to us, and by whose means we had formed the hope of making known, with God's help, the truths of Christianity to these poor people of Thibet.

When we re-entered our house, we found the Cashmerian governor awaiting us; he had brought us some provisions for our journey; some excellent dried fruits from Ladak, cakes made of flour, butter, and eggs. He insisted upon passing all the evening with us, to assist us in packing our trunks. As he intended shortly to visit Calcutta, we charged him to give intelligence of us to the first Frenchman he should meet in the English possessions in India. We also gave him a letter, which we entreated him to get forwarded to the representative of the French government at Calcutta. In this letter, we briefly explained the circumstances of our stay in the capital of Thibet, and the reasons of our departure.

It seemed to us advisable to take this measure, when we were about to commence a journey of a thousand leagues, along frightful roads continually bordered with precipices. We thought that, if it should be the will of God for us to be buried amid the mountains of Thibet, our friends in France would at least know what had become of us.

The same evening, Samdadchiemba came to bid us adieu. On the day that the Chinese ambassador had resolved to make us leave Thibet, our dear neophyte had been taken from us. It is needless to say how hard and painful this trial was; but to this measure we could not, either the Regent or ourselves, offer any objection. Samdadchiemba was a native of the province of Kan-Sou, directly subject to the Chinese authority. Although our influence with Ki-Chan was not very great, yet we got him to promise that

Samdadchiemba should suffer no injurious treatment, and should be sent back safe to his family. Ki-Chan promised this, and we have since ascertained that he was true to his word. The Regent was full of kindness towards our neophyte. As soon as he was separated from us, he took care that he should want for nothing; he even gave him a sum of money to provide for his journey. With what circumstances allowed us to add to this, Samdadchiemba was enabled to amass a small fortune, and to place himself in a position to return in a fitting manner to his paternal dwelling. We recommended him to go to his aged mother, and fulfil the duties which filial affection dictates, to instruct her in the mysteries of the Christian faith, and to cause her to enjoy at her last moments the benefit of baptismal regeneration; then, when he had closed her eyes, to return and pass his days among the Christians.

To say the truth, Samdadchiemba was not an amiable young man; sour, savage, and sometimes saucy, he was by no means an agreeable fellow-traveller; yet he had in him a groundwork of honesty and devotion, quite capable, in our opinion, of compensating for the perversities of his nature. We felt at parting from him a deep affliction, and all the more so, that we had never suspected the existence at the bottom of our hearts, of so strong an attachment to this young man. But we had made together a long and painful journey; we had endured together so many privations, and so much misery, that, unconsciously, our existence was, so to speak, fused with his. The law of affinity which unites men to each other, acts with much more power amidst suffering than in prosperity.

On the day appointed for our departure, two Chinese soldiers came, early in the morning, to inform us that the *Ta-Lao-Ye*, Ly-Kouo-Ngan [*Ta-lao-yeh* Li Kuo-an]; that is to say, his Excellency

Ly, Pacificator of Kingdoms, awaited us at breakfaſt. This personage was the Mandarin whom the ambassador Ki-Chan had appointed to accompany us to China. We fulfilled his invitation ; and, as the departure was to take place from his house, we had our luggage transported thither.

Ly, the Pacificator of Kingdoms, was a native of Tcheng-Tou-Fou [Ch'eng-tu-fu], capital of the province of Sse-Tchouen ; he belonged to the hierarchy of the military mandarins. For twelve years he had served in Gorkha [Gurkha], a province of Boutan, where he obtained rapid promotion, and reaching the dignity of *Tou-Sse*, with the general command of the troops guarding the frontiers bordering on the English possessions, he was decorated with the blue button, and enjoyed the privilege of wearing in his cap seven sable tails. Ly-Kouo-Ngan was only forty-five years old, but you would have taken him for seventy, so broken and battered was he : he had hardly any teeth left in his head ; his scanty air was grey ; his dull and glassy eyes endured a ſtrong light with difficulty ; his flabby wrinkled face, his totally withered hands, and his enormous legs, upon which he could scarcely support his frame, all bespoke a man exhauſted by great excesses. We thought at firſt that this premature senility resulted from an immoderate use of opium, but he informed us himself, in our very firſt conversation, that it was brandy which had reduced him to this ſtate. Having obtained permission to quit the service, he was now about to seek, in the bosom of his family, and by a careful and severe diet, the reſtoration of his shattered health. The ambassador Ki-Chan had in faƈt hurried our departure that we might go in company with this Mandarin, who in his quality of *Tou-Sse* was entitled to an escort of fifteen soldiers.

Ly-Kouo-Ngan was very well instruƈted for a

THIBET, AND CHINA

military Mandarin; the knowledge he had of the Chinese literature, and above all, his eminently observant character, rendered his conversation effective and full of interest. He spoke slowly, almost in a drawling manner, but he had the faculty of giving to his stories and general conversation a dramatic and picturesque turn. He was very fond of philosophical and religious discussions; he had even, he said, magnificent projects of perfection for the time, when quiet and unembarrassed in his family, he should have nothing to do but to play at chess with his friends, or go and see the play. He believed neither in the Bonzes nor in the Lamas; as to the doctrine of the Lord of Heaven, he scarcely knew what it was, and required to be initiated in it before he embraced it. Meanwhile, all his religion consisted in a fervent veneration for the Great Bear. He affected aristocratic manners and exquisite polish; unfortunately, he happened sometimes to forget himself, and to expose his altogether plebeian origin. It is superfluous to add that his Excellency the Pacificator of Kingdoms was passionately fond of silver ingots; otherwise it would have been difficult to recognize in him a Chinese, much less a Mandarin. Ly-Kouo-Ngan had a luxurious breakfast prepared for us; and his table seemed to us all the finer as for two years we had been used to live almost like savages. The habit of eating with our fingers had nearly made us forget the use of the Chinese chop-sticks. When we had finished, Ly-Kouo-Ngan informed us that everything was ready for departure, but, that before setting out, it was his duty to go to the palace of the ambassador, with his company of soldiers, to take leave. He asked us if we would not accompany him. "By all means," we replied, "let us go together to the residence of the ambassador; you will fulfil your duty, and we a politeness."

TRAVELS IN TARTARY,

We entered, our guide and ourselves, the apartment where Ki-Chan sat. The fifteen soldiers drew up in file at the threshold of the door, after proſtrating themselves thrice and ſtriking the earth with their foreheads. The Pacificator of Kingdoms did the same, but the poor wretch could not himself get up again without our assiſtance. According to our cuſtom, we saluted by placing our caps under our arms. Ki-Chan opened the discourse, and addressed a short speech to each of us.

Addressing us firſt, he assumed a wheedling tone: "You," said he, "are going to return to your country; I do not think you have any complaint to make of me; my conduct towards you has been irreproachable. I do not allow you to ſtay here, but this is the will of the Grand Emperor, not mine. I do not suffer you to go to India, because the laws of the empire forbid it; if it were otherwise, I, old as I am, would accompany you myself to the frontiers. The road you are about to travel is not so horrible as you are led to imagine; you will have, it is true, a little snow, you will pass some high mountains, and some of the days will be cold. You see I do not conceal the truth from you. Why should I try to mislead you? but at all events, you will have attendants to wait upon you, and every evening you will have a lodging for the night ready for you; you will have no need to put up a tent. Is not this travelling better than that on your way hither? You will be obliged to travel on horseback; I cannot give you a palanquin; there are none to be got in this country. The report I am going to address to the Grand Emperor will be sent in a few days. As my couriers go day and night they will pass you. When you have reached in safety the capital of Sse-Tchouan, the viceroy, Pao, will take charge of you, and my responsibility will be at an end. You may depart in confidence and with joyful hearts. I have

THIBET. AND CHINA

sent on orders that you shall be well treated throughout. May the ſtar of happiness guide you in your journey from beginning to end." "Although we consider ourselves oppressed," replied we to Ki-Chan, "we do not the less on that account offer up wishes for your prosperity. Since it is to dignities you aspire, may you recover all those you have loſt, and attain ſtill higher." "Oh, my ſtar is unlucky! my ſtar is unlucky!" cried Ki-Chan, taking a vigorous pinch of snuff from his silver box.

Then addressing himself to the Pacificator of Kingdoms, his voice assumed a grave and solemn tone, "Ly-Kouo-Ngan," said he, "since the Grand Emperor allows you to return to your family, you depart; you will have these two fellow-travellers, and this circumſtance ought to cause you great joy, for the way, you know, is long and tedious. The charaƈter of these men is full of juſtice and gentleness; you will therefore live with them in perfeƈt harmony. Take care never to sadden their hearts, by word or deed. Another important thing I have ſtill to say: As you have served the empire for twelve years on the frontiers of Gorkha, I have commanded the paymaſter to send you 500 ounces of silver; it is a present from the Grand Emperor." At these words Ly-Kouo-Ngan, finding all at once an unwonted suppleness in his legs, threw himself on his kness with vehemence: "The heavenly benificence of the great Emperor," said he, "has always surrounded me on every side, but unworthy servant that I am, how could I receive a further signal favour without blushing? I address my heartfelt supplications to the ambassador, that I may hide my face from him, and withdraw myself from this undeserved graciousness." Ki-Chan replied, "Do you imagine the Grand Emperor will thank you for your disintereſtedness? What are a few ounces of silver? Go, receive this small sum, as it is offered to you ; it will furnish you with tea to offer to your friends ; but when you get home, take care not to begin drinking brandy again. If you wish to live a few years longer, you must deny yourself brandy. I say to you this, because a Father and Mother ought to give their children good advice." Ly-Kouo-Ngan struck the earth thrice with his forehead, and then rose up and placed himself beside us. Ki-Chan than harangued the soldiers, and changed his tone for the third time. His voice was sharp, abrupt, and sometimes bordering on anger. "And you soldiers ! " at these words the fifteen soldiers as though moved by one string, fell together on their knees, and retained that position all the time of the harangue. " Let me see, how many are there of you ? You are fifteen, I think," and at the same time he counted them with his finger ; " yes, fifteen men ; you, fifteen soldiers, are about to return to your own province ; your service is fulfilled ; you will escort your *Tou-Sse* to Sse-Tchouan, and also these two strangers. On the way you will serve them faithfully, and take care to be always respectful and obedient. Do you clearly understand what I say ? " " Yes, we do." " When you pass through the villages of the Poba (Thibetians) beware that you do not oppress the people. At the stations take care not to rob or pillage the property of any person. Do you clearly understand ? " " Yes, we do." " Do not injure the flocks, respect the cultivated fields, do not set fire to the woods. Do you clearly understand me ? " " Yes, we do." " Among yourselves let there always be peace and harmony. Are you not all soldiers of the empire ? Do not then abuse or quarrel with one another. Do you understand clearly ? " " Yes, we do." " Whoever conducts himself badly, let him not hope to escape chastisement ; his crime will be investigated attentively, and severely punished.

THIBET, AND CHINA

Do you clearly underſtand?" "Yes, we do." "As you underſtand, obey and tremble." After this brief but energetic peroration, the fifteen soldiers ſtruck the ground with their foreheads thrice and rose.

Juſt as we were leaving the residence of the ambassador, Ki-Chan drew us apart, to say a few words in private. "In a little while," said he, "I shall leave Thibet, and return to China.[1] In order that I may not be too much encumbered with luggage on my departure, I am going to send two large cases with you; they are covered with the hide of a long-haired ox." He then told us the charaƈters with which they were marked. "These two cases," added he, "I recommend to your care. Every evening, when you reach the ſtation, have them deposited in the place where you yourselves pass the night. At Tcheng-Tou-Fou, capital of Sse-Tchouan, you will commit them to the care of Pao-Tchoung-Tang [Pao chung-t'ang], viceroy of the province. Keep a good eye on your own property, for in the route you will pursue, there are many petty thieves." Having assured Ki-Chan that we would observe his recommendation, we rejoined Ly-Kouo-Ngan, who was waiting for us on the threshold of the great entrance gate.

It was rather curious that the Chinese ambassador should think fit to confide his treasure to us, whilſt he had at his disposal a Grand Mandarin, who was naturally called upon by his position to render him this service. But the jealousy which Ki-Chan felt towards strangers did not make him forget his own intereſts. He considered, no doubt, that it would be more safe to truſt his cases to missionaries than to a Chinese, even though the Chinese was a Mandarin. This token of confidence gave us great pleasure. It was a homage rendered to the probity of Chriſtians, and, at the same time, a bitter satire upon the Chinese charaƈter.

[1] Ki-Chan, in faƈt, is now viceroy of the province of Sse-Tchouan.

We proceeded to the house of Ly-Kouo-Ngan, where eighteen horses, ready saddled, were awaiting us in the courtyard. The three beſt were ſtanding apart, reserved for the *Tou-Sse* and ourselves. The fifteen others were for the soldiers, and each was to take the one which fell to him by lot.

Before we mounted, a ſtrong-limbed Thibetian female, very fairly dressed, presented herself: she was the wife of Ly-Kouo-Ngan. He had been married to her six years, and was about to leave her for ever; he only had one child by her, which had died in its infancy. As these two conjugal halves were never again to see each other, it was but natural that at the moment of so afflicting a separation there should be a few words of adieu. The thing was publicly done, and in the following manner: "We are going to part," said the husband, "do you ſtay here and sit quietly in your room." "Go in peace," replied the wife, " go hence in peace and take care of the swellings in your legs." She then put her hand before her eyes, to make believe she was crying. "Look here," said the Pacificator of Kingdoms, turning to us, "they are odd people these Thibetian women. I leave her a well-built house, and plenty of furniture almoſt new, and yet she is going to cry—is she not content?"

After this adieu, so full of unction and tenderness, everyone mounted, and the party set out down the ſtreets of Lha-Ssa, taking care to seleƈt those less encumbered with Lamas.

When we were out of the town, we perceived a large group awaiting us. They were those inhabitants of Lha-Ssa with whom we had had more intimate acquaintance during our ſtay in that town. Many of them had begun to learn the truths of Chriſtianity, and seemed to us sincerely disposed to embrace our holy religion; they had assembled on our road to salute us and offer us a farewell *khata*. We observed,

THIBET, AND CHINA

amongſt them, the young physician, ſtill wearing on his breaſt the cross we had given him. We dismounted, and addressed to these Chriſtian hearts a few words of consolation; we exhorted them courageously to renounce the superſtitious worship of Buddha, to adore the God of the Chriſtians, and ever to have full truſt in his infinite mercy. Oh, how cruel was that moment, when we were obliged to part from these well-beloved catechumens, to whom we had as yet only pointed out the path of eternal salvation without being able to guide their first ſteps! Alas! we could do nothing further for them, except to implore Divine Providence to have compassion on these souls redeemed by the blood of Jesus Chriſt.

As we were remounting, we saw a horseman advancing towards us at full gallop. It was the governor of the Cashmerians, who had resolved to accompany us as far as the river Bo-Tchou. We were extremely tonched by so friendly an attention, which, however, did not surprise us at all on the part of a sincere and devoted friend, who had given us repeated proof of his attachment during our ſtay at Lha-Ssa.

The arrival of the governor of the Cashmerians occasioned us to ride on slowly, for we had much to say. At length, after an hour's march, we reached the borders of the Bo-Tchou. We found there a Thibetian escort, which the Regent had ordered to conduct us to the frontiers of China; it was composed of seven men and a Grand Lama, bearing the title of *Dheba* [*sde-pa*] " governor of a diſtrict." With the Chinese escort, we formed a caravan of twenty-six horsemen, without counting the drivers of a large herd of oxen that carried our baggage.

Two large ferry-boats were ready to receive the horsemen and the horses; the latter jumped in at a single bound, and drew up in a line, one beside the other. It was easy to see that this was not the firſt time they had performed this manœuvre. The men then entered, with the exception of the *Dheba*, Ly-Kouo-Ngan, and ourselves. We saw that they were going to convey us across the river in a rather more aristocratic manner; we looked in every direction, but saw no means of transit. "How, then, are we to go over?" "Look below there," they replied, "see the boat coming." We turned our eyes in the direction indicated, and we perceived, in fact a boat and a man coming across the fields, but, contrary to the usual practice, it was the boat that was carried by the man, and not the man by the boat. This boatman, running with his back laden with a large boat, was a thing monstrous to behold. As soon as he reached the river side, he quietly set down his load, and pushed the boat into the water without the least effort. It was clearly one thing or the other: either the man was of prodigious strength, or the boat of extreme lightness. We looked at the man, and saw nothing extraordinary in him; we approached the boat, examined it, touched it, and the problem was solved. This large boat was made of ox-hide solidly sewn together; inside, a few light bamboo sticks served to keep it in shape.

After having heartily shaken hands with the Cashmerian governor, we entered the boat, but we nearly burst it the first step we made. They had forgotten to tell us that we must only tread on the bamboo rods. When we were all embarked, the boatman pushed off with a long pole, and in the twinkling of an eye we were on the other side of the river; we sprang ashore, and the owner taking the boat on his back, went off across the fields.

These hide-boats have the disadvantage of not remaining long in the water without rotting. Each time they are done with, the boatmen take care to turn them upside down on the beach, to let them dry.

Perhaps by varnishing them well, they might be preserved from the action of the water, and rendered capable of enduring a longer navigation.

When we were mounted, we cast a last look on the town of Lha-Ssa, still visible in the distance, and said in our hearts: " Oh, my God, thy will be done!" and followed in silence the progress of the caravan. It was the 15th of March, 1846.

CHAPTER VIII

LEAVING Lha-Ssa we travelled for several days, amid a large valley entirely cultivated, and where we remarked on every side numerous Thibetian farms, generally surrounded by trees. The labours of agriculture had not yet commenced, for in Thibet the winters are always long and severe. Herds of goats and bellowing oxen were wandering dejectedly about the dusty fields, biting every now and then at the hard roots of the *tsing-kou*, with which the ground was covered; this species of barley is the chief culture of these poor regions.

The entire valley is composed of a number of small fields, separated from one another by thick low fences, made of large stones. The clearing of this stony ground doubtless cost the original cultivators much fatigue. These enormous stones had to be dug out of the ground one after another, and rolled with labour to the borders of the fields.

At the time of our passing, the country presented, a dull and melancholy aspect. The landscape, however, was animated at intervals by caravans of Lamas, who, singing and dancing, were going to the solemn festival of the *Lha-Ssa-Morou*. Shouts of joy and laughter issued now and then from the farm-houses on the roadside, and informed us that the rejoicings for the new year were not yet at an end.

Our first stage was a short one. We stopped some time before sunset, at Detsin-Dzong [Dechen-jong (bDe-ch'en rdzong)], a large village, six leagues (60 lis) distant from Lha-Ssa.

THIBET, AND CHINA

A large house had been previously got ready for the accommodation of the caravan. As soon as we had alighted, we were introduced, by the governor of the village, to a room, in the midst of which flamed a magnificent fire of *argols*, in a large earthen basin. We were invited to seat ourselves on thick cushions of green *pou-lou* and we were served immediately with buttered tea. We were, in fact, surrounded by such care and attention that our hearts began to open. This kind of travelling seemed marvellous to us. What a contrast to the hard and laborious life we had spent in the desert, where a halt was only an aggravation of misery to us. To travel without being obliged to pitch a tent and to see to the animals; without being put to any straits for fuel and food, seemed the realization of a brilliant utopia. As soon as we dismounted, to find a warm room, and a large pitcher of buttered tea was for us absolute sybaritism.

Soon after our arrival we received the official visit of the Grand Lama, whom the Regent had appointed to accompany us to the frontiers of China, and with whom we had as yet merely exchanged a few compliments as we crossed the river. This individual called Dsiamdchang [Jamjang (? 'Jam-dbyans)], that is to say, "the musician," was a thick-set man, about 50 years of age, who had fulfilled administrative functions in several parts of Thibet. Before being recalled to Lha-Ssa, he occupied the post of *Dheba*-general, in a district some little distance from Ladak. His large and somewhat wrinkled countenance was full of good nature. His character partook of the frankness and open disposition of a child. He told us that the Regent had commanded him to come here expressly on our account, that he might see we wanted nothing during the time we were in the regions subject to the Talé-Lama. He then presented to us two young

Thibetians, on whom he pronounced a long and pompous eulogium. "These two men," said he, "have been specially appointed to serve you on the way. Whatever you command them to do, that they muſt do punctually. As to your refreshments," added he, "as you are not accuſtomed to the Thibetian cookery, it has been arranged that you shall take them with the Chinese Mandarin."

After a brief conversation with the Lama Dsiamdchang, we had, in fact, the honour to sup in the company of Ly, the Pacificator of Kingdoms, who lodged in a chamber contiguous to our own. Ly-Kouo-Ngan was very complaisant, and gave us a great deal of information about the route we were to pursue, and which he himself was now travelling for the eighth time. That we might be enabled to have every day correct notions of the countries through which we were passing, he lent us a Chinese work, containing an itinerary from Tcheng-Tou, the capital of Sse-Tchouan to Lha-Ssa. This book is entitled, *Oui-Tsang-Thou-Tchi* [*Wei-Tsang-t'u-chih*], that is to say, "A description of Thibet, with engravings." This compilation, from various Chinese notices of Thibet, was drawn up by a Mandarin named Lou-Houa-Tchou [*Lu-Hua-chu*], who, in the 51st year of Kien Loung (1786), was charged with the commissariat of the Chinese army. Father Hyacinthe, the Russian archimandrite at Peking, published a translation of this sort of geography of Thibet. M. Klaproth, after having revised, corrected, and enriched with notes, the work of the Russian translator, inserted it in the *Journal Asiatique*.[1] The portion of this Chinese work which concerns the route from Lha-Ssa to the province of Sse-Tchouan, and which we had daily before us during our journey, is extraordinarily exact; but this dry and laconic itinerary

---

[1] *Nouveau Journal Asiatique*, 1st series, tome iv and vi.

can be of no interest except to persons occupying themselves especially in geography, or who travel through the places it mentions. It is merely an arid nomenclature, stage by stage, of the places you find on the way. To give an idea of it, we will transcribe the article relative to our first day's journey.

From Detsin-Dzong to the halt of Tsai-Li [Ts'ai-li].
From Tsai-Li to the inn at Lha-Ssa.

At Detsin-Dzong there are several inns, in which travellers generally stop for some time ; near the road is a post-house. Thence a journey of 40 lis takes you to the convent of Tsai-Li .... 40 lis
" At Tsai-Li, there is a *Dheba* who supplies travellers with wood and hay ; this district is separated only by a river from the territory of Lha-Ssa ; you reach this last place, after a journey of 20 lis ; there is a military commandant there .... 20 lis

Total 60 lis.

We set out from Detsin-Dzong before daybreak, for we had a long way to go. We followed the same valley we had entered on quitting the town of Lha-Ssa. But as we advanced, the mountains, with which this large plain is surrounded, rose insensibly in the horizon, and seemed to draw near us ; the valley grew narrower and narrower ; the ground became more and more stony ; the farms less frequent ; and the population lost by degrees that appearance of refinement and civilization which is always observable in the environs of large towns. After a rapid and uninterrupted march of 80 lis we stopped to take a little repose and refreshment in a large and ruinous Buddhist convent, which served as a residence for some old ragged Lamas. The poverty in which they lived rendered them unbale to offer to the ſtaff of the caravan anything but tea with milk, a pot of beer, and a small roll of butter. However, by adding to these provisions some biscuits and a leg of mutton which the cook of Ly-Kouo-Ngan had been civil enough to prepare for us on the previous evening, we realized a sufficiently subſtantial repaſt.

As soon as we had satisfied our appetite and refreshed our limbs, we thanked these poor religious Buddhiſts with a *khata*, or scarf of blessing, and then remounted our horses. It was already late, and we had yet 40 lis to go before we reached our night ſtage. It was pitch dark when we arrived at Midchoukoung [Medu Kougkar]. Our firſt care was to summon our Thibetian grooms, and bid them get ready our beds as soon as possible. We considered that after a long journey on a bad horse, we might dispense with ceremony. After partaking of a light repaſt, and saying our prayers, we wished a good night to the Pacificator of Kingdoms, and to the Lama musician, and proceeded to bury ourselves under the coverlid.

Next day, when we put our heads out of bed, the sun was already shining in all its splendour, yet all was quiet in the courtyard of the inn; we could hear neither the bellowing of the yaks, nor the neighing of the horses, nor anything indicating preparations for the departure of a caravan. We rose, and after rubbing our eyes, opened the door of our room to see how matters ſtood. We found Ly-Kouo-Ngan and the Lama Dsiamdchang, seated in a corner of the courtyard, quietly basking in the rays of the sun. As soon as they saw us they approached, and told us in an infinitely roundabout manner, that we should be obliged to halt for one day, as there were difficulties in procuring horses and a change of oxen. "This is very bad news," said they; "this mischance is very unfortunate, but we cannot help it; the circumstance of the new year's festival is the sole cause of this delay." "On the contrary," said we, "this is excellent news; we are in no sort of hurry. Let us go quietly, and rest frequently on the way, and all will go well." These words relieved our two guides from a great embarrassment. These good people imagined that we should quarrel with them because it was necessary to make a day's halt; they were prodigiously mistaken. If, in our previous travels, delays had been sources of grievous vexation to us, the reason was that we had an object in view, and that we were eager to attain it. But now this was not the case, and we wished, as much as possible, to travel like gentlemen. We felt, besides that it was not logical to go at a running pace from a place from which we had been expelled.

Midchoukoung is a stage where you change your *oulah* [*ulaga*], that is, the horses, beasts of burden, and guides. These services are kept up by the Thibetian government, all the way from Lha-Ssa to the frontiers of China. The Chinese or Thibetian public officers, who make official inspections of the roads, are alone allowed to avail themselves of these sources. The government of Lha-Ssa gives them a passport, upon which is stated the number of men and animals that the villages, subject to the contribution of the *oulah*, must furnish.

The Chinese account of Thibet gives the following account of this compulsory service: "As respects the local service called *oulah*, all those who have any fortune, whether men or women, are compelled to supply it; even those who come from the most distant countries, if they occupy a house to themselves, are not exempt from it. The number of men each person must furnish for this service is regulated by the fortune of each individual. The elders and the

Dhebas determine, according to the size of each house, the number of men, etc., it muſt furnish to the oulah; each village provides three, four, and sometimes as many as ten men. The smaller families employ poor people as subſtitutes, paying them wages. People beyond sixty years of age are exempt from the burden. If the public service requires it, they exaƈt oxen and horses, asses and mules from the dwellings of the rich; the poor people club together, and three or four houses give one beaſt."

The Chinese Mandarins, who always try to make money out of everything, find means to speculate in the *oulah* with which the Thibetian government furnishes them. Before leaving Lha-Ssa, they manœuvre, by all imaginable means, to have set forth on their road-bill a great number of animals; they then take as many as are aƈtually necessary, and receive, inſtead of the reſt, a compensation in money, which the wealthy Thibetians much prefer to give them than to expose their animals to the perils of the road. Others claim the whole *oulah*, and employ it to transport into China Thibetian merchandise. Ly-Kouo-Ngan, whom we had heard declare so energetically his disintereſtedness, when the ambassador Ki-Chan offered him a present on the part of the Emperor, showed feelings much less generous in relation to the *oulah*.

During the day we passed at Midchoukoung, his road-bill accidentally fell into our hands, and we were much surprised to read there that we had been allotted two horses and twelve long-haired oxen. Yet our entire baggage was two portmanteaus and a few bed things. "What do all these oxen mean?" inquired we of the Pacificator of Kingdoms; "do we need twelve beaſts to carry two portmanteaus?" "Oh, it's a miſtake of the secretary," replied he; and out of politeness we affeƈted to be perfeƈtly satisfied with the answer.

It often happens, however, that the Chinese make gross mistakes as to their speculations in the *oulah*; they find, on the way, for example, some Thibetian tribes who are not at all disciplined to this kind of contribution. It is in vain they point out to these rude and fierce mountaineers the road-bill sealed with the seal of the Talé-Lama and that of the Chinese ambassador; they remain inexorable. To everything that is said to them as an inducement to submit to the law, they have but this answer: " For a guide you will give so much; for a horse, so much; for a yak, so much;" until, at last, Chinese diplomacy is pushed into a corner, and the *oulah* is paid. The inhabitants of the district of Midchoukoung treated us with great politeness and courtesy; the chiefs of the village had a spectacle got up for us, by a troop of buffoons who were assembled for the new year's festival. The large courtyard of the inn, where we lodged, served for a theatre: first, the artists, masked and fantastically dressed, performed for some time, wild, deafening music, in order to summon to the play the inhabitants of the neighbourhood. When all were come, and arranged in a circle round the stage, the *Dheba* of Midchoukoung approached in a solemn manner to offer to our two guides, and to ourselves, a scarf of blessing, and invited us to take our places on four thick cushions which had been placed at the foot of a large tree, that rose from an angle of the court. As soon as we were seated, all the troop of players put themselves in motion, and executed to the sound of music a sort of satanic round, the rapidity of which nearly made our heads swim; then came leaping, jumping, pirouetting, feats of strength, combats with wooden sabres; the whole accompanied alternately by songs, dialogues, music, and imitations of the cries of wild beasts. Among this troop of comedians there was one more grotesquely masked than the others, who acted as a sort of clown to the ring, monopolizing the jests and repartees. We had not knowledge enough of the Thibetian language to appreciate his sallies ; but judging from the stamping of feet and the shouts of laughter of the audience, he seemed to acquit himself wonderfully as a wit. Altogether, the exhibition was amusing enough ; the Thibetians were perfectly enthusiastic. When they had danced, leaped and sang for upwards of two hours, the performers ranged themselves in a semi-circle around us, took off their masks, and put their tongues in their cheeks at us, with profound bows. Each of us presented to the chief of the troop a scarf of blessing, and the curtain fell.

In the afternoon, we invited Ly-Kouo-Ngan to a short walk. Notwithstanding the indifferent elasticity possessed by his legs, he acceded to our proposal with good grace, and we proceeded together to explore the country. The village of Midchoukoung is populous ; but everything announces that its inhabitants are living in anything but a state of comfort. The houses are generally built of stones, strongly cemented with glazed earth ; a great many are crumbling away, the ruins serving as a retreat for troops of large rats. Some small Buddhist altars, carefully lime-washed, are the only constructions that exhibit any cleanliness, and their whiteness presents a remarkable contrast with the grey, smoky hue of the village. Midchoukoung has a Chinese guard, composed of four soldiers and an under-corporal. These men keep a few horses, and their barracks serve as a stage for the couriers who carry the dispatches of the Chinese government.

On re-entering the inn, we found in the courtyard, which in the morning had been used as a theatre, a noisy assembly of men and beasts. They were occupied in collecting our *oulah*, which was settled at twenty-eight horses, seventy oxen, and twelve guides.

THIBET, AND CHINA

At the commencement of the night, the *Dheba* came to inform us that all was done in accordance with the sacred ordinance of the Talé-Lama, and that on the morrow we could depart at an early or late hour as we pleased. At the dawn of day, we mounted our horses and bade adieu to Midchoukoung. After some hours' journey, we left, as through the extremity of a large funnel, the great valley in which we had been travelling since we left Lha-Ssa, and emerged into a wild uncultivated region. For five days we journeyed on in a labyrinth, now to the right, now to the left, and sometimes retracing our steps in order to avoid abysses and inaccessible mountains. We were perpetually in the depths of ravines, or on the precipitous and rocky banks of torrents; our horses rather leaped than walked. The moſt vigorous animals, not accustomed to these dreadful places, could not resiſt for any length of time the fatigues of such a route. For half a day only could we travel with any pleasure and security. We came again to the river we had crossed on quitting Lha-Ssa; it was tranquilly flowing over a slightly inclined bed, and its broad banks offered an easy and even path to travellers. Amid these wild regions you find no place wherein to pass the night, except cold, damp hovels, exposed to all the winds of heaven. However, you arrive there so overcome by fatigue that you always sleep profoundly.

Before reaching the town of Ghiamda [Giamda], we crossed the mountain Loumma-Ri [Lu-ma-ri (Nimaring)]. " This mountain," says the Chinese itinerary, " is high and somewhat declivitous; it extends over a space of about forty lis. The snow, ice, and menacing peaks which travellers meet with on the way, before reaching this mountain, and which intimidate the heart and dim the eye, may cause this to be regarded, in comparison, as a plain easily traversed." The summit of Mount Loumma-Ri, although very lofty, is, in fact, very easy of access. We reached it by an easy slope, without being obliged to dismount once, a very remarkable circumstance in the mountains of Thibet. We found, however, on the other side of the mountain a somewhat serious difficulty, on account of the snow, which fell that day in abundance. The animals frequently slipped, sometimes their hind feet came suddenly in contact with their fore feet, but they never fell. The only result to the horseman was a sort of jerking swing, to which we grew gradually accustomed.

The Pacificator of Kingdoms took it into his head to dismount, and walk, to warm himself a little ; but after a few stumbling steps, he staggered for an instant on his poor legs, fell, and made in the snow a broad, deep furrow. He rose in a fury, ran to the nearest soldier, and loaded him with curses and cuts of his whip, because he had not dismounted to support him. All the Chinese soldiers immediately jumped from their steeds, and fell at the feet of their colonel, making excuses. All, in fact, had been deficient in their duty ; for, according to the Chinese code of politeness, when a chief sets his foot on the ground, all the subalterns must on the instant dismount.

When we were at the base of the mountain of Loumma-Ri we continued our march along a little river, which meandered through a forest of firs so thick that the light of day scarce penetrated it; the snow lay deeply on the broad branches of the trees, whence the wind shook them on thick flakes on the caravan. These small avalanches, falling unexpectedly upon the horsemen, made them start and utter cries of surprise ; but the animals, which, doubtless, had crossed the forest before in similar weather, were in no degree affected. They continued at their ordinary pace, without taking fright, contenting themselves with quietly shaking off the snow from their ears whenever it incommoded them.

We had scarcely emerged from the forest when we were all obliged to dismount, for the purpose of scaling, during a full hour, some horrible rocks. When we had reached the summit, we laid the bridles on the necks of the horses, and left the animals to the sagacity of their instinct as a guide over this rapid and precipitous descent. The men descended, now backwards, as down a ladder, now seated, and letting themselves slide down the snow; everyone extricated himself victoriously from this dangerous position, and arrived at the bottom, without breaking or bruising arms or legs.

We still went on five lis more, in a narrow valley, and then perceived, at the foot of a high mountain, a large collection of houses, amongst which rose two Buddhic temples of colossal proportions. This was the station of Ghiamda. A little before reaching the town, we found on the road, a company of eighteen soldiers, drawn up in file, and having at their head two petty Mandarins, decorated with the white button. Mandarins and soldiers had their sabres drawn and their bows in their shoulder-belts. It was the garrison of Ghiamda, which, under arms and in full uniform, awaited Ly, the Pacificator of Kingdoms, to pay him military honours. When the caravan had come within proper proximity, the eighteen soldiers and the two Mandarins fell on their knees, turning the points of their sabres to the ground, and crying out with one voice, " To the *Tou-Sse*, Ly-Kouo-Ngan, the humble garrison of Ghiamda wishes health and prosperity." At these words, Ly-Kouo-Ngan and the soldiers of his suite stopped their horses, dismounted, and ran to the garrison, to invite them to rise. On both sides there was an infinity of bowing, during which we quietly continued our journey. On entering the town, we had in our turn, our little official reception. Two Thibetians, in holiday attire, seized, to do us honour, the bridles of our horses, and conducted us to the house which had been prepared for our reception. There the *Dheba*, or chief magistrate of the district, awaited us ; he offered us a scarf of blessings, and led us into an apartment where was a table already laid out with tea, butter, cakes, and dried fruits. In all these marks of friendship and attention, we could not help discerning the effect of orders forwarded by the Regent. Whilst we were doing honour to this modest collation we were informed that we should be obliged to stop two days at Ghiamda, because the *Dheba* of the district, having received only that morning the announcement of our approaching arrival, had not had time to send for the animals, which were grazing at a great distance from the town. This news was very welcome to us ; but it plunged Ly-Kouo-Ngan and the Lama Dsiamdchang into despair. We essayed to console them, by telling them that when one cannot direct events, one bears them with resignation. Our two conductors acknowledged our doctrine to be very fine in theory, but the practice was not to their taste. However, they were obliged to admit afterwards that this delay was very opportune, as, during the two days that we remained at Ghiamda, the sky was so overcast, the north wind blew with so much violence, and the snow fell so abundantly, that, in the opinion of the people of Ghiamda, we could not have proceeded with safety in such boisterous weather. In fact, judging from what passed in the valley, it was easy to imagine that a frightful storm must have laid waste the mountains.

The day after our arrival at Ghiamda we received a visit from the two Chinese officers stationed in the town. The one bore the title of *Pa-Tsoung* [*Pa-tsung*], and the other that of *Wei-Wei* [*Wai-wei*]. The *Pa-Tsoung* was a fine man, strongly made, with a sounding voice and quick movement. A large scar across his face, and great black muſtachios, contributed not a little to give him a highly military look. For four years he had served in the Kachkhar [Kashgar] as a private soldier, and had returned thence with the title of *Pa-Tsoung* and the decoration of the peacock's feather. The *Wei-Wei*, a young man of two-and-twenty, was also a well-built person, but his languid and effeminate mien presented a singular contraſt with the manly bearing of his colleague. His face was pale, flabby, and extremely delicate, his eyes were conſtantly humid and languishing. We asked him if he was ill. "No," replied he, with a scarcely audible voice; "my health is excellent"; and, as he spoke, his cheeks were slightly tinged with an angry redness. We saw that we had been guilty of an indiscretion, and we turned to another subject of conversation. This poor young man was an insane smoker of opium. When they were gone, Ly-Kouo-Ngan said, "The *Pa-Tsoung* is a man born under a very favourable ſtar; he will ascend rapidly the grades of the military mandarinship; but the *Wei-Wei* was born under a cloud. Since he has become addicted to the European smoke, heaven has forsaken him. Before a year has elapsed, he will have said good-bye to the world."

The torrents of rain which fell almoſt without interruption during our ſtay at Ghiamda prevented us from visiting in detail this populous and commercial town. You find a great number of Pebouns or Indians of Boutan, who monopolize here, as at Lha-Ssa, all that appertains to the arts and induſtry. The agricultural products of the country are next to nothing. They cultivate in the valley some black barley, but scarcely sufficient for the consumption of the inhabitants. The wealth of the diſtrict is derived from its wool and goat's hair, out of which they manufacture large quantities of stuffs. It appears that amid these frightful hills there are excellent pastures, where the Thibetians feed numerous flocks. The lapis lazuli, stag's horn, and rhubarb, are also materials of a great commercial intercourse with Lha-Ssa and the provinces of Sse-Tchouan and Yun-Nan. They affirm here, that it is in the mountains about Ghiamda that the best rhubarb grows. This district abounds in game of every description. The forest, which we crossed after leaving Mount Loumma-Ri, was full of partridges, pheasants, and several varieties of wild fowl. The Thibetians have no idea how to make the best of these meats, so admired by the gourmands of Europe. They eat them boiled, and without any kind of seasoning. The Chinese, in this respect, as in every other, are much more advanced than their neighbours. The cook of Ly-Kouo-Ngan dressed our venison in a manner that left us nothing to desire.

The appointed day of departure having arrived, the *oulah* was ready early in the morning. The wind had fallen, and the rain had ceased, yet the weather was by no means fine ; a cold and thick fog enveloped the valley, and intercepted the view of the surrounding mountains. We resolved, however, to proceed, for the people of the place agreed in saying that, for the time of year, the weather was all that could be expected. " So long as you are in the valley," they said, " you will not see very distinctly, but once on the heights, the obscurity will disappear ; as a general rule, whenever there is a fog in the valley, snow is falling on the mountains." These words were far from encouraging. We were fain, however to be resigned to our position, fortifying ourselves against the snow, for everyone assured us that from Ghiamda to the frontiers of China, every day, without a single exception, we should have it on our road. Just as we were mounting, the *Dheba* of Ghiamda made us a present of two pairs of spectacles to protect our eyes from the dazzling whiteness of the snow. We could not, at first, help laughing at the sight of these optical instruments, so entirely novel to us was their form.

The place occupied by glass in ordinary spectacles was here occupied by a sort of gauze horsehair work, carved out like a half walnut-shell. To fasten these two lids against the eyes, there was on each side a string which passed behind the ears, and was then tied under the chin. We thanked the excellent *Dheba* most heartily; for, under the circumstances, the present was inestimable. On crossing the mountain of Loumma-Ri, we had already suffered much from the reflection of the snow.

On quitting the town, we found, as on entering it, the soldiers of the garrison awaiting Ly-Kouo-Ngan, in order to give him the military salute. These men, ranged in file, in the fog, and holding in their hands a sabre that gleamed in the obscurity, had so odd an appearance that almost all the horses in the caravan shied at them. These military salutes were renewed on the way, wherever there was a Chinese garrison, to Ly-Kouo-Ngan's extreme exasperation. As he was unable, on account of his diseased legs, to dismount and remount with facility, these ceremonies were a regular torment to him. It was in vain that at each point he sent forward one of his soldiers to direct the garrison not to come out to receive him. This made them only more eager and more earnest for display, thinking that it was mere modesty prompted him to withdraw himself from the honours due to his rank.

Four lis from Ghiamda we crossed a large and rapid torrent, over a bridge composed of six enormous trunks of fir trees, not planed, and so badly joined, that you felt them shake under your feet. No one ventured to cross on horseback, and the precaution was most valuable to one of our soldiers; his horse, slipping over the wet and trembling bridge, one of its legs passed between two trees, and ſtuck there as in a vice. If the man had been on it, he would have inevitably been precipitated into the torrent, and dashed to pieces on the rocks. After long and painful efforts, we managed to extricate the unfortunate animal from its frightful position; to the aſtonishment of everyone, it had not broken its leg, nor even received the leaſt wound.

Beyond this wretched bridge, we resumed our wild pilgrimage across rugged and snow-clad mountains. For four days, we did not find in these wild regions a single Thibetian village. Every evening we lay in the Chinese guard-houses, around which were grouped a few shepherds' huts, made with the bark of trees. During these four days, however, we changed the *oulah* three several times without experiencing the leaſt delay. The orders had been so well given beforehand, that on our arrival at each ſtage, we found everything ready arranged for our departure on the morrow.

If we had not known that in these countries, desert in appearance, there were shepherds living in the gorges of the mountains, it would have been impossible for us to underſtand this prompt organization of the *oulah*. Generally speaking, it was only in large towns that the service of the caravan experienced delays and difficulties.

On the fourth day of our departure from Ghiamda, after having crossed a great lake on the ice, we ſtopped at the ſtation Atdza [Atsa], a small village, the inhabitants of which cultivate a few acres of land, in a little valley encircled by mountains, the tops of which are covered with hollies and pines. The Chinese Itinerary says, on the subjeƈt of the lake you see before your arrival at Atdza, " The unicorn, a very curious animal, is found in the vicinity of this lake, which is 40 lis long."

THIBET, AND CHINA

The unicorn, which has long been regarded as a fabulous creature, really exists in Thibet. You find it frequently represented in the sculptures and paintings of the Buddhic temples. Even in China, you often see it in the landscapes that ornament the inns of the northern provinces.[1] The inhabitants of Atdza spoke of it, without attaching to it any greater importance than to the other species of antelopes which abound in their mountains. We have not been fortunate enough to see the unicorn during our travels in Upper Asia. But all we were there told about it serves to confirm the curious details which M. Klaproth has published on this subject in the new *Journal Asiatique*. We think it not irrelevant to give here an interesting note which that learned orientalist has added to his translation of the *Itinerary of Lou-Houa-Tchou*.

"The unicorn of Thibet is called, in the language of this country, *serou* [*seru* (*bse ru*)]; in Mongol, *kere* [*gere*]; and in Chinese, *tou-kio-cheou* [*tu-chio-shou*]; which means the one-horned animal, or *kio-touan* [*chio-tuan*], the straight horn. The Mongols sometimes confound the unicorn with the rhinoceros, called in Mantchou, *bodi-gourgou* [*bodi-gurgu*]; and in Sanscrit, *khadga*; calling the latter also, *kere*."

The unicorn is mentioned, for the first time, by the Chinese, in one of their works which treats of the history of the first two ages of our era. It is there said that the wild horse, the *argali*, and the *kio-touan* are animals foreign to China; that they belong to Tartary, and that they use the horns of the latter to make the bows called unicorn bows.

The Chinese, Mahometans, and Mongol historians agree in the following tradition, relative to a fact which

---

[1] We had for a long time a small Mongol treatise on natural history, for the use of children, in which a unicorn formed one of the pictorial illustrations.

TRAVELS IN TARTARY,

took place in 1224, when Tchinggiskhan was preparing to attack Hindoſtan. "This conqueror having subdued Thibet," says the Mongol hiſtory, "set out to penetrate into Enedkek (India). As he was ascending Mount Djadanaring [Jadanaring], he perceived a wild beaſt approaching him, of the species called *serou*, which has but one horn on the top of the head. This beaſt knelt thrice before the monarch, as if to show him respeƈt. Everyone being aſtonished at this event, the monarch exclaimed: 'The Empire of Hindoſtan is, they say, the birth-place of the majeſtic Buddhas and the *Buddhiſtavas* [*budhisattva*], and also of the powerful *Bogdas* [*bogda*] or princes of antiquity. What then can be the meaning of this dumb animal saluting me like a human being?' Having thus spoke, he returned to his country." Although this circumſtance is fabulous, it demonſtrates, nevertheless, the exiſtence of a one-horned animal on the upper mountains of Thibet. There are further, in this country, places deriving their name from the great number of these animals, which, in faƈt, live there in herds; for example, the diſtriƈt of Serou-Dziong [Seru-jong (bSe-ru-rdzong)], which means "the village of the land of unicorns," and which is situate in the eaſtern part of the province of Kham [Kham (Khams)], towards the frontier of China.

A Thibetian manuscript, which the late Major Lattre had an opportunity of examining, calls the unicorn the one-horned *tsopo*. A horn of this animal was sent to Calcutta: it was fifty centimetres[1] in length, and twelve centimetres in circumference from the root; it grew smaller and smaller, and terminated in a point. It was almoſt ſtraight, black, and somewhat flat at the sides. It had fifteen rings, but they were only prominent on one side.

[1] A centimetre is 33-100 of an inch.

THIBET, AND CHINA

Mr. Hodgson, an English resident in Nepaul, has at length achieved the possession of a unicorn, and has put beyond doubt the question relative to the existence of this species of antelope, called *tchirou* [*chiru-(gchig-ru)*], in Southern Thibet, which borders on Nepaul. It is the same word with *serou*, only pronounced differently, according to the varying dialects of the north and of the south.

The skin and the horn, sent to Calcutta by Mr. Hodgson, belonged to a unicorn that died in a menagerie of the Rajah of Nepaul. It had been presented to this prince by the Lama of Digourtchi [Digurchi] (Jikazze [Shikatse]), who was very fond of it.

The persons who brought the animal to Nepaul informed Mr. Hodgson that the *tchirou* mostly frequented the beautiful valley or plain of Tingri [Dingri], situated in the southern part of the Thibetian province of Tsang, and watered by the Arroun [Arun]. To go from Nepaul to this valley, you pass the defile of Kouti [Kuti] or Nialam [Nilam]. The Nepaulese call the valley of Arroun Tingri-Meidam [Dingri-meidam], from the town of Tingri, which stands there on the left bank of the river; it is full of salt-beds, round which the *tchirous* assemble in herds. They describe these animals as extremely fierce, when they are in their wild state; they do not let anyone approach them, and flee at the least noise. If you attack them, they resist courageously. The male and the female have generally the same aspect.

The form of the *tchirou* is graceful, like that of all the other animals of the antelope tribe, and it has likewise the incomparable eyes of the animal of that species; its colour is reddish, like that of the fawn in the upper parts of the body, and white below. Its distinctive features are, first a black horn, long and pointed, with three slight curvatures, and circular annulations towards the base; these annulations are more prominent in front than behind; there are two tufts of hair which project from the exterior of each nostril, and much down round the nose and mouth, which gives the animal's head a heavy appearance The hair of the *tchirou* is rough, and seems hollow, like that of all the animals north of the Himalaya that Mr. Hodgson had the opportunity of examining. The hair is about five centimetres long, and so thick that it seems to the touch a solid mass.

Beneath the hair, the body of the *tchirou* is covered with a very fine and delicate down, as are almost all the quadrupeds that inhabit the lofty regions of the Himalaya mountains, particularly the famous Cashmere goats.

Doctor Abel has proposed to give to the *tchirou* the systematic name of *Antelope Hodgsonii*, after the name of the learned person who has placed its existence beyond a doubt.[1]

At Atdze we changed our *oulah*, although we had only fifty lis to go before we reached the residence of Lha-Ri [Lha-ri]. We required fresh animals accustomed to the dreadful road we had below us. One single mountain separated us from Lha-Ri, and to cross it it was, we were told, necessary to get out early in the morning, if we wished to arrive before night. We consulted the Itinerary, and we found there the following agreeable account of the place: " A little further on you pass a lofty mountain, the summits of which rise in peaks. The ice and snow never melt

[1] The unicorn antelope of Thibet is probably the *oryx-capra* of the ancients. It is still found in the deserts of Upper Nubia, where it is called Ariel. The unicorn (Hebrew, *reem*; Greek, *monoceros*), that is represented in the Bible, and in Pliny's *Natural History*, cannot be identified with the *oryx-capra*. The unicorn of holy writ would appear rather to be a pachydermous creature, of great strength and formidable ferocity. According to travellers, it still exists in Central Africa, and the Arabs call it *Aboukarn* [*abu-garn*].

THIBET, AND CHINA

here throughout the year. Its chasms resemble the declivitous shores of the sea; the wind often fills them with snow; the paths are almoſt impraćticable, the descent is so rapid and slippery." It is obvious that this brief but emphatic sketch did not hold out to us any very agreeable pleasure trip for the morrow. Oh, how readily we would have given up our places to some of those intrepid touriſts, whom the love of ice and snow, of rocks and precipices, leads every year amidſt the Alps, those mountains of Thibet in miniature.

Another thing, very little calculated to encourage us, was that the people of the caravan, the villagers, everybody seemed anxious and uneasy. They asked one another whether the snow, which had fallen in abundance for five days, and had not had time to settle, would not render the mountains impassable; whether there was not a danger of being buried in the chasms, or of being overwhelmed by the avalanches; whether, in a word, it would not be prudent to wait a few days, in the hope that the snow would be dispersed by the wind, or partly melted by the sun, or consolidated by the cold. To all these queſtions, the answers were anything but encouraging. In order to guard againſt the effećts of mere pusillanimity of presumption, we held, before going to bed, a council, to which we summoned the old mountaineers of the country. After long deliberation, it was decided firſt, that if, on the morrow, the weather was calm and serene we might set out without temerity; secondly, that in the supposition of departure, the long-haired oxen laden with the baggage, and condućted by some people of the diſtrićt, should precede the horsemen, in order to trace out for them, in the snow, a more easy path. The matter being thus determined, we tried to take a little reſt, relying little on the advantages of this plan, and much on the Divine protećtion.

TRAVELS IN TARTARY,

When we rose, a few stars were still shining in the heaven, contending with the first rays of light; the weather was wonderfully beautiful. We quickly made our preparations for departure, and as soon as the last shades of night were dissipated, we began to ascend the formidable Mountain of Spirits (Lha-Ri). It rose before us like a hugh block of snow, whereon we perceived not a single tree, not a blade of grass, not a dark spot to interrupt the uniformity of the dazzling whiteness. As had been arranged, the long-haired oxen, followed by their drivers, went first, advancing one after the other; next came the horsemen, in single file, in their steps, and the long caravan, like a gigantic serpent, slowly developed its sinuosities on the mountain side. At first the descent was by no means rapid, for we encountered frightful quantities of snow, that threatened every instant to bury us. We saw the oxen at the head of the column, advancing by leaps, anxiously seeking the least perilous places, now to the right, now to the left, sometimes disappearing all at once in some deep rut, and struggling amidst these masses of moving snow like porpoises amid the billows of the ocean. The horsemen who closed the cavalcade found a more solid footing. We advanced slowly along the steep and narrow furrows traced out for us between the walls of snow that rose to the height of our breasts. The air resounded with the bellowing of the oxen; the horses panted loudly, and the men, to keep up the courage of the caravan, raised, every now and then, a simultaneous shout like that of mariners at the capstan. Gradually the route became so steep, so precipitous, that the caravan seemed suspended from the mountain's side. It was impossible to remain on horseback; everyone dismounted, and each clinging to his horse's tail, resumed his march with renewed ardour. The sun, shining in all its splendour, darted its rays on these vast piles of snow, and caused them to emit innumerable sparks, the flashing of which dazzled the eyes. Fortunately, our visuals were sheltered by the ineſtimable glasses that the *Dheba* of Ghiamda had given us.

After long and indescribable labour, we arrived, or rather, were hauled up to the summit of the mountain. The sun was already on the decline. We ſtopped for an inſtant, both to re-adjuſt the saddles and faſten the baggage, and to remove from the soles of our boots the masses of snow that had accumulated upon them, and become consolidated into the form of cones reversed. Everyone was transported with joy. We felt a sort of pride in being mounted so high, and in finding ourselves ſtanding on this gigantic pedeſtal. We took a pleasure in following with our eyes the deep and tortuous path that had been hollowed out in the snow, and the reddish tint of which was markedly outlined in the otherwise spotless white of the mountain.

The descent was more precipitous than the ascent, but it was much shorter, and did not require the exertion we had been obliged to make on the other side of the mountain. The extreme ſteepness of the way assiſted us, on the contrary, in the descent, for we had merely to let ourselves go; the only danger was that of rolling down too faſt, or of ſtepping out of the beaten path, and being thus for ever buried in the bottom of some abyss. In a country such as this, accidents of this description are by no means chimerical. We descended easily then, now ſtanding, now seated, and without any other mischance than a few falls and some protraćted slides, more calculated to excite the merriment than the fear of travellers.

Shortly before arriving at the base of the mountain, the whole caravan halted on a level spot, where ſtood an *Obo*, or Buddhic monument, consisting of piled up ſtones, surmounted by flags and ſtones covered with Thibetian sentences. Some enormous and majestic firs encircling the *Obo*, sheltered it with a magnificent dome of verdure. " Here we are, at the glacier of the Mountain of Spirits," said Ly-Kouo-Ngan. " We shall have a bit of a laugh now." We regarded with amazement the Pacificator of Kingdoms. " Yes, here is the glacier; look here." We proceeded to the spot he indicated, bent over the edge of the plateau, and saw beneath us an immense glacier jutting out very much, and bordered with frightful precipices. We could distinguish, under the light coating of snow, the greenish hue of the ice. We took a stone from the Buddhic monument, and threw it down the glacier. A loud noise was heard, and the stone gliding down rapidly, left after it a broad green line. The place was clearly a glacier, and we now comprehended partly Ly-Kouo-Ngan's remark, but we saw nothing at all laughable in being obliged to travel over such a road. Ly-Kouo-Ngan, however, was right in every point, as we now found by experience.

They made the animals go first, the oxen, and then the horses. A magnificent long-haired ox opened the march; he advanced gravely to the edge of the plateau; then, after stretching out his neck, smelling for a moment at the ice, and blowing through his large nostrils some thick clouds of vapour, he manfully put his two front feet on the glacier, and whizzed off as if he had been discharged from a cannon. He went down the glacier with his legs extended, but as stiff and motionless as if they had been made of marble. Arrived at the bottom, he turned over, and then ran on, bounding and bellowing over the snow. All the animals, in turn, afforded us the same spectacle, which was really full of interest. The horses, for the most part, exhibited, before they started off, somewhat more hesitation than the oxen; but it was easy to see that all of them had long been accustomed to this kind of exercise.

The men, in their turn, embarked with no less intrepidity and success than the animals, although in an altogether different manner. We seated ourselves carefully on the edge of the glacier, we ſtuck our heels close together on the ice, as firmly as possible, then using the handles of our whips by way of helm, we sailed over those frozen waters with the velocity of a locomotive. A sailor would have pronounced us to be going twelve knots an hour. In our many travels we had never before experienced a mode of conveyance at once so commodious, so expeditious, and above all, so refreshing.

At the foot of the glacier each caught his horse as soon as he could, and we continued our journey in the ordinary ſtyle. After a somewhat rapid descent, we left behind us the Mountain of Spirits, and entered a valley, sprinkled here and there with patches of snow that had withſtood the rays of the sun. We rode for a few minutes along the frozen banks of a small river, and reached at length the ſtation of Lha-Ri. We had, at the gate of this town, as at Ghiamda, a military reception. The *Dheba* of the place came to offer us his services, and we proceeded to occupy the lodging that had been prepared for us, in a Chinese pagoda, called Kouang-Ti-Miao [Kuan-ti-miao],[1] which means the temple of the god of war. From Lha-Ssa to Lha-Ri, they reckon 1,010 lis, (101 leagues); we had been fifteen days travelling the diſtance.

[1] Kouang-Ti was a celebrated general who lived in the third century of our era, and who, after many and famous victories, was put to death with his son. The Chinese, indeed, say that he did not really die, but that he ascended to heaven, and took his place among the Gods. The Mantchous, who now reign in China, have named Kouang-Ti the tutelary spirit of their dynaſty, and raised a great number of temples in his honour. He is ordinarily represented seated, having on his left hand his son Kouang-Ping [Kuan P'ing], ſtanding, and on his right his squire, a man with a face so very dark as to be almost black.

TRAVELS IN TARTARY,

As soon as we were installed in our residence, it was agreed unanimously, among Ly-Kouo-Ngan, the Lama Dsiamdchang, and ourselves, that we should stop one day at Lha-Ri. Although the oulah was all ready, we considered it better to make a brief halt, in order to reinstate, by a day's repose, the strength we should require for climbing another formidable mountain that lay in our way.

The large village of Lha-Ri is built in a gorge, surrounded by barren and desolate mountains; this district does not exhibit the least signs of cultivation, so that the people have to get their flour from *Tsing-Kou*. The inhabitants are nearly all shepherds; they breed sheep, oxen, and, especially, goats, the fine silky hair of which is used in the fabric of *poulou* of the first quality, and of those beautiful manufactures, so well known by the name of Cashmere shawls. The Thibetians of Lha-Ri are much less advanced in civilization than those of Lha-Ssa; their physiognomy is hard and rugged; they are dirty in their clothing; their houses are merely large, shapeless hovels, made of tough stone, and rudely plastered with lime. You remark, however, on the side of the mountain, a little above the village, a vast Buddhic monastery, the temple of which is fine enough. A *Kampo* [*mkhan-po*] is the superior of this Lamasery, and, at the same time, temporal administrator of the district. The numerous Lamas of Lha-Ri lead an idle, miserable life; we saw them, at all hours of the day, squatting in the different quarters of the town, trying to warm, in the rays of the sun, their limbs, half covered with a few red and yellow rags,—it was a disgusting sight.

At Lha-Ri the Chinese government maintains a magazine of provisions, under the management of a learned Mandarin, bearing the title of *Leang-Tai* [*liang t'ai*] "purveyor," and decorated with the button of white crystal. The *Leang-Tai* has to pay the

THIBET, AND CHINA

various garrisons quartered on his line of road. There are, between Lha-Ssa and the frontiers of China, six of these provision magazines. The first and most important is at Lha-Ssa; the *Leang-Tai* of which town superintends the five others, and receives an annual salary of seventy ounces of silver, whereas his colleagues have only sixty. The maintenance of the provisional magazine at Lha-Ssa costs the Chinese government 40,000 ounces of silver per annum; while that at Lha-Ri costs only 8,000 ounces. The garrison of the latter town consists of 130 soldiers, having at their head a *Tsien-Tsoung* [*ch'ien-tsung*], a *Pa-Tsoung*, and a *Wei-Wei*.

The day after our arrival at Lha-Ri, the *Leang-Tai*, or purveyor, instead of coming to pay an official visit to the staff of the caravan, contented himself with sending us, by way of card, a leaf of red paper on which were inscribed the letters of his name; he added, by the mouth of his messenger, that a severe illness confined him to his room. Ly-Kouo-Ngan said to us, in a whisper, and with a sly laugh, " The *Leang-Tai* will recover as soon as we are gone." When we were left alone, he said, " Ah, I knew how it would be: every time a caravan passes, Leang-Tai-Sue [liang t'ai Hsieh] (the name of the Mandarin) is at death's door; that is well understood by everybody. According to the usages of hospitality, he should have prepared for us to-day a feast of the first class, and it is to avoid this that he feigns illness. The Leang-Tai-Sue is the most avaricious man imaginable; he never dresses better than a palanquin bearer; he eats *tsamba* like a barbarian of Thibet. He never smokes, he never plays, he never drinks wine; in the evening his house is not lighted; he gropes his way to bed in the dark, and rises very late in the morning, for fear of being hungry too early. Oh, a creature like that is not a man; 'tis a mere tortoise-egg! The

TRAVELS IN TARTARY,

ambassador Ki-Chan is resolved to dismiss him, and he will do well. Have you any *Leang-Tais* of this kind in your country?" "What a question! The *Leang-Tais* of the kingdom of France never go to bed without a candle, and when the *oulah* passes through their town, they never fail to get ready a good dinner." "Ah, that is the thing! those are the rites of hospitality! but this Sue-Mou-Tchou [Hsieh Mu-chin]—" at these words we burst into a hearty fit of laughter. "By-the-by," asked we, "do you know why the Leang-Tai-Sue is called Sue-Mou-Tchou; the name seems to us very ignoble?" "Ignoble, indeed; but it has reference to a very singular annecdote. Leang-Tai-Sue, before he was sent to Lha-Ri, exercised the functions of Mandarin in a small district of the province of Kiang-Si [Kiangsi]. One day two labourers presented themselves at his tribunal, and besought him to give judgment in the matter of a sow, which they both claimed. Judge Sue pronounced thus his decision: 'Having separated truth from fiction, I see clearly that this sow belongs neither to you, nor to you; I declare, therefore, that it belongs to me: respect this judgment.' The officers of the court proceeded to take possession of the sow, and the judge had it sold in the market. Since that occurrence, Mandarin Sue has always been called Sue-Mou-Tchou (Sue the sow)." The recital of this story made us deeply regret that we must depart without seeing the physiognomy of this interesting individual.

We left the town of Lha-Ri in changeable weather; our first day's march was only sixty lis, and offered nothing remarkable, except a large lake which they say is eight lis in breadth and ten in length: it was frozen, and we crossed it easily, thanks to a slight coating of snow with which it was covered. We lodged in a miserable hamlet, called Tsa-Tchou-Ka [Chachukha (Ts'a-chu'-k'a)], near which are hot springs. The

Thibetians bathe there, and do not fail to attribute to them marvellous properties.

The next day was a day of great fatigue and tribulation; we crossed the mountain Chor-Kou-La [Shar-kou-la], which, for its height and ruggedness, may well rival that of Lha-Ri. We began its ascent, our hearts full of anxiety, for the clouded and lowering sky that hung over us seemed to presage wind or snow; the mercy of God preserved us from both the one and the other. Towards mid-day there rose a light north wind, the cutting cold of which soon chapped our faces; but it was not ſtrong enough to raise the thick coat of snow which covered the mountain.

As soon as we had reached the summit, we reſted for a moment under the shade of a large ſtone *obo*, and dined on a pipe of tobacco. During this frugal repaſt the Mandarin Ly-Kouo-Ngan told us, that in the time of the wars of Kien-Loung againſt Thibet, the Chinese troops, exasperated by the fatigues and privations of a long journey, mutinied as they were passing Chor-Kou-La. "On this plateau," said he, "the soldiers arreſted their officers, and after having bound them, threatened to precipitate them into this gulf, unless they promised them increased pay. The generals having agreed to do right to the claims of the army, the sedition was appeased, the Mandarins were set at liberty, and they quietly continued their march to Lha-Ri. As soon as they arrived in this town, the generals made good their promise, and increased the pay; but, at the same time, the insubordinate soldiers were mercilessly decimated." "And what did the soldiers say?" inquired we of Ly-Kouo-Ngan. "Those upon whom the lot did not fall, laughed heartily, and declared that their officers had shown great ability."

On quitting the summit of Chor-Kou-La, you follow a somewhat inclined path, and continue for several days on an extensive, high ground, the numerous ramifications of which stretch afar their pointed tops and the sharp needles of their peaks. From Lha-Ssa to the province of Sse-Tchouan, through all this long route, nothing is to be seen but immense chains of mountains, intersected with cataracts, deep gulfs, and narrow defiles. These mountains are now all heaped up together, presenting to the view the most varied and fantastic outlines; now they are ranged symmetrically, one against the other, like the teeth of a huge saw. These regions change their aspect every instant, and offer to the contemplation of travellers landscapes of infinite variety; yet, amidst this inexhaustible diversity, the continuous sight of mountains diffuses over the route a certain uniformity which after awhile becomes tiresome. A detailed account of a journey in Thibet being extremely susceptible of monotony, we abstain, that we may not fall into unnecessary repetitions from describing the ordinary mountains. We shall content ourselves with mentioning the most celebrated—those which, in the Chinese phrase, "claim the life of travellers." This method, besides, will be conformable with the style of the inhabitants of these mountain countries, who call whatever is not lost in the clouds, *plain*; whatever is not precipice and labyrinth, *level road*.

The high grounds we traversed, after surmounting the Chor-Kou-La, are considered by the natives level ground. "Thence to Alan-To [Alado (A-ra-mdo)]," said the Thibetian escort to us, "there is no mountain; the path is all like that," showing us the palms of their hand. "Yet," said they, "it is necessary to use a good deal of precaution, for the paths are sometimes very narrow and slippery." Now hear what, in reality, was this same road, "as flat as the palm of your hand." As soon as you had quitted the summits of Chor-Kou-La, you encounter a long series of frightful chasms, bordered on each side by mountains cut perpendicularly, and rising up like two vast walls of living rock. Travellers are obliged to pass these deep abysses by following, at a great height, so narrow a ledge that the horses frequently find only juſt enough room to plant their feet. As soon as we saw the oxen of the caravan making their way along this horrible path, and heard the low roar of the waters rising from the depths of those gulfs, we were seized with fear, and dismounted, but everyone at once told us immediately to remount, saying that the horses, accuſtomed to the journey, had surer feet than we ; that we muſt let them go their own way, contenting ourselves with keeping firmly in our ſtirrups, and not looking about us. We recommended our souls to God, and followed in the wake of the column. We were soon convinced that, in point of faċt, it would have been impossible for us to keep our equilibrium on this slippery and rugged surface ; it seemed as though, at every moment, an invisible force was drawing us towards those fathomless gulfs. Leſt we should get giddy, we kept our heads turned towards the mountain, the declivity of which was sometimes so perpendicular that it did not even offer a ledge for the horses to plant their feet on. In such places we passed over large trunks of trees, supported by piles fixed horizontally in the mountain side. At the very sight of these frightful bridges, we felt a cold perspiration running from all our limbs. It was essential, however, to advance, for to return or to dismount were two things beyond possibility.

After having been for two days conſtantly suspended between life and death, we at length got clear of this route, the moſt dreadful and moſt dangerous imaginable, and arrived at Alan-To. Everyone was rejoiced, and we congratulated each other on not having fallen into the abyss. Each recounted, with a sort of feverish excitement, the terrors he had experienced in the most difficult parts of the passage. The *Dheba* of Alan-To, on hearing that no one had perished, expressed his opinion that the caravan had been unprecedentedly fortunate. Three oxen laden with baggage had indeed been swallowed up, but these mischances were not worth talking about. Ly-Kouo-Ngan told us that he had never passed the defile of Alan-To without witnessing frightful accidents. In his previous journey, four soldiers had been precipitated from the top of the mountain with the horses they rode. Everyone was able to recount catastrophes, the mere recital of which made our hair stand on end. They had forborne to mention them before, for fear of our refusing to continue the journey. In fact, if we could have seen at Lha-Ssa the frightful abysses of Alan-To, it is probable that the ambassador Ki-Chan would scarcely have succeeded in inducing us to attempt this journey.

From Alan-To, where we changed *oulah*, we descended through a thick forest of firs, into a valley where we stopped, after eighty lis march, at a village called Lang-Ki-Tsoung [Lang-chi-tsung (Namgialgon, rNam-rgyal-rdzong)]. This post is one of the most picturesque and most agreeable we had met throughout our journey. It is situate amidst the centre of a plain, bounded on all sides by low mountains, the sides of which are covered with trees of fine growth. The country is fertile, and the Thibetians of the district seem to cultivate it with much care. The fields are watered by an abundant stream, the waters of which drift down a large quantity of gold sand, for which reason the Chinese give this valley the name of Kin-Keou [Chin-kou] "Golden Valley."

The houses of Lang-Ki-Tsoung are very singularly constructed; they are absolutely nothing more than trunks of trees, stripped of their bark, and with the two extremities cut off; so that they may be nearly of the same size throughout. Enormous piles are first driven into the earth at a great depth ; the part remaining above ground being at moſt two feet in height. Upon these piles they arrange horizontally, one beside the other, the trunks of fir which they have prepared ; these form the foundation and the floor of the house. Other fir trees similarly prepared, and laid one upon the other, serve to form walls remarkable for their thickness and solidity. The roof is likewise formed of trunks, covered with large pieces of bark, arranged like slates. These houses exactly resemble enormous cages, the bars of which are closely fixed againſt each other. If between the joiſts they discover any cracks they ſtop these up with *argols*. They sometimes build in this fashion very large houses, of several ſtories high, very warm and always free from damp. Their only inconvenience is their having very uneven and disagreeable floors. If the inhabitants of Lang-Ki-Tsoung ever take it into their heads to give balls, they will, it is moſt likely, be obliged to modify their plan of house conſtruction. Whilſt we were waiting patiently and in silence in our big cage until they should please to serve up supper, the *Dheba* of Lang-Ki-Tsoung, and the corporal of the Chinese guard, came to tell us that they had a little point to settle with us. " What point ? " cried Ly-Kouo-Ngan, with an important air, " what point ? Oh, I see, the *oulah* is not ready." " It is not that," answered the *Dheba*. " Never at Lang-Ki-Tsoung has anyone to wait for his *oulah* ; you shall have it this evening, if you like, but I muſt warn you that the mountain of Tanda [Damta (Dambtag)] is impassable ; for eight consecutive days, the snow has fallen in such abundance that the roads are not yet open." " We have passed the Chor-Kou-La, why should we not with equal success pass the Tanda ?" " What is the Chor-Kou-La to the Tanda ? these mountains are not to be compared with each other. Yesterday, three men of the district of Tanda chose to venture upon the mountain, two of them have disappeared in the snow, the third arrived here this morning alone and on foot, for his horse was also swallowed up. However," said the *Dheba*, " you can go when you like ; the *oulah* is at your service, but you will have to pay for the oxen and horses that will die on the way." Having thus ſtated his ultimatum, the Thibetian diplomatiſt put out his tongue at us, scratched his ear, and withdrew. Whilſt the Pacificator of Kingdoms, the Lama Dsiamdchang, and a few other experienced persons belonging to the caravan, were discussing earneſtly the queſtion of departure, we took up the Chinese Itinerary, and read there the following passage : " The mountain of Tanda is extremely precipitous and difficult of ascent ; a ſtream meanders through a narrow ravine : during the summer it is miry and slippery, and during the winter it is covered with ice and snow. Travellers, provided with ſticks, pass it, one after the other, like a file of fish. It is the moſt difficult passage on the whole way to Lha-Ssa." On reading this laſt sentence the book fell from our hands. After a moment's ſtupor, we resumed the book in order to assure ourselves that we had read correctly. We were right ; there it was written : " It is the moſt difficult passage all the way to Lha-Ssa." The prospect of having to pursue a ſtill more arduous route than that of Alan-To was enough to ſtagnate the blood in our veins. " The ambassador Ki-Chan," said we to ourselves, " is evidently a cowardly assassin. Not having dared to kill us at Lha-Ssa, he has sent us to die in the midſt of the snow." This fit of depression laſted but for an inſtant ; God, in his goodness, gradually reſtored to us all our energies, and we rose to take part in the discussion which was proceeding

THIBET, AND CHINA

around us, and the result of which was that, on the morrow a few men of the caravan should set out before daybreak to sound the depth of the snow, and to assure themselves of the real state of the case. Toward mid-day the scouts returned, and announced that Mount Tanda was impassable. These tidings distressed all of us. We ourselves, although in no great hurry, were annoyed. The weather was beautiful, and we apprehended that if we did not profit by it, we should soon have fresh snow, and thus see our departure indefinitely adjourned. Whilst we were anxiously deliberating what we should do, the *Dheba* of the place came to relieve us from our embarrassment. He proposed to send a herd of oxen to trample down, for two days, the snow that encumbered the path up the mountain. " With this precaution," said he, " if the weather continues fine, you may, without fear, depart on your journey." The proposition of the *Dheba* was eagerly and gratefully adopted.

Whilst we waited until the long-haired oxen had made us a path, we enjoyed at Lang-Ki-Tsoung a few days of salutary and agreeable repose. The Thibetians of this valley were more kindly and civilized than those we had encountered since our departure from Lha-Ri. Every evening and morning they furnished us abundantly with the appliances of cookery; they brought us pheasants, venison, fresh butter, and a sort of small sweet tubercle which they gather on the mountains. Prayer, walks and some games of chess, contributed to the delights of these days of leisure. The chessmen which we used had been given to us by the Regent of Lha-Ssa; the pieces were made of ivory, and represented various animals sculptured with some delicacy. The Chinese, as is known, are passionately fond of chess, but their game is very different from ours. The Tartars and the Thibetians are likewise acquainted with chess; and singularly enough, their chessboard is absolutely the same as our own; their pieces, although differently formed, represent the same value as ours and follow the same moves, and the rules of the game are precisely the same in every respect. What is still more surprising, these people cry *chik* when they check a piece, and *mate* when the game is at an end. These expressions, which are neither Thibetian nor Mongol, are nevertheless used by everyone, yet no one can explain their origin and true signification. The Thibetians and the Tartars were not a little surprised when we told them that, in our country, we said in the same way, *check* and *mate*.

It would be curious to unravel the archaiology of the game of chess, to seek its origin and its progress amongst various nations, its introduction into Upper Asia, with the same rules and the same technical phrases that we have in Europe. This labour appertans, of right, to the *Palamède, Revue française des èchecs*. We have seen among the Tartars first-rate players of chess; they play quickly, and with less study, it seemed to us, than the Europeans apply, but their moves are not the less correct.

After three days' rest, the *Dheba* of Lang-Ki-Tsoung having announced to us that the long-haired oxen had sufficiently trampled down the mountain paths, we departed; the sky was clouded, and the wind blew briskly. When we reached the foot of Tanda, we perceived a long dark line moving, like a huge caterpillar, slowly along the precipitous sides of the mountain. The guides of Lang-Ki-Tsoung told us that it was a troop of Lamas returning from a pilgrimage to *Lha-Ssa-Morou*, and who had encamped for the night at the other end of the valley. The sight of these numerous travellers restored our courage, and we resolutely undertook the ascent of the mountain. Before we reached the top, the wind began to blow violently, and drove about the snow in every direction. It seemed as though the whole mountain was falling to pieces; the ascent became so steep, that neither men nor animals had strength enough to climb it. The horses stumbled at almost every step, and if they had not been kept up by the large masses of snow, on more than one occasion they would have been precipitated into the valley of Lang-Ki Tsoung. M. Gabet, who had not yet recovered from the illness which our first journey had occasioned him, could scarcely reach the top of Tanda; not having sufficient strength to grasp the tail of his horse, he fell from exhaustion, and became almost buried in the snow. The Thibetian escort went to his assistance, and succeeded, after long and painful exertions, in getting him to the top, where he arrived more dead than alive; his face was of a livid paleness, and his heaving breast sent forth a sound like the death-rattle.

We met on the top of the mountain the Lama pilgrims, who had preceded us; they were all lying in the snow, having beside them their long iron-feruled sticks. Some asses, laden with baggage, were packed one against the other, shivering in the cold wind, and hanging down their long ears. When we had sufficiently recovered breath, we resumed our march. The descent being almost perpendicular, we had only to sit down, and leave it to our own weight to secure our making a rapid journey. The snow, under these circumstances, was rather favourable than otherwise; it formed on the asperities of the ground a thick carpet which enabled us to slide down with impunity. We had only to deplore the loss of an ass, which, choosing to get out of the beaten path, was precipitated into an abyss.

As soon as we reached Tanda, the Mandarin, Ly-Kouo-Ngan, shook off the snow which covered his clothes, put on his hat of ceremony, and proceeded, accompanied by all his soldiers, to a small Chinese pagoda we had seen on our entrance into the village. It is reported that at the time of the wars of Kien-Loung against the Thibetians, one of the *Leang-Tai*, charged with victualling the Chinese army, crossed during the winter the mountain of Tanda on his way to Lha-Ri. On passing the brink of an abyss filled with snow, a long-haired ox let fall a coffer of silver with which it was laden. On seeing this, the *Leang-Tai* sprang from his horse, threw himself upon the coffer, which he grasped in his arms, and rolled, without relaxing his hold of the treasure, to the bottom of the gulf. Tradition adds, that in the spring, the snow having melted, they found the *Leang-Tai* standing on his coffer of money. The Emperor Kien-Loung, in honour of the devotion of this faithful commissary, who had so faithfully abided by his trust, named him the Spirit of the Mountain of Tanda, and raised a pagoda to him in the village. The Mandarins who journey to Lha-Ssa never fail to visit this temple, and to prostrate themselves thrice before the idol of the *Leang-Tai*. The Chinese emperors are in the habit of deifying in this manner civil or military officers whose lives have been signalized by some memorable act, and the worship rendered to these constitutes the official religion of the Mandarins.

On leaving the village of Tanda, you travel for sixty lis on a plain called Pian-Pa [Pemba (sPen-pa)], which, according to the Chinese Itinerary, is the most extensive in Thibet. If this statement be correct, Thibet must be a very detestable country; for, in the first place, this so-called plain is constantly intercepted by hills and ravines, and in the second place, it is so limited in extent that anyone in the centre of it can easily distinguish a man at the foot of the surrounding mountains. After passing the plain of Pian-Pa, you follow, for fifty lis, the serpentine

THIBET, AND CHINA

course of a small mountain stream, and then reach the Lha-Dze [Lha-'che], where you change the *oulah*.

From Lha-Dze to the stage of Barilang [Bari-nang] is 100 lis journey ; two-thirds of the way are occupied by the famous mountain of Dchak-La [Chag-la], which is of the number of those that are reputed murderous, and which, for that reason, the Chinese call Yao-Ming-Ti-Chan [Yao-ming-ti-shan] ; that is to say, Mountain that claims life. We effected its ascent and descent without any accident. We did not even get tired, for we were becoming used, by daily practice, to the hard employment of scaling mountains.

From Barilang we pursued a tolerably easy route, whence we observed, rising here and there, the smoke from a few poor Thibetian dwellings, isolated in the gorges of the mountains. We saw some black tents, and numerous herds of long-haired oxen. After a journey of 100 lis we reached Chobando [Shobando (Shug-pa-mdo)].

Chobando is a small town, the houses and Lamaseries of which, painted with a solution of red ochre, present, in the distance, a singular and not disagreeable appearance. The town is built on the slope of a mountain and is enclosed in front by a narrow but deep river, which you cross on a wooden bridge, that shakes and groans under the feet of travellers, and seems every moment about to break down. Chobando is the most important military station you find after quitting Lha-Ri ; its garrison consists of twenty-five soldiers and of an officer bearing the title of *Tsien-Tsoung*. This military Mandarin was an intimate friend of Li, the Pacificator of Kingdoms ; they had served together for several years on the frontiers of Gorkha. We were invited to sup with the *Tsien-Tsoung*, who managed to give us, amidst these wild and mountainous regions, a splendid repast, where were displayed Chinese delicacies of every description.

333

During supper the two brothers-in-arms enjoyed the satisfaction or recounting to each other their former adventures.

Just as we were going to bed, two horsemen, having belts adorned with bells, came into the courtyard of the inn; they stopped for a few minutes, and then set off again at full gallop. We were informed that it was the courier-extraordinary, bearing dispatches from the ambassador Ki-Chan to Peking. He had quitted Lha-Ssa only six days before, so that he had already travelled more than 2,000 lis (200 leagues). Ordinarily, the dispatches only occupy thirty days between Lha-Ssa and Peking. This speed will, doubtless, seem in no way prodigious when compared with that of the couriers of Europe; but, making allowance for the excessive difficulties of the journey, it will perhaps be considered surprising. The express couriers, who carry the mails in Thibet travel day and night; they always go in twos, a Chinese soldier and a Thibetian guide. At about every hundred lis, they find on the road a change of horses, but the men are not relieved so often. These couriers travel fastened to their saddles by straps; they are in the habit of observing a day of rigorous fast before mounting their horses, and all the time they are on duty they content themselves with swallowing two raw eggs at every stage. The men who perform this arduous labour rarely attain an advanced age; many of them fall into the abysses or remain buried in the snow. Those who escape the perils of the road fall victims to the diseases which they readily contract in these dreadful regions. We have never been able to conceive how these couriers travelled by night among these mountains of Thibet, where almost at every step you find frightful precipices.

You see at Chobando two Buddhic monasteries, where numerous Lamas reside, belonging to the sect of the Yellow Cap. In one of these monasteries there is a great printing press, which furnishes sacred books to the Lamaseries of the province of Kham.

From Chobando, after two long and arduous days' march, in the turnings and windings of the mountains, and through immense forests of pine and holly, you reach Kia-Yu-Kiao [Chia-yü-ch'iao]. This village is built on the rugged banks of the river Souk-Tchou [Sug-ch'u], which flows between two mountains, and the waters of which are wide, deep, and rapid. On our arrival we found the inhabitants of Kia-Yu-Kiao in a state of profound grief. Not long before, a large wooden bridge, thrown over the river, had broken down, and two men and three oxen who were upon it at the time perished in the waters. We could still see the remains of this bridge, built of large trunks of trees; the wood, completely rotten, showed that the bridge had fallen from decay. At sight of these sad ruins, we thanked Providence for having kept us three days on the other side of the mountain of Tanda. If we had arrived at Kia-Yu-Kiao before the fall of the bridge, it would probably have sunk under the weight of the caravan.

Contrary to our expectation, this accident caused us no delay. The *Dheba* of the place hastened to construct a raft, and on the morrow we were able, at daybreak, to resume our march. The men, baggage, and saddles crossed the river on the raft, the animals swimming.

Thirty lis from Kia-Yu-Kiao, we came to a wooden bridge, suspended over a frightful precipice. Having our imagination still full of the accident at Kia-Yu-Kiao, we felt, at sight of this perilous pass, a cold shudder of terror pervade all our limbs. As a matter of precaution, we made the animals pass first, one after the other; the bridge trembled and shook under them, but held firm; the men went next. They advanced gently on their toes, making themselves as light as possible. All passed safely, and the caravan proceeded again in its usual order. After having surmounted a rocky and precipitous hill, at the foot of which roared an impetuous torrent, we ſtayed for the night at Wa-Ho-Tchai [Wa-ho-chai], a ſtation composed of a barracks, a small Chinese temple, and three or four Thibetian huts.

Immediately after our arrival the snow began to fall in great flakes. In any other place, such weather would have been merely disagreeable; at Wa-Ho-Tchai, it was calamitous. We had next day to travel a ſtage of 150 lis, on a plateau famous throughout Thibet. The Itinerary gave us the following details as to this route: " On the mountain Wa-Ho, there is a lake. That people may not lose themselves in the thick fogs which prevail there, there have been fixed on the heights wooden signals. When the mountain is covered with deep snow you are guided by these signals; but you muſt take care not to make a noise; you muſt abſtain from even uttering a word, otherwise the snow and ice will fall upon you in abundance, and with aſtonishing rapidity. Throughout the mountain you find neither beaſt nor bird, for it is frozen during the four seasons of the year. On its sides, and within 100 lis diſtance, there is no dwelling. Many Chinese soldiers and Thibetians die there of cold."

The soldiers of the garrison of Wa-Ho-Tchai, finding that the weather seemed really made up for snow, opened the gates of the little pagoda, and lighted a number of small red candles in front of a formidable-looking idol, brandishing a sword in its right hand, and holding in the other a bow and a bundle of arrows. They then ſtruck, with repeated blows, on a small tam-tam, and executed a flourish on a tambourine. Ly-Kouo-Ngan assumed his official coſtume, and went to proſtrate himself before the

THIBET, AND CHINA

idol. On his return we asked in whose honour this pagoda had been raised. "It is the pagoda of the *Kiang-Kian*[1] Mao-Ling." "And what did the *Kiang-Kian* do, that he is thus honoured?" "Oh, I see that you are ignorant of these events of times gone by. I will tell you about him. In the reign of Khang-Hi the empire was at war with Thibet. Mao-Ling was sent against the rebels in the rank of generalissimo. Just as he was going to pass the mountain Wa-Ho, with a body of 4,000 men, some of the people of the locality who acted as guides, warned him that everyone, in crossing the mountain, must observe silence, under penalty of being buried beneath the snow. The *Kiang-Kian* issued forth an edict to his soldiers, and the army proceeded in the most profound silence. As the mountain was too long for the soldiers, laden with baggage, to cross it in a single day, they encamped on the plateau. Conformably with the established rule in large towns of the empire, and of camps in time of war, as soon as it was night, they fired off a cannon, Mao-Ling not daring to infringe this rule of military discipline. The report of the cannon had scarcely subsided, when enormous blocks of snow came pouring down from the sky upon the mountain. The *Kiang-Kian* and all his men were buried beneath the fall, and no one has ever since discovered their bodies. The only persons saved were the cook and three persons of the *Kiang-Kian*, who had gone on before, and arrived that same day in the village where we are. The Emperor Khang-Hi created the *Kiang-Kian* Mao Ling tutelary genius of the mountain Wa-Ho, and had this pagoda erected to him, on the condition of protecting travellers from the snow."

[1] The *Kiang-Kian* are the highest dignitaries of the military hierarchy in China; they are decorated with the red button. Each province has a *Kiang-Kian*, who is its military governor, and a *Tsoung-Tou* [*tsung-tu*], or viceroy, who is its chief literary Mandarin.

TRAVELS IN TARTARY,

Ly-Kouo-Ngan having finished his story, we asked him who was the potent being that sent down these terrible masses of snow, ice, and hail, when anyone presumed to make a noise in crossing the mountain Wa-Ho ? "Oh, that is perfectly clear," answered he; "it is the Spirit of the Mountain, the Hia-Ma Tching-Chin [Ha-ma-ching-shên]" (the deified toad). "A deified toad!" "Oh, yes; you know that on the top of Wa-Ho there is a lake." "We have just read so in the Itinerary." "Well, on the borders of this lake there is a great toad. You can scarcely ever see him, but you often hear him croaking 100 lis round. This toad has dwelt on the borders of this lake since the existence of heaven and earth. As he has never quitted this solitary spot, he has been deified, and has become the Spirit of the Mountain. When any one makes a noise and disturbs the silence of his retreat, he becomes exasperated against him, and punishes him by overwhelming him with hail and snow." "You seem to speak quite in earnest; do you think that a toad can be deified and become a spirit ?" "Why not, if he makes a point every night of worshipping the Great Bear ?" When Ly-Kouo-Ngan came to his singular system of the Great Bear, it was futile to reason with him. We contented ourselves with smiling at him and holding our tongues. "Ah!" said he, "you laugh at me because I speak of the Seven Stars; and, indeed, as you do not believe in their influence, it is wrong of me to speak to you of them. I ought merely to have told you that the toad of Wa-Ho was deified, because he had always lived in solitude, on a wild mountain, inaccessible to the foot of man. Is it not the passions of men that pervert all the beings of the creation, and prevent them from attaining perfection ? Would not animals in the course of time become spirits if they did not breathe an air poisoned by the presence of man ?" This argument seeming to us somewhat more philosophical than the first, we vouchsafed the honour of a serious answer. Ly-Kouo-Ngan, who possessed a fair judgment, when he was not confused with this Great Bear, doubted at length the power of the deified toad, and the protection of *Kiang-Kian* Mao-Ling. Just as we were going to repeat our evening prayer, Ly-Kouo-Ngan said to us : " Whatever may be the actual case with the toad and *Kiang-Kian,* this is certain, that our journey to-morrow will be fatiguing and perilous ; since you are Lamas of the Lord of Heaven, pray to him to protect the caravan." " That is what we do every day," answered we ; " but on account of to-morrow's journey, we shall do so in an especial manner this evening." We had scarcely slept two hours when one of the soldiers noisily entered our room, hung on a peg in the wall a large red lantern, and announced that the cock had already crowed once. We had, therefore, to rise, and make, with expedition, the preparations for departure, for we had 150 lis to march before we reached the next stage. The sky was studded with stars, but the snow had fallen the evening before in such abundance that it had added to former layers another of a foot thick. This was precisely what we wanted, by way of carpet, to facilitate the passage of Wa-Ho, a mountain perpetually covered with frozen snow, almost as slippery as a glacier.

The caravan set out long before daybreak ; it advanced slowly and silently along the tortuous paths of the mountain, sufficiently lighted up by the whiteness of the snow and the lustre of the stars. The sun was beginning to tinge the horizon with red when we reached the plateau. The fear of the Great Toad having dissipated with the night, everyone now broke the silence to which he had been condemned. First the guides commenced vituperating the long-haired oxen that were wandering beyond the beaten path. By-and-by the travellers themselves hazarded some reflections on the mildness of the air and the unexpected facility of the route. At length we altogether scorned the anger of the Toad, and everyone talked, hallooed, chattered or sang, without seeming in the least apprehensive of the fall of snow or hail. Never, perhaps, had the caravan been so noisy as on this occasion.

The aspect of the plateau of Wa-Ho is extremely melancholy and monotonous. As far as the eye can reach, nothing is to be seen but snow; not a single tree, not even a trace of wild animals, interrupts the monotony of this immense plain. Only, at intervals, you come to a long pole, blackened by time, which serves to guide the march of caravans. Throughout this extended mountain travellers do not find even a place to prepare their tea and take refreshment. Those who have not strength enough to pass twenty hours without eating or drinking, swallow, as they go a few handfuls of snow, and a little *tsamba* previously prepared.

Throughout the day, the sky was pure and serene, not a single cloud obscuring for a moment the rays of the sun. This excess of fine weather was to us the source of the greatest suffering; the glare of the snow was so intensely dazzling that the hair spectacles did not suffice to keep our eyes from severe inflammation.

When darkness began to spread over the mountain, we had reached the edge of the plateau. We descended by a narrow, rugged path and after a thousand twistings and turnings in a deep gorge, we reached at length the stage of Ngenda-Tchai [En-ta-chai], where we passed the night in intolerable suffering. Everybody was continually crying and groaning as though his eyes had been torn out. Next day it was impossible to proceed. The Lama

Dsiamdchang, who knew something of physic, made a general distribution of medicine and eye-salve, and we all spent the day with our eyes bandaged.

Thanks to the drugs of the Lama, the next day we were able to open our eyes and continue our journey. Three stages separated us from Tsiamdo [Tsiamdo (Ch'amdo)] ; and they were very laborious and annoying stages, for we were obliged to cross a number of those odious wooden bridges, suspended over torrents, rivers, and precipices. The recollection of the recent catastrophe at Kia-Yu-Kiao haunted us incessantly. After having pursued for twenty lis a narrow path on the rugged banks of a large river called the Khiang-Tang-Tchou [Ch'iang-tang-ch'u (Chang-tu-ch'u ?)] we at length reached Tsiamdo. Thirty-six days had elapsed since our departure from Lha-Ssa. According to the Chinese Itinerary we had travelled 2,500 lis (250 leagues).

CHAPTER IX

THE Chinese government has established at Tsiamdo[1] a magazine of provisions, the management of which is confided to a *Leang-Tai*. The garrison is composed of about 300 soldiers and four officers, a *Yeou-Ki* [*you-chi*], a *Tsien-Tsoung* and two *Pa-Tsoung*. The maintenance of this military station, and of the garrisons dependent upon it, amounts annually to the sum of 10,000 ounces of silver.

Tsiamdo, the capital of the province of Kham, is built in a valley surrounded by high mountains. Formerly it was enclosed by a rampart of earth, now broken down everywhere, and the remnants of which are taken away every day to repair the floors of the houses. Tsiamdo, indeed, has little need of fortifications; it is sufficiently defended by two rivers, the Dza-Tchou [Za-ch'u], and the Om-Tchou [Om-ch'u (Nom-ch'u)], which, after flowing the one to the east, the other to the west of the town, unite on the south, and form the Ya-Loung-Kiang [Ya-lung-chiang (mistake for Lan-tsiang-chiang)], which crosses from north to south the province of Yun-Nan and Cochin-China, and falls at length into the sea of China. Two large wooden bridges, one over the Dza-Tchou, the other over the Om-Tchou, to the right and left of the town, lead to two parallel roads, the first called the Sse-Tchouan road, the other the Yun-Nan road. The couriers who convey the mails from Peking to Lha-Ssa, and all the civil and military servants of the

[1] On Andriveau-Goujon's map, this place is called Chamiton [Chamiton (for Chamitou.)]

Chinese government, are obliged to use the Sse-Tchouan road; that of the Yun-Nan is almoſt deserted. You only see there, from time to time, a few Chinese merchants, who purchase from the Mandarins of their provinces the privilege of going to Thibet to sell their merchandise.

The military ſtations which the court of Peking has eſtablished in the ſtates of the Talé-Lama were at one time maintained and managed by the joint authorities of Sse-Tchouan and Yun-Nan. This combination having been, for a long time, the source of dissensions and quarrels between the Mandarins of the two provinces, it was determined that the viceroy of Sse-Tchouan should be sole director of the Chinese resident in Thibet.

Tsiamdo presents the appearance of an ancient town in decay; its large houses, conſtructed with frightful irregularity, are scattered confusedly over a large tract, leaving on all sides unoccupied ground or heaps of rubbish. Except a few buildings of later date, all the reſt bear the ſtamp of great antiquity. The numerous population you see in the different quarters of the town are dirty, uncombed, and wallow in profound idleness.

We could not divine what were the means of exiſtence of the inhabitants of Tsiamdo; they are without arts, induſtry, and we may add, almoſt without agriculture. The environs of the town present, generally speaking, nothing but sands, unfavourable to the cultivation of corn. They grow, however, some poor crops of barley, but these are, doubtless, insufficient for the supply of the country. Possibly musk, skins of wild beaſts, rhubarb, turquoises, and gold-duſt, provide the population with the means of a petty commerce, and thus with the necessaries of life.

Although Tsiamdo is not a place remarkable for its luxury or elegance, you admire there a large and magnificent Lamasery ſtanding towards the weſt, on an elevated platform which commands the reſt of the town. It is inhabited by about 2,000 Lamas, who, inſtead of each having his own house, as in the other Buddhic monaſteries, live all together in the large buildings, with which the principal temple is surrounded. The sumptuous decorations that ornament this temple make it regarded as one of the fineſt and moſt wealthy in Thibet. The Lamasery of Tsiamdo has for its ecclesiaſtical superior a Houtouktou Lama, who is at the same time temporal sovereign of the whole province of Kham.

Five hundred li from Tsiamdo, towards the frontiers of China, there is a town called Djaya [Jaya (Draya)], which, with the countries dependent on it, is subjeƈt to a Grand Lama bearing the title of Tchaktchouba [Phyag-mdzod-pa]. This Lamanesque dignity is somewhat inferior to that of Houtouktou. At the time we were in Thibet, there arose a great conteſt between the Houtouktou of Tsiamdo and the Tchaktchouba of Djaya. The latter, a young, bold and enterprising Lama, had declared himself Houtouktou in virtue of an old diploma, which he affirmed had been granted to him, in one of his former lives, by the Talé-Lama. He asserted, accordingly, his rights to supremacy, and claimed the see of Tsiamdo and the government of the province of Kham. The Houtouktou of Tsiamdo, a Lama advanced in years, did not choose to resign his authority, and, on his side, alleged authentic titles, sent by the court of Peking, and confirmed by the Grand Lama of Lha-Ssa. All the tribes, and all the Lamaseries of the province, entered into this quarrel, and took part, some with the young Lama, some with the old. After long and futile discussions, written and verbal, they resorted to arms, and for a full year these wild and fanatic tribes were engaged in bloody confliƈts. Whole villages were destroyed, and their inhabitants cut in pieces. In their terrible fury, these ferocious combatants devastated everything; they pursued into the desert, with arrows and fusils, the herds of goats and long-haired oxen, and in their destructive course, set fire to the forests they found on their way.

When we arrived at Tsiamdo, the war had ceased some days, and all parties had consented to a truce, in hopes of effecting a reconciliation. Thibetian and Chinese negociators had been sent by the Talé-Lama and the ambassador Ki-Chan conjointly. The youthful Houtouktou of Djaya had been summoned to this congress, and fearful of treachery, he had come with a formidable escort of his bravest partisans. Several conferences had been held without producing any satisfactory result. Neither the one nor the other of the two pretenders would withdraw his claims; the parties were irreconcilable, and everything presaged that the war would soon be resumed with fresh fury. It appeared to us that the party of the young Houtouktou had every chance of success, because it was the most national, and consequently the most popular and strongest. Not that his title was really better founded or more valid than that of his competitor, but it was easy to see that the old Houtouktou of Tsiamdo had hurt the pride of his tribes by invoking the arbitration of the Chinese, and relying upon the aid of the government of Peking. All foreign intervention is odious and detestable. This is truth, alike in Europe and in the mountains of Thibet, wherever people care for their independence and their dignity.

Our residence at Tsiamdo was quite exempt from the irritation and rage that reigned about us. We were treated with all those marks of attention and kindness which we had experienced on all our journeys since our departure from Lha-Ssa. Both the young and the old

Houtouktou sent us a scarf of blessing, with a good provision of butter and quarters of mutton.

We ſtayed at Tsiamdo three days, for our guide, the Pacificator of Kingdoms, had great need of reſt. The fatigues of this arduous route had sensibly affected his health. His legs were so swollen that he could not mount or dismount from his horse without the assiſtance of several persons. The physicians and sorcerers of Tsiamdo, whom he consulted, gave answer, the cleareſt meaning of which was, that if the malady diminished, it would be no great matter; but that if it should grow worse, it might become a serious affair. The moſt reasoned counsellors advised Ly-Kouo-Ngan to continue his journey in a palanquin. A Chinese Mandarin of the place offered to sell him his own, and to engage carriers. This advice was perfectly prudent; but avarice interposed, and the sick man proteſted that he should be more fatigued in a palanquin than on horseback.

To the illness of Ly-Kouo-Ngan was added another source of delay. A Chinese caravan which had left Lha-Ssa a few days after us, had arrived at Tsiamdo on the same evening with ourselves. This caravan consiſted of a *Leang-Tai*, or commissary, of his son, a young man of eighteen, and of a numerous suite of soldiers and servants. We wanted to let these pass on before, for, if we travelled in company, it was to be feared that we should not find lodgings and *oulah* sufficient for so great a number. The *Leang-Tai* and his son travelled in palanquins; but, notwithſtanding the conveniences of this mode of conveyance, the two illuſtrious travellers were so extenuated with fatigue, and so languid, that it was the general impression their ſtrength would not suffice to carry them into China. The literary Mandarins being used to an easy life, are little adapted for supporting the innumerable miseries of the journey into Thibet. Among those who are sent to fulfil the duties of commissary, few are fortunate enough to return to their country.

The day of our departure, the old Houtouktou of Tsiamdo sent us an escort of four Thibetian horsemen, to guard us until we reached the territory of the Tchaktchouba of Djaya. On quitting the town, we passed over a magnificent bridge entirely built of large trunks of fir, and we then found ourselves on the Sse-Tchouan road, which meanders along the sides of a high mountain, at the base of which runs the rapid river Dza-Tchou. After proceeding twenty lis, we met, at a turn of the mountain, in a deep and retired gorge, a little party of travellers, who presented a picture full of poetry. The procession was opened by a Thibetian woman astride a fine donkey, and carrying an infant, solidly fastened to her shoulders by large leathern straps. She led, after her, by a long cord, a pack-horse, laden with two panniers, which hung symmetrically on its sides. These two panniers served as lodgings for two children, whose laughing, joyous faces we saw peeping out from little windows in their respective baskets. The difference in the age of these children seemed slight; but they could not be of the same weight, for to keep the equilibrium between them, a large stone was tied to the side of one of the panniers. Behind the horse laden with these child-boxes followed a horseman, whom one easily recognized, by his costume as a retired Chinese soldier. He had behind him, on the crupper, a boy of twelve years old. Last of all, an enormous red-haired dog, with squinting eyes, and an expression altogether of decided bad temper, completed this singular caravan, which joined us, and took advantage of our company as far as the province of Sse-Tchouan.

The Chinese was an ex-soldier of the garrison of Tsiamdo. Having performed the three years' service required by law, he had obtained leave to remain in

Thibet, and to engage in commerce. He had married, and after having amassed a little fortune, he was returning to his country with all his family.

We could not but admire the fortitude, the energy, and the devotion of this brave Chinese, so different from his selfish countrymen, who never scruple to leave their wives and children in foreign lands. He had to bear up, not only against the dangers and fatigues of a long journey, but also against the raillery of those who themselves had not the heart to follow his good example. The soldiers of our escort soon began to turn him into ridicule. "This man," said they, "is evidently insane; to bring from foreign countries money and merchandise, that is reasonable; but to bring into the central nation a large-footed woman and all these little barbarians, why, it is contrary to all established usages. Has the fellow an idea of making money by exhibiting these animals of Thibet?"

More than once observations of this kind excited our indignation. We always made a point of defending this worthy father, of commending his honourable conduct, and of reproving loudly the barbarity and immorality of the Chinese customs.

Shortly after we had admitted into our caravan the interesting little party from Tsiamdo, we left the river Dza-Tchou to our right, and ascended a high mountain covered with large trees and enormous rocks, themselves covered with thick coats of lichen. We afterwards again came upon the river, and proceeded along its banks, by a rugged path, for a few lis, till we arrived at Meng-Phou [Mengphu (Mong-phud)]. We had travelled scarcely eight leagues, but we were overcome with fatigue. The three days' rest we had taken at Tsiambo had modified our equestrian powers, so that we had some difficulty in getting our legs into riding order again. Meng-Phou consists of seven or eight huts, built of rough stone, in a large and deep ravine.

Next day we travelled along the crest of a lofty mountain, having continually to mount and dismount, in order to get from one eminence to another. On this route we had frequently to cross precipices on wooden bridges, which, to use the expression of the Chinese Itinerary, are " suspended from the region of the clouds." After a march of 60 lis we reached Pao-Tun, where we changed the *oulah*, and where we began to find the Thibetians less complaisant and docile than on the other side of Tsiamdo. Their mien was hautier and their manner more abrupt. On the other hand, the Chinese of the caravan became more humble, less exacting, and prudently abstained from speaking in a domineering fashion. All the way from Pao-Tun to Bagoung you see nothing for ten leagues but calcareous mountains, entirely bare and rough. No trees are to be seen, nor grass, nor even moss. Below you only remark, in the fissure of the rocks, a little verdant stone-crop, which seems to protest against the desolate sterility around. One of these mountains, which the Chinese call Khou-Loung-Chan [K'u-lung-shan], which means the perforated mountain, presents a very singular appearance. You see here a great number of holes and hollows, in infinite variety of form and size. Some of these apertures resemble huge doorways. The smaller look like bells, some like round and oval sky-lights.

The mountain being in the peak form, we were not able to go and visit these caverns. However, we approached sufficiently near to them to be able to judge that they are all of a considerable depth. These numerous cavities resulting, probably, from old volcanic eruptions, are attributed by the Chinese to the *Kouei* [*kuei*] or evil genii. The Thibetians, on the contrary, affirm that they were dug by the tutelary deities of the country; that, in ancient times, some Lamas of great sanctity made them their retreat, and that therein they were transformed into Buddha ; and that at certain periods of the year you still hear within the mountain the murmur of Lama prayers.

In Thibet, we had never observed on our route other mountains than those of a granite nature, always remarkable for masses of enormous stones, heaped upon one another, generally assuming a form originally quadrangular, but rounded at the angles by the incessant action of the wind and the rain. These enormous calcareous masses, which we observed on our way to Bagoung, could not fail to fix our attention. In fact, the country began entirely to change its aspect. For more than a fortnight we saw nothing but calcareous mountains, producing a marble as white as snow, of a fine and very close grain. The shepherds of these regions are in the habit of cutting from them large slabs, on which they carve the image of Buddha, or the formula *Om mani padme houm*, and which they afterwards place on the roadside. These carvings remain for many years, without being in the least defaced, for this marble having a great quantity of silex closely intermixed with carbonate of chalk, is extremely hard. Before our arrival at Bagoung, we journeyed for four of five lis, along a road bordered on both sides by two unbroken lines of these Buddhic inscriptions. We saw some Lamas engraving the *mani* on marble slabs.

We reached the little village of Bagoung a little before nightfall, and proceeded to dismount at a Chinese barracks, composed of a few huts built of magnificent fragments of white marble, cemented with mud and dung. As soon as we arrived, they announced to us the death of the *Leang-Tai*, named Pei [P'ei], who had overtaken us at Tsiamdo. It was two days before that his caravan had passed through

THIBET, AND CHINA

Bagoung. Having reached the barracks, the bearers of the Mandarin, after setting down the palanquin, had opened the curtains, as usual, to invite his excellency to enter the apartment that had been prepared for him. But, in the palanquin, they only found a corpse. In accordance with the Chinese usages, the son of the departed could not leave the body of his father in a foreign land, but muſt take it to his family, in order to deposit it in the sepulchre of his anceſtors. Now, we were ſtill in the heart of Thibet, and the family of the Mandarin Pei was in the province of Tche-Kiang [Chêkiang], altogether at the extremity of China. The route, as has been seen, was difficult and long ; but hesitation in the matter was out of the queſtion : filial piety had to surmount all obſtacles. A coffin, ready-made, was, by chance in the guard-house. The son of the Mandarin bought it at a high price from the soldiers ; he deposited therein the remains of his father. They adapted the shafts of the palanquin to the coffin, and the carriers, in consideration of increased pay, agreed to carry to the frontiers of China, a dead inſtead of a living man. The caravan had quitted Bagoung the evening preceding our arrival.

The announcement of his death aſtonished and affeɕted all of us.

Ly-Kouo-Ngan particularly, who was in no satisfaɕtory ſtate of mind, was thunderſtruck. The fear he felt prevented him from taking any supper ; but, in the evening, another matter occurred to divert his attention from these sad thoughts of death. The chief of the Thibetian village came to the guard-house, to announce to the travellers that it had been resolved in that country, that thereafter they would not supply the *oulah* gratuitously ; that for a horse, people muſt pay one ounce of silver, and for a yak half an ounce. " The caravan which passed

yesterday," added he, " was obliged to agree to this."
.... To make it manifest that this regulation would not admit of any discussion, he abruptly put his tongue in his cheek at us, and withdrew.

A manifesto so plain and definite was a complete thunderbolt to the Pacificator of Kingdoms. He entirely forgot the melancholy death of the poor *Leang-Tai*, in the thought of this frightful catastrophe which threatened his purse. We charitably participated in his affliction, and tried, as well as we could, to conform our words to his sombre thoughts. But, in reality, it was a matter of utter indifference to us. If they refused to supply us with the means of continuing our journey, we should merely have to stay in Thibet, which, after all, was a result to which we should without difficulty become reconciled. Meantime, we went to bed, and left the people of the escort to discuss politics and social economy.

The next day, when we rose, we found neither oxen nor horses in the court of the barracks. Ly-Kouo-Ngan was in utter despair. " Shall we have the *oulah* ? " inquired we ; " shall we depart to-day ? " " These barbarians," answered he, " do not comprehend the merits of obedience. I have resolved to address myself to Proul-Tamba ['Phrul-bstan-pa] ; I have sent a deputation to him ; I have known him a long time, and I hope he will procure the *oulah* for us." This Proul-Tamba was a person of whom we had already heard a great deal. He was at the head of the party of the young Tchaktchouba of Djaya, and consequently the avowed enemy of Chinese influence. He was, we were informed, learned as the most learned Lamas of Lha-Ssa. No one came up to him in valour ; never in battle had he experienced defeat. Accordingly, among all the tribes of the province of Kham, his name alone had potency, and acted like a talisman in the minds of the multitude. Proul-Tamba was, in some measure, the Abd-el-Kader of these wild mountaineers.

The dwelling of Proul-Tamba was distant from Bagoung not more than five or six lis. The deputation that had been sent to him, soon returned, and announced that the great chief himself was coming. This unexpected news put in commotion the whole Thibetian village and the soldiers. Every one said to everyone, excitedly, " The great chief is coming, we are going to see the great chief! " Ly-Kouo-Ngan hastened to attire himself in his best clothes, his silk boots and his hat of ceremony. The Chinese soldiers also improved, as well as they could, their toilet. Whilst the Thibetians ran to meet their chief, Ly-Kouo-Ngan selected from his baggage a magnificent *khata*, or scarf of blessing, and then posted himself on the threshold of the door, to receive the illustrious Proul-Tamba. As for us, the department we selected was to study the physiognomies of the different parties. The most interesting was, doubtless, that of the Pacificator of Kingdoms. It was curious to see this Chinese Mandarin, generally so haughtily insolent in the presence of Thibetians, become all at once humble and modest, and awaiting, tremblingly, the arrival of a man whom he deemed strong and potent.

At last the great chief appeared ; he was on horseback, escorted by a guard of honour, consisting of four horsemen. As soon as all had dismounted, the Pacificator of Kingdoms approached Proul-Tamba, made him a low bow, and offered him the scarf of blessing. Proul-Tamba motioned to one of his attendants to receive the present, and without saying a word, quickly crossed the court, and went straight to the room prepared for his reception, and where we awaited him with the Lama Dsiamdchang. Proul-Tamba made us a slight bow, and sat down without ceremony, in the place of honour, on a carpet of grey felt. Ly-Kouo-Ngan placed himself on his left, the Lama Dsiamdchang on his right, and we in front of him. Between us five there was such a respectful distance, that we formed a sort of large circle. Some Chinese soldiers and a crowd of Thibetians stood behind us.

There was a minute of profound silence. The great chief (Proul-Tamba) was at most forty years of age; he was of middle height, and his sole attire was a large robe of green silk, bordered with beautiful wolf-fur, and fastened at the waist by a red girdle. Large purple leather boots, an alarming fox-skin cap, and a broad, long sabre, passed through the girdle horizontally, completed his costume. Long hair, black as ebony, which hung down over his shoulders, gave to his pale, thin face, a marked expression of energy. The eyes were, however, the most remarkable features in the physiognomy of this man; they were large, glittering, and seemed to breathe indomitable courage and pride. The whole appearance and bearing of Proul-Tamba denoted a man of real superiority, born to command his fellows. After having attentively looked at us, one after the other, his hands resting one on each end of his sabre, he drew from his bosom a packet of little *khatas*, and had them distributed amongst us by one of his men. Then turning to Ly-Kouo-Ngan : " Ah, thou art back again," said he, with a voice that resounded like a bell ; " if they had not told me this morning it was thee, I should not have recognized thee. How thou hast aged since thy last visit to Bagoung." " Yes, thou art right," answered the Pacificator of Kingdoms, in soft and insinuating tones, drawing himself along the felt carpet nearer to his interlocutor ; " yes, I am very feeble ; but thou art more vigorous than ever."
" We live in circumstances under which it is necessary

to be vigorous: there is no longer peace in our mountains." "True, I heard yonder that you have had here amongſt you a little dispute." " For more than a year paſt, the tribes of Kham have been waging a bloody war, and thou calleſt that a little dispute. Thou haſt only to open thy eyes, on thy way, and thou wilt behold, on every side, villages in ruins, and foreſts burnt down. In a few days, we shall be obliged to resume our work, for no one will hear the words of peace. The war, indeed, might have been brought to a conclusion after a few skirmishes; but, since you Chinese have chosen to meddle in our affairs, the parties have become irreconcilable. You Chinese Mandarins are good for nothing but to bring disorder and confusion into these countries. It cannot go on in this way. We have let you alone for some time, and now your audacity knows no bounds. I cannot, without shuddering all over, think of that affair of the Nomekhan of Lha-Ssa. They pretend that the Nomekhan committed great crimes. It is false: these great crimes, it is you that invented them. The Nomekhan is a saint, a Living Buddha. Who ever heard that a Living Buddha could be tried and exiled by Ki-Chan, a Chinese, a layman?" " The order came from the Grand Emperor," answered Ly-Kouo-Ngan, in a low and tremulous voice. "The Grand Emperor!" cried Proul-Tamba, turning with an angry air to his interrupter, "thy Grand Emperor is only a layman. What is thy Grand Emperor compared with a Grand Lama, a Living Buddha?" The great chief of the province of Kham inveighed for a length of time againſt the domination of the Chinese in Thibet. He assailed in turns the Emperor, the viceroy of Sse-Tchouan, and the ambassador at Lha-Ssa.

Throughout these energetic philippics, he frequently reverted to the affair of the Nomekhan. One could see that he felt a deep interest in the fate of the Grand Lama, whom he regarded as a victim of the court of Peking. The Pacificator of Kingdoms took care not to contradict him; he affected to concur in the sentiments of Proul-Tamba, and received each proposition with an inclination of the head. At length he hazarded a word as to departure and the *oulah*.

"The *oulah*," replied Proul-Tamba; "henceforth there will be none for the Chinese, unless they pay the price for them. It is enough that we allow the Chinese to penetrate into our country, without adding the folly of furnishing them with the *oulah* gratuitously. However, as thou art an old acquaintance, we will make an exception in favour of thy caravan. Besides, thou are conducting two Lamas of the Western Heaven, who have been recommended to me by the chief *Kalon* of Lha-Ssa, and who are entitled to my services. Where is the *Dheba* of Bagoung? Let him advance."

The individual who, the evening before, had come to tell us, "no more money, no more *oulah*," presented himself. He bent his knee before the great chief, and respectfully put his tongue in his cheek at him. "Let them get ready the *oulah* immediately," cried Proul-Tamba, "and let everyone do his duty." The Thibetians, who were in the courtyard, sent forth a simultaneous shout of submission, and ran off to the adjacent village.

Proul-Tamba rose, and after having invited us to take tea in his house, which stood on our road, sprang on his horse, and returned home at full gallop. The *oulah* soon appeared, and the caravan found itself organized, as it were, by magic. After half an hour's march, we reached the residence of the great chief. It was a lofty, large structure, not unlike a stronghold of the feudal times. A broad canal, bordered with large trees, encircled it. A drawbridge descended for us. We dismounted to cross it, and entered, through an immense gateway, a square court, where my lord Proul-Tamba awaited us. They tied the horses to poſts planted in the middle of the court, and we were introduced into a vaſt saloon, which seemed to serve as the domeſtic temple, or caſtle chapel. The enormous beams which supported the roof were entirely gilt. The walls were hung with flags of all colours, covered with Thibetian inscriptions. At the end of the saloon were three colossal ſtatues of Buddha, before which were placed large butter lamps and censers. In the corner of the temple, they had prepared a low table, with four thick cushions, covered with red ſtuff. Proul-Tamba graciously invited us to take our places, and as soon as we were seated, the chatelaine made her appearance in ſtate coſtume, that is to say, with her face frightfully daubed over with black, her copious tresses adorned with spangles, red coral beads, and small mother-of-pearl buttons.

In her right hand she carried a majeſtic tea-pot, the vaſt circumference of which reſted on her left arm. Each of us presented his cup, which was filled with a bumper of tea, on the surface of which floated a thick coat of butter: the tea was of the best quality. While we were sipping the hot fluid, our hoſtess re-appeared, bearing two dishes of gilt wood, the one full of raisins, the other of nuts. "These are fruits of our country," said Proul-Tamba to us; "they grow in a fine valley not far diſtant. In the Weſtern Heaven have you fruits of this kind?" "Oh, yes, plentifully; and you cannot conceive how much pleasure you give us in presenting to us these fruits, for they recall to us our country," and, as we spoke, we took a handful of raisins from the gilt plate. Unfortunately, they were only remarkable for a tough and sour skin, and for a number of pips, which cracked under our teeth like gravel. We turned to the nuts, which were of a magnificent size, but were again deceived; the kernel was so solidly fixed in its hard shell, that it was as much as we could do to extract a few morsels with the tips of our nails. We returned to the raisins, then again to the nuts, travelling from one plate to the other in search, but vainly, of something wherewith to quiet the gnawings of our stomach. We were growing convinced that Mrs. Proul-Tamba had resolved to play us a trick, when we saw two vigorous Thibetians approach, carrying another table, on which was a whole kid, and a superb haunch of venison. This unexpected apparition gladdened our hearts, and an involuntary smile must have announced to our Amphitryon how favourably his second service was received. They removed the skins of raisins and the nut shells; Thibetian beer took the place of the buttered tea, and we set to work with incomparable energy. When we had triumphantly achieved this Homeric repast, we offered to the grand chief a scarf of blessing, and remounted our horses. Not far from the feudal castle of the illustrious Proul-Tamba we came to a calcareous hill, with great apertures on its summit, and on its rugged sides numerous Buddhic sentences cut in gigantic characters. All the Thibetians stopped, and prostrated themselves thrice to the ground. This mountain was the retreat of a hermit Lama, for whom all the tribes of the province of Kham entertained profound veneration. According to the statement of the natives, this holy Lama had withdrawn, twenty-two years before, to one of the caverns of the mountain; since that time, he had remained in it, without quitting it once, passing day and night in prayer, and in the contemplation of the ten thousand virtues of Buddha. He allowed no one to visit him. Every three years, however, he gave a grand audience of eight days, and, during that period, the devout might present themselves freely at his cell, and consult him about things paſt, present, and to come. At this time, large offerings failed not to pour in from every quarter : the sainted Lama kept none for himself, but diſtributed them among the poor of the diſtrict. What did he want with riches and the good things of this world ? His cell, dug out of the living rock, never required the leaſt repair ; his yellow robe, lined with sheepskin, served him alike in all seasons of the year. On every sixth day only did he take a repaſt, consiſting of a little tea and barley-meal, which charitable persons in the vicinity passed to him by means of a long cord, which descended from the top of the grotto to the foot of the mountain.

Several Lamas had placed themselves under the direction of this hermit, and had resolved to adopt his manner of life. They dwelt in cells, dug near that of their maſter. The moſt celebrated of his disciples was the father of the great Proul-Tamba. He, also, had been a famous warrior, and ever at the head of the people of this country. Having reached an advanced age, and seeing his son capable of being his successor, he had conferred on him the title of Grand Chief. Then, shaving his head, and assuming the sacred habit of the Lamas, he had retired into solitude, leaving to younger and more vigorous hands the charge of terminating the conteſt which had commenced between the two Houtouktous of the province of Kham.

The sun had not set when we reached the ſtation of Wang-Tsa [Wang-k'a], fifty lis from Bagoung. Wang-Tsa is a small village built at the foot of a hill of black loam, covered with thickets of holly and cypress The houses, built of the black soil, communicate to the village an entirely sombre and funereal aspect. At Wang-Tsa, we began to observe traces of the civil war, which was laying waſte these countries. The Chinese barracks, built of large fir planks, had been entirely burnt; its remains, half charred, which lay about, served throughout the evening to keep up a magnificent fire. Upon setting out next morning, we observed a singular alteration in the caravan. The horses and oxen were the same that we had taken from Bagoung, but all the Thibetian guides had vanished not one of them remained: women of Wang-Tsa had taken their place. Upon inquiring the meaning of this new and surprising arrangement: "To-day," answered the Lama Dsiamdchang, "we shall reach Gaya which is a hostile village. If the Bagoung men went there, there would inevitably be a fight, and the inhabitants of Gaya would seize the animals of the caravan. The *oulah* being conducted by women, we have nothing to fear. Men, who would have the cowardice to fight with women, and take the animals confided to their care, would be despised by the whole world. Such is the usage of these countries." We were not a little surprised to find, among the wild mountains of Thibet, sentiments so like those of our own country. This was pure French chivalry. We were eager to see in what courteous and gallant fashion the ladies of Wang-Tsa would be received by the gentlemen of Gaya.

After passing a lofty mountain, covered with large masses of rock, partly buried in old layers of snow, we entered a valley thoroughly cultivated, and of a mild temperature. We perceived in the distance, in a hollow, the houses of Gaya. They were high, flanked with watch-towers, and not unlike castles. When we were some hundred paces from this large village, there issued from it all at once a formidable squadron of cavalry, who dashed forward to meet the caravan. The horsemen, armed with fusils and long lances, seemed quite disposed for a skirmish. Their martial humour, however, vanished, when they perceived that the caravan was conducted by women; and they contented themselves with hearty shouts of laughter, and with expressions of contempt at the cowardice of their foes. As we entered Gaya, men, women, and children were all in motion, and sending forth cries, that seemed to us anything but amicable. No mischance, however, occurred. We dismounted in the court of a large three-storied house, and as soon as they had unsaddled the horses, and unyoked the long-haired oxen, the ladies of Wang-Tsa drank hastily a cup of buttered tea, which was courteously handed round to each, and immediately returned with their *oulah*.

We found at Gaya a tolerably comfortable lodging, but we did not know on what condition we should proceed. The important question of the *oulah* occupied everyone's mind, yet no one ventured to put the question openly, and we went to bed, leaving the consideration of serious matters to the morrow.

It was scarce day when the court of the house where we lodged was filled with a crowd of Thibetians, who had come to deliberate on the degree in which they should tax our caravan. From a second floor balcony, we could enjoy at our leisure the spectacle which this council presented. Of the immense multitude there was not an individual who was not an orator; everybody spoke at once; and, judging from the sounding altitude of the voices, and the impetuous animation of the gestures, there must certainly have been some very fine speeches there. Some orators mounted upon the luggage that was piled in the court, and made of it a pulpit, whence they overlooked the multitude. Sometimes it seemed that the eloquence of words was insufficient to convey conviction to the minds of the audience, for the disputants would fight and pull each other's hair, and beat each other without mercy, until an orator of superior influence came and called the honourable members to order. This calm, however, would not be of long duration : the tumult and disorder would soon recommence with increased vigour. The thing became so serious, that we were convinced these people would end with drawing their sabres, and massacring each other. We were miſtaken. After the assembly had vociferated, geſticulated, and manipulated for more than an hour, there was a great shout of laughter ; the council rose, and everybody withdrew perfeƈtly calm. Two deputies then ascended to the second-floor, where the ſtaff of the caravan lodged ; and informed Ly-Kouo-Ngan that the chiefs of the family of Gaya, after deliberating on the organization of the *oulah*, had decided that they would furnish gratuitously animals for the two Lamas of the Weſtern Heaven, and for the Thibetians of Lha-Ssa ; but that the Chinese muſt pay half an ounce of silver for a horse, and a quarter for a long-haired ox. At this intimation, Ly-Kouo-Ngan colleƈted his ſtrength, and inveighed with energy againſt what he called a tyranny, an injuſtice. The Chinese soldiers of the caravan, who were present, co-operated with loud cries and menaces, for the purpose of intimidating the delegates of the national assembly of Gaya ; but the latter preserved an attitude deliciously haughty and contemptuous. One of them advanced a ſtep, placed, with a sort of wild dignity his right hand on the shoulder of Ly-Kouo-Ngan, and after piercing him with his great black eyes, shaded with thick eyebrows, " Man of China," said he, " liſten to me ; doſt thou think that with an inhabitant of the valley of Gaya there is much difference between cutting off the head of a Chinese and that of a goat ? Tell thy soldiers, then, not to be too fierce, and not to talk big words. Who ever saw the fox that could terrify the terrible yak of the mountains ? The *oulah* will be ready presently ; if you do not take it, and go to-day, to-morrow the price will be doubled." The Chinese perceiving that violence would only involve disagreeable results, had recourse to cajolery, but to no purpose. Ly-Kouo-Ngan found no resource except that of opening his strong-box, and weighing out the required sum. The *oulah* soon arrived, and we occupied ourselves busily with the organization of the caravan, in order to leave as soon as possible this village of Gaya, which the Chinese deemed barbarous and [un]inhabitable, but which seemed to us extremely picturesque.

From Gaya to Angti [Ang-ti], where we were to change the *oulah*, was only a short stage of thirty lis. The Chinese were in despair at having been obliged to spend so much money to effect so short a distance; but they had only come to the commencement of their miseries; for we were destined to meet with Thibetian tribes still less tractable than those of Gaya.

The snow, which had given us a few days' respite since our departure from Tsiamdo, again assailed us on the very evening of our arrival at Angti. During the night, and on the following day, it fell in such abundance that we were unable to go out without having it up to our knees. As a climax of misfortune, we had, on leaving Angti, to ascend one of the rugged and most dangerous mountains on this route. The Chinese Itinerary thus describes it: " At Angti, you cross a great snow-clad mountain; the road is very steep; the accumulated snows resemble a silvery vapour. The fog which the mountain exhales penetrates the body, and makes the Chinese ill."

According to a popular tradition of the country, in the olden time, a chief of the tribe of Angti, a famous warrior, held in awe by all his neighbours, was buried under an avalanche one day when he was crossing the mountain. All the efforts to recover his body were fruitless. A holy Lama of the period, having declared that the chief had become the genius of the mountain, they raised a temple to him, which still exists, and where travellers never fail to burn a few incense sticks, before proceeding on their way. In tempests, when the wind blows with violence, the genius of Mount Angti never fails to appear; there is no one about who has not seen him several times. He is always seen mounted upon a red horse, clothed in large white robes, and quietly sauntering upon the crest of the mountain. If he meets any traveller, he takes him on his crupper, and vanishes forthwith at full gallop. The red horse being so light that he leaves no trace, even on the snow, no one, to this day, has been able to discover the retreat of the White Knight, for so they call him in the country.

As to us, we were not much concerned about the red horse and the white knight. What we feared, was the mountain itself. We could not help shuddering at the sight of the frightful quantity of snow which had fallen, and which would render the road extremely dangerous. We were obliged to await the return of fine weather, and then to send, as we had before done under similar circumstances, a herd of long-haired oxen to trample down the snow, and trace out a path over the mountain.

We stayed five days at Angti. Ly-Kouo-Ngan took advantage of this long halt to doctor his legs, the malady in which assumed every day a more alarming character. The question of the *oulah*, long discussed in several assemblies, was resolved, at last, in the same way as at Gaya; a result which did not fail greatly to annoy the Chinese, and to elicit from them infinite clamour.

What we found most remarkable at Angti was, certainly, the *Dheba* or chief of the tribe. This individual, named Bomba, was at most three feet high; the sabre which he carried in his girdle was, at least, twice his own length; notwithstanding this, the man had a magnificent chest, and a face, broad, energetic in its expression, and beautifully regular in its features. The exiguity of his stature arose from an entire abortion of the legs, which, however, did not in the least affect his feet; nor did the almost total absence of legs prevent the chief of the tribe of Angti from being surprisingly active. He was always running about with as much agility as the longest legged of his people; he could not, indeed, make very extended strides, but he compensated for this by the rapidity of his movements. By dint of working about right and left, skipping and jumping, he always arrived as soon as any one else; he was, they said, the most expert horseman, and the most intrepid warrior of the tribe. When they had once hoisted him on his horse, where he held on, at once standing and seated, he was invincible. In the popular assemblies, which the mountaineers of these regions are in the habit of holding very frequently, and always in the open air, to discuss all questions of public and private interest, the chief Bomba always made himself remarkable by the ascendancy of his eloquence and his resolute character. When they were discussing at Angti the tax on the *oulah*, no one was seen, no one heard, but the astonishing Bomba. Perched on the shoulders of a big, tall Thibetian, he pervaded, like a giant, the tumultuous assembly, and dominated it, by word and gesture, still more than by his factitious stature.

The chief of Angti omitted no opportunity of giving us special proofs of kindness and sympathy. One day, he invited us to dine with him. This invitation served the double end of exercising towards us the duty of hospitality, and, in the next place, of piquing the jealousy of the Chinese, whom he hated and despised with all his soul. After dinner, which offered nothing remarkable but a profusion of uncooked and boiled meat, and tea richly saturated with butter, he asked us to go and see a saloon full of pictures and armour of every description. The pictures which lined the walls consisted of portraits, rudely coloured, representing the most illustrious ancestors of the family of Bomba. We observed there, a numerous collection of Lamas of every age and dignity and some warriors in war costume. The arms were numerous, and in great variety. There were lances; arrows; two-edged sabres, spiral and scythe-shaped; tridents; long sticks with large iron rings; and matchlocks, the stocks of which were of most singular shapes. The defensive arms were round bucklers of the hide of the wild yak, ornamented with red copper nails; armlets and greaves of copper, and coats of mail of iron wire, of a thick and close web, but, notwithstanding, very elastic. The chief Bomba told us that these coats of mail were the armour of very ancient times, which had been put aside since the use of the gun had become general in their country. The Thibetians, as we have said, are too indifferent in matters of chronology, to be able to assign the time when they began to make use of fire-arms. It may be presumed, however, that they were not acquainted with gunpowder until towards the thirteenth century, in the time of the wars of Tchingghiskhan, who had, as we know, artillery in his army. A rather remarkable circumstance is, that in the mountains of Thibet, as well as in the Chinese empire and the plains of Tartary, there is no one but knows how to make powder. Every family makes it for its own use. In passing through the province of Kham we often remarked women and children busily employed in pounding coal, sulphur, and salt petre. The powder thus made is certainly not so good as that of Europe, yet, when it is put in a fusil, with a ball upon it, it is sufficiently potent to project the ball, and make it kill stags in hunting, and men in battle.

After five days' repose we resumed our route. Immediately at the outset, the caravan began to ascend the lofty mountain of Angti. We met neither red horse nor white knight, and no genius took us on his crupper, to bear us away to his solitary abode. On every side we saw only snow, but that snow was so abundant that even on the most noted mountains we have never found so frightful a quantity. Frequently the guides, mounted upon long-haired oxen, entirely disappeared in gulfs, from which they could only disengage themselves with great difficulty. More than once we were on the point of retracing our steps and giving up all hopes of reaching the summit.

The small Sinico-Thibetian caravan that had joined us at Tsiamdo, and that had never left us since, presented a spectacle worthy of the utmost compassion. We forgot, in some degree, our own sufferings, when we saw these poor little creatures almost at every step buried in the snow, and with hardly strength enough to cry. We admired the intrepid energy of the Thibetian mother, who, so to speak, multiplied herself, in order to rush to the assistance of her numerous offspring, and who derived, from maternal tenderness, superhuman strength.

The mountain of Angti is so lofty and steep that it took us the whole day to ascend and descend it. The sun had already set when we managed to roll to the bottom. We halted a few minutes, under some black tents inhabited by nomad shepherds, swallowed a few handfuls of *tsamba*, diluted with brackish tea, and then resumed our route along a rocky valley where the snow was all melted. We followed for two hours, in utter darkness, the steep banks of a river, of which we heard the waters without seeing them. Every instant we trembled lest we should be precipitated into it;

but the animals, which knew the road, and which we left to their inſtinct, conducted us safely to Djaya.

Our arrival in the middle of the night put all the town in commotion. The dogs, by their fierce barking, gave the alarm. Soon after, the doors of the houses were opened, and the inhabitants of the town rushed out in a crowd into the ſtreets, with horn lanterns, torches, and weapons of every description, the general impression being that there was an invasion of the enemy. However, when they observed the peaceful and even timid bearing of the caravan, their apprehensions were quieted, and each person returned home. It was paſt midnight before we were able to get a sleep, having previously resolved to ſtay a day at Djaya, with a view to taking a few hours' reſt after crossing the famous mountain of Angti,—not more than was necessary.

Djaya is, as we have ſtated already, the residence of the young Lama Houtouktou, who at the time was warring with the Houtouktou of Tsiamdo. The town, situated in a beautiful valley, is tolerably large; but at the time we passed through it, it was half in ruins; scarce twenty days had elapsed since it had been attacked by the partisans of the Grand Houtouktou. The two parties, we were informed, had had terrific combats, wherein on both sides the victims had been numerous. In passing through the town, we found whole quarters laid waſte by fire; nothing remained but enormous heaps of calcined stones, and woodwork reduced to ashes. All the trees of the valley had been cut down, and the trampling of horses had utterly laid waſte the cultivated fields. The celebrated Lamasery of Djaya was deserted, the cells of the Lamas and the walls, of more than 400 yards in circuit, which surrounded them, had been demolished, and presented nothing but a terrible mass of ruins. The assailants had only respected the principal temples of Buddha.

THIBET, AND CHINA

The Chinese government keeps at Djaya a small garrison, composed of twenty soldiers, commanded by a *Tsien-Tsoung* and a *Pa-Tsoung*. These military gentlemen wore anything but a satisfied aspect. They seemed to be very indifferently pleased in this country, a prey to all the horrors of civil war. The warlike attitude of the mountaineers left them no rest, day or night. It was in vain they tried to preserve neutrality, or rather to have the appearance of belonging to both parties; they none the less found themselves constantly between two fires. It would appear, indeed, that Djaya has never furnished to the Chinese an easy and agreeable residence. At all times Chinese domination has met with invincible resistance from the fierce tribes around it. The Chinese Itinerary, which was written in the reign of the Emperor Kien-Loung, expresses itself thus concerning these countries: "The Thibetians, who inhabit the district of Djaya, are of a haughty and fierce character; all attempts to subdue them have been fruitless, they are considered very ferocious; it is their natural character." What the Chinese writer calls "fierce character," is nothing more in reality than ardent patriotism, and a very just hatred of a foreign yoke.

A day's rest having sufficiently repaired our strength, we quitted Djaya. It is unnecessary to add that the Chinese were obliged to pay, and in ready money, for the hire of the *oulah*. The Thibetians of the country were too ferocious to furnish us gratuitously with oxen and horses. We travelled for two days through a country extremely low, where we frequently found small villages and black tents grouped in the valleys. We were often obliged to traverse wooden bridges, in order to cross sometimes calm and quiet streams, and at other times torrents, the impetuous waters of which rolled on with a terrible noise. Shortly before our arrival at the station of Adzou-Thang

[A-tsu-t'ang], we overtook the party which was accompanying the coffin of the deceased *Leang-Tai* from Bagoung. The son also had juſt died in a black tent, after a few hours' frightful agony. The caravan, having no chief, was in a complete ſtate of disorganization ; most of the soldiers of the escort had dispersed, after pillaging the baggage of their Mandarin; three only had remained, who were devising the beſt means of effecting the conveyance of the two bodies to China. They despaired of being able to continue their journey in so small a number ; so that the arrival of our caravan extricated them from a great difficulty. The conveyance of the father's body had been arranged at Bagoung ; that of the son remained unsettled. The carriers of his palanquin had refused to undertake the carriage, for they foresaw that there would not be money enough to pay them for their trouble. To place the coffin on an ox was impracticable ; there was no inducing a Thibetian guide to allow one of their animals to carry a corpse, much less the corpse of a Chinese. We were obliged to have recourse to ſtratagem. The body of the laſt deceased Mandarin was secretly cut into four pieces, and then packed in a box, which we put among the general luggage, making the Thibetians believe that in honour of filial piety, the body of the son had been laid beside that of his father, in the same coffin.

The two corpses, that had become our fellow-travellers, communicated to the caravan a mournful aspect, which had great influence upon the Chinese imagination. Ly, the Pacificator of Kingdoms, whose strength decreased daily, was particularly alarmed by the circumſtance ; he would fain have removed the sad spectacle, but this he could not effect without exposing himself to the terrible accusation of having impeded the sepulture of two Mandarins, who had died in a foreign country.

THIBET, AND CHINA

From Adzou-Thang, we went on to sleep and change *oulah* in a small village of the valley of Che-Pan-Keou [Shih-pan-kou] "Valley of Slates." According to the testimony of the Chinese Itinerary, the inhabitants of this valley are a rude, wicked, and obstinate people; that is to say, in other words, they do not fear the Chinese, and are in the habit of making them pay a good price for the yaks and horses with which they furnish them.

The valley of Che-Pan-Keou, as its name indicates, abounds in quarries of argillaceous schist. The Thibetians of these countries raise from them beautiful slate, which they use in tiling their houses; they also raise very thick pieces, upon which they engrave images of Buddha with the form, *Om mani padme houm*. This slate is of very fine texture. The small portions of mica or talc which it contains, gives it a brilliant and silky lustre.

The stream which flows through the centre of the valley contains a large quantity of gold dust, which the natives do not neglect to collect and refine. As we walked along the stream, we found fragments of crucibles, to which were still attached a few particles of gold; we showed them to the Pacificator of Kingdoms, and this sight seemed to reanimate his strength, and to renew the bonds which attached him to life. The blood suddenly rushed into his face, his eyes, which had been almost extinct, shone with an unwonted fire. One would have said the sight of a few grains of gold had made him completely forget both his malady and the two corpses which accompanied him.

Musk deer abound in this schistous valley. Although that animal, addicted to cold climates, is met with on almost all the mountains of Thibet, nowhere, perhaps, is it seen in such large numbers as in the neighbourhood of Che-Pan-Keou. The pines, cedars, hollies, and cypresses, which cover this country, contribute, no doubt, a great deal to attract these animals thither, peculiarly fond, as they are, of the roots of these trees, which have a strong aromatic perfume.

The musk deer is of the height of a goat; it has a small head; its nose is pointed, and ornamented with long white mustachios; its legs are small, its haunches large and thick; two long crooked teeth, which grow out of the upper jaw, enable it to tear up from the ground the odiferous roots upon which it subsists; its hair is generally from two to three inches long, and is hollow, like that of almost all the animals which live north of the Himalaya mountains, extremely rough, and always bristling; its colour is black below, white in the middle, and inclining to grey above. A bladder, suspended from the belly, near the navel, contains the precious substance, the musk.

The inhabitants of the schistous valley capture in the chase such a number of these musk deer that you see nothing in their houses but the skins of these animals, hung on the walls by pegs. They use the hair to stuff the thick cushions, on which they sit during the day, and the sort of mattress which serves them for a bed; they have in the musk the source of a very lucrative trade with the Chinese.

The day after our arrival at Che-Pan-Keou we bade farewell to the inhabitants of the valley, and proceeded on our way. At the three next stations, they were quite inexorable on the question of the *oulah*. The Chinese were disgusted at the behaviour of these rude mountaineers, who, as they said, did not comprehend hospitality, and had no notion of what was right and what was wrong. As to us, on the contrary, we sympathized with these men and their rude, spirited temperament; their manners, it is true, were not refined, but their natural disposition was

THIBET, AND CHINA

generosity and frankness itself, and in our eyes matter was of more moment than manner. At length we reached Kiang-Tsa [Chiang-k'a (Gartok)], and the Chinese now began to breathe more freely, for we were entering upon a less hostile district. Kiang-Tsa is a very fertile valley, the inhabitants of which seem to live in plenty. We remarked among them, besides the soldiers of the garrison, a great number of Chinese from the provinces of Sse-Tchouan and Yun-Nan, who keep a few shops and exercise the primary arts and trades. A few years, they say, enable them, in this country, to amass a tolerably large fortune. The two military Mandarins of Kiang-Tsa, who had been companions in arms of Ly-Kouo-Ngan, were alarmed at the deplorable state in which they found him, and advised him strongly to continue his journey in a palanquin. We joined our entreaties to theirs, and we were fortunate enough to triumph over the avarice of the Pacificator of Kingdoms. He appeared at last to comprehend that a dead man had no need of money, and that first of all he should see to the saving of his life. The son of the Mandarin Pei seemed to have died just in the nick of time for placing at Ly-Kouo-Ngan's disposal his palanquin and his eight Chinese bearers, all of whom were at Kiang-Tsa. We halted for one day to repair the palanquin and to give the bearers time to prepare their travelling sandals.

The countries which we passed to the south of Kiang-Tsa seemed to us less cold and less barren than those we had journeyed through previously. The ground perceptibly declined ; we were still, indeed, completely surrounded by mountains, but they gradually lost their savage and mournful aspect. We no longer saw those threatening forms, those gigantic masses of granite with sharp and perpendicular declivities. High grass and forests showed themselves on every side, cattle became more numerous and everything announced that we were rapidly advancing towards more temperate climes; only the tops of the mountains still preserved their crowns of snow and ice.

Four days after our departure from Kiang-Tsa, we reached the banks of the Kin-Cha-Kiang "River of Gold-duft," which we had already crossed on the ice with the Thibetian ambassador, two months before our arrival at Lha-Ssa. Amid the beautiful plains of China, this magnificent river rolls on its blue waves with an imposing majefty; but among the mountains of Thibet, it is ever bounding about, throwing the great mass of its waters to the bottom of gorges and valleys, with terrible impetuosity and noise. At the spot where we came to the river, it was enclosed between two mountains, the sharp flanks of which rising perpendicularly on its banks, made for it a narrow but extremely deep bed; the waters ran rapidly, sending forth a low and lugubrious sound. From time to time we saw huge masses of ice approach, which, after having whirled round in a thousand eddies, at laft were dashed to pieces againft the sharp projections of the mountain.

We followed the right bank of the Kin-Cha-Kiang for half a day. Towards noon, we reached a small village, where we found everything prepared beforehand for crossing the river. The caravan divided itself among four flat boats, and in a little while we were on the opposite bank. Near it, at the entrance to a narrow valley, was the ftation of Tchon-Pa-Loung. [Chu-pa-lung (Gru-ba-nang)]. The *Dheba* of the place furnished us by way of supper, with some excellent fresh fish; and, for sleeping, with a very snug wind-tight chamber, and thick mattresses ftuffed with the hair of the musk deer.

Next day we travelled along a small river, which subsequently joins the River of Gold-duft. Our hearts were lighter than usual, for we had been told that we should arrive the same day in a charming country. As we went along, we accordingly looked first on one side and then on the other, with an uneasy curiosity; from time to time we rose on our stirrups in order to see further; but the landscape was a long time before it became poetical. On our left we had still the aforesaid river, prosaically running over great stones, and on our right a large red mountain, dismal, bare, and cut up in all directions by deep ravines; masses of white clouds, driven onwards by a cutting wind, flitted over the sides of the mountain, and formed, ahead of us, a sombre horizon of mist.

Towards midday, the caravan halted at some ruins, to drink a cup of tea and eat a handful of *tsamba*; we then clambered on to the top of the red mountain, and from the height of this great observatory admired on our right the magnificent, the enchanting plain of Bathang [Ba-t'ang].[1] We found ourselves all at once transported, as it were by magic, into the presence of a country which offered to our view all the wonders of the richest and most varied vegetation. The contrast, above all, was striking. On one side, a sombre, barren, mountainous region, almost throughout a desert; on the other, on the contrary, a joyous plain, where numerous inhabitants occupied themselves in fertile fields in the labours of agriculture. The Chinese Itinerary says: "The canton of Bathang is a beautiful plain, a thousand lis in length, well watered by streams and springs; the sky there is clear, the climate pleasant, and everything gladdens the heart and the eyes of man." We quickly descended the mountain, and continued our journey in a real garden, amid flowering trees and verdant rice fields. A delicious warmth gradually penetrated our limbs, and

[1] Bathang signifies in Thibetian, plain of cows.

we soon felt our furred dresses oppressive; it was nearly two years since we had perspired, and it seemed very odd to be warm without being before a good fire.

Near to the town of Bathang, the soldiers of the garrison were drawn up in line to do military honours to the Pacificator of Kingdoms, who, perched up, at the bottom of his palanquin, went through the ranks in a very unwarlike manner. The Thibetian population, who were all on foot, accompanied the caravan to a beautiful Chinese pagoda which was to serve for our lodging. The same evening, the Mandarins of the Chinese garrison and the Grand Lamas of the town came to pay us a visit, and to offer us some beef and mutton, butter, corn, candles, bacon, rice, nuts, raisins, apricots, and other products of the country.

At Bathang there is a magazine of provisions, the fourth from Lha-Ssa; it is, like all the others, managed by a literary Mandarin, bearing the title of *Leang-Tai*. The Chinese garrison, consisting of three hundred soldiers, is commanded by a *Cheou-Pei* [*shou-pei*], two *Tsien-Tsoung*, and a *Pa-Tsoung*. The annual maintenance of the Chinese troops who belong to this post amounts to nine thousand ounces of silver, without reckoning the rations of rice and *tsamba*. We observed, among the population of Bathang, a very great number of Chinese; they are engaged in various arts and trades; several of them, indeed, occupy themselves with agriculture, and make the most of the Thibetian farms. This plain, which you find, as by enchantment, amid the mountains of Thibet, is wonderfully fertile: it produces two harvests each year. Its principal products are, rice, maize, barley, wheat, peas, cabbages, turnips, onions, and several other varieties of vegetables. Of fruits, you find grapes, pomegranates, peaches, apricots and water melons. Honey is also very abundant there. Lastly, you find there mines of cinnabar (sulphur of mercury), from which they extract a large quantity of mercury. The Thibetians get the mercury in all its purity by disengaging the sulphur by combustion, or by combining it with slack-lime.

The town of Bathang is large and very populous, and its inhabitants seem to be well off. The Lamas there are very numerous as they are in all the Thibetian towns. The principal Lamasery, which they call the Grand Monastery of Ba ['Ba], has for its superior a *Kampo*, who holds his spiritual authority from the Talé-Lama of Lha-Ssa.

The temporal power of the Talé-Lama ends at Bathang. The frontiers of Thibet, properly so called, were fixed in 1726, on the termination of a great war between the Thibetians and the Chinese. Two days before you arrive at Bathang you pass, on the top of the Mang-Ling mountain, a stone monument, showing what was arranged at that time between the government of Lha-Ssa and that of Peking, on the subject of boundaries. At present the countries situated east of Bathang are independent of Lha-Ssa in temporal matters. They are governed by the *Tou-Sse*, a sort of feudal princes, originally appointed by the Chinese Emperor, and still acknowledging his paramount authority.

These petty sovereigns are bound to go every third year to Peking, to offer their tribute to the Emperor.

We halted at Bathang three days, the illness of our guide Ly-Kouo-Ngan being the cause of this delay. The daily fatigues of this long journey had so overpowered the poor Mandarin, that he was in an almost hopeless state. His best plan was to take advantage of the fine climate of Bathang, and to let the caravan proceed on its way. His friends advised him to do so, but without success. He insisted upon continuing his journey, and sought, in every way, to deceive himself as to the serious nature of his malady. As for us, we considered his case so dangerous that we felt it our duty to profit by the repose we enjoyed at Bathang, to talk seriously to him on the subject of his soul and of eternity. Our previous conversations on the way had already sufficiently enlightened him as to the principal truths of Christianity. Nothing now remained but to make him clearly perceive his position, and to convince him of the urgency of entering frankly and fully into the path of salvation. Ly-Kouo-Ngan concurred with us, admitting our observations to be replete with reason. He himself spoke with great eloquence on the frailty and brevity of human life, of worldly vanities, of the impenetrability of God's decrees, of the importance of salvation, of the truth of the Christian religion, and of the obligation on all mankind to embrace it. He said to us, on all these subjects, some very sensible and very touching things; but when it came to the point, to the practical result, to the declaring himself Christian, there was a dead stand; he must absolutely wait till he had returned to his family, and had abdicated his mandarinate. It was in vain that we represented to him the danger he incurred by postponing this important matter; all was useless. "So long as I am a Mandarin of the Emperor," said he, " I cannot serve the Lord of Heaven," and he had got this absurd idea so deep in his brain, that it was impracticable to dislodge it.

On leaving the station at Bathang, we were obliged to turn for some distance, quite northwards, in order to resume an eastern direction; for since our departure from Tsiamdo we had continually progressed towards the south during twenty consecutive days. The caravans are compelled to lengthen this route considerably, in order to reach a secure passage across the great river Kin-Cha-Kiang.

THIBET, AND CHINA

Our first day's march from Bathang was full of charms, for we travelled in a delightful temperature, through a country of an infinite variety of landscape. The narrow path we followed was throughout bordered with willows and apricot trees in flower. Next day, however, we again found ourselves amid all the horrors and dangers of our old route. We had to ascend a very high mountain, upon which we were mercilessly assailed by the snow and the north wind. It was a complete reaction against the sybaritism we had enjoyed in the warm and flowery plain of Bathang. At the foot of the mountains, the snow was succeeded by torrents of cold rain, which seemed to filter through into the very marrow of our bones. As a climax of misfortune, we were obliged to pass the night in a habitation, the roof of which, cracked in several places, gave free passage to the wind and rain. We were, however, so exhausted with fatigue that this did not prevent our sleeping. The next day, we awoke in the mire ; we found our bedclothes entirely soaked, and our limbs stiff with cold. We were obliged to rub ourselves violently with pieces of ice, in order to restore circulation to the blood. The abominable village which afforded us this horrible lodging, bears the name of Ta-So [Ta-So (sDag-shod)]. On emerging from the valley of Ta-So, you ascend, by a narrow gorge, an elevated plain, which we found covered with snow. Here we entered a magnificent forest, the finest we had seen in the mountains of Thibet. The pines, cedars, and hollies entwined their vigorous branches, and formed a dome of verdure impenetrable to the sun, and under which there is much better protection from the rain and snow than in the houses of Ta-So. The trunks and branches of these large trees are covered with thick moss, which extends in long and extremely delicate filaments. When this stringy moss is new, it is of a beautiful green hue ; but when it is old, it is black, and bears an exact resemblance to long tufts of dirty and ill-combed hair. There is nothing more grotesque or fantastic than the appearance of these old pines, with this very long hair suspended from their branches. The prickly holly that grows on the mountains of Thibet is remarkable for the extraordinary development it attains. In Europe, it never exceeds the size of a shrub, but here it always grows to the size of a large tree. If it does not rise as high as the pine, it equals it in the size of its trunk, and it is even superior to it in the richness and abundance of its foliage.

This day's march was long and fatiguing. The night had set in when we reached the station of Samba where we were to change the *oulah*. We were just going to bed, when we missed a Thibetian, belonging to the escort, precisely the very man who had been assigned as our servant. We sought him, but without success, in every corner of the small village in which we had arrived. We concluded he had lost his way in the forest. We at first thought of sending in search of him, but in so dark a night, how could one possibly find a man in that vast and thick forest? We contented ourselves with going in a body to a neighbouring hill, where we shouted, and lit a large fire. Towards midnight, the lost man reappeared, almost dead with fatigue. He carried on his back the saddle of his horse, which, no doubt, finding the journey too long, had thought fit to lie down in the midst of the forest, and it had been impossible to get him up again. The return of this poor young man filled everyone with joy, and we all then went to rest.

The next day, we rose late. Whilst the inhabitants of Samba were bringing the horses and the beasts of burden to form the caravan, we went for a little walk, and to have a view of the place, which we had reached over night. The village of Samba is a collection of thirty small houses, built of large flint stones, rudely cemented, some with *argols*, others with mud. The aspect of the village is mournful, but the environs are tolerably cheerful. Two streams, one coming from the west, the other from the south, join near the village, and form a river, the transparent waters of which flow over a vast prairie. A small wooden bridge, painted red, herds of goats and long-haired cattle, which sported amid the pastures, some storks and wild ducks, fishing for their breakfast on the banks of the water, a few gigantic cypresses here and there, even the smoke which rose from the Thibetian cottages, and which the wind gently wafted over the adjacent hills, all contributed to give life and charm to the landscape. The sky was clear and serene. Already the sun, having risen a little above the horizon, promised us a fine day, and a mild temperature.

We returned to our lodgings, walking slowly. The caravan was ready, and on the point of departure; the beasts were laden with their burdens; the horsemen, their robes tucked up, and whip in hand, were ready to mount. "We are behindhand," said we, "let us make haste," and at a run we were in our places. "Why are you in such a hurry?" said a Chinese soldier, "Ly-Kouo-Ngan is not ready; he has not yet opened the door of his room." "To-day," answered we, "there is no great mountain ahead; the weather is fine: there is no objection to our starting a little later; go, however, and tell the Mandarin that the caravan is ready." The soldier pushed open the door and entered the chamber of Ly-Kouo-Ngan; he rushed out again pale and with haggard eyes. "Ly-Kouo-Ngan is dead!" said he to us, in a low tone. We rushed into the room, and saw the unfortunate Mandarin, stretched on his bed, his mouth open, his teeth clenched, and his eyes shrunk up by death. We placed our hands on his heart, which gently moved. He had yet a spark of life in him, but all hope was vain; the dying man had altogether loſt the use of his senses; there was another rattle or two in his throat, and he expired. The humours with which his legs were swollen had gone up to his cheſt, and suffocated him.

The death of our guide had not been unexpected; there was nothing in it to surprise us, but it occurred in such a sudden, melancholy manner, that everyone of us was greatly agitated. As for ourselves, in particular, we were afflicted at it beyond all expression. We bitterly regretted that it had not been our good fortune to assiſt at the laſt moments of this unfortunate man, whom we had so desired to bring from the darkness of paganism into the light of the faith. Oh, how impenetrable are the decrees of God! Some hope, however, mingled with our but too juſt grounds for fear. As this poor soul had been sufficiently enlightened as to the truths of religion, it is permissible to suppose that God, of his infinite mercy, perhaps accorded to him, in his laſt moments, the grace of the baptism of volition.

That day the caravan did not proceed on its march, the animals were unsaddled and sent out to paſture; and then the soldiers of the escort made all the necessary preparations, according to the Chinese rites, for conveying the body of their Mandarin to his family. We will not enter here into the details of what was done in this matter, for whatever concerns the manners and cuſtoms and ceremonies of the Chinese will find a place elsewhere. We will merely say that the defunct was enveloped in a large white pall, which had been given him by the living Buddha of Djachi-Loumbo, and which was covered with Thibetian sentences, and with images of Buddha, printed in black.

THIBET, AND CHINA

The Thibetians, and other Buddhists, have unlimited confidence in the printed winding-sheets which are distributed by the Talé-Lama and the Bandchan-Remboutchi. They are persuaded that those who are fortunate enough to be buried in them, cannot fail to have a happy transmigration.

By the demise of Ly-Kouo-Ngan, the caravan found itself without a leader and without a guide. There was, to be sure, the Lama Dsiamdchang, to whom the power should have fallen by right, and by legitimate succession; but the Chinese soldiers being very little disposed to acknowledge his authority, we passed from the monarchic state to the republican, democratical form. This state of things lasted at most half a day. Perceiving that the men of the caravan, both Thibetians and Chinese, were not yet prepared for so perfect a government, and considering that anarchy was developing itself in every direction, and that matters threatened to go to rack and ruin, consulting only the public interest and the safety of the caravan, we assumed the dictatorship. We immediately issued several decrees, in order that everything might be in readiness for us to proceed on the morrow at daybreak. The necessity of being governed was so completely understood, that no one made any opposition, and we were obeyed punctually.

At the appointed time, we left Samba. The caravan bore a sad and melancholy aspect. With its three corpses, it absolutely resembled a funeral procession. After three days' march across mountains, where we generally found wind, snow, and cold, we arrived at the station of Lithang [Li-t'ang] " copper plain." The Chinese government keeps here a magazine of provisions, and a garrison consisting of 100 soldiers. The Mandarins of Lithang are: a *Leang-Tai*, a *Cheou-Pei*, and two *Pa-Tsoung*. A few minutes after our arrival, these gentlemen came to pay us a visit. In the first place, the illness and death of our guide were discussed at full length; then we were required to state our quality, and by what authority and in what position we were in the caravan. By way of answer, we simply showed him a large scroll, fortified with the seal and signature of the ambassador Ki-Chan, and containing the instructions which had been given to Ly-Kouo-Ngan about us. "Good, good," said these persons to us, " the death of Ly-Kouo-Ngan will make no change in your position; you shall be well treated wherever you go. Up to this time you have always lived peaceably with the men of the caravan, doubtless this good understanding will continue to the end." We hoped so too. Yet, as considering human frailty, difficulties might possibly arise on the way, particularly among the Chinese soldiers, we wished to have with us a responsible Mandarin. We made this request, and were informed that of the four Mandarins who were at Lithang, not one could be spared to conduct us; that we could go along quietly enough as far as the frontiers, with our Thibetian and Chinese escort; and that there we should readily find a Mandarin to conduct us to the capital of Sse-Tchouan. "Very well," said we, "as you cannot give us a Mandarin we shall travel as we think fit, and go where we please. We are not even sure that on quitting this place we shall not return to Lha-Ssa. You see that we deal freely with you; reflect upon the point." Our four magistrates rose, saying that they would deliberate on this important matter, and that in the evening we should have an answer.

During our supper, a *Pa-Tsoung*, one of the four Mandarins, presented himself in his state robes. After the usual compliments, he told us that he had been selected to command our escort as far as the frontiers; that he had never, in his dreams of ambition, imagined he should have the honour of conducting people such as we; that he was ashamed on the firſt day of seeing us, to have to ask us a favour; it was, that we would reſt for two days at Lithang, in order to recover our ſtrength, which muſt be exhauſted by so long and arduous a journey. We perceived that our friend had need of two days to arrange some affairs of his own previous to a journey which he had not expected. " Ah," we replied, " already how full of solicitude is your heart for us. We will reſt then two days as you wish it." Authority having thus been reorganized, our dictatorship was at an end. But we thought we perceived that this was anything but agreeable to our people, who would much rather have had to do with us than with a Mandarin.

The town of Lithang is built on the sides of a hill which rises in the middle of a plain, broad but almoſt ſterile. Nothing grows there but a little barley, and a few poor herbs, which serve for paſturage to some miserable herds of goats and yaks. Seen from a diſtance, the town has some promise. Two large Lamaseries, richly painted and gilt, which are built quite on the top of the hill, especially contribute to give it an imposing aspect. But, when you pass through the interior, you find nothing but ugly, dirty, narrow ſtreets, so ſteep that your legs muſt be accuſtomed to mountain travelling to keep their equilibrium. This side of the River of Gold-duſt, you observe among the tribes a rather remarkable modification in the manners, cuſtoms, coſtume, and even in the language. You see that you are no longer in Thibet, properly so called. As you approach the frontiers of China, the natives have less ferocity and rudeness in their character; you find them more covetous, flattering, and cunning; their religious faith is no longer so vivid, nor so frank. As to the language, it is no longer the pure Thibetian that is spoken at Lha-Ssa, and in the province of Kham; it

TRAVELS IN TARTARY,

is a dialect closely connected with the idiom of the Si-Fan, and in which you remark various Chinese expressions. The Thibetians of Lha-Ssa who accompanied us had the greatest difficulty in the world in understanding and being understood. The costume, for the most part, only differs as to the head-dress. The men wear a hat of grey or brown felt, somewhat similar to our own felt hats when they first come from the hatter's board and have not been rounded to the form. The women form with their hair a number of small tresses, which flow over their shoulders. They then place on their heads a large silver plate somewhat similar to a dinner-plate. The more elegant wear two of these, one on each side, so that the two ends meet above the head. The precept of daubing the face with black does not apply to the women of Lithang. This kind of toilet operates only in the countries temporally subject to the Talé-Lama.

The most important of the Lamaseries of Lithang possesses a great printing press for Buddhic books, and it is hither that, on holidays, the Lamas of the neighbouring countries come in for their supplies. Lithang carries on also a large trade in gold dust, in chaplets of black beads, and in cups made with the roots of the vine and box-tree. As we departed from Lithang, the Chinese garrison was under arms, to render military honours to Ly-Kouo-Ngan. They acted as if he had been alive. When the coffin passed, all the soldiers bent their knees and exclaimed : "To the *Tou-Sse*, Ly-Kouo-Ngan, the poor garrison of Lithang wishes health and prosperity." The petty Mandarin, with the white button who had become our guide, saluted the garrison in the name of the deceased. This new commander of the caravan was a Chinese of Moslem extraction ; but one could find nothing about him which seemed to belong in the

THIBET, AND CHINA

least to the fine type of his ancestors: his puny, stunted person, his pointed smiling face, his shrill treble voice, his trifling manners, all contributed to give him the air of a shop-boy, and not in the least that of a military Mandarin. He was a prodigious talker. The first day he rather amused us, but he soon became a bore. He thought himself bound, in his quality of Mussulman, to talk to us, on all occasions, about Arabia, and of its horses that are sold for their weight in gold; about Mahomet, and his famous sabre that cut through metals; about Mecca and its bronze ramparts.

From Lithang to Ta-Tsien-Lou [Ta-chien-lu], a frontier town of China, is only 600 lis, which we divided into eight stages. We found the end of that frightful route to Thibet exactly like its middle and its beginning. We in vain climbed mountains; we found still more and more before us, all of a threatening aspect, all covered with snow and rugged with precipices; nor did the temperature undergo any perceptible change. It appeared to us that, since our departure from Lha-Ssa, we had been doing nothing but move round and round in the same circle. Yet, as we advanced, the villages became more frequent, without, however, losing their Thibetian style. The most important of these villages is Makian-Dsoung [Ma-rgan-rdzong], where some Chinese merchants keep stores for supplying the caravans. One day's journey from Makian-Dsoung, you pass in a boat the Ya-Loung-Kiang a large and rapid river. Its source is at the foot of the Bayen-Kharat mountains, close to that of the Yellow River. It joins the Kin-Cha-Kiang, in the province of Sse-Tchouan. According to the traditions of the country, the banks of the Ya-Loung-Kiang were the first cradle of the Thibetian nation, As we were passing the Ya-Loung-Kiang in a boat, a shepherd crossed the same river on a bridge merely composed of a thick rope of yak skin tightly stretched from one bank to the other. A sort of wooden stirrup was suspended by a solid strap to a moveable pulley on the rope. The shepherd had only to place himself backwards, under this strange bridge, with his feet on the stirrup, and hold on to the rope with both his hands; he then pulled the rope gently; the mere weight of his body made the pulley move, and he reached the other side in a very short time. These bridges are very common in Thibet, and are very convenient for crossing torrents and precipices; but one must be accustomed to them. We ourselves never ventured on them. Iron chain bridges are also much in use, particularly in the provinces of Oui and Dzang [Tsang (gTsang)]. To construct them, as many iron hooks are fixed on both sides of the river as there are to be chains, then the chains are fastened, and on the chains planks, which are sometimes covered with a coating of earth. As these bridges are extremely elastic, they are furnished with hand-rails.

We arrived at length safe and sound at the frontiers of China, where the climate of Thibet gave us a very cold farewell. In crossing the mountain which precedes the town of Ta-Tsien-Lou, we were almost buried in the snow, it fell so thick and fast; and which accompanied us into the valley where stands the Chinese town, which, in its turn, received us with a pelting rain. It was in the early part of June, 1846, and three months since we had departed from Lha-Ssa; according to the Chinese Itinerary, we had travelled 5,050 lis.

Ta-Tsien-Lou signifies the forge of arrows, and this name was given to the town because in the year 234 of our era, General Wou-Heou [Chu-ko Chung-wu-hou], while leading his army against the southern countries, sent one of his lieutenants to establish there a forge of arrows. This district has by turns belonged to the Thibetians and to the Chinese; for the last hundred years it has been considered as an integral part of the empire.

"The walls and fortifications of Ta-Tsien-Lou," says the Chinese Itinerary, "are of freestone. Chinese and Thibetians dwell there together. It is thence that the officers and troops which are sent to Thibet quit China. Through it passes also a large quantity of tea coming from China and destined to supply the provinces of Thibet; it is at Ta-Tsien-Lou that is held the principal tea fair. Although the inhabitants of this canton are very addicted to the worship of Buddha, they seek to get a little profit; yet they are sincere and just, submissive and obedient, so that nothing, even death, can change their natural good nature. As they have been long accustomed to the Chinese domination, they are the more attached to it."

We rested three days at Ta-Tsien-Lou, and each day had several quarrels with the principal Mandarin of the place, who would not consent to our continuing our route in a palanquin. However, he had at length to give way, for we could not bear even the idea of mounting once more on horseback. Our legs had bestrid so many horses of every age, size, quality and colour, that they refused to have anything further to do with horses at all, and were full of an irresistible resolution to stretch themselves at ease in a palanquin. This was granted them, thanks to the perseverance and energy of our remonstrance.

The Thibetian escort which had accompanied us so faithfully during the long and arduous route, returned after two days' rest. We gave the Lama Dsiamdchang a letter for the Regent, in which we thanked him for having assigned us so devoted an escort, and which had throughout kept in our memory the good treatment we had received at Lha-Ssa. On parting from these good Thibetians we could not help shedding tears, for insensibly, and as it were without our knowledge, ties had been formed between us which it was painful to sever. The Lama Dsiamdchang secretly told us that he had been charged to remind us, at the moment of separation, of the promise we had made to the Regent. He asked us if they might reckon on seeing us again at Lha-Ssa. We replied that they might, for at that time we were far from anticipating the nature of the obstacles that were to prevent our return to Thibet.

The next morning, at daybreak, we entered our palanquins, and were conveyed, at the public expense, to the capital of the province of Sse-Tchouan, where, by order of the Emperor, we were to undergo a solemn judgment before the Grand Mandarins of the Celestial Empire.

POSTSCRIPT

AFTER a few months journey through China, we arrived at Macao, in the early part of October, 1846. Our long and painful journey was at an end; and at laſt we were able, after so many tribulations, to enjoy a little quiet and repose. During two years we applied our leisure moments to the preparation of a few notes made in our journey. Hence these *Reminiscences of Travel*, which we address to our European brethren, whose charity will no doubt be intereſted in the trials and fatigues of the missionaries.

Our entrance into China, for the purpose of returning to our mission in Mongol-Tartary, compels us to leave unfinished the labour we had undertaken. It remains for us to speak of our relations with the Chinese tribunals and Mandarins, to give a sketch of the provinces we have traversed, and to compare them with those which we had occasion to visit in our former travels in the Celestial Empire. This omission we will endeavour to supply in the leisure hours we may be able to snatch from the labours of the sacred miniſtry. Perhaps we shall be in a position to give some correct notions about a country, of which, at no time, certainly, have men's ideas been so erroneous as they are at this day. Not that we are without abundant books about China and the Chinese. On the contrary, the number of works on these subjects that have appeared in France, and particularly in England, within the laſt few years, is really prodigious. But the zeal of a writer will not always suffice to describe countries in which he has never set his foot. To write travels in China, after a saunter or two through the factories of Canton and the environs of Macao, involves the danger of speaking of things that one is not thoroughly acquainted with. Although it has been the good fortune of the learned orientalist, J. Klaproth, to discover the Potocki Archipelago without quitting his closet, it is, generally speaking, rather difficult to make discoveries in a country which one has not visited.

INDEX

Aboucha [Ubashi], a Torgot chief, I 325
Adzon-Thang [A-tsu-t'ang], II 370
Akayé [Aka-yeh], a Lama, II 33 *et seq.*
Alani, I 308
Alan-To [Alado (A-ra-mdo)], II 324 *et seq.*
Alechan [Alashan], I 175, 208, 287, 288, 289, 294, 295, 296, 343, 358, 359, 365, 369
Altai mountains, II 196
Altan-Somé [Altan-sümé], I 21, 107
Altère [Altere], a Grand Lama, II 129 *et seq.*
Amdo, land of, II 29, 39, 45; people of, II 53
Amour [Amur], I 109, 123
Angti [Ang-ti], II 363, 367
Aral lake, I 322
Archery, Mantchou skill in, I 130
Argali, the wild horse, II 311
Argol, dried dung used as fuel, I 18 *passim*
Armour, Thibetian, II 366
Arroun [Arun], II 313
Arsalan, name of a dog, I 18, *et passim*
Asof, I 317
Atdza [Atsa], a village, II 310, 311, 314
Azaras [Hazaras], White, Indian Buddhists, II 189, 193, 229

Ba ['Ba], Grand Monastery of, II 377
Babdcho [babjo], a brother, I 380
Bactriana, I 308

Bagoung ['Ba-gong] II 349 *et seq.*
Baikal, Lake, I 109, II 322
Balk [Balkh], II 255
Bandchan-Remboutchi [Pan-ch'en-Rim-bo-ch'e], I 157; II 130 *et seq.*, 193 *et seq.*, 247, 383
Bankers, Chinese, I 295, 317
Barains, *see* Barin
Barbaro, Josaphat, I 317, 318
Barka, mountains, I 109
Barilang [Bari-nang] II 333
Barin, a principality north of Peking, I 214, 324
Barrow, Mr, I 364
Bathang [Ba-t'ang] " the plain of cows," II 375 *et seq.*
Batou [Batu], I 318
Batourou [Baturu], a title, I 329; II 3
Bayen-Kharat [Bayen-khara], a chain of mountains, II 12, 116, 142 *et seq.*, 387
Beïlé [beilé], a title, I 331; II 116
Beïssé [pei-tzŭ], a title, I 331; II 116
Birds in Tartary, I 190
Bochehons [Khoshigun], I 44
Bochkhon [Khoshigun], I 324
Bokhara, I 314
Bokté [Bogda], name of a Lama, I 244, 245
Bokte-Oula [Bogda-ula] sacred mountains, I 109, 327
Bomba, name of a chief of tribe at Angti, II 364, *et seq.*
Bonnets of Amdo women, II 39
Bonzes, I 155, 320; II 53, 261
Borax, supplies of, II 136

393

INDEX

Borhan [burkhan], I 157
Bo-Tchou, a river, II 291
Boukaria [Bukharia], I 323
Bouldeselle, Guillaume de, I 314
Bourhan-Bota [Burkhan-Buddha], name of a mountain, II 137
Boutan [Bhutan], II 170, 181, 187, 258, 284, 307
Brandy, II 69, 134
Bridge of ropes, II 383
Brigands, I 17, 361; II 2, 12, 105, 116, 124
Bronze foundries, I 33
Buddha-La [Potala], II 167 et seq., 248 et seq., 261
Buddhas, Living, I 219 et passim
Burial customs, I 92 et seq.; II 251
Butchering, methods of, I 116, 274; II 19

Calcutta, II 183, 184, 189, 211, 228, 254, 255, 258, 282 (see also Galgata)
Calendars, Mongol and Thibetian, II 268-270
Cambalech [Khan-balik], Peking, I 338 et seq.
Camels, treatment and use of, I 9, 148, 149, 178, 264 et seq.; II, 100, 149, 159, 162
Canton, II 200, 201, 214, 255, 256, 264, 267
Caravans, I 164, 286, 346; II 3, 125, 126, 137, 147
Cashmere, II 183, 188, 255
Cave-dwellings, Chinese, I 229 et seq.
Chaberon [shabron], appellation of Living Buddhas, I 157, 219 et seq.; II 163, 192, 247 et seq.
Chabi [Sha-bi, corruption of Sha-mi (Sraman)], a Lama disciple, I 102, 110, 224 et passim; II 31 et passim

Chaborté [Shabartai=Slough] a trading station, I 66 et seq., 80
Chakdja [Sa-skya], name of a lama, II 48, 49
Chakdja-Mouni [Sâkya-muni], the Buddha, II 46 et seq., 83
Chamiton [Chamiton (for Chamitou)], II, 342, footnote
Chamo [Shamo], Gobi Desert, I 359
Chan-ly-Houng [shan-li-hung], I 18
Chan-Si [Shansi], I 33, 39, 93, 94, 114, 133; II 19, 53
Chan-Toung [Shan-tung], I 121, 328; II 19, 201
Charadchambeul, name of a cameldriver, II 113, et passim.
Chara-Mouren [Shira-müren], I 16
Charmanas [sramana], monks, II 85
Chen-Si [Shensi] province, I 307; II 19
Cheou-pei [shou-pei], a title, II 376
Ché-Pan-Keou [Shih-pan-kou] = " valley of slates," II 371
Chess, in Thibet and China, II 329
Ché-Tsui-Dze [Shih-tsui-tzŭ], a frontier town on the Hoang-Ho, I 305, 342 et seq.
Chen-Yan [Shen-Yang] (Mukden), I 127
Chingtsa-Tsio [Shing-bza-'a-ch'os], a woman's name, II 45
Chobando [Shobando (Shuy-pamdo)], a town, II 333
Cho-Kan [sho-gang], a coin, II 180
Chor-Kou-La [Shar-ku-la], a mountain, II 323
Christians in Tartary, I 337 et seq.
Chronology, Lamanesque, II 271, 272

INDEX

Chuga [Shugan], Mount, II 139
Chun-T'che [Shun-chih] I 95, 112, footnote, 123; II 271
Chun-Ti [Shun-ti], I 320
Cochin China, I 309; II 342
Coinage, Chinese, I 140; Thibetian, II 179, 180
Conon de la Gabelentz, I 125
Conversion, method to be followed by missionaries, II 72 *et seq.*
Coſtume of missionaries, I 12
Cotton, cultivation of, I 128
Couriers between Lha-Ssa and Peking, II 334
Creation, legend of, II 94
Crusades, the, I 312
Cycles in Mongol and Thibetian calendars, II 268

Dabsoun-Noor [Dabsun-Nôr], I 262, 263, 264, 270
Dauria, I 127
Dchagar [rGya-gar], I 157
Dchak-La [Chag-la], a mountain, II 333
Dcha-Mi [rGya-mi], " Chinese," I 157
Dchassak [Jassak], miniſter of the King-Lama, I 113, 114, 331
Dchiahour [rgya-hor], I 15, *et passim*; description of, I 370
Dchos [*jôs* (*jo'os*)], a coin, I 140
Dchou-Ganga [Jün-Ganga (Ja'ün-Ganga)], Eaſtern Ganges, I 376
Demons frightened by prayer, II 75
Deserted cities in Tartary, I 82
Detsin-Dzong [Dechen jong (bDech'en-rdzong)], a village, II 294, 297
Dheba [*sde-pa*], governor of a diſtrict, II 291
Digourtchi [Digurchi] (Jikazze [Shikatse]), II 313

Divorce among Tartars, I 238
Djachi-Loumbo [Jashilumbo (bkrashis-Lhun-po)], I 157; II 193 *et seq.*, 247, 382
Djadanaring [Jadanaring], Mount, II 312
Djaya [Jaya (Draya)], II 344 *et seq.*, 368 *et seq.*
Djo-Naiman-Soumé [Jo-naimansümé], " The Hundred and Eight Convents," I 32
Dogs in Lha-Ssa, II 251
Dsiamdchang [Jamjang (? 'Jamdbyans)], a grand Lama, II 291 *et seq.*
Duhalde, Father, I 132
Dzang [Tsang (gTsang)], II 388
Dza-Tchou [Za-ch'u], a river, II 342, 347, 348

Eagles in Tartary, I 117
Eating-houses, I 30
Efe [Efu], kingdom of, I 95, *et seq.*
Eleuts [Ölet], I 209, 387 (*see also* Oelets)
Elliot, Mr, English plenipotentiary, II 201, 241
Emperor of China, I 290-294, 330; II 185, 195, 241
Enedkek (India), II 312
England, Chinese war with, I 43, 329, 372; II 241
English, Thibetian dislike of, II 189, 191, 222
Eul [Ol (?or Erh)] Mountain, II 65

Faculties, at Kounboum Lamasery, II 56
Famines, I 5
Fan (Fan-Lan-Mo), Brahma, II 88
Farsie [Persian] language, II 253
Ferns, as food, II 98
Fishing, methods of, I 192 *et seq.*
Flowers, Feaſt of, II 37 *et seq.*

395

INDEX

Fô, the living, Grand Lama, I 105, 157
Forty-two Points of Instruction, an edition of this work in four languages, II 83, 88
Fou-Y [Fu-I], a sage, II 88
Franba [Framba], the French, II, 94

Gabet, M., I 9, 35, 36, 56, 98, 102, 103, 147, 207, 249, 378; II 7, 140, 142, 144, 151, 152, 155, 258, 331
Galgata (Calcutta), I 376
Garlic, II 69, 112
Gaya, II 360
Gayouk [Güyük], Emperor, I 313, 314
Gechekten [Keshikten], I 16, 20 *et seq.*, 46, 324
Gé-Ho-Eul [Jehol], I 19, 114
Gepidæ, I 308
Getæ, the [Yüeh-chih], I, 307
Ghiamda [Giamda], a town, II 303 *et seq.*
Ghirin [Girin], I, 127
Gobi desert, I 84, 108, 111, 169, 215, 309, 334, 359
Gold in Thibet, II 179
Gorkha [Gurkha], a province, II 284, 287, 333
Goucho [*Gusl ti*], a title, II 96
Great Kouren (*see* Kouren).
Grosier, Abbé, I 209
Guard-houses, on Chinese roads, I 348
Guison-Tamba [Jebtsun-Damba (rJebtsun-Dampa)], King-Lama, I 108 *et seq.*, 150 *et seq.*, 324, 332; II 3, 247
Gunpowder in China, I 317

Hada, mosque at, II 20, 21
Hager, I 318
Han dynasty, I 308; II 87

Hares, as food, II 96
Hé-Chuy [Hei-Shui], Black Waters, Valley of, I, 2
Hedgehogs in Thibet, II 64
Heliogabalus, I 269
He-Loung-Kiang [Hei-lung-chiang], I 132
Herat, II 255
Hermits in Thibet, II 81, 115
Hia [Hsia], I 208
Hia-Ho-Po [Hsia-ho-p'o], a village, I 354, 356
Hia-Ma-Tching-Chin [Ha-ma-ching-shên], the deified toad, II 338
Hia-Tcheou [Hsia-chou], capital of Hia, I 208, 353
Hioung-Nou [Hsiung-nu], I 307, 337
Hoang-Ho [Huang-ho], Yellow River, I 16, 168 *et passim*
Hoang-Sse [Huang-Ssŭ], I 63
Hobilgan [Hubilgan], Great Lama, I 150, 157
Hodgson, Mr, English resident in Nepaul, II 313
Hoei-Hoei [Hui-hui], Chinese name for Moslems, I 327; II 18 *et seq.*
Ho-Kiao-Y [Ho-Chiao-i] another name for Tai-Toung-Fou, I 376, 377, 379, 381, 382
Ho-Nan, I 175; II 200
Hong-Kong, II 201
Hong-Lon-Ssé [Hung-lu-ssŭ], II 88
Hormoustha [Khormusta] (Persian Hormuzd), I 88, 279
Horsemanship among Tartars, I 54, 77
Horses of paper, II 73
Houlagou [Hulagu], Mongol Khan, I 314, 317
Houng-Mao-Eul [Hung-mao-êrh] Long Hairs, a Thibetian tribe, I 387; II 12, 14, 15, 16, 30, 39

INDEX

Houng-Wou [Hung-wu], Emperor, I 320
Houtouktou [Hutuktu], Lamas, I 157; II 192 *et seq.*, 236, 248, 344, 368
Huc, M., I 9, 36, 147, 207, 251, 378; II 7, 157, 266
Hundred Wells, the, I 283, 286
Huns, history of, I 307 *et seq.*
Hyacinthe, Father, II 296

Ili, principality of, I 326; river of, I 308, 326, 363
Illu (Ilü), II 192
In-Chan [Yin-shan] mountains, I 309
Ing-Kie-Li (Ying-chi-li], the English, I 372
Inns, in Tartary and China, I 10, 134, 166, 342, 351, 354, 362, 365, 372, 378, 383
Inventions, Chinese, I 317, 318
Itinerary of Lou-Hoa-Tchou, II 311 *et passim*

Jacquet, M., I 338
Jehol, *see under* Gé-ho-eul
Jen-y-Ting [Jên-i-t'ing] "Hotel of Justice and Mercy," I 342
Jin-seng [*ginseng*], a product of Manchuria, I 128, 129
Jou-Tchen [Juchen], I 317
Jovio, Paulo, I 319

Ka-Gan [*Ka'-gang*], a coin, II 180
Kai-Tcheou [Kai-chou], I 127
Kaldan [Galdan (dGa'-ldan)], lamasery of, I 157; II 50, 198, 278
Kalon [*Gelong (dge-slong)*], a clerical degree among Lamas, I 246; in all other places = *Kalon* (*bka'-bha*)

Kampo [*mkhan-po*], superior of lamasery, II 320, 377
Kang [*k'ang*], a kind of stove, I 11, 137, 160, 229, 367, 373, 379, 382
Kan-Sou [Kan-Su], province, I 175 *et passim*; II 118 *et passim*
Kao-Leang [*kao-liang*]=Indian corn, I 128
Kao-li-seng [*Kao-li-shên*], Corean jin-seng, I 129
Kao-Tan-Dze [Kao-tan-tzŭ] I 360 *et seq.*
Kara Koroum [Karakorum], I 313, 325
Karatsin [Kharachin], a Mongol tribe, I 324
Kas'yamatanga [kâśyapamatanga], II 88
Katchi [K'a-chê], "High Carts," Moslems in Lha-Ssa, II 172, 183, 184, 188, *et seq.*, 221, 259, 275
Keou-Ho [Kou-Ho], I 386; II 16
Keroulan [Kerulen], a river, I 21
Khachghar [Kashgar], I 327, 328, 329; II 307
Khalifat [Caliphate], I 311, 316
Khalkhas [Khalkha], I 21, 38, 39, 44, 78, 84, 95, 96, 109, 110, 111, 112, 151, 152, 153, 215, 321, 323, 324, 332, 333, 372; II 3 *et seq.*, 130, 154
Khalmoukia [Kalmuky], I 323
Khalmouks [Kalmuks], Calmucks, II 117
Kham [Kham (Khams)], province, II 312, 335, 342 *et seq.*, 385
Khan, the Grand, I 310 *et seq.*
Khan-Balik (Peking), I 316, 338
Khang-Hi [K'ang-hsi], Emperor, I 19, 84, 119, 123, 128, 132, 150, 152, 169, 209, 212, 321; II 55, 271, 337
Khan-Khoubilai [Khubilai-Khan], I 309, 314

INDEX

Khara-Oussou [Khara-usu], " Black Waters," II 161
Khartchin [Kharachin], Kingdom of, II 163
Khata [*kha-btags*], scarf of blessing, II 29 *et passim*
Khiang-Tang-Tchou [Ch'iang-tang-ch'u (Chang-tu-ch'u ?)], II 341
Khilian-Chan [Ch'i-lien-shan], II 118
Khinggan mountains, I 21, 323
Khou-Loung-Chan [K'u-lung-shan], II 349
Kia-King [Chia-ch'ing] I 1, 19; II 271
Kiaktha [Kiakhta], I 32, 84, 85
Kiang-Kian [*chiang-chün*], " military commandant," I 120, 150; II 337 and footnote.
Kiang-Si [Kiangsi], province, II 323
Kiang-Sou [Kiangsu], I 175
Kiang-Tsa [Chiang-k'a (Gartok)], II 373
Kian-Ngan-Remboutchi[rGyal-ba-rin-po-che], Thibetian name of the Dalai-Lama, II 192
Kia-Yu-Kiao [Chia-yü-ch'iao], a village, II 335
Ki-Chan [Ch'i-shan], Mandarin, II 200 *et seq.*, 258 *et passim*
Kien-loung [Ch'ien-lung], Emperor, I 95, 123, 124; II 186, 187, 271, 296, 323, 332, 369
Kin-Cha-Kiang [Ching-sha-chiang], river, II 142, 145, 374, 378, 387
Kin-Keou [Chin-Kou], " Golden Valley," II 326
Kin-Tchai [*Ch'in-ch'ai*], Delegates Extraordinary, I 327 ; II 185 *et seq.*, 202, 259
Kin-Tcheou [Chin-chou], I 127

Kio-nio-eul [*chia-niao-êrh*], " Bird of the family " (sparrow), I 231
Kitat Lama=" The Chinese Lama," II 34, *et seq.*
Kitats [Kitat]=The Chinese, I 22, *et passim*
Ki-Tou-Sse [Chi-t'u-ssu], Dchiahour tribe, I 371 ; II 214
Kiun-Wang [*Chün-wang*], noble, I 331 ; II 116
Knitting in China, I 382
Klaproth, II 244, 296, 311
Koiran mountains, II 164
Kolo [Kolo (mGo-log, Ngo-log)], appellation of Thibetian brigands living in the Bayen-Kharat Mts., II 3, 4, 117, 124, 152
Kolos [Kolo], I 387
Komans [Comans], I 316
Kongour [Khongor] mountains, I 108
Koua-mien [*kua-mien*], a paste, I 18
Kouang-Ping [Kuan-P'ing], II 319, footnote
Kouang-Ti-Miao [Kuan-ti-miao], " Temple of the God of War," II 319 and footnote
Koui-Hoa-Tchen [Kui-hua-Ch'eng], I 119, 133
Koukou-Khoton [Kôkô-khoto], " Blue Town," I 119, 120, 131, *et seq.*, 148, 343.
Koukou-Noor [Kôkô-nôr], I 112, 153, 175, 297, 298, 324, 325, 386 ; II 5, 6, 9, 12, 45, 78, 113 *et seq.*, 161
Kou-Kouo [*k'u-kuo*], a medicinal bean, I 198, 199
Koumis [*Kumis*], wine, I 333
Kounboum [*Kum-bum*], Lamasery, II, 7, 25 *et seq.*, 110, 112, 130, 231, 233
Koung [*Kung*], a title, I 331

INDEX

Kouren [Küren], the Great, Lamasery, I 84, 108 *et seq.*, 151, 152, 157, 324 ; II 130, 247
Koutcheou-Dcham [Kinju-jam], " Road of the Emperor's daughter," I 84
Kouti [Kuti], defile, II 313

Ladak, II 221, 222, 253 *et seq.*, 282
Lakto (?lag-'don, a mistake for rkang-'gro), footmen, II 125
Lama-Miao (Tolon-Noor), I 31
Lamas, characters and doctrines of, I 33, 63, 76, 87, 104 *et seq.*, 152 *et seq.*, 244, 258, 277 ; II 28 *et seq.*, 36 *et seq.*, 55, 69, 77, 181, 204, 207, 245, 276, 320, 330, 358
Lamaseries, I 34, 102 *et seq.*, 218 *et seq.*, 331 ; II 28 *et seq.*, 58, 277 *et seq.*, 344
Lam-Rim-Tsien-Bo [*Lam-rim-ch'en-po*], " The Progressive Path to Perfection," a work by Tsong-Kaba, II 50
Langles, M., I 318
Land-vapours, period of, II 99, 100
Landza [Lantsa], II 244
Lang-Ki-Tsoung [Lang-chi-tsung (Namgialgon, rNam-rgyal-rdzong)], II 326, 329
Lan-Tcheou [Lan-chou], capital of Kan-Sou, II 18, 68
Lao-Chan [Lao-Shan], I 307
Lao-Tseu [Lao-tzŭ], I 125
Lao-Yan [Lao-Yang], I 127
Lao-Ya-Pu [Lao-ya-p'u], " Valley of the Duck," I 382
Leang-Tai [Liang-t'ai], a mandarin, II 320 *et seq.*, 332, 346
Léao-Ho [Liao-ho], I 17
Leeches in Thibet, II 65
Lha, spirit, II 48
Lha-Dze [lha-'che], II 333

Lha-Ri, " Mountain of Spirits," II 314, 316, 319 *et seq.*
Lha-Ssa [Lha-sa], I 34, 112, 152, 156, 157, 169, 289, 326, 371 ; II 13, 48, 63, 118, 123, 129, 132 *et passim*
Lha-Ssa-Morou [*Lha-sa-Mo-ru*], a festival, II 276, 294, 330
Liao-Toung [Liao-tung], province, II 119
Lice, cures for, I 184
Lin, a Chinese commissioner, II 201
Li-Pai-Sse [*li-pai-ssŭ*], Chinese name for a mosque, II 20
Lithang [Li-t'ang] " Copper plain," II 383, *et seq*
Lobzan [Lobzang (blo-bzang)], a Lama, II 66
Lombo-Moke [Lubumge (k'Lu-'bum-dge)], name of a shepherd, II 45
Lo-Pou, name given to Lo and Pou, Chinese ambassadors, interpreted by Thibetians as *la-p'ug*, a radish, II 186
Loudiana [Ludhiana], II 255
Lou-Houa-Tchou [Lu-Hua-Chu], a mandarin, II 296, 311
Lou-joung [lu-jung], I 19
Louk-so [*lug-so*], a festival, II 273 *et seq*
Loumma-Ri [Lu-ma-ri (Nimaring)] II 303
Loung-Kio [*lung-chio*], a curious bird, I 191
Lo-Yang, II 88
Ly-kouo-Ngan [Li-kuo-an], name of a mandarin, II 283 *et passim*

Macao, II 201, 266, 267, 391
Macartney, Lord, I 364
Magic, practised by Lamas, I 244 *et seq.*
Makian-Dsoung [Ma-rgan-rdzong], II 387

INDEX

Malte-Brun, I 322
Mandeville, John de, I 314
Mang-Lin, a mountain, II 377
Mani, name of the prayer *Om mani padme houm*, II 244 *et seq.*
Mantchou [Manchu] language and literature, I 123 *et seq.*
Mantchou Tartars, I 120 *et seq.*, 321
Mao-Ling, a soldier mandarin, II 337
Maps, Chinese and Thibetian fear of, II 218, 222, 227
Marco Polo, I 314, 316
Marriage Customs of the Mongols, I 235
Martini, Father, I 318
Matanga [Kâśyapamatanga], II 88
Medicine, practised by Lamas, I 87 ; II 78, 108, 110
Mendoça, I 319
Meng-Phou [Mengphu (Mongphud)], II 348
Miao, " pagoda," I 173, 174, 176, 177
Microscope, Thibetians wonder at, II 226, 238, 281
Midchou-koung [Medu kongkar], II 298 *et seq.*
Mingan-Lamané-Kouré [Mingan-Lama-yin-küren], The Monastery of the Thousand Lamas, I 112
Ming dynasty, I 120, 121
Ming-Tchen-Tou-Sse [Ming-chen-t'u-ssŭ], II 248
Ming-Ti dynasty, II 87
Miracles by Lamas, I 244 *et seq.*
Monhe-Dchot [Möngke-jot], " the Eternal Sanctuary " (Lha-Sa), I 34 ; II 163
Mont Corvin, Jean de, I 338 ; II 51
Moorcroft, an Englishman at Lha-Ssa, II 222, 253 *et seq.*

Morou [Mo-ru] lamasery at Lha-Ssa, II 277
Moslems in Tartary and China, I 311, 316, 327, 328, 344 ; II 18 *et seq.*, 386
Moukden [Mukden], I 127
Mourguevan [Murgevan], I 38, 39, 40, 84
Mouroui-Oussou [Murui-usu], " tortuous river," II 145
Moussour [Muzart] mountains, I 308, 326
Mou-Wang, Emperor, II 87
Mules, wild, in Tartary, II 146
Musk deer, II 371

Nadan-Omo [Tolon-Noor], I 31
Naiman kingdom, I 2, 3, 6, 7, 16
Nan-chan [Nan-shan] mountains, II 127
Nanking, I 126
Na-Ptchu [Nag-ch'u], river and village in Thibet, II 161 *et seq.*
Nasamboyan, I 62
Nepaul, II 313
Nepaulese tribes, II 186
Nertechink [Nerchinsk], I 21
Nestorians in China, I 339
Nettles as food, II 99
New Year ceremonies, I 292 ; II 22, 23, 273 *et seq.*
Ngao-la-Eul [ao-li-êrh], I 18
Ngari province, II 254
Ngenda-Tchai [En-ta-chai], a village, II 340
Nialam [nilam], defile, II 313
Ning-Hia [Ning-hsia], I 208, 346, 349, 350, 351, 353, 355, 358
Ningouta [Ninguta], town, I 127
Ning-Pey-Hien [Nien-po-hsien], I 383
Nisan, servant to Moorcroft, II 253 *et seq.*

INDEX

Nomekhan [Nomun-khan], Spiritual Emperor, called by the Chinese Tsan-Wang, at Lha-Ssa, II 174, 186, 192, 198, 202, 206, 260, 355
Nourou-Tchayn [niru-i-jangir], I 44, 46
Nymbo [Nimbo], a Mongol singer, I 75

Obo, the great, name of places of pilgrimage in Tartary, I 20; II 317, 323
Oelets [Ölet], I 150; origin of name, I 321 (*see also* Eleuts)
Okhous-Han [Oquz-khan], conqueror of the Scythians, I 307
Om mani padme houm [*om mani padme hûm*], Thibetian prayer, II 244 *et seq.*
Om Tchou [Om-ch'u [Nom-ch'u)], a river, II 342
Oros=Russians, I 84, 276, 373, 376; II 196
Ortous [Ordos] the, I 161, 168, 175, 198, 204 *et seq.*, 226, 229, 234, 240, 244, 247, 261, 263, 264, 280, 284, 289, 295, 302, 324, 345, 365
Oudchou-Mourdchin [Ujumchin], I 33
Ou-Fou-Tien [Wu-fu-tien], Hotel of the Five Felicities, I 354
Ou-Gourdha [*uberi-da*], a Banner chief, I 44, 46
Oui [Wei; Dbus; Üi; Ü] province in which Lha-Ssa is situated, II 48, 118 *et seq.*, 277, 278, 388
Oui-Tsang-Thou-Tchi [*Wei-Tsang-t'u- chih*], "A description of Thibet," a Chinese work, II 296
Oula [*ula*], grass of Mantchouria, I 128, 129

Oulah [*ulaga*], II 299 *et seq.*
Ouniot [Ougniut] kingdom of, I 3, 23, 24, 324
Ourianghai [Uriangkhai], I 153; II 195
Ou-San-Kouei [Wu-San-Kuei], an Imperial general, I 121
Ou-Tay [Wu-t'ai], "The Five Towers" lamasery, I 93

Paga-Gol [Baga-gol], "Little river," I 182, 193, 194, 198, 204, 234
Paintings by Lamas, I 106, 107
Palmerston, II 241
Pampou [Pampu], plain near Lha-Ssa, II 165
Pan-tan [*pan-tan*], oatmeal diluted with water, I 65
Pao-Tchoung-Tang [Pao-chung-t'ang], II 289
Pao-Tun, a town, II 349
Paquette, a woman of Metz carried into Tartary, I 314
Pa-Tsoung [*Pa-tsung*], an official title, II 306
Paul, a Lama convert, I 102, 103
Pawning at New Year, II 26
Pe-Tche-Li [Pechili], I 121, 175; II 19, 54, 201, 228
Pebouns [Pebung?='Bras-spungs] inhabitants of Lha-Ssa, I 109; II 172, 181, 188, 189, 259, 275, 307
Pei [P'ei], name of a mandarin, II 350 *et seq.*, 370, 373
Peking, I 1 *et passim*; II 124 *et passim*
Peling [Phyiling (Phyi-gling)], English, I 375, 376; II 183, 189, 228
Pheasants' eggs, sent to Peking, I 290
Phou-Hai [P'o-hai] Gulf, I 127, 323

INDEX

Pian-pa [Pemba (sPen-pa)], a plain of Thibet, II 332
Pié-lié-keou [Pieh-lieh-kou], I 2
Ping-Fang [P'ing-fan], I 371, 376
Ping-Keou [Ping-kou], mountain, I 381, 382
Ping-Lou-Hien [P'ing-lu-hsien], a town, I 347, 348, 349
Plan Carpin, Jean de, I 314
Playing-cards, a Chinese invention, I 318
Po-ba, [Poba], Thibetian name for Thibet, II 94, 120, 288
Polygamy in Tartary, I 237
Potala, see Buddha-La
Pou, a Chinese Ambassador at Lha-Ssa, II 186
Pouhain-Gol [Bukhaïn-gol], a river, II 127, 133
Pou-lou [p'u-lu], a fabric, II 176, 178
Pou-Ssa [P'u-sa], idols [of Bodhisatvas], I 105, 174, 176, 177
Prayers of Thibetians, II 56, 57, 75, 107, 243
Praying-wheels, I 260
Preboung [Prebung (?—Brasspungs)], "ten thousand fruits," a lamasery, II 278
Printing in China and Thibet, I 318, 319 ; II 62
Proul-Tamba ['Phrul-bŝtan-pa], II 352, 353

Rache-Tchurin [Rash'e-churin (bkra-shis . . .?)], a lamasery, I 243, 258
Racon [Zaitun], I 338
Rala-Tchembe [Rala-chembe], a Thibetian, II 154, 157
Ran-Tchan [Ran-chan] lamasery, II 206
Ratchico [Rachico] mountains, II 113

Red Cap Lamas, II 48
Rémusat, Abel, I 310 et seq.
Robert (a singer), I 314

Sable fur, I 129
Sa-Dcha-Fo [Sa-skya-Fo], II 247
Sain-Nai [Saïn-nai], Good old woman, I 16
Sain-Oula [Saïn-ûla], a mountain, I 16
Sakhalien-Oula [Sakhalyan-ula], I 132, 323 ; II 203
Samarcand, I 310
Samba [San-pa, (Zam-pa)], II 94, 380, 383
Samdadchiemba [Samda-chiemba (bSam-gtan-'dzin-pa)], chief cameleer to MM. Huc and Gabet, I 9 et passim
Samoiede [Samoyed], I 322
Samtche-Mitcheba [Sangs-rgyas-mi-skye-va], I 157
Sandara, a young Lama, who helped MM. Huc and Gabet with their translations, II 7, et seq.
San-Kan-Tien, Hotel of the Three Social Relations, I 372
San-Tchouan [San-ch'uan], I 60, 298, 370, 371 ; II 214
San-Yen-Tsin [San-yen-tsing], I 365, 367, 368
Sarliques [Sarlik], long haired cattle, II 45
Se-Eul [Ssŭ-êrh], a dweller in the Blue City, I 136
Sem-pad, the Orbelian, I 313
Sera Lamasery at Lha-Ssa, II 63, 198, 204 et seq., 278, 279
Serou [Seru (bse-ru)], an antelope, II 311 et seq.
Serou-Dziong [Seru-jong (bSe-ru-rdzong)], II 312
Sheep in Tartary, I 72, 270, 272

INDEX

Siao [Liao], a river, I 309
Sié-fa [*hsieh-fa*], supernatural doings of Lamas, I 246, 247
Sie-kia [*hsieh-chia*], "Houses of Repose," I 386, 387; II 1 *et seq.*, 24
Si-Fan [Hsi-fan], Eastern Thibetians, I 157, 208, 323, 324, 343, 353; II 6 *et seq.*, 27, 30, 39 *et seq.*, 81, 89 *et seq.*, 106, 116, 198, 248, 386
Si-Hai [Hsi-hai], I 115
Si-Ngan-Fou [Hsi-an-fu], II 19
Si-Ning [Hsi-ning], I 386
Si-Ning-Fou [Hsi-ning-fu], I 383, 385, 386, 387; II 61, 131
Si-Po [Hsi-po (Sibo)], I 122
Si-Ta-Dze [Hsi-ta-tzŭ], Western Tartars and Mongols, I 323
Si-wan [Hsi-wan], I 2, 103, 146, 229
Slavery among Tartars, I 226
Small-pox in Thibet, II 250
Snuff, prized by Thibetians, II 158
Sok-Po-Mi [Sog-po-mi], Tartars, I 157
Solon, I 43, 108, 122, 130
Songari, I 109, 122
Souan-pan [*suan-p'an*], the, I 141, 142, 143, 318; II 180
Souk-Tchou [Sug-ch'u], a river, II 335
Soume [*sŭmé*], I 218, 221
Souniot [Suniut], I 46, 84, 324; king of, II 61
Sousdal [Susdal], I 311
Spectacles for snow, II 309
Srong-Bdzan-Gombo [Srong-btsan-sgam-po], II 244
Ssampa [Samba], II 247
Ssang [Tsang], province, II 276
Sse-Pin-Ssé [Ssŭ-pin-ssŭ], Hotel II 88
Sse-Tchouan [Ssŭ-chuan] province, of, I 371; II 19, 63, 67, 132, 145, 187, 188, 201, 205, 284, 286, 288, 289, and footnote 296, 308, 342 *et seq.*, 373, 384, 387, 390
Sue [Hsieh], a *Leang-Tai* mandarin, II 321
Suen-hoa-Fou [Hsüan-hua-fu], I 2

Tahai [Ta-hai], designer of the Mantchou system of letters, I 123
Tai-Toung-Fou [Ta-t'ung], I 376
Taitsi [*taiji*], Tartar nobles, I 215, 216, 233, 289; II 116
Tai-Tsou-Kao-Hoang-Ti [T'ai-tsu-Kao-huang-ti], chief of the Eastern Tartars, I 123
Talé-Lama [Dalai-Lama], I 33, 151, 152, 157; II 124 *et passim*
Tamerlane, I 73, 310; *see under* Timour
Tanda [Damta (Dam-btag)] Mountain, II 327, 330
Tang-Keou-Eul [Dangar], I 386, II 1 *et seq.*, 9, 12 *et seq.*, 22, 29, 30, 61, 111
Tang-pou [*tang-pu*], pawnshop, I 146, 155; II 23
Tansan, lamasery, II 113
Tant-La [Dang-la] Mountains, II 155, 161
Tao-Kouang [Tao-kuang] Emperor, I 5, 19, 110, 122, 328; II 201, 267, 271
Tao-Ssé [Tao-shih], II 89
Ta-So [sDag-shod], a village, II 379
Ta-Tsien-Lou [Ta-chien-lu], II 387 *et seq.*
Tchagan-Kouren [Chagan-kuren], "White Enclosure," I 161, 162 *et seq.*, 181 *et seq.*, 205, 207, 234, 248

INDEX

Tchakar [Chakhar], "Border Land," I 24, 26, 43, 44, 46 et seq., 84, 96, 117, 209, 290, 296, 324

Tchaktchouba [Phyag-mdzod-pa], lama, II 344

Tchanak-Kampo[rGya-nag-mkhan-po], II 124, 125, 134

Tchang-Kia-Fo [Chang-chia-Fo], living Buddha, II 247

Tchang-Lieou-Chouy [Ch'ang-liu-shui], I 359, 360

Tchang-mao-nieou [*ch'ang-mao-niu*], cattle, II 91

Tchang-Tcheou-Fou [Chang-chou fu], I 318

Tchan-ka [*tang-ka*], Thibetian coin, II 180, 188, 229

Tchankoeul [Chang-ko-êrh (Jihangir)], I 328, 329

Tchao-Wang [Chao-wang], Emperor, II 87, 88

Tche-Kiang [Chê kiang], Chinese province, II 351

Tcheng-Tou-Fou [Ch'eng-tu-fu], capital of the province of Sse-Tchouan, II 284, 289, 296

Tcheou [Chou], dynasty, I 349; II 89

Tcheou-ta-dze [*Sao-ta-tzŭ*], I 205

Tche-Ptche [*Khapch'e (kha-phyed)*], a coin, II 180

Tchinggis, Tchinggiskhan [Chingiz Khan], I 53, 68, 110, 156, 208, 215, 219, 309, 310, 321, 322, 325, 332, 337, 353; II 312, 366

Tchirou [*Chiru (gchig-ru)*], an antelope, II 313 et seq.

Tcho-Fa-Lan [Chu-Fa-Lan], II 88, 89

Tchoang-Long [Chuang-lang], see Ping-Fang [P'ing-fan], I 371, 376

Tchogortan [Ch'u-'khor-tang], lamasery, II 78 et seq., 102, 105, 113

Tchong-Wei [Chung-wei], I 358, 360

Tchortchi [Chorchi], lamasery, I 100, 101, 102, 103, 114

Tchouanda [*juvani-da*], military rank, I 43, 44

Tchoung-Tang [Chung-t'ang], a Chinese title, II 201, 242

Tchoung-Teou-Y [Chung-t'ou-i], Chamber of Deputies, II 242

Tchou-Pa-Loung [Chu-pa-lang (Gru-ba-nang)], II 374

Tchou-Youen-Tchang [Chu-Yüenchang], I 320

Tchu-Kor [*Ch'u-'khor*], praying wheel, I 260; II, 248

Tchurtchun [*churchun*], an augur, I 220

Tchutgour [*jetker*], a demon, I 87, 88, 89, 300

Tea, Tartar and Chinese, I 37

Tea-generals, at Lamaseries, II 59

Tents, Mongol, I 51

Thang [T'ang], dynasty, II 19

Thien-Chan-Pé-Lou [T'ien-shanpei-lu], prophecies concerning, II 195, 196

Thou-Pa [T'o-Pa], Tartars, I 208

Thsin-King [*Ch'in-Ching*], an officer, II 88

Thsin-Wang [*Ch'in-wang*], nobles, I 331

Tien-Chan [T'ien-shan], Chinese holy mountain, I 327

Tien-Tsin-Veï [T'ien-chin-wei (Tientsin)], I 44

Timkouski, M., I 53, 85

Timour [Tamerlane], Invocation to, I 73, 74, 321, 322

Tingri-Meidam [Dingri-Meidam], Valley, II 313

Toad, the deified, II 338

Tobacco, prohibition against, II 69

404

INDEX

Tokoura [Tokura], a chief, I 89, 93, 94
Tolon-Noor [Dolôn-Nôr], I 6, 7, 14, 28 *et seq*., 59, 114, 156, 157, 321
Tongous [Tungus], Tartar Tribe, I 322
Tonking, I 309
Tonmi-Sambhadha [Tonmi-Sambhota], II 244
Toolholos [*da'ulgachi, dôlgachi*], Tartar minſtrels, I 73, 74, 75, 237
Torgot [Torgût], I 94, 109, 308, 323 *et seq.*; II 129, 135
Tortche [*dorje (mdo-rje)*], the sacred thunderbolt, II 279
Touchimel [tushimel], I 215
Toudzelaktsi [*tusalakchi*], Miniſter of State, I 205, 206, 215
Toula [Tula], a river, I 84, 108, 109, 110
Toulain-Gol [Taolai-yin-gol], II 135
Toumet [Tümet], I 46, 117, 118, 119, 159, 324
Toung-Ta-Dze [Tung-ta-tzŭ], Eaſtern Tartars, I 322
Tou-Pa [T'o-pa], a town, I 353
Tou-Sse [*t'u-ssŭ*], a title, I 371; II 198, 284
Tou-Toun [*tu-t'ung*], a title, I 113
Transmigration of Souls, belief in, I 219; II 237, 246
Trebeck, M., II 255
Tsaidam, I 325; II 118, 136
Tsa-in [Ts'ai-Yin], II 88
Tsai-Li [Ts'ai-li], II 297
Tsamba [*tsam-pa*], barley meal, II 112, 148
Tsam-Wang [Tsang-Wang], *see under* Nomekhan
Tsang, province, II 313
Tsan-Hiang [*tsang-hsiang*], paſtileſticks, II 176

Tsa-Tchou-Ka [Chachuka (Ts'a-chu'-p'a)], II 322
Tsien [*ch'ien*], a coin, I 140
Tsien-tsoung[*ch'ien-tsung*], a captain, II 321, 333
Tsiamdo [Ch'amdo], II 341 *et seq.*
Tsin-Chi-Hoang-Ti [Ch'in-Shih-Huang-ti], builder of the Great Wall, I 307, 363, 365
Tsing-Hai [Ch'ing-hai], " Blue Sea," I 324; II 115
Tsing-Kou [*Ch'ing-k'uo*], barley, II 179, 294, 320
Tsong-Kaba-Remboutchi [Tsongkha-pa Rim-po-ch'e], I 157; II 6, 46 *et seq.*, 182, 192, 231, 278
Tsopo, one-horned, II 312
Tsot-Dun [mts'o-bdun], " Seven Lakes," I 31
Tsot-Ngon-Po [mTs'o-sngo-po], " Blue Lake," II 115
Tsoung-Tou [*tsung-tu*], Viceroy, II 337
Turkeſtan, I 309; II 255

Unicorn in Thibet, II 311 *et seq*
U-Pi-Ta-Dze [Yü-p'i-ta-tzŭ], Fish-skin Tartars, I 109

Varnish, used by Thibetian women, II 174 *et seq.*
Verolles, M., Vicar Apoſtolic, I 126, 127
Veſtments, Lama, II 43, 50
Victoria, Queen, II 241
Vitry, Jacques de, I 318
Vladislavitch, M., I 84
Vritanes [*vritranes (virkharân ?)*], I 340

Wa-Ho, mountain and plateau, II 336 *et seq.*
Wa-Ho-Tchai [Wa-ho-chai], II 336

INDEX

Wang, a title, I 3 footnote, 331
Wang-Ho-Po [Wang-ho-p'o], I 345
Wang-Tsa [Wang-k'a], II 359
Wang-Tsun, a man of letters, II 88
Wan-li-Tchang-Tching [Wan-li-ch'ang-ch'eng], the Great Wall of China, I 121, 307, 344, 358, 363 et seq.
Wei-Wei [*Yu-wei*], a title, II 306
Wou-Heou [Chu-ko Chung-wu-hou], II 388

Yak, the, II 91
Ya-Loung-Kiang [Ya-lung-Chang (mistake for Lan-tsiang-chiang)], river, II 342, 387
Yang, a Mandarin and General, I 328, 329
Yang-Dze-Kiang [Yang-tzŭ-chiang], river, II 145
Yang-Kouei-Dze [Yang-kui-tzŭ], " sea devils "=English, I 372
Yang-Tou-Sse [Yang-t'u-ssŭ], I 371 ; II 198 et seq.
Yan-pa-eul [Yang-pa-êrh], I 10, 16
Yao-Ming-Ti-Chan [Yao-ming-ti-shan], II 333
Yao-Tchang-Ti [Yao-chang-ti], a debt collector, I 162

Yarou-Dsangbo [Yaru-dzang-po], a river, II 47
Yellow Cap Lamas, II 48, 65
Yeou-ki [*you-chi*], a title, II 342
Ycou-Wang [Yu-Wang], Emperor of the Chou Dynasty, I 349
Yeroslaf [Yaroslav] of Sousdal, I 313
Y-jin [*I-jen*], stranger, I 376 footnote
Youé [Yueh], Sea, I 309
Youei-Tchi [Yüeh-chi] (the Getae), I 307 ; II 88
Youen [Yüăn], dynasty, I 209, 309
Youen-pao [yüan-pao], I 143, 144, 145
Youen-Yang [*Yuan-yang*], an aquatic bird, I 191
Yong-Mon [Yung-men], gate, II 88
Young-Lo [Yung-lo], Emperor of the Ming Dynasty, I 83, 320
Young-Ping [Yung-p'ing], Emperor of the Later Han Dynasty, II 88
Young-Tching [Yung-cheng], Emperor, II 271
Yuè-Ping [*yüeh-ping*], " Loaves of the Moon," I 68, 69
Yun-Nan province, II 19, 47, 187, 233, 308, 342, 373

Zipangri [Zipangu], I 316

For Product Safety Concerns and Information please contact our EU representative GPSR@taylorandfrancis.com
Taylor & Francis Verlag GmbH, Kaufingerstraße 24, 80331 München, Germany

www.ingramcontent.com/pod-product-compliance
Lightning Source LLC
Chambersburg PA
CBHW060549230426

43670CB00011B/1747